Eben Greenough Scott

The development of constitutional liberty in the English colonies of

America

Eben Greenough Scott

The development of constitutional liberty in the English colonies of America

ISBN/EAN: 9783337150990

Printed in Europe, USA, Canada, Australia, Japan

Cover: Foto ©ninafisch / pixelio.de

More available books at **www.hansebooks.com**

THE DEVELOPMENT

OF

CONSTITUTIONAL LIBERTY

IN THE

English Colonies of America

BY

EBEN GREENOUGH SCOTT

" *The Spirit of Liberty is, indeed, a bold and fearless spirit.*"
DANIEL WEBSTER.

"*Les nations libres sont superbes.*"—MONTESQUIEU·

NEW YORK
G. P. PUTNAM'S SONS
27 & 29 WEST 23D STREET
1890

Press of
G. P. Putnam's Sons
New York

THIS WORK IS DEDICATED TO

FRANKLIN B. GOWEN

IN TOKEN OF ANCIENT FRIENDSHIP, AND IN RECOGNITION OF
HIS CONSTANT SYMPATHY WITH LITERARY EFFORT.

PREFACE.

THIS work embraces a comprehensive view of those things in the life of the American people, previous to the War for Independence, which are necessary to be known in order to clearly understand why we are what we are. It discloses the Plan of Development contained in the histo.y of colonial life in America.

It is shown, that these United States are the direct and legitimate offspring of that great intellectual movement, which, for want of a better term, men called the Reformation; that the Free Inquiry thence evolved, passed from religious subjects to political, and gave us, at last, as it had before given the people of England, a really constitutional government established on Freedom of Conscience and the Liberty of the Citizen. The change that came over us, as we passed from the age of Religious Inquiry through that of State Development, is described; and the causes which made us what we are, and those which prompted us to do what we did, having been set forth, the events are narrated and the impulses disclosed, which, step by step, impelled us to assume the responsibility of independence and to take our place among the great powers.

In considering this plan of Development the three great Eras into which it is divided are observed in connection :—The Era of Constitutional Development in England; the Era of State Devel-

opment in America ; and the Era of Constitutional Development
in America. The motive of each of these is likewise revealed : that
of the First Era being Freedom of Conscience, that of the Second
the Development of Tribal Institutions, and that of the Third
being the Longing for Popular Sovereignty. Throughout this
Trilogy of Eras glowed the Spirit of Liberty, which, in the final
stage, became fierce, and crowned its long task by giving to our
people political, religious, and personal freedom guaranteed by
constitution.

It is only when surveying its course from the eminence upon
which the lapse of time has placed us, that the action of the law
of development can be viewed in its entirety, and the constant
force of its energy be calculated. Then we see, that this energy
has expanded or advanced by steps of unequal length ; that the
development of the race or tribe is marked by successive stages ;
and that the law which controls this energy is to be found in
these stages or eras, and not in the individual phenomena which
have been but its temporary expressions. Thus it is, that historical eras—which may be described as historical phenomena
grouped into organic systems—are of greater importance to human
knowledge than individual phenomena ; and thus it is, that the
philosopher will seek the truth of history in eras rather than in
the events of a day or the acts of individuals, however striking to
the eye they may be.

This work is the result of an endeavor to extract the truth of
our early history by an application of the principle thus disclosed ;
and hence it is, that it is not a history but a philosophical contemplation of what is known to be history. As such, therefore,
it makes no pretension to the discovery of new facts or the display of learning ; but, leaving the domain of original research untouched in that respect, and presuming a knowledge of accepted
history to be in the reader, it confines itself strictly to the work of
evolving therefrom the historical plan of development. The lapse

of time and the patient research of earnest and conscientious workers have at last enabled this to be done. The notes and the matter in the Appendix, then, are given rather to assist, or to explain, than to instruct, and, whenever possible, are drawn from sources familiar to the general reader, or easily to be referred to by him.

The Commercial Relations of the Colonies to the mother-country and to each other are set forth at large, and in connection with the causes that, according to Mr. Burke, made the spirit of our liberty fierce. This is the first time they have appeared in our literature as a cause of Revolution, although we have had, staring us in the face for three fourths of a century, the positive assertion of no less an actor in the achievement of our independence than John Adams, that "if any man wishes to investigate thoroughly the causes, feelings, and principles of the Revolution, he must study this Act of Navigation and the Acts of Trade, as a philosopher, a politician, and a philanthropist."

This done, a remarkable hiatus is filled up, and the story of our development from feeble communities to being a great power is believed to be here presented with all its stages defined and complete.

WILKES BARRÉ, PA., *January*, 1882.

TABLE OF CONTENTS.

PART I.—The Era of Constitutional Development in England.

CHAPTER I.

INTRODUCTION.

To what the Anglican migration westward was due—The United States the result of the Great Movement or Revolution of the 16th century—The destructive and constructive periods of this movement—The course of the Great Revolution in the British Isles—The first stage of its Destructive Era, terminating with the accession of Charles I.; the second with the investiture of the Protector—Results of these Eras of Effort, and their effect upon absolutism—The Constructive Era, which began with the Protectorate—The absolutism of the Restoration and its inherent weakness—The Nomenclature of the Great Revolution—Meaning of the word Puritanism—What was Puritanism, and what did it do for England?—What was the Revolution of 1688, and what did it do for England?—The law of historical development does not act with the regularity of physical laws; characteristic of its advance and retrogression—In respect to the Colonies, the effects of the Revolution of 1688 were moral, not physical—What the Revolution of 1688 did not do for the Colonies—Conditions of colonial life favorable to liberty—In what the Revolution of 1688 worked positive ill to the Colonies—William the Third an absolutist in America—The relations of the Colonies to the Government during the reigns of Anne and the early Hanoverians—The good feeling terminated by the accession of George III.—The plan of absolutism, which, in attacking colonial liberty, was really aimed at the liberty of England—The popular feelings which aided the absolutists.

The two Houses of Parliament and the people unite with the throne against the Colonies—The immediate cause of the outbreak in America—The Revolution of 1776 a manifestation of the same force which produced the Revolution of 1688—The Revolution of 1776 accomplished the last great step of Revolution, namely, the transfer of sovereignty from the throne to the people—How society regarded the Revolution of 1776—Its cause at first negative—Character of the revolutionists—Character of the Colonies—The conditions of Colonial life favorable to local self-government—Revolutions not affairs of battle-fields—The Revolution of 1776 instructive to those who would know how to be free.

Advantage possessed by the history of the Caucasian tribes in America over that of others—The Trilogy of Eras which embraces the historical development of colonial British America—The controlling Force or Motive of each of these Eras—The Spirit of Liberty manifest in all.　.　.　.　.　.　.　.　.　.　.　5-26

PART II.—The Era of State Development in America.

CHAPTER II.

**DESCENT.   REMOTENESS OF SITUATION.   THE FORMS OF THE CO-
LONIAL GOVERNMENTS, AND THE POLITICAL RELATIONS OF
THE COLONIES.**

Mr. Burke's Six Capital Sources whence the fierceness of Liberty in the Colonies was
derived—Two additional sources or causes: the *Political Relations of the Colonies*, and
their *Commercial Relations*—1. *Descent*—2. *Remoteness of Situation*: the *Laissez-faire*
policy, or policy of Governmental indifference.
    3.   *The Forms of the Colonial Governments*, and the *Political Relations of the Colonies*.
(*a.*) Comparison of the nature of the English Colonies with that of the Roman and
Greek: (1) the Roman Colonies; (2) the Greek Colonies—The English more like the
Greek than the Roman; points of resemblance and difference; the self-sustaining nature
of the English. (*b.*) Three kinds of English Colonies in America: (1) The Royal or Provincial Colonies; (2) the Proprietary or Palatine, and (3) the Charter—Political separateness
or distinction of these colonies from each other, and effect of their common allegiance to
the same suzerain—Dr. Robertson's surprise respecting the charters commented upon—
The Charters as compacts: they recognized local self-government—Amplification of the
meaning of the term " chartered liberties." (*c.*) The colonial governments one in spirit
though differing in form—Virginia: its exceptional character—Maryland—Pennsylvania,
New Jersey, and Delaware— Massachusetts — New Hampshire—Connecticut—Rhode
Island—New York—Colonies south of Virginia—Georgia—These Colonies free and self-
governing: their self-taxing power not regarded as sources of revenue—Virginia's resistance to royal monopoly.
    (*d.*) The institutional nature of the English colonies—Definition of the word institu-
tions—This institutional nature a race characteristic—The institutional development of
the English colonies shown by contrast with the French colonies—The English carried
with them institutional vigor; the French did not: illustrations—The extinction of French
power in America to be attributed to the paucity and weakness of institutions—The institutions of British America as ancient as the race.
    (*e.*) English colonization under the Stuarts—How it was that franchises were lavished
so freely on the colonists—The predisposition of the English colonists to self-government a tribal characteristic—Love of the soil closely allied with disposition for self-
government—Self-government coincident with the landing of a colony, and simultaneous
appearance of institutions—Effect upon the colonists of the contempt maintained by the
English commercial classes: loyalty of the former—Political independence a natural
sequence of the fierceness of liberty.   29-58

CHAPTER III.

RELIGION IN THE NORTHERN PROVINCES.

Mysticism : Rationalism : Faith.

Religion in the Northern Provinces: its chief feature toleration and freedom of conscience—The localities where the principle of freedom of conscience were most apparent—
This freedom a natural progenitor of political freedom—Free Inquiry passed from religious to secular subjects in America as it did in England, but without violence—The Colonies at the first glance unfavorable to religious freedom: intolerance, nevertheless, shown
to be inherently feeble—State religion, how regarded by the English previous to the Commonwealth ; dissent regarded as heretical—Rule for ascertaining the existence of toleration
or intolerance in a community—Intolerance natural at the time of colonial settlement, and
universal—Maryland and Pennsylvania exceptions.

I.—*The Mysticism of West Jersey and Pennsylvania.*

Quakerism : its mysticism, and the illustration it affords of a union of freedom of conscience and state instead of a union of church and state : effect of its appearance in
America—Rise of the sect of Quakers, and character—What Quakerism attempted, and
what it failed to attain—Its decline—Appearance of the Quakers in West Jersey and Pennsylvania—Apathetic condition of Freedom of Conscience at the time of their arrival—
Their advent propitious to its continued existence as a social force—Freedom of Conscience in Rhode Island—To what the favorable influence of Quakerism upon this principle was due—The Quakers of West Jersey—Their first enactment is declarative of freedom of conscience as a political principle—The constitution of their polity : its glory and
its defects—Their notion of government, a government by the people—Pennsylvania a result of West Jersey—The Quakerism of Pennsylvania a necessary expression of freedom
of conscience—The times propitious to the settlement of Pennsylvania—Charter of Pennsylvania : it recognizes local self-government—Comparison of it with the charters of
Maryland and Rhode Island—Steps taken by Penn before leaving England—Declaration
of Toleration—The Great Law of Chester : its provisions—It shows Penn to be in advance
of his followers in respect to freedom of conscience—The prudence and foresight displayed in the settlement of Pennsylvania : early prosperity of the colony—Passiveness of
Quakerism : its effect in saving freedom of conscience to America—Freedom of conscience
in Pennsylvania the gift of an individual, and not a conquest won by society.   . 59–81

CHAPTER IV.

RELIGION IN THE NORTHERN PROVINCES—*Continued.*

II.—*Rationalism of New England.*

In New England Freedom of Conscience rises from Society instead of descending upon
it—Puritanism of New England a direct expression of the Great Revolution or Movement—One and the same thing with the Puritanism of England—Historical importance of
the New England colonization—The most emphatic expression of insubordination the
times afforded—The immediate cause of the Puritan migration—Its motive one with that
of the Puritan Revolution.

The Pilgrim or Brownist migration—The Mayflower Compact—Not democratic—
Analysis of the Compact—Importance of its assertion of autonomy—An oligarchy flowed
from it.

The real Puritan migration begins with Winthrop's band of colonists—Character of
these colonists—Their love of learning—The early Puritan a reformer—Not to be confounded with the Independents or Separatists—Early Puritans a class rather than a sect—
Distinction between the Pilgrim and the Puritan Fathers—The Puritan of the reign of
James I.

The Puritan emigration brought Puritanism pure and simple into New England, and
assumed a sectarian character—Motive of this emigration—The object of emigration did
not include the foundation of a State free in politics and religion—Freedom came by
natural development—Political well-being dependent upon natural development—The
true greatness and well-being of a people to be ascertained only by observing its growth
—The law of development—Its action is slow—This action illustrated by the career of
Freedom of Conscience among the English.

To what the development of New England character is due—Early Puritanism in
America uneventful—Inefficacy of the early Puritan literature—The polemical strifes—
Extraordinary diffusion of education among the Massachusetts and Connecticut Puritans—
Adverse effects of an oligarchy upon the development of literature—The part performed
by the rage for disputation—Its ultimate inclusion of secular as well as religious subjects,
and its final change from disputation to discussion : the Debating Society—Effects of early
controversial theology.

Advent of Roger Williams in Massachusetts: the part he performed in his life: the first to make Freedom of Conscience a constitutional principle of polity—His life previous to his arrival in America—His personal character at the time of his coming—The facts concerning his trial and expulsion from Massachusetts—The action of his judges not censurable—Historical significance of the trial of Roger Williams—The condition of the doctrine of toleration in the Plantations it disclosed—That doctrine involved in the issue of the trial—Development of Williams' ideas into a system—Soul-liberty—His disunion of Church and State—His notion of the relations held toward each other by the civil and ecclesiastical powers—The new subjects his doctrines gave to discussion—Growth and expansion of these doctrines—His ultimate view of Freedom of Conscience—The view taken by him of the relations between the Indians and civilization—Character of Williams—Effect of his doctrines on American society—Effect of his doctrines on Vane and Milton.

III.—_Faith of Maryland._

Settlement of Maryland—Sketch of Calvert—His character—His early attempts at colonization—Condition of the Roman Catholics under the _præmunire_ statutes—Calvert first seeks Virginia, but ineffectually—Difference between the New England and Proprietary Charters—The Maryland Charter—Aristocracy and faith serve Freedom of Conscience along with democracy and rationalism. 82-123

CHAPTER V.

MANNERS IN THE SOUTHERN PROVINCES; MANNERS OF THE FRONTIER.

1. _Southern Life and Manners._—Enlargement of this capital source—The type to be found in Virginia and Maryland—Topography of these two provinces—Their distribution of population, and character of the people—Contrast between distribution of population in New England and in the South—What caused the difference—Disassociation the characteristic of Southern distribution; it was enhanced by the topography of the country—Personal effect of isolation—Simplicity and purity of the language preserved—Uncorrupted by the planters' foreign tours—Political effect of isolation—Class feeling and sense of individuality heightened by absence of middle class and isolation—Rare development of domestic life—Haughtiness of the planter—His hunger after land—His love of field sports—Freedom and purity of manners in the South between the sexes—Southern hospitality: its refinement—The winter visit to the colonial capital—The simplicity of life and manners extended to commercial transactions—The English squirearchy—The Southern squirearchy—Society in the Piedmont and the Valley—Its antagonism to the intolerance of the sea-board—How it differed from the planter society.

2. _Manners of the Frontier._—The Leatherstockings and Pioneers—Their mode of life—Their military efficiency—The actual process of social organization on the frontier, from the block-house to the city—The love of local self-government manifests itself at every step as the directing force—The sense of personal freedom in the frontiersman greater than the sense of political responsibility. 124-153

CHAPTER VI.

MANNERS IN THE MIDDLE PROVINCES.

3. _Pennsylvania._—The colonists commercial and agricultural—The different classes—Opposition to Quakerism—Greater diversity of nationality and manners than in the South—Philadelphia: its opulence; culture; famous men—Its social life: Black's Diary—The colonial metropolis: its printing presses; schools; learned societies—The German element in Pennsylvania, or "Pennsylvania Dutch": the Scotch-Irish—Greater diversity of population than in any other colony—Was highly conservative—The progressive party—The spirit of liberty in Pennsylvania stubborn but not fierce. . . . 154-163

CHAPTER VII.

NEW ENGLAND'S FIVE ADVANTAGES AS ENUMERATED BY JOHN ADAMS; AND HEREIN OF EDUCATION.

The Five Advantages possessed by New England over the other colonies—(*a*) *Purity of the English blood*—(*b*) *The institutions for the support of religion, morals, and decency.*
(*c*) *Education.*—The New England school system aided by concentration of population: contrary effect produced by the dispersion of Southern society—Education in the South—Education in the North more general than in the South—Education in Pennsylvania—Education in New England—It contemplated the highest culture possible: Yale and Harvard—Learning in itself not productive, but preservative of freedom—Effect of Northern education upon conceptions of government—The support lent by Northern school system to democracy.
(*d*) *The Township.*—What it is physically and politically—Its character more administrative than parliamentary—Its structure—The selectmen, and their duties; the other officers—Excellence of the township in political education—Division and concentration of its forces—The township a purely local self-government—Its development of active, practical citizenship—The part performed by the citizen in administering its affairs; a corrective to tendency to excessive abstraction—Attachment of the New Englander to his township—Its prominence in New England social life—Its effect in making the spirit of liberty fierce.
(*e*) *Distribution of Intestates' Estates, etc.*—Real estate in New England held in small parcels—Northern society democratic—The course of descents, etc., are there expressions of democratic tendency—Effects of diversity of principle in this respect, between North and South—Why the conflicting social constitutions of North and South united in a common republic—Land as assets for payment of debts—Decline of Gothic attachment to the soil—Curtailment of entails, abolition of right of primogeniture, repugnance to long trusts, and facilities for alienation of realty
Review of the Six Capital Sources: their tendency to make liberty fierce. . 164-184

CHAPTER VIII.

THE COMMERCIAL RELATIONS OF THE COLONIES.

Effect of the downfall of the French power in America upon the relations of the colonies to the mother-country: enforcement of the Acts of Trade, and growing restiveness of the colonists—The Navigation Act of Richard II.; the Navigation Act of the Commonwealth, and the policy it expressed—Effect of the discovery of America upon commercial supremacy: Rise of the Dutch—The decline of Holland a result of the Navigation Act—What led England to adopt this measure—Effect of the Act upon Monopoly.
I. *The Legislation concerning Trade and Navigation:*—The Three Acts: the Restrictive System—England becomes the colonial Factor—The Acts extended to intercolonial trade: the angle of intercolonial commerce—The compensation for Monopoly, derived by the colonists from the Restrictive System: (1) the pecuniary or material compensation, (2) the political or moral.
II. *The Literature having colonial trade for its subject: its significance.*—Political Economy takes its place as a science and divides the English into two schools—Early English writers on Political Economy: (*a*) *Sir Josiah Child* and his *New Discourse of Trade*—Object of the work—This object as it appeared to the Americans—Their view justified by the work itself—Child's aspersions of Virginia and Barbadoes—Selections from the work; comments upon them—Analysis of its propositions—Designs of the English commercial classes disclosed by the treatise—The sentiments are generally adopted, and the Government marks its approval of them. (*b*) *Joshua Gee* and his work *The Trade and Navigation of Great Britain Considered*—He advocates colonial taxation for revenue—Local self-government now definitely established in the colonies—Political

effect of taxing the colonies for revenue—Their character of dominions wholly distinct from that of commercial dependencies—Gee's propositions tend to the destruction of the character of dominions—His views acceptable to the Government ; a later administration circulates his work in 1767. (c) *John Ashley* and his *Memoirs and Considerations concerning the Trade and Revenues of the British colonies in America*—Follows Child and Gee, and also advocates colonial taxation for revenue—Drift of public opinion shown by these treatises to be unfriendly toward the colonies--No respect exhibited by them for the Charters—Review of the Restrictive System—The persistent rage for regulation—Motive of the System : the right of Great Britain to impose it upon the colonies, and the duty of these to obey it—Acceptance of it by the emigrants not compulsory—the inherent defect of the Restrictive System—The conservative disposition of the Government toward the political status of the colonies: the *laissez-faire* policy ; the true policy, and Walpole's rejoinder—Policy of the Government as to the commercial status an active one—Meaning of the change from policy of indifference to interference in political affairs of the colonies —How such change was regarded by the colonists : their alarm and excitement.   185-229

PART III.—*The Era of Constitutional Development in America.*

CHAPTER IX.

THE WOODEN HORSE.

Encroachments of the Restrictive System—The forerunner of rebellion—Ashley's proposition—His object : terminology of the Revenue Acts--Governmental construction of "the Molasses Acts"—Writs of Assistance—Their nature—Otis' Argument—Its effect upon those who heard it—Its effect upon the people of all the colonies.   .   .   233-246

CHAPTER X.

THE CONFLICT WITH ABSOLUTISM.

Barren victory of the Government ; its irresolute action—Dissension between the mother-country and the colonies—George Grenville ; his character—The grounds of his change of policy—Their falsity shown—What the colonists had done and were doing—Revenue from the colonies resolved upon ; the Port Duty Act ; Resolution to charge stamp duties—Deliberate action of Grenville—Passage of the Stamp Act—How the colonies acted by way of protest—Feeling in America—The New York Congress—Debates in Parliament and Repeal of the Stamp Act—Joy in the colonies—The four new facts which constitute the outcome of the Stamp Act matter—The Declaratory Act—Character of Charles Townshend —His sentiments respecting British rule in America—The Townshend Acts—A trick of absolutism—England defective in moral qualifications for the coming struggle—Reception of the Townshend Acts in America—The Massachusetts Circular Letter ; the action of the ministry thereon, and the action of the colonial legislatures : troops quartered on Boston—The feeling of resentment displayed in Parliament—Revival of the law to transport offenders for trial—Action of Virginia—Botetourt's appointment : the Virginia Resolutions of 1769—Attempts of the ministry to throw the *onus* on the colonies—Partial repeal of the Townshend Acts ; the Tea Act remains—Government of the colonies by Royal Instructions, or ukase administration—The subordinate part played by " Parliamentary absolutism "—Apathetic reaction in the colonies ; Boston Massacre—The order to pay the colonial judges from the imperial treasury ; the Boston Committee of Correspondence—The " Gaspee " Commission—The Virginia Legislative Committee of Correspondence the first effective step to colonial union.   247-272

CHAPTER XI.

THE CONFLICT WITH ABSOLUTISM—*Continuea.*

Embarrassment of the East India Company, and plan of the Government to relieve it at the expense of the colonies—The sordid way in which England looked at American affairs—The tea thrown overboard in Boston Harbor--Resentment of the English—The Boston Port Bill—The Massachusetts Government Bill or Regulating Act—Another cargo pitched into the water—The sad state of affairs due to the attempt to set up a paternal government—England retrograding, America advancing: what the English people might have done—The Revolution of 1688 powerless to arouse sympathy in the English masses with the Revolution of 1776—The way the news of the Boston Port Bill was received in America—Impending physical force becomes an element in the conflict--General impulse in favor of a colonial Congress—Twelve colonies agree to send delegates; effect of feeling in Virginia on the rest of the country—The Congress created; its character, and relations to the English Parliament and to the colonies—The First Congress; two parties—The Suffolk Resolutions—What this Congress did—Chatham's eulogium upon this Congress sustained by the judgment of time—The course pursued by Massachusetts—The elections of 1774 sustain the ministry—Lord Chatham's fruitless endeavor to have the troops withdrawn from Boston—His Provisional Bill for settling the troubles in America; its failure—Why this bill would not have been acceptable to the Americans—Plans of conciliation: Lord North's plan—Edmund Burke's plan; his great speech—Affair of Lexington and Concord—Its effect on the colonists; Boston invested by the Americans—Rejection by Congress of Lord North's plan—Bunker Hill—Last Petition to the King—An army raised and Washington appointed commander-in-chief: measures to obstruct the enemy—The Petition rejected and Proclamation of Rebellion made—Vigorous policy of the ministry—the King's Speech—Failure of the Opposition—Action of Congress—The Middle Colonies conservative—Effect of Tom Paine's " Common Sense " —Futile opposition of the Conservatives to revolution—Resolution of the 15th of May—Opposed by the Conservatives; their decline—Congress takes steps to bring forward the question of independence—Resolutions of Richard Henry Lee—The Great Debate, and the resolutions—The Declaration of Independence—The War for Independence and triumph of local self-government—Retrospect—Verification of the Motive and Law of Development. .   .   . 273-302

PART I.

THE ERA OF CONSTITUTIONAL DEVELOPMENT IN ENGLAND.

"*Cette nation aimerait prodigieusement sa liberté, parceque cette liberté serait vraie.*"

Esprit des Lois, liv. xix, chap. xxvii.

INTRODUCTION.

"Ce n' est pas la fortune qui domine le monde. * * * *Il y a des causes générales, soit morales, soit physiques, qui agissent dans chaque monarchie, l' élèvent, la maintiennent, ou la précipitent ; tous les accidents sont soumis à ces causes ; et si le hasard d' une bataille, c' est-à-dire une cause particulière, a ruiné un État, il y avait une cause générale qui faisait que cet État devait périr par une seule bataille. En un mot, l' allure principale entraine avec elle tous les accidents particuliers."*

Grandeur et Decadence des Romains, chap. xviii.

CHAPTER I.

Introduction.

THE growth of the English colonies in America was due to causes peculiar to the times. The wilderness was an inviting one, the climate was favorable to race development, society would have no traditionary limits set upon its expansion, and men's needs were pressing. Yet, though the virgin stood before their eyes, whole generations of Northmen were born, lived out their days and passed away, without heeding the gentle bidding which every western gale bore across the waters. The bridegroom tarried.

All at once, however, Europe stirred, and the North Atlantic was dotted with sails moving westward. Why this restlessness ; why this migration ; why happened it then instead of before ; why did it occur at all ? The answer is short and emphatic. So long as men were satisfied with their condition, there was no reason for their moving. But, when a sudden and marvellous expansion of the human intellect occurred ; when, under that expansion, old bonds were broken and the ancient systems were left inadequate to supply the new demands of society ; when these systems failed to readily adapt themselves to the changed order of things, then life fast became intolerable, and men who were determined upon having something better, were forced to seek elsewhere what they could not find at home. Thus arose something which compelled movement, and as society could only move westward, hence began the great Anglican migration which other impulses from time to time sustained.

The United States of America, then, are results of that mighty force, which, bounding into existence through the throes of the Reformation, still continues its triumphant march. The disintegra-

5

tion of ancient manners, ancient notions, and ancient principles, consequent upon the upheaval of the ancient structure, continued for many generations, until at last it embraced every element of the old European civilization. When this disintegration was ended, however, a process just the contrary set in, and under the cohesive forces of society the different fragments crystallized into new forms and into new organizations. Thus the course of the great movement may be distinguished by two periods: one of destruction, and the other of construction. In the latter the English-speaking race is living to-day, but the former continued in England until 1688, or less than two centuries ago, while in America it was not completely at an end until 1776, or about one century ago.

In the British Isles the first great step of the destructive era terminated in the accomplishment of the Reformation proper, when the new conditions of religious life were fixed and settled. Then it ended; but after this period of activity, and before the more amazing one that followed, there occurred what might be termed an interval of volcanic repose. Flames did not shoot toward the zenith, streams of fire did not lay waste the vineyards, nor were the temples overthrown. All this was indeed to come; but for the present, that is to say, from the accession of Elizabeth to the accession of Charles the First, there was, to outward appearance, tranquillity. Men went on cutting and grafting upon the slopes, though at times a tremor ran through the ground, and though the ear, in spite of itself, would turn to catch the smothered muttering that betokened a fast-brimming crater. This interval was characterized by the transition of the lately awakened force from purely religious subjects to those that were purely intellectual; and though it was but a period of transition from one part of the destructive era to another, we behold the constructive forces of society bursting forth in every direction; just as on the sides of Vesuvius we see vegetation pushing its blades through the scarcely cooled lava. Nevertheless, the time is not yet come for the full action of these forces; old systems, which others must replace, still survive, and until they are in ruins, the era of construction cannot be said to have set in.

Accordingly, the next stage is destructive, and, as it proves, is the most destructive of all. The constructive forces cease from acting altogether, and the destructive are seen in full possession of the field. This embraces the short period between the accession of Charles the First and the investiture of the Protector, and in the annals of the great Revolution it may be characterized as that in which Free Inquiry advanced in religious matters still further toward the substitution of reason for credulity, and in which, passing to secular subjects, it attacked the existing political structure of society and asserted the supremacy of personal liberty over absolutism. The struggle between these forces was one which, even yet, men shudder at the thought of. The forces of society acted only in violence, and in violence which sent England reeling to the ground. When the conflict was ended, and men paused to take breath and look about them, marvellous were the changes wrought. In religion, freedom of conscience held the ground, and intolerance, or the doctrine that the civil power was at the service of the ecclesiastical in prescribing faith, in regulating doctrine, and in extirpating heresy, had sheathed its sword, or, at best, was standing on a weak defence. Its voice no longer thundered its decrees, but in shrill treble quavered its apologies. In politics, though a dictator "protected" the land, that dictator was an uncrowned and unanointed one, and in every thing he said or did, was careful to ascribe his omnipotence to the people only as the sole source of power.

Absolutism, the world over, has never recovered from the shock then given it ; English absolutism from that day has borne the mark of the beast. In commercial matters, the old system of monopoly was overthrown, though the monstrous principle still held its own ; and a new system took its place, in which a whole people were substituted as monopolists instead of courtiers and guilds. Though monopoly itself, as we shall see, was as strong as ever, its enjoyment was shared by all the inhabitants of England, and in this change, as in every other that had occurred, one invariable fact presents itself—the emphatic assertion of individuality in matters pertaining to the common weal. In short, control of the social forces was more in the hands of the people, enjoyment of franchises and liberties was much more general, and religion had become a thing of the individual and not of the state.

The Protector, Oliver Cromwell, was, to all appearance, the veriest of dictators, and absolutism seemed to be enthroned in his person : but such were really not the facts. That wonderful man saw clearly that the absolutism of the past was over, and that the absolutism of which he was the figure was a make-shift ; and, with singular self-control, he set to work to secure to England the advances toward liberty it had gained from the conflict just ended. While the strife was going on, he had kept just ahead of events, with the revolutionary spirit of the day following hard after him ; but when, exhausted by its efforts, revolution paused, Cromwell, who never paused, distanced it, and the result was, that, unsustained by public opinion, death caught him with his work unfinished. Nevertheless, the people, whose hesitating steps still carried them forward, did reach his ground in course of time, and the feeble absolutism of the Restoration found itself face to face with an England far more united against it than ever that which confronted Charles I. had been. Indeed, such was now the pervading sense of freedom, and such the universal appreciation of personal rights, that when absolutism, under James II., arrayed itself against liberty for its last struggle, there was no conflict worthy of the name. It threw down the gauntlet only to retire from the lists, and it fled panic-struck from the presence of the warrior it had itself called into the field. Thus the Revolution of 1688 was almost a bloodless revolution ; and personal freedom had nothing to do but to take possession of abandoned ground, and to proclaim a constitution which none have disputed from that day to this. Since then the era of construction and enjoyment has been uninterrupted in England, and the last violent effort of the great movement which had been initiated by the Reformation may be said to have there terminated in the Revolution of 1688. The Middle Ages were ended.

This whole movement, from beginning to end, has been unfortunate in its names. Indeed, unless we call it " The Great Movement " or " The Great Revolution," it is nameless : for the term " The Reformation " applies only to a part, and the term " Puritanism," which never expressed but a part of a part, and which at most is the name of a quality or characteristic only, is actually misleading. Used at first to designate anti-formalism in religious matters, and, afterward, what would be called to-day " reform " in politics, it has been extended so as to embrace the whole expansion which resulted in substituting freedom of conscience for credulity, freedom of trade for monopoly, and constitutional freedom for absolutism. This distinction it does not deserve ; for Puritanism, as a political force, did not make its appearance until long after the Reformation, and it ended with the death of Cromwell. It was during these two periods that the English people did the most of the task that had been set them to do, and the rest of the work, which was accomplished in 1688, was simply that of garnering the crop. Nevertheless, the final stage is as distinct as either of those which precede it, and to complete the designation of the movement which so changed the character of the English and wrought such great good, we must add to its nomenclature the name of the Revolution of 1688.

The American colonies owed so much to the Great Movement, that it may be well, once for all, and at this point, to set forth the nature of its different phases. We know what the Reformation was, and what it did for all people—it changed the subjects of mental activity, by substituting, as the impelling motive, free inquiry for credulity. But what was Puritanism, and what did it do for England ?

It was a reformation of the Reformation ; and it left an indelible mark upon English character. Modern England dates from its expiration, and with it ended a heroic age. Politically, it was a revolt of the Middle Class ; intellectually and spiritually, it was a violent, uncontrollable expansion of the mind and soul ; historically, it was the latest popular development of Free Inquiry in the British Isles. Taking it altogether, it was a convulsive effort toward freedom. The Middle Class wanted representation in the government ; they would no longer be left out of every thing but the revenue acts and the press-gang. The Intellectual Class, whose field had been broadened by Free Inquiry, would no longer stay pent up within the schools ; and the Religious Class, stimulated by the sight of an open Bible, and frantic from the stings of intolerance, insisted upon absolute freedom of conscience. All three got what they wanted. After the storm was over, England apparently settled down into what she had been ; but only in appearance. The divisions of society remained the same, the church resumed her services, parliament betook itself to the old business of granting royal supplies, and the king went out hawking as usual. But there was a change ; the ancient life was gone, the new life had leavened the lump, and things were not what they had been. The old liberties looked more vigorous than ever, the new ones already seemed as enduring, and together they resisted with easy indifference the dangers that threatened them from the frivolity, the bigotry, and the obstinacy of kings, and those that would assault them from the tyranny of mobs. Had Puritanism done nothing else than develop manly self-respect, the sense of individuality, and the consciousness of a power which could and would compel a reverent regard for personal rights, it had deserved well of the people. Had it limited its efforts solely to assuring the old liberties, to advancing the new, and to establishing both, it had deserved well of civilization. It did these things, and, in spite of its violence and cruelty, and of all its manifold offences, it deserves and has the good word of mankind. It started England upon the career which she has run as head of the human family; upon her career of conquest; not her conquest of brute force, but her conquest of civilization, which has subdued continents to the plough, and which has rooted her principles of liberty as sturdily in the islands of far-off seas as ever they were rooted in the soil of Runnymede. It was much to demonstrate, if but for a single day, that conscience could be free—and this it did: it was much to teach rulers that the possession of power is a trust for the benefit of society—and this it did: it was much to return a parliament which really represented the people—and this it did: it was much to propose reforms which it is still the endeavor of England to effect—and this it did: it was more, far more, to actually accomplish them, though but for a parliament's sitting—and this it did.

It may be urged against Puritanism, that its greatest services to freedom were given during the riot of that worst of afflictions, a people run mad, and that it was in the days of its fanaticism that liberty reaped its richest gains. But that some of these services were involuntary by no means deprives Puritanism of the credit due her for what she did freely and from good-will. The gains of liberty, too, before and since that time, have been due as often to the indolence, the vices, and the necessities of rulers, to the brutality of the rabble, to the passions and blunders of citizens, and to the mere accretions of time, as to the merits and virtues of mankind. All these things have proved quite as efficient for her ends as patriots and heroes. Does a prince become impecunious? Riches are his, if she is only given another foothold. Does a mob break in the doors of a Parliament House? Immunity from punishment is accorded, if the right of free speech—speech as secure from a mob as from a ruler—is guaranteed for the future. Does the legislature encroach on the administration or the administration on the legislature? Swarms of precedents, whose presence is justified simply because they have existed time out of mind, straightway confront the outrage and turn it to liberty's account. All this only goes to show that this ever-watchful spirit does not disdain to make use of the stones which the builders reject. She may not be nice in her agents, but she uses them to good ends and with good effect. So with Puritanism : it made use of the tools it had, not what it would have. Conservative England may have done more to hedge old liberties with safeguards ; but Puritanism is good, and is to be honored for this, that it produced more new liberties which have lived, and it proposed, and, what is better, set the example of more reforms which have lasted, than ever conservatism did. It gave, too, the two great parties necessary to every free government, and of these one has made it its duty to preserve what the other originates. Beneath the froth and scum the waters of life still ran in pure and steady current. Puritanism was indeed fanatical, but it used its fanaticism in the end, to the advancement of the human race and the greater glory of God.

What, then, as the next inquiry, was the Revolution of 1688, and what did it do for the people of England?

The nerveless rule of Cromwell's successor disclosed how abruptly the work of reconstruction had been interrupted by the Protector's death, and laid bare the necessity of its continuance. The country was exhausted by convulsion ; reaction naturally followed, and the conservatism of the race having nothing to withstand it, the result was, that the king had his own again. So practical a people as the English, had not, however, gone through tribulation for nothing, and when absolutism dropped its mask, the temper which had beheaded one king was not disposed to palter with another. The past was scrutinized after reflection had cooled the judgment, and the discrimination between the good and bad it disclosed was made with just severity. Nothing could be more timely for popular rights, than that royal absolutism should choose for its attempts a moment when the recollection of what they had done was still fresh enough to show the people what they could do, and when the resolution to maintain their rights was made inflexible by the lately acquired sense of having earned them. Accordingly, as if by instinct, the whole mass set to work to secure what had been gained. The Writ of *Habeas Corpus* was wrung from Charles, and, in fact, during no period of English history were so many rights secured as there were under the reigns of that monarch and his brother, two of the most inveterate absolutists that ever sat upon the throne. The reason was, that though these rights were not embodied in a constitution, they were alive in the people, who were bent upon seeing them recognized elements of the law of the land ; and so strong was this determination, that when, at last, the king obstructed the work, he was pushed aside, and another was called in who took his place upon the express condition, that, henceforth, the crown should act under the limitations imposed by the constitution. Thus the Restoration bestowed liberties, and the Revolution of 1688 secured them. It did more : it gave the English the solid assurance, that all their liberties, old and new, were of equal weight before the constitution, and were alike constituent elements of their social organization. No matter when this liberty or that had risen to the surface, all were now made living elements of the body politic, and when the Declaration of Rights was put forth, and Majesty did it reverence, personal freedom was set upon immovable foundations.

Such were the three periods of the Great Revolution, of which the first two may be styled emphatically the Eras of Effort, and such were what they accomplished. In surveying this mighty movement from beginning to end, we cannot but be struck with this fact, that, though history repeats itself, the law of a people's development does not act, at any time or in any place, with the uniformity of those physical laws whose action can be measured and determined mathematically. The retrogression of the intellect is indicated by a regular and gradual relinquishment of its ground ; but its advance is marked by successive steps of unequal length, taken after unequal pauses ; and its expansion is characterized by efforts of increasing vehemence. In its condition of effort, its action is irregular and spasmodic; it advances, rests, takes breath, and once more rushes onward. In all progress of the mind, one thing strikes the observer with a force secondary only to its achievements—its intermittent periods of repose, when, laying aside its aggressive character and patiently rebuilding the demolished fabric in another form, it gains a new point of departure for a still further advance. As each of these stages comes to an end and takes its place in the recorded past, it becomes a known and written chapter in the history of human development.

The spectacle of such results as the Revolution of 1688 displayed, had a great effect upon the English colonies in America ; but there were no physical effects (for the conflict did not reach these shores), except the settlement of certain portions of American territory, notably New England and Pennsylvania, which was a direct result of the intellectual and religious disturbance of the times. But, apart from this, the importance of which can scarcely be overestimated, the colonies, when they had come to maturity, were profoundly impressed by the historical example presented : it concentrated their regards more steadfastly upon ·their chartered liberties, which were great, and upon those which time and their situation had brought to hand, which were greater ; it popularized among them the knowledge of constitutional government ; it excited a keener appreciation of the freedom they enjoyed, and it inflamed their resolution to maintain its integrity. Such were the moral effects of the Revolution of 1688 upon all the colonies in the course of time, and such was its generating influence upon the northern part of the British territory in America. Further than that, however, it did not go.

The Revolution of 1688 did not establish in America the constitutional government it had secured to England. What freedom existed, existed by the force of race instinct, of franchises expressed in charters, or by the force of time and custom. The colonies, it is true, had already been in the enjoyment of some of the liberties the English did not secure to themselves until then ; but these had been quietly appropriated from time to time, or had grown up of themselves, thanks to the inducements to colonization which had to be offered in the shape of franchises, to the distance which rendered interference impracticable, to the distractions of the government by civil wars and discord, to the indifference of kings and cabinets, to the necessity of fostering good-will which the neighborhood of an aggressive rival created, and, above all, to their character of mere commercial dependencies. What liberty they had, then, was theirs by the force of circumstances, and not by the force of the English constitution ; it was liberty, but the liberty only of England before the Bill of Rights. They could not, therefore, be said to be in the constitutional enjoyment of popular representation, for their legislatures could be convened only by the breath of a king, by the same breath could they be dissolved, and their acts were subject to the scrutiny of a Board commissioned during the pleasure of the sovereign ; nor could justice be considered constitutionally administered, for the judges were not independent of the crown. As the laws of England were made for that country only, and therefore were confined in their action to the British Isles, the *Habeas Corpus* Act was of no force in the colonies. Thus, in three essential elements of free government, viz.: popular representation, administration of justice, and inviolability of the person, the colonies lacked the safeguards of either a constitution or the law. They practically enjoyed these rights, it is true, but the enjoyment was without any such guaranty of continuance as Anglican liberty now insists upon and obtains the world over.

In one thing, however, their condition was superior to that of their fellow-subjects at home : they were not weighed down by an Established Church, and, though toleration as a principle was not accepted, save in Pennsylvania and Rhode Island, toleration as a fact existed from the absence of any power which could prescribe faith or extirpate heresy. Moreover, their circumstances were not conducive to the division of society as it existed in Europe, and the expansion of social life was therefore unrestrained. These two conditions were extremely favorable to the growth of liberty, and they account for the exercise of many rights which came to the surface when a state of society existed which imposed no limitations upon their growth but those of nature. But they were the results of natural law, regulated by municipal law ; they were not guaranteed by any constitution of the colonies, nor were they recognized by the constitution of England.

On the other hand, the Revolution of 1688, in one way, worked

positive ill to the colonies : it permitted the forces of absolutism
to concentrate upon the weaker portions of the empire. The
downfall of the Stuarts was the downfall of personal government·
in England, but not in America, and this country was forthwith.
regarded as the one where British absolutism had its last chance
of success, and whither it must betake itself if it would regain
what had been lost at home.

The Americans owe no thanks to William the Third. Whatever he may be to England, to America he is the embodiment of
Stuart absolutism. In colonial administration he simply took up
the thread those arbitrary rulers had dropped, and, though king·
by the grace of a constitution, he went right on from where
they had left off. He refused the colonies the liberty of the press,
he withheld from them the writ of *Habeas Corpus*, and what he
acknowledged as the personal rights of Englishmen he denied to
be the personal rights of Americans. During his reign the Acts
of Trade multiplied, not in the interest of commerce but of arbitrary power, and, in a word, though compelled to play the part of
liberator in England, he maintained, as covertly as he could, that
of absolutist in the colonies. The administration of their affairs
was taken from the Privy Council and was placed in a Board of
Lords of Trade and Plantations, which, established in the time of
Charles the Second, was now revived and invigorated with the
energy that characterized the reign of the Deliverer.[1] The osten-
sible purpose of this Board was the care of provinces, whose
wealth and importance demanded an administration exclusively
devoted to them ; but its constitution was such that it could be.
readily used by the crown for direct interference in the internal
affairs of the colonies. Happily, colonial liberty was favored by
the existing French occupation of the country beyond the St.
Lawrence and the Alleghenies. So long as the British possessions
were threatened from that quarter, the government felt itself under the necessity of cultivating the good-will of the colonies, and,
to effect this, any thing like intrusion into their private affairs was
discountenanced. Thus the dependencies were left to themselves
to work out their political welfare, and when the time came for
absolutism to show its hand, and to effect its bidding by means of
the Board of Lords of Trade and Plantations, it was too late :

[1] See Appendix A.

the colonies were by that time strong enough to take care of themselves, and to retain, in spite of the throne, the self-government that had become as dear to them as it was to the people of England.

During the reigns of Anne and the early Hanoverians, the dread of civil commotion which might disturb the placidity of the palace, or endanger the hold of a ministry upon office, discountenanced any encroachment on popular rights at home, while, abroad, the menacing presence of the French on the Lakes and the Mississippi constrained the government, as has been said, to the cultivation in the colonies of a spirit of cordiality and affection. There existed at this time between the government and the people what politicians style an era of good feeling, and it was during this period that material prosperity and enjoyment of personal freedom attained their height in America. Although the first half of the eighteenth century is stained by the scandalous corruption which rendered the bribes of Walpole possible, the people everywhere were left to themselves. They were injured, not by assault, but by having their defences taken away : for this corruption, with its rotten boroughs and sinecures, had the effect of diminishing the representative character of Parliament. That branch of government deserted the people, and, obedient to a law of political forces, the further it receded from the commons the nearer it approached the throne. With this dangerous symptom appeared another : the sense of security had persuaded the English that their rulers did not need watching ; their ancient dread of the prerogative, consequently, became torpid, and, forgetting that arbitrary power never so much as slumbers, they suffered themselves to sleep. This lethargy, and the absence of defenders, invited attack, and, accordingly, a different order of things than any warranted by the constitution, raised its head and sought to gain a footing upon the accession of George the Third. It had not long to wait. The necessities of the government, which had been exhausted by a war that had embraced the globe in its struggles, supplied a pretext, and a course of action was pursued which was destined to end in the most remarkable attempt of arbitrary power to prevent the expansion of constitutional government known to English-speaking people since the times of Strafford. In the end it proved futile, and so signal was its failure, that the wonder is that it could ever be contemplated. But the scheme was a cunning one, and, at the time, had every promise of success; for, whatever injury ensued would seem the unavoidable result of a rightful performance of a function of government, while resistance, if any there were, would call forth the whole power of an empire whose integrity that resistance would threaten. Thus those who so lately had bound arbitrary power with fetters of brass, would be forced to do its work, and thus the hand which was mining the citadel would distract the attention of the garrison by inciting a revolt of the outposts.

A deep-rooted feeling, which was general, also lent its support to the scheme. Ever since England possessed dependencies, there had always been manifested toward the dependent a sense of superiority on the part of the home citizens ; and, from time immemorial, the sentiment had prevailed, that, for the protection accorded by their government and for the tranquillity not paid for by the colonists, the latter should evince a due sense of subordination, and should not affect to be upon the same level with their protectors. This feeling, akin to that with which every people regard foreigners, was not original with the English, as the marks left by it long before upon the chronicles of other people abundantly testify : but, not to go back to the troubles which arose on this score between Rome and her provinces, it is enough to recall its sanguinary records in the revolts which, from time to time, stain the history of the relations that existed between Spain and her foreign possessions. In these, indeed, the feeling toward dependencies which usually had been acquired by conquest, and whose inhabitants were of a different blood and a different tongue from their conquerors, manifested a spirit of oppression in keeping with the despotic character of governments, which, far from considering their dependents exempt from burdens for which they were not responsible, regarded them as objects of imperial rapacity and plunder. Of such spirit and conduct toward their colonies, however, it need not be said that the freedom-loving Britons were not guilty—the less so, as the inhabitants of these distant countries were not a conquered people, but were the conquerers, and, being of the same race, were as English as themselves. Nevertheless, this sentiment, always strong enough to make itself felt, was, moreover, sufficiently energetic to play a part in politics, and thus it became an ally worthy the effort of short-sighted or unscrupulous ministers.

Nothing was easier in those days of closed parliaments and sluggish circulation of news, than to delude the populace and arouse their passions ; and no means were more effective to carry a measure than wounded pride and insular prejudice. A word was sufficient—that mere colonial dependencies, fostered for the benefit of home trade, actually interpreted their charters as erecting them into dominions ; that subordinates beyond the sea claimed for their puny legislatures the independence and the powers of Parliament ; and that those who slept under the shield of Great Britain insisted upon doing so, exempt from paying for their repose : these, and other like things, struck the vulgar mind as impudent in the extreme, and aroused in a moment the arrogance which set its face like flint against any thing that looked like an attempt on the part of inferiors to put themselves upon an equality with their masters. The House of Lords, thronged with creations whose patents were still too fresh to be worm-eaten, naturally sided with the throne ; and the House of Commons, which, though Walpole and Newcastle had passed away, still knew too well its master's crib, hurried off in the same direction. Thus arbitrary power, when it precipitated upon the country the same conflict with freedom which England had terminated so gloriously less than a century before, had upon its side not only public opinion, but the only means public opinion had to express itself, save the press ; and this it endeavored to silence before the last argument of kings had been reached. Never was a more singular spectacle beheld than that of a people who had been the only ones to establish constitutional government, frantically protesting against the extension of that boon to others of their race. But so it was ; and, though London and Bristol made demonstrations in favor of the colonies, the isolation of these great markets served only to show more plainly the general sentiment. No fact in history is clearer, than that, throughout this struggle, public opinion in the British Isles was on the side of arbitrary power ; and that when friends were needed, constitutional freedom found few among that constitution-loving people.

What appears from the history of those times is, that, until a tax, other than one imposed by themselves, was laid upon the colonies, the colonists were quiet, law-abiding, aad loyal. The moment the offence which afterward led to rupture was committed, it was resented, but as soon as it was expiated, they relapsed into tranquillity, which was stirred only by the fervent expression of their loyalty, and broken only by the convulsion which followed the discovery that the government had been untrue to them. Then arms were taken up, not to avenge wrongs, nor to achieve independence, but to redress grievance—a distinction received in England with scorn. The immediate cause, then, of this outbreak was the arbitrary action of the home government. That the Americans were content with their liberties as they had them before the first act of oppression was committed ; that, upon the warning given by this act, they sought to constitutionalize these liberties ; that they did not take up arms with a view to independence, but to enforce a recognition of their rights by the constitution of England ; and that what grew into a revolt became such only when that recognition had become hopeless, is proof convincing that the Revolution of 1776 is a manifestation of the same force which produced the Revolution of 1688, and that the Americans simply fought over the same fight which the English themselves had fought before them. The motive of the conflict was the same ; the parties to it were the same, arbitrary power being on one side and the people on the other, and so far as the attainment of constitutional government is concerned, the results were the same. There, however, the parallel stops. Each succeeding revolution always takes a step further forward than its predecessor, and the American Revolution was no exception to the rule. The English Revolution stopped when constitutional limitations had been placed upon the sovereignty by popular rights : the American Revolution went still further, and boldly transferred the sovereignty from the throne to the people. In doing this, revolution seems to have culminated ; for no revolution since this has done more. This last step could not have been taken had not the Revolution of 1688 set the Americans at a point of departure whence it must be taken ; and thus the Revolution of 1776 is a necessary sequence to that of England, or at least the final chapter of a broken tale.

No event had ever before made so profound an impression on

modern society as the American Revolution.   History, it is true, exhibited a growing list of victories which freedom had gained over usurpation, but it was not an unbroken series, and the minds of men still refused to accept as an axiom the truth then established, that, with a just cause and unity of action, those who are determined to be free can be free.   When, then, the world beheld communities which had been fostered solely for the purposes of peace,—communities harmless, unwarlike, feeble, remote from the sympathy of friends, cut off from human aid, and encouraged only by the dangerous applause of those who would make use of them ; when the world beheld such pigmies standing boldly on their defence against such odds, it washed its hands of the doom that awaited them.   But when, the contest ended, it beheld arbitrary power lying in the dust, while what had been but colonial factories stood erect as free states, great was the revulsion of feeling.   Pity and scorn gave way to admiration, and everywhere the oppressed took heart again ; for they could see for themselves how powerless force and cunning are against the resolution of the fierce spirit of liberty, and how impotent a giant clothed in brass can be before the stripling who comes in the name of the Lord.   Henceforth the lad whose days had been passed in herding flocks was accepted in the sight of all the people.

Patriots have at different times and in different places astounded the world and won its admiration by achieving at a blow the independence of their country or the sanctity of their hearths, and nations have earned the respect of mankind by the patience which has at last wrung freedom from niggardly time.   Not so these people : they righted their wrongs too speedily to merit praise for the heroism that waits and is patient, and they valued their cause too highly to stake it upon the hazard of a single throw.   What respect and admiration men gave them was given for more sober conduct : for their breadth and clearness of vision, their profound knowledge of constitutional liberty, their intense earnestness, their faith in the justice of their cause, their prudence which left nothing to chance, their endurance and self-sacrifice, their restraint in the hour of victory, and for the reason and judgment with which they rebuilded their violated temple. This is an exhibition of qualities rather than of deeds ; of qualities which may not be dramatic but which certainly are heroic.   Had these people sprung to arms from the bosom of society, and had they come before the world clothed with the traditions and manners of a past familiar to their neighbors, they could claim the sympathy of old associations, or, at least, engross the attention of the startled family of commonwealths. Or could they present such a motive as the overthrow of a foreign oppressor, the exclusion of a religion not their own, or even proclaim independence of present rule as their object, they might expect the immediate and attentive regards of mankind. But there was nothing of the sort: their present condition was as negative as their past had been, no foreigner oppressed them, their religion was their own, and independence, though a result, was not a motive.

They were a remote people ; the Atlantic Ocean fixed its gulf between them and their kindred blood, and thus removed from Europe, they took no part in its affairs and affected it in neither one way nor another. They did not even constitute a separate state ; they were mere dependencies of a power which could number others like them in every quarter of the globe, and which power itself was not continental but insular. Scattered along an immense stretch of coast and back-lying uplands, they passed their existence in trade and in the fields, and, so far from any thing occurring in this simple life to call forth genius or heroism, hardly a bubble rose to the surface to indicate what was going on beneath. They had no literature, no great men, no ruins, no tradition, no history. Neither art nor song was beholden to them ; no past glory was theirs, nor the enforced respect of acknowledged power, and, without long years of oppression to move the hearts of their fellow-men, they had not even a claim to the world's compassion. They may have added to the comfort of society, but that is all, and the history of civilization might have been written without their absence from its pages being regretted. Nor was the motive which impelled them on their glorious career much more positive. They took arms, not to gain more, but to keep what they had ; their material prosperity could hardly be bettered, and greater freedom than theirs it was not possible to attain ; for they governed themselves, and, exempt from imperial taxation, were yet protected by the empire. Of all people upon the earth, the Americans enjoyed the happiest lot, save in one thing,—the assurance of its continuance as a thing of right and not of grace ;

they had no Declaration of Rights. Thus without the attractive-
ness or the misfortune which appeal alike to the sensibilities of
ancient societies, devoid of antecedents, without which those
organizations eye the intruder askance, and with no better reason
for disturbing the common peace than the resolution to make
sure what was already theirs, these little communities of planters
and tradesmen betook themselves to their task, after invoking
the God of Nations and appealing to the judgment of mankind.
Yet, before their work was ended, the attention of the whole
civilized world was riveted upon them. Humanity became
moved to its deepest depths; its hopes and fears rose and fell
with their successes and defeats, and people held their breath
lest a sigh should disturb the balance in which the pretensions
of arbitrary power and the rights of free men hung so long in
equal poise.

Such were, or, rather, thus appeared to the beholder, the adversaries of the most powerful empire the world has seen since the
days of ancient Rome, and when the contrast between the contestants is regarded, allowance must be made for the lukewarmness with which society at first met their appeal. But appear-
ances were deceptive. Obscurity is not unfriendly to the growth
of manly virtues, and the remoteness of these people from the
agitation of the world had permitted the silent but vigorous development of qualities which make men heroic. The seclusion of
their fields induced a contemplative disposition, and their afflu-
ence preserving them from the sordidness of daily care, they could
safely let the imagination wing its steady flight. Free inquiry
never enjoyed better conditions of existence than among these
men, and freedom of conscience was theirs by inheritance. They,
therefore, did have something, though it was not striking to the
eye; they had much, and, had their liberties been guaranteed by
a constitution, the political philosopher would have beheld in
their condition the realization of Utopia. But, so long had
they been in the enjoyment of these liberties, they never contemplated their loss, and they gave themselves up to the exercise of
their rights without restraint. This taught them their use, and
self-government made these men law-givers and statesmen. Liberty was to them as substantial a fact as their plantations, and
they estimated its value as coolly; it was certainly as essential to

their well-being as their possessions were. They did not approach it timidly, nor as *dilettanti*, but boldly and with the confidence that grows out of habitual contact; and to their familiarity with the practical working of constitutional maxims must be ascribed that mastery in the art of governing which moved Lord Chatham to direct the eyes of those who would know how to conduct states, not to the works of Greece or Rome, to the cabinets of Europe, nor yet to its parliaments, but to the little senates in the woods of America.

What led these people, one after another, to throw themselves at the feet of the mother that bore them and implore her to withdraw her heavy hand; what made them rise as one man in passionate outcry against her; what they did to avert her unjust wrath; and how, one step leading to another, they at last cut themselves off from maternal rule, and started out into the world by themselves;—all this is worth the telling.

Events, such as wars, which close the action of violent forces, are too apt to exclude the attention from the course of that action and from its causes. Men love to dwell upon what strikes the eye, and nothing so fills the view as the sight of warring hosts. But revolutions are not affairs of battle fields. They run their course in the hearts and minds of men where batallions cannot enter, and they are ended when they have given a community something for it to protect against the world. Revolutions do not fight for society, but society fights to make good its revolutions; for, what they bring forth needs protection, and, as revolutions are intangible, there is no power but that of society which can give the protection required. Hence, revolutions are followed by physical conflicts (for the intruder is never welcomed by the one whose place it usurps), which must not be confounded, however, with the revolutions themselves. The real Revolution of 1688 was at an end long before the Battle of the Boyne was fought; and the real French Revolution was over when the National Guard was organized. In the same way, the Revolution in America was ended when the conflict of opinion terminated in the Declaration of Independence; it was not the Revolution of 1783, when the War for Independence came to a close, but it was the Revolution of 1776. The war was the closing scene only of a long struggle, and the real revolution was over before this began.[1]

The story of no successful attempt for freedom is richer in the qualities which are necessary to make men worthy of being free, in the circumstances which impel men to be free, in the means they use to attain freedom, and in the knowledge of when, where, and how to strike the blow, than that which sets forth the different stages through which the American Revolution passed to the War for Independence. This it is which is here designed to be told, and the story of the final conflict will be permitted to rest as it has already been narrated, or as it is to be again told by others.

First, however, to a better understanding of the causes and the events of the American Revolution, it is necessary to observe the nature of the ground and of the actors ; what relations they maintained toward each other, toward the mother-country, and toward the world ; what they really were and what made them such ; and then shall we better appreciate what impelled them to become something else.

The history of the Caucasian tribes in America has this advantage over the history of those tribes in Europe—the tribal advent is known, and its history, unbegotten by fable and unclouded by legend, can be followed, step by step, from one recorded fact to another, and in the clear light of day. When we reflect, that the colonists were English in origin, that they remained English as long as they were subjects of the king of England, that the accessions to their number were chiefly from the British isles, and that the Anglican migration owed its impulse in a great measure to the Great Movement or Revolution, we cannot but accept the period of constitutional development in England as one which profoundly affected American character. Reviewing, then, the career of the American people, from the time they came to these shores as Britons, to the time they became Americans, as well in fact as in name, it will be found that they passed through three successive stages or eras of development :

---

[1] "But what do we mean by the American Revolution ? Do we mean the American war? The revolution was effected before the war commenced. The revolution was in the minds and hearts of the people ; a change in their religious sentiments of their duties and obligations. * * * This radical change in the principles, opinions, sentiments, and affection of the people was the real American Revolution."—John Adams, " Life and Works," x, 283.

1st, the Era of Constitutional Development in England ;

2d, the Era of State Development in America ;· and

3d, the Era of Constitutional Development in America.

Looking back from the heights up which we are still toiling, it is plainly to be seen, that, from the beginning to the end of the First Era, the mastering spirit was Freedom of Conscience,—the form Free Inquiry took after it had once got its foothold, and which includes the free action of the mind as well as of the soul. This freedom the colonists brought with them, as in the cases of Rhode Island, New Jersey, Pennsylvania, Maryland, and Georgia, or, as with the rest of the colonies, developed after their arrival.

During the Second Era a great step was taken. ‹ From the force of location and circumstances, certain qualities, which were inherent in the colonists as members of a Teutonic tribe, enjoyed unmolested exercise, and, of a consequence, the controlling force of this Era will be found to lie in the undisturbed, free, and natural growth of Tribal Institutions. The State had silently grown to maturity, and had but to await the next and inevitable change to assert its existence.

The Third Era is brief and convulsive. Free Inquiry, which, passing from things spiritual to secular matters, had given a constitutional government to England, now did the same for America. The freely-grown tribal institutions stood the shock of civil war unmoved, and displayed a degree of maturity little suspected. Under their protection, the Americans took a step further forward than any yet taken in the history of constitutional government —they transferred the sovereignty from the throne to the people ; or, as they would term it, returned the sovereignty to the hands whence it had first emanated. The individuality, which during the First Era, had been asserted in religion, and which, in the Second Era, had manifested itself in institutions, displayed itself, in the Third Era, in politics, and the ruling force of this stage of the country's development, may, therefore, be said to be Popular Sovereignty.

Throughout all these eras the Spirit of Liberty is manifest, and the freedom of the individual is clearly the expansive force. During the First Era liberty was violent. It had to force its way ; and, uncertain of its footing, it hacked at obstacles it could not wait for time to remove. Its action, therefore, was characterized more by vehemence than reason. But, transferred to America, it appears wholly changed ; and the Second Era finds it watchful, patient, ruminative, and constructive. It became a tiller of the soil ; it pruned with discretion ; and its business seemed to be, to wait on time, to tend the growth of institutions, and to see that nothing interfered with them. This task accomplished, it again, in the Third Era, took upon itself another character. It resented intrusion ; it stood upon its defence ; it defied assault ; it was bitter, uncompromising, and fierce. It ran to meet its enemies ; activity was in every motion. To save an institution, it did not hesitate at staking the existence of a people ; and, provided the institutions were left unharmed, the country itself might lie in ruins. But, in this Era, it was any thing but irrational ; its vehemence was controlled by reason ; and, as it was not so much violent as fierce, it drew the sword only after calculating the blow. As soon as it had achieved its purpose of establishing popular sovereignty under the limitations of a constitution, its fierceness departed from it : the work for the time was over, and it became calm.

In order to understand the American Revolution, this whole Trilogy of Eras requires equal study and reflection ; but, according to the design of this work, the First Era needs no more discussion than what it has here received. We can, accordingly, pass to the Second Era, which is the first that is purely American.

PART II.

THE ERA OF STATE DEVELOPMENT IN AMERICA.

* * * "*ce gouvernement portant avec lui la prosperité, on verrait se former de grands peuples dans les forêts mêmes qu' elle enverrait habiter.*"

Esprit des Lois, liv. xix, chap. xxvii

CHAPTER II.

*Descent—Remoteness of Situation—The Forms of the Colo-
nial Governments, and the Political Relations of the
Colonies.*

WHEN Mr. Burke, in his speech on conciliation with
America, sought the causes that made liberty in Ameri-
ca fierce, his analysis led him to these six capital sources: (1)
Descent ; (2) The Colonial Forms of Government ; (3) Religion
in the Northern Provinces ; (4) Manners in the Southern ; (5)
Education ;.and (6) Remoteness of Situation.

Political philosophy has accepted this analysis as true, so far as
it goes, but not as altogether complete. The *political relations*
of the colonies to the mother-country and to each other, for instance, were such as assisted their self-development in an extraordinary manner, and thereby served to render their spirit of liberty
fierce ; and their *commercial relations* to Great Britain were so peculiar as to affect their character no less remarkably. Doubtless
these political relations were included by Mr. Burke in his medi-
tations upon the Forms of Government, although in the Speech he
neither drew the distinction that existed between them nor exhibited their relationship ; and though it is hardly possible that
this thoughtful and sagacious philosopher overlooked the political
and moral effects exerted upon the colonial constitution by the
commercial relations which he himself recognized as "the corner-
stone of the policy of this country with regard to its colonies,"[1]

---

[1] Speech on American Taxation. See, also, *post* p. 209, the positive utterances of John Adams to the same effect.

yet these relations were treated by him simply as components of an existing system which affected the interests of the whole empire. Time, however, has at last set us at that point where an ordinary observer can gain a broader view of the subject than was possible for even the most far-seeing of those days; and the political relations are perceived to be such adjuncts to the forms of government as to justify their being coupled with them as political forces, while the commercial relations are seen to be so peculiar and so comprehensive, and to exert such force in developing constitutional liberty and rendering it aggressive, as to warrant their distinct addition to the causes of fierceness already assigned. It shall be one of the aims, then, of this treatise to set forth the extent to which these political and commercial relations were exponents of American character, and to show, also, how, as active elements, they affected its formation and development, and served to render the spirit of colonial liberty fierce. Accordingly, the political relations of the colonies will be found embraced in the consideration of the Forms of Government, and the commercial relations will be the subject of distinct discussion.

I, II.—*Descent, and Remoteness of Situation.*

Concerning the "capital source," *Descent*, it is to be remarked, that, if purity of tribal blood is meant thereby, this is to be accepted or rejected as a cause according to the notions of the subject entertained by the observer. There are those who maintain that purity of tribal blood is essential to vigor of race; but there are others who, asserting purity of race to be indispensable, see in the mixture of tribal bloods an element of greater race vigor and activity. A discussion of the subject would only be argumentative[1]; a style foreign to a process which seeks in facts only that are established the historical plan they contain. This cause, therefore, may be dismissed without further consideration.

The source, *Remoteness of situation*, likewise, needs but brief observation. It may be styled the *physical* one of the six causes,

---

[1] Burke, himself, confined his observation on Descent as a cause of fierceness to the fact that the colonists were Englishmen, and "therefore not only devoted to liberty, but to liberty according to English ideas and on English principles." The term "descent" thus scarcely appears sufficiently expressive of the true cause.

and as such it is the one most tangible and most striking to the eye. It speaks for itself, though it is more exact to say, that, by this term, the *laissez-faire* policy of Great Britain toward the colonies is meant rather than distance ; a policy which was induced in the beginning by the fact that the colonies were too remote to allow of governmental interference in their affairs. It is obvious that the indifference, as it has been called, of the home government to the domestic affairs of the colonies, was, in a measure, compelled by the impossibility of immediate action at so great a distance, supposing interference to be contemplated. This was in the highest degree beneficial to the colonists, inasmuch as they were thus enabled to develop by themselves their character and powers in a condition that had no restraints put upon it other than those imposed by the law of nature. Nothing stunts the growth of freedom so much as the paternal care of government ; and it requires no argument to prove, that, unembarrassed by external interference, one at least of the conditions of colonial life was exceedingly favorable to the self-development that always invigorates liberty.

With this brief notice of two of the sources whence, according to Mr. Burke, there flowed a fierce spirit of liberty in the British-American colonies, we shall pursue the consideration of the others mentioned by him, in the order in which he has placed them.

III.—*The Forms of the Colonial Governments, and the Political Relations of the Colonies.*

The forms of colonial government and the character of the relations existing between the English colonies in America and the mother-country appear at a glance, when those forms and character are compared with the forms of Roman and Greek colonial government and the relations which the Roman and Greek colonies held toward their sources of origin.

The colonies of Rome were of four kinds : Roman, Latin, Italian, and Military. The Roman colonies were so called from the fact that they were composed of Roman citizens; the Latin, from their being selected from the Latins ; the Italian from natives of Italy who were neither Roman nor Latin ; and the Military were made up of garrisons and discharged soldiers.

These last had the same rights as the Roman colonies. Some
of these colonies were established in Italy, but others, like the
Italian, were planted outside the boundaries of the peninsula.
Neither the Latin nor the Italian colonies possessed the same
rights as did the Roman and the Military. All these colonies
resembled the municipal towns with right of suffrage, in that
they received the laws of Rome ; and differed from the allied
states, in that they adopted also her form of government and institutions. Since the municipal towns generally imitated these
of their own accord, it was natural that the difference between
them and the colonies should be very slight. We, consequently,
find the same names of magistrates and institutions in both.[1]

From the earliest times the inexorable law of Roman conquest
was, that the lands of the conquered were seized upon by the
state. As soon, therefore, as the Romans got possession of a
conquered territory, they sent colonists from Rome to inhabit it
in conjunction with its former inhabitants, or to build a new city
—for every province had, for its capital, a walled town. In this
way Rome gained two benefits : additional territory, and relief
from the surplusage of its dangerous classes. Each colony was
the result of deliberation, and was conducted in accordance with
a law passed for the especial circumstance. After the proper
preliminaries, political and religious, had been performed, commissioners were appointed, and, under their guidance and the
protection of the military, the colony proceeded to its appointed
place. There, if a new city was to be built, the ploughshare ran
its lines. If no new city was necessary, but all that was required
was, that the colonists should be mingled with the ancient inhabitants in sufficient force to overawe and control them, then their
chief work seems to have been to assimilate the subjugated to
Rome, as closely and as rapidly as possible, in language, laws,
customs, manners, and institutions.[2]

In this brief sketch of Roman colonization, it is impossible to
overlook the fact, that the government was the head and front of
the undertaking. The territory was almost invariably that which
had been reduced to the possession of the commonwealth by the
force of the public arms. No colony could be thought of, until,

---

[1] "Fuss Rom. Antiq.," Oxford trans., 1840, cap. i, §§ 118, *et seq.*
[2] *Id.*, cap. ii, §§ 241 *et seq. ; Brachet.*

not only the consent of the state had been given, but the mode in
which the work should be performed had been signified through
an act of the legislature.   Then, under the guidance and control
of commissioners selected by the government, it started on its
journey under the armed protection of the state, and found, on its
arrival at its destination, its immediate duty to be that of creating
a subordinate and miniature Rome.   In modern times, when we
observe attentively the settlements of the French in Canada and
Algiers, we cannot but be struck with a resemblance to the colonies of Rome, which can be accounted for only by that natural
proclivity which springs from an infusion of Latin blood, and
from the impressions stamped on the Gallic character in those
ages which reach back to the colonies of Narbo and Lutetia.   In
France, the founding of a colony is the work of the government ;
it is planted under the protection of the military ; it relies upon
the armed force of the state, and its first and last duty is to assimilate the new acquisition in language to the French, in laws
to the Code Napoléon, and in manners to those of Paris.   When
the military assures ample security for the experiment, the capital
of the colony becomes, as we have seen, a miniature Paris, just as
Verona, Treves, or Lutetia became miniature Romes.

Among the Greeks, the usual object in founding a colony was,
either to relieve the state of its redundant population, or to facili-
tate trade.   These colonies date from a very early period, from
the invasion of the Heraclidæ, in fact, and being chiefly situated
on the coasts of the adjacent seas, they frequently rose, through
the advantages of their situation, to a pitch of prosperity surpassing even that of their parent states.   The Greeks were far
more truly a colonizing people than the Romans.

Though the colonies went forth under the auspices of the state,
and though their connection with it was marked by the same em-
blems of coinage, the same deities and the same festivals, the
government assumed no such paternal attitude in respect to it as
did Rome toward its colonies, which were ever looked on as *in
statu pupillari*.   The colony was regarded, indeed, in its relations
to the state, as a daughter to the mother ; but it was regarded, too,
as a daughter who was to have her natural growth, and who, in
the course of time, was to assume the rights and duties of adolescence.   In a political point of view, therefore, the mother country

and the colony, though united, were properly quite distinct, and
the former never interposed but on extraordinary emergencies,
when its aid was implored against foreign enemies, or its media-
tion required in civil broils.   In all matters of common interest,
the colony gave precedence to the parent state, but this did not
imply any sovereignty or permanent ἡγεμονία of the latter, any
right to trench on the political independence of its offspring, nor
any closer connection than that imposed by the ties of kindred.[1]

Moreover, the Grecian system of colonization differed from that
of the Romans in this, that under the former the colony always
had a founder, to whom were eventually given the honors of a
hero, or demi-god.   This fact of itself marks a great difference
from that system under which the state, and the whole state, was
the founder.   The Greek colony was expected to grow of itself ;
an expectation which, their history shows, was uniformly realized.

It will at once be seen, that, differing though they do from both
Grecian and Roman, the English colonies resemble more closely
those of the Greeks.   In their foundation the government acts no
great part, but they are led forth by some prominent leader or by
a company.   In their political relations, they are connected with
the parent stock as daughters are with their mothers ; but they
are expected to make their own way, when able to do so, and
to assume the rights and obligations which time imposes on all
who set up for themselves.   While they are unquestionably united
with the mother-country, they are, nevertheless, distinct from her,
and owe allegiance only to the person of the ruler, who never
interferes with them except on extraordinary occasions.   They are
self-governing, and, in every thing but allegiance and what affects
the empire in common, are independent of the parent and of each
other.   In fact, if the resemblance between the French and Roman
systems of colonization is a marked one, still more so is that existing between the Greek and English.

---

[1] For the subject of the Greek colonies see the work of Heeren, and also
Hermann's " Politic. Antiq. of Greece," cap. iv, §§ 73, *et seq.* See further,
" History of Colonization of the Free States of Antiquity Applied to Contest
between Great Britain and her American Colonies," 1777 ; John Symond, in
opposition to preceding, in " Remarks upon an Essay," etc.; Adam Smith's
"Wealth of Nations " ; Sainte Croix, " De l'état et du sort des colonies des an-
cins peuples," Philadelphie, 1779 ; Barthélémy, " Voy. du j. Anach."; Raoul-
Roch., t. iii, 15-50.

Though resembling the Grecian system of colonization, the English differed from it in this, that, except indirectly, the crown took no such prominent part in the foundation of the colonies as the Hellenic governments did. It granted them franchises, and, in return for their allegiance, the throne owed them protection ; but this was the whole extent of governmental action and responsibility. Sometimes the crown followed the examples set by other colonizing powers, and ruled the colony as a province, with a governor appointed by itself with something like vice-regal powers ; sometimes the crown granted large tracts of land to individuals, as is seen in the case of the proprietary colonies, and these were invested with palatine powers ; and again the crown permitted the settlement of a colony by individuals who organized society under laws which were not to conflict with those at home, nor with the interests of the throne. But whether the colonies were royal, proprietary, or chartered, their development was left to the enterprise of the colonists ; and the government, which stood ready to share in the advantages of the undertaking, while, at the same time, it held guardedly back from incurring any risk, limited its action to simple encouragement and to the barest direction it was forced to exercise as a ruler.[1]

As is here indicated, the thirteen colonies were of three kinds :
First, the Royal or Provincial Governments ;
Second, the Proprietary Governments ; and,
Third, the Charter Governments.

The Royal or Provincial Governments were characterized by a delegation of the royal authority to a Governor, as the King's deputy. At the same time, and by the same authority, a Council to assist the Governor was appointed. When the Legislature of the colony met, this Council formed the Upper House. The

---

[1] This was clearly shown in the case of Virginia, where the government suffered the colonists to take all the trouble and risk ; and only awoke to a knowledge of their existence, when it could share the tobacco crop. In the same way Pennsylvania and New England were left to shift for themselves, until they affected trade and revenue. Then they received attention. The Council of Massachusetts used the following language, January, 1773, in an " Answer to Gov. Hutchinson."

" The dominion of the crown over this country before the arrival of our predecessors was merely ideal. Their removal hither realized that dominion ; and has made the country valuable both to the crown and nation, *without any cost to either of them from that time to this. Even in the most distressed state of our predecessors, when they expected to be destroyed by a general conspiracy and invasion of Indian natives, they had no assistance from them.*"

Council was thus not only a cabinet but a senate, which assisted in making the laws of the colony. Over this legislation the Governor exercised the veto power, and the right to prorogue and dissolve. When a law was passed and signed, the King signified his approval or disapproval. In the Governor's hands, also, was lodged the power to establish courts, to raise military forces, and, in general, to perform all needful executive acts.

The Royal or Provincial colonies were New Hampshire, New York, New Jersey, Virginia, North and South Carolina, and Georgia. New Jersey and the Carolinas, once Proprietary, had become Provincial Governments before the Revolution.

The Proprietary Governments were where the King granted rights and privileges to subjects who were Proprietaries of those colonies, and who held the territory, according to the general tenor of legal opinion, as a feudal principality.[1] Certain it is, that the Proprietary exercised regal power in appointing the Governor, in calling together the Legislature, and in approving or disapproving the laws enacted. They were *quasi* Palatinates.

Maryland, of which Lord Baltimore had been the first Proprietary, and Pennsylvania and Delaware, of which William Penn had been the first Proprietary, were the only governments of this description at the time of the Revolution.

The Charter Governments, unlike the Royal and Proprietary, were democratic in their nature ; the powers and rights being vested by a charter in the colonists, who selected their own Governor, Council, and Assembly, though in Massachusetts the Governor was appointed by the King.

Massachusetts, Rhode Island, and Connecticut were the only charter governments existing at the time of the Revolution.

This diversity of constitution is owing to the different times and circumstances of settlement, and also to the different character of the settlers ; and it shows how distinct the colonies were from one another.[2] They were, in fact, separate and distinct bodies in separate and distinct territories. Each held the title to

---

[1] J. Adams, " Canon and Feudal Laws ": but see " Story on the Constitution," i, c. xvii, § 172, and 14 " Pennsylvania State Reports," 492.

[2] " I know of no American constitution ; a Virginia constitution, a Pennsylvania constitution we have ; we are totally independent of each other,"—Galloway's speech, " Life and Works of John Adams," ii, 390: " Story on the Constitution," i, prelim. chap., c. xvii, § 177.

its territory by a grant separate and distinct from its neighbors, and, as allegiance was an act of the person and related to the crown, there was nothing else political whatever in common between them. The colony of Massachusetts was as distinct from the colony of Pennsylvania, as it was from the colony of Jamaica. As colonies they were distinct and separate peoples; as far as their relations to the crown were concerned, each owed it its own individual allegiance, and the crown, in return, owed it protection and the free enjoyment of granted franchises, without the slightest reference to any other colony. Had Virginia owed her allegiance to the crown of France, and Maryland her allegiance to the crown of Spain, they could not have been more distinct and separate bodies politic, in relation to each other, than they were when both bore allegiance to the crown of Great Britain. A British subject indeed, residing in one of these colonies, would have had certain rights within the territory of the other, had he chosen to transfer his residence thither and exercise them, and some did he not so choose : as the right to own property there, to inherit lands, and the like. But this he had from no unity of the colonies, express or implied, but simply from the force of his being a British subject; a fact which gave him these rights in whatever part of the empire they might fall—as well in the Bermudas or Bengal, as in New York or the Barbadoes. In a word, they were separate and distinct autonomies, of which the citizens of one, from the fact of bearing allegiance to the same crown, were not aliens to the citizens of the others. As subjects they could make no treaties with each other ; as subjects they could not be taxed without their consent ; and as, from their remoteness from the capital, representation was impracticable, they really taxed themselves, and under whatever form they might be, Royal, Proprietary, or Charter, they were practically self-governed.

Dr. Robertson expresses his surprise, that the charters should have found favor in the eyes of the colonists, since, in their terms, they bestowed so little and withheld so much.[1] Had he reflected, however, that, of the thirteen colonies, three only had charters at the time he wrote, he would have seen that it was not these few charters which caused the feeling so general throughout the land, and which was common with all whether chartered or not,

---

[1] " America," b. 9.

but that it was something else. What charters there were, it is true, did not, in their terms, bestow every thing free men could desire ; but they did give something to a colonist which was not conceded to an Englishman.   They gave him freedom of conscience, either expressly or by implication, and they had to recognize the fact, that communities planted in a distant desert, must, of necessity, govern themselves in very many respects.   These were all important concessions by the sovereign ; concessions important not only in the franchises granted, but in what they threw open the doors to.

The charters were always looked upon as compacts between the king, acting on the behalf of the nation, and the first planters or settlers.   Though this view of them might not satisfy the strict technicalities of legal construction, it was one never disputed until the days of the Stamp Act ; but was accepted by political writers in England and acted upon by both the crown and the colonists.   By this compact, it was considered, the nation solemnly promised, that if the adventurers, at their own cost and charge, and at the hazard of their lives and every thing dear to them, would purchase a new world, subdue a wilderness and thereby enlarge the king's dominions, they and their posterity should enjoy such rights and privileges as were expressed in their respective charters ; which, in general, were all the rights, liberties, and privileges of his majesty's natural-born subjects within the realm of England.[1]

The charters, then, being inducements to settlers to undertake what was a hazardous venture, the same reasons which urged the crown to hold out these inducements, led it also, after the settlement had taken place, to abstain from any act which might add the weight of its hand to the burdens nature lays upon every community that invades its wilds.   The first steps of the colonies were thus unhampered ; the more so as the poverty of the settlers

---

[1] *Extract from a letter from the House of Rep. of the Mass. Bay to their agent Dennys de Berdt*, London, 1770: "Although the crown might not have a right to grant such exclusive privileges, yet the grants having once been made, and the colonists having settled upon the faith of them, they doubtless acquire a sanction and an authority which nothing but the most urgent necessity can justly alter.   Though wrongly given, they are rightly established, and it would be much more wrong to take them away." "A Short View of the History of the New England Colonies," by Israel Mauduit, 4th ed., 1776,7.   Even Sir Joshua Child admitted the sanctity of the charters, though neither he, Gee, nor Ashley showed any deference to them.

and the hazard of the venture offered little temptation to the doubtful patronage of monarchs. Thus left to themselves to make good their footing, the colonists were compelled to exercise powers which belonged solely to the sovereign, and they did so unchallenged by the only power that had a right to question them. This was liberty ; and no vigorous people, after once enjoying liberty, have ever been known to show any thing but pleasure at its possession. The public mind does not affect nicety of distinction, and as it was natural that the people should unite in the same view, the liberties they had acquired with those which had been granted, it was natural, too, that they should accept what was visible and tangible as the representative of what was not so, and symbolize by the word " charter " every liberty they possessed. Thus, what Dr. Robertson deemed an attachment to charters was really an attachment to personal liberty. If this be not so ; if it be not the many liberties acquired, but rather the few franchises granted, which the colonists regarded with such veneration, how are we to account for the same feeling in the ten colonies which had no charters? Only by that fact. The same conditions of colonial existence caused the same benign indifference on the part of the crown, and this benignity was recorded in the commissions of the governors in terms to which time soon lent the force of custom, and which, in the royal colonies, became equivalent to charters, so far as franchises are concerned.[1] The people of these colonies, likewise, had to exercise the powers of governments as those of the chartered colonies did, and this exercise was recorded in the laws ; the crown had to recognize the acts of sovereignty in their case as in that of the others ; precedent was as forcible here as there, and thus, in the course of time, liberty

---

[1] " The commissions to the governors contained the plan of government, and the contract between the king and the subject in the former [*i. e.* the royal governments], as much as the charters in the latter " [*i. e.*, the charter governments.]. Novanglus, " Life and Works," John Adams, iv, 126 : " As to those colonies which are destitute of charters, the commissions to their governors have ever been considered as equivalent securities, both for property, jurisdiction, and privileges, with charters ; and as to the crown being absolute in those colonies, it is absolute nowhere." *Id., id.*, 127.

" If the first commissions from the crown to the governor of any colony, and the forms of government prescribed by such commissions, are a precedent to be followed in all succeeding commissions, and a system of laws once approved by the crown cannot be repealed (all which is contended by the inhabitants of the royal governments) the charter to the Massachusetts was not so great a boon as our forefathers generally imagined."—" Hist. of Prov. of Mass. Bay " (Hutchinson). Ed. 1767. ii, 11.

became as well assured among them as among their neighbors. The term "chartered liberties" lost in the three colonies its strictly technical sense, and, in all, it acquired the meaning of liberties which had recorded precedents to sustain them ; and thus it is that so significant an attachment to charters originated, and that the Americans made so much of this term.

These governments, though diverse in constitution, were, nevertheless, one in spirit, as a comparison of the annals of the most important ones clearly shows. For, though the terms of the charters varied, and we find the utmost dissimilarity existing between the ideas and institutions of the different colonies in the early stages of their growth, nevertheless, the operation of time, the similarity of circumstances, the identity of motives, and, above all, the same common law,[1] seem to have bent the whole family in one direction, so that, when ready to assert their independence, common notions of free government and of what constituted civil liberty governed all the members alike, and community of interest caused all to act together.

The first colonial government that we are to notice may be said to differ from the rest of the mass. It was so thoroughly monarchical, that, at one time, James I., and afterward Charles I., might be styled the absolute monarchs of what, at a later day, was formally annexed by Charles I. to the realm of England, and adherence to monarchical rule was so much the characteristic of the people, that they not only exulted in the name of their territory derived from the virgin queen, but their pride of loyalty added still another designation to the land, that of the Old Dominion. Yet, when the time came, Virginia was among the foremost in the assertion of independence.

The first charter under which Virginia was colonized was one granted to a company, and it may be briefly and negatively described as one which did not concede in terms the right of self-government. This charter was from time to time revised. The

---

[1] The colonists carried with them the common law. See Lord Mansfield in Hall *v.* Campbell, Cowp. R. 204, 211, 212 ; and Lord Ellenborough in Rex *v.* Brampton, 10 East R. 282, 288, 289.   But, even if they did not, as Blackstone maintains, 1 "Comm.," 107, nevertheless, with the single exception of Pennsylvania, every charter contained a clause expressly declaring that all subjects and their children should be deemed natural-born subjects, and as such enjoy all the privileges and immunities thereof ; and, either expressly, or by implication, it was provided that the laws of England, so far as applicable, should be in force. See further, Stokes' "Hist. Colon.," 20, 23, 149, 184, 185.

company was authorized to engage as colonists any of the subjects of the British crown who should be disposed to emigrate.
All persons being British subjects and inhabiting the colony, and
their children born therein, were declared to have all the liberties, franchises, and immunities within any other dominion of the
crown, to all intents and purposes, as if they had been abiding in
the realm of England. The patentees were to hold their lands in
free and common socage, and not *in capite.*[1] In respect to political organization, the colony was to be governed by a local council, appointed and removable at the pleasure of the crown. This
council was to be under the supreme management and direction
of another council sitting in England, and a duty was imposed on
all persons trafficking with the colony, and the colonists themselves were prohibited from trading with foreign countries.[2] This
charter, similar to the one under which New England was afterward settled, was altered in 1609 and 1612, without any important change, however, as to the civil or political rights of the colonists, and it is the illiberal tenor of this instrument which caused
Dr. Robertson[3] to express his surprise, that the colonists were
satisfied with what gave so little and withheld so much. But, as
the colony increased in numbers and importance, its tone waxed
more and more self-reliant and independent, until, under the continued relaxation of company rule, it called together, in 1619, a
general assembly composed of its own citizens, and this first representative legislature in America, whose existence was sanctioned
by an ordinance of council, in 1621, remained ever after, except
during a suspension in the reign of Charles I., a permanent
feature of the colonial government. The company having lived
long enough to confer on Virginia the boon of what was practically self-government, had its grant of franchises forfeited in proceedings under a writ of *quo warranto* in 1624, and the government of the colony became immediately dependent on the crown.
Henceforth, Virginia was a royal province.[4] It was annexed by
Charles I. to the crown, its assembly was not convened, and it
might have continued to be ruled despotically, had not the neces-

---

[1] That is, by services which are free, honorable, and *certain*, as opposed to
those that were free, honorable, but *uncertain*.

[2] 1 Haz. "Coll.," 50 ; Marshall's " Colon.," 26.

[3] " America," b. 9.

[4] 1 Haz. " Coll.," 220, 225.

sities of the king responded to the demands of the colonists (who, having once tasted the sweets of self-government, were not disposed to give them up), by calling together the legislature under the direction of Sir William Berkeley, whose favorable disposition toward the colonists enabled them to take great steps in the art of governing themselves. The natural proclivity of the colonists assisted the direct efforts of the government, and the common law, itself favorable to the growth of free principles, was established as the law of the land. The effect of this ancient body of laws and free customs, however, was in some degree counterbalanced by the establishment of the Church of England as the colonial church, and the adoption of all the intolerant notions then characteristic of the age and family that sat upon the throne. The distribution of property on the death of the owner followed the course prescribed by the laws of England, and, thoroughly conservative and aristocratic in disposition and in its social structure, Virginia displayed, to an overweening extent, the fondness of the race for the soil, and its love of territorial accumulation, by going beyond the mother-country in obstructing the alienation of land, and by supporting entailments in a manner which surpassed the rest of English society in stringency. She constituted the most prominent example of a royal colony, or what might almost be called a royal province. She was conservative ; she loved royalty and its belongings ; her large estates, the absence of any great, balancing middle class, and the absolute, personal ownership of her labor, made her extremely aristrocratic ; and her pride lay in her fidelity to what the northern colonies were learning to dislike. But as, reacting, this very social organization strengthened the conservatism and haughtiness of which it was the expression, so it made her sensitive to the infringement of personal rights, and called into existence ideas of personal liberty which stubbornly maintained their position. While the constitution of her government was verging on absolute rule, the individuals who were governed were fiercely free. As long as they had their freedom, they snapped their fingers at the terms of charters, the commissions of governors, and the avidity of kings. In fact, the growth of no colony displays so forcibly the rise of positive liberty under the quickening influence of benign indifference on the part of the home government for the management of colonial affairs, and in spite of fettering charters, as does that of Virginia.[1]

With this exception of Virginia, the governments of all the other colonies may be said to be very much alike in character and form, and may all be described in a breath as being of the very opposite in nature from that of Virginia. In a word, as she was aristocratic in social constitution, they were democratic, with the exception of New York, Maryland, and, to a certain extent, the colonies south of her. The share taken by the people in the government was much greater in the colonies north of her ; for, popular representation having been, in their cases, assured to them by the crown at a very early day in their history, some of them might almost lay claim to being styled veritable democracies.

Proceeding north, we come at once to Maryland, where the distribution of power, involving as it did that of the people, seems to have been dictated by great sense and prudence. In its charter, probably composed by Calvert himself, an independent share in the government was reserved to the colonists ; for representative government was secured by the provision that the assent of the people, in assembly convened, was requisite to the validity of the proprietaries' levies of taxation. As this assembly made the laws and ratified the action of the proprietary or governor, Maryland was really self-governed.

In Pennsylvania and New Jersey, including Delaware, society was expressly organized on the basis of self-government, and this feature of their colonial life was always inviolably preserved.

In New England, though settled under what might be called the same kind of charter as that of Virginia, the people had a voice in every thing that pertained to the administration of their affairs, and the charters granted from time to time to the colony of Massachusetts Bay, to its offshoots, and to those established independently of it, seemed to vie with each other in emphasis of the right of the colonies to govern themselves. There, too, the charter of the Plymouth company was transferred at an early day to the colony,[2] and thus the colonists themselves became the recipi-

---

[1] For characteristics of the colonial constitution of Virginia and other colonies, see "Story on the Constitution," b. i, chaps. 2, *et. seq.*, whom I have quoted at large.

[2] Sept. 1, 1629.

ents of the franchises granted. As this charter provided for general assemblies of the company, the colonists had the immediate enjoyment of self-government. That they erected an oligarchy, only proves the existence of self-government more conclusively; inasmuch as they did it of their own motion, and in making choice of a form so different from the one under which they had previously lived, they exercised the liberty of governing themselves at the very first step and in the most positive way. But, as under the exercise of this franchise, the oligarchical feature of their organization melted away, in the course of time, before the popular element, no further notice need be taken of it.

In the address of the General Court of Massachusetts to Parliament, in 1646, it is said: " The highest authority here is in the General Court, both by our charter and by our own positive laws."[1] This General Court, or representative assembly, was invested with full authority to erect courts of justice, to levy taxes, and to make all wholesome laws and ordinances, " so as the same be not repugnant or contrary to the laws of England"; to settle annually all civil officers, and to grant lands. Certainly, here was self-government; self-government that, including all freemen, bordered on simple democracy. Had it been denied the power of regulating faith and extirpating heresy, liberty would have little to complain of it.

In New Hampshire, which was not Puritan in its social constitution, but of the Church of England, with liberty of conscience to all Protestants, the government was, in 1679, defined in a commission issued by the crown. This commission, among other things, provided for a colonial legislature to be composed of the representatives of the colonists themselves, and thus the people of New Hampshire were self-governed.

Connecticut was, by its charter of 1662, entitled to *two* general assemblies annually, and to such an extent was the right of self-government conceded, that Chalmers complains that the constitution of the colony was "a mere democracy or rule of the people."[2]

Rhode Island, in 1663, obtained a charter, which, as we might suppose from a knowledge of its founder and his principles, pre-

---

[1] 1 Hutch. " Hist.," 145, 146; 3 Hutch. " Coll.," 199.
[2] " Annals," 296.

served, in remarkably emphatic language, "full liberty in religious concernments." Liberty is rarely found in fragments, and we consequently find that, in this colony, the exercise of self-government is conceded to the fullest extent.[1]

New York was a royal colony ; but, as under the first governor, an assembly was called in 1691, and the right to representation was never abrogated, self-government must, likewise, be said to be an inherent feature of its colonial organization.

South of Virginia, the Carolinas, at first one but afterward divided, having tried in vain the ideal aristocracy of Locke, constituted also royal colonies. As their assembly was composed of their own representatives, and, like the other colonies, managed their own affairs in conjunction with the coördinate branches of government, they, too, were self-governed.

As for Georgia, its colonial life was too short, and its population too scanty, to illustrate the growth of liberty, or the exercise of self-government, even if it had any. Its real life may properly be said to date only from the time it became an independent state.

Thus we see that the colonies were self-governed, and, were we to follow their history in detail, we should see, moreover, that, from the periods of their inception, this tribal disposition to self-government asserted itself successfully. It was this characteristic, indeed, as has been said, which made States of them. When, therefore, we observe, that this freedom of government went hand in hand with freedom of thought, of conscience, of speech, and of action, it must be admitted that the colonies of Great Britain in America were very free ; more free, in fact, than were the English themselves in England.

But, in no respect did they more emphatically display their free condition, than in their exemption from all taxation, save what they imposed on themselves. Had not this fact existed, they would in truth have been at the mercy of the crown, and would have been mere dependencies, of which the inhabitants would have found to be very apples of Sodom, filled with dust and ashes, those saving clauses, so pleasant to the eye, that secured to them the rights and liberties of English citizens. This exemption, however, existing in their favor from a time anterior to the fixed

---

[1] The government of this province (Rhode Island) is entirely democratical. Burnaby's "Travels," 123.

establishment in England itself of the principle of no taxation without representation, early instilled into them the sense of a responsibility to take care of themselves, a knowledge of the power that lay in them, and a feeling of independence, which, nevertheless, was remarkably slow in reaching a development that involved political disjunction.   Though the needs of government often directed attention to them as sources of revenue, yet, until the last stage of colonial existence was reached, no king approved and no cabinet dared the enforcement of a policy which would constitute them such.   On that point the temper of the colonies was not to be mistaken.   Colonies they were, colonies they expected, nay, hoped to remain, but satrapies they were determined to be never.

It is true, that, at an early day, the value of the tobacco trade, by exciting the cupidity of the Stuarts, threatened to pave the way to a revenue system which would benefit the crown at the expense of the colonies.   But the efforts of those monarchs to control the staple[1] were not so much political as personal, and bore not so heavily on the rights of the Virginians as on their pockets.   Those efforts met with an opposition from America which rendered them wholly abortive as acts of oppression.   As early as 1624, Sir Edwin Sandys secured to this crop protection against foreign competition.[2]   So valuable had it already become, and so destitute were the colonists of ready money, that, for a long while, it was transferred from hand to hand as currency, until, in 1645, this barter was prohibited, and Spanish pieces were substituted as the standard.[3]   From the very beginning, however, tobacco was made the subject of governmental regulation, and orders, acts of Parliament, and proclamations concerning it, succeed each other,[4] as a matter of course, in the list of those which

---

[1] "The Staple appears originally to have meant a particular port, or other place, to which certain commodities were brought to be weighed or measured for the imposition of customs duties previous to being exported or sold." Eccleston's "Eng. Ant.," b. iv, chap. v.   McCulloch's "Comm., Dic.," Tit. Staple.

[2] Stith, 328 ; Haz., I, 193 ; Parl. Hist., I, 1489, et seq.

[3] Jefferson's "Notes on Virginia," Query xxi.

[4] Here are those which I have extracted from Mr. Jefferson's list, "Notes on Virginia," Query xxiii. I give the titles of several : The first is, "Commissio specialis concernens le garbling herbae Nocotianae," 1620, Apr. 7, 18 Jac. I. 17 Rym. 190.   "A proclamation for the utter prohibition of the importation and use of all tobacco which is not of the proper growth of the colony of Virginia and the Somer islands, or one of them," 1625, Mar. 2, 22 Jac. I. 17 Rym. 668.

are devoted to the ordinary subjects of government. The proclamations concerning the protection of tobacco in the colonies [1]
having set a premium on its cultivation, and, thus, rapidly enlarged
the area of its planting and the quantity and value of the crop,
were soon followed by what showed that the monarchs, father
and son, were not altogether disinterested in the aid thus royally
extended. For, in 1628, in a letter addressed to the governor
and council of Virginia, the king, Charles I., offers to buy of the
planters their whole crop of tobacco. This was royal merchan-
dising, indeed ; and, with the mistrust of a huckster, that this
wholesale forestalling might not prove altogether palatable to the
colonists, it was sweetened by an express desire that a colonial
assembly be convened to consider the proposal.

It has been already noticed in this work, how apparently capri-
cious liberty is in her choice of instruments whereby to establish
herself, and how quick she is to adopt any means of gaining a
footing. We have here another instance of her readiness to take
advantage of circumstances. In this case, the cupidity and necessity of a king were the means employed ; to satisfy which, a
monarch, for the first time, conceded to a portion of his people
the exercise of the highest attribute of free government, and, by
admission, yielded that concerning which the title-deed to colonial
existence had maintained a guarded and forbidding silence. [2] The

---

"De proclamatione de signatione de tobacco," 1627, Mar. 30, 3 Car. I. 17 Rym.
668. "Id. pro ordinatione de tobacco," same year, 18 Rym. 920. "A proclamation restraining the abusive venting of tobacco," 1633 ; and another,
"concerning the landing of tobacco," and also "forbidding the planting thereof
in the king's dominions." Both in 19 Rym. 522, 553. Of these, there are
twenty in all : four under James I., fifteen under Charles I., and one under
Charles II. There does not appear to be any under the Commonwealth, and
they extend from 1620 to 1644. In consequence of the rise in price under these
restrictions of competition, the legislature enacted that "no man need pay
more than two thirds of the debts" which had been contracted to be paid in
that commodity, and that creditors should not have a legal right to more than
"forty pounds for a hundred,"—a most despotic act, which ignored the inviolability of contracts and was the first instance of "repudiation" in America,
Hening, I, 225 *et seq.;* Brockenborough's "Virginia," 586.

[1] 1624, Sept. 29, 22 Jas. I, 17 Rym. 621 ; 1625, Mar. 2, 22 Jas. I. 17 Rym.
668 ; 1626, Feb. 17, 2 Chas. I. Rym. 848 ; 1627, Mar. 30, 3 Chas. I, 18 Rym.
886 ; 1627, Aug. 9, 3 Chas. I, 18 Rym. 920.

[2] Bancroft's remarks on this subject are, in view of what I have said concerning it, and the let-alone demeanor of England toward her colonies, worthy of
quotation :—" Hitherto," says he, "the king had, *fortunately for the colony,
found no time to take order for its government.* His *zeal for an exclusive contract* led him to observe and to sanction the existence of an elective legislature.
"Hist U. S." I, chap. vi.

impecuniosity of princes has always been favorable to liberty. But it was the fate of the unlucky Charles, in all his schemes of aggrandizement, to fall short of his object, and, yet, at the same time, to strengthen the hands of those of whom he expected to make something.   This very tobacco speculation illustrated his miscalculations, or bad fortune.   The colonists met, but they declined the offer, and thus the king failed to get the tobacco, while the colonists not only kept what they had, but gained a representative government besides.   They at once followed up their advantage.[1]

This attempt to establish a monopoly was, for some time, not altogether abandoned[2]; but the firm attitude of the planters, and the rapidly thickening crowd of events at home finally compelled its relinquishment.   In the meantime, the Virginians had learned two things: first, that their productions were of value to the crown; and, secondly, that they occupied a position sufficiently independent to enable them to make their own terms in any bargain with the government.   That they did not forget this lesson was clearly shown in after days, when they came to make a truce with the Commonwealth,[3] and while Charles I. sat upon the throne, the understanding seems clear, that, so long as the planters made great profits, the crown might impose what duties it liked on the staple at home.

What distinguishes the English colonies from all others is their institutional character.   The English, or, as it was originally, the Saxon blood, has always sought and found its natural expression in institutions—those self-acting means by which the social forces of free peoples express themselves; which are themselves independent creations endued with the capacity of self-government and the tendency to self-development, and which, having frequently

[1] To what extent the Virginians took advantage of this concession, see note to chap. vi, Bancroft, "Hist. U. S.," vol. i., where a list of assemblies extending from 1630 to 1642, sixteen in all, has been extracted from Hening's "Statutes at Large"; which list refutes, too, the statement of Story, "Comm. on the Constitution," c. 2, § 49, that, during this time, there was not the slightest effort made to convene an assembly.   In 1660, representation had acquired such force, that Berkeley, the governor, who had just taken his seat as such, said, "I am but a servant of the assembly."   Smith's "Hist. New York," 27.

[2] See "A Commission Concerning Tobacco," 10 Car. I, June 19, 1634.

[3] "Notes on Virginia," Query xiii; Hening, I, 363, *et seq.*; Hazard, I, 560, *et seq.*; Burk, II, 85, *et seq.*

the power of self-production, are, thus far in the history of the human race, the very highest forms or expressions of social force.

This institutional nature is the tribal characteristic, and, as it has always distinguished the body of the tribe, so, too, it invariably characterizes the offshoots ; and, as institutions are vital organizations which grow by their own inherent force, the institutional nature is, therefore, progressive. Hence it is, that the English colonies have never stood still, but, once planted, have grown right on, adapting themselves to the conditions of soil, climate, and circumstance, and each developing into a state, precisely as its parent had done before it. The colonies of other people are but fragments of themselves broken off and set into the western world, as a piece of stone is set in mosaic. They toil and they spin ; but they do not grow. They stop short when the conquest or the settlement is terminated, and for them the law of development seems hardly to exist. Not so with the English colonies : their colonists bear with them the ark which contains self-development, and no sooner is this ark set down than the law of their being springs into action, and, like those organisms of which we read, that a member straightway begins to develop a body analogous to that from which it has been torn, the little group at once proceeds to organize its social forces, to root itself in the soil, to draw thence its sustenance, to acquire strength, and to develop, sometimes rapidly, sometimes slowly, but always surely, a state, in principles, modes of action, polity, nature, and even form, like that from which it sprung.

No more forcible illustration of this institutional development can be imagined, than that which the English colonies in America presented ; an illustration rendered still more forcible by the contrast it offers to the French colonies in the same quarter. We see what the historic growth of the former was ; but where was the historic growth of the latter ? The French were just as early on the ground ; they displayed as great personal energy, and in one respect outstripped their neighbors, for they had pushed their way from the St. Lawrence to the Gulf of Mexico before the more sluggish English had crossed the Alleghenies. At this day, we know little more of the general topography of the Mississippi valley than what the early French did. They were brave—the plains of Abraham and the grass-covered lines around the ruins of Fort Carillon still bear silent but eloquent testimony to that virtue. But that is all : their activity was individual, not national ; their development was personal, but not social. While the Frenchman's canoe was pushing its way into waters where the Englishman would not follow for a century, his people on the St. Lawrence were doing nothing ; yet, France was dreaming of empire and of the glory that was to follow her adventurers, while the whole English frontier was steadily and surely, albeit slowly, advancing. The French settlements of Canada never developed, in the sense felt by every one who speaks English. They were mere pieces of Normandy and Brittany tesselated in American wood, and, as soon as they were once fixed in position, they were the same that they are to-day. They have not changed. Picturesque, dreamy, poetic they may be, with their old Norman and Breton songs, their musical tongue, their seigniories, and their quaint villages, each grouped around a glittering-roofed church which has a name as tuneful as its own chimes, but they have not advanced an inch, they have not produced a single new thing for the good of the human race or of themselves ; they stand still, and they survive simply by the sufferance of the rigorous climate which envelopes them, and under the protection of the tortoise that passed them in the race. Even the genius of Montcalm could not save them. The laws of nature would have prevailed just the same had the French gained the upper hand, and the French in America display to-day a picture of what French America would have been had Wolfe failed to take Quebec.

The reason of this, of course, lies in the difference of race ; and that difference is shown in the contrast which the institutional character of one of these peoples makes with the uninstitutional character of the other.

It would be as easy to imagine the Anglican tribe without the power of speech, as to imagine it without institutions ; for these are as much a characteristic of the tribe as that is of the human race. First conceived and born in the forests of Germany,[1] they have made the Teutonic race, and especially the English branch of it, what it is, no matter where and under what circumstances it has

---

[1] Montesquieu, " Esprit des Lois," l. xi, c. vi : " Ce beau système a été trouvé dans les bois." Voltaire, however, doubted this.

been placed. Not a kingdom rules the seas ; not a colony plants itself on the other side of the globe ; not a State knocks for admission at the door of the American Union ; not a new county, nor so much as a township, is laid off from an old one, but what the fact is due to the institutional character of the race. In America, where, unrestricted by ancient limitations, the growth of institutions has been prolific beyond measure, the exhibition of institutional development has lost its impressiveness from triteness, and the mind turns to the contemplation of the subject with much the same feeling that it would have if called upon to observe the familiar organization of household life. It would be interesting, but it would not have novelty to increase the interest.

With the French it was different. When they planted a colony, the first thing it did was to make itself a miniature France. It did not strike out for itself, and leave the formation of its character to time and circumstance. It did not even rely on itself : it depended upon the military under whose guns it had landed, and on the officials of the bureaucracy it was sure to bring along. Its sole object seemed to be to imitate what it had left behind. No institutions grew of themselves : what there were of them were like posts stuck in the ground. The structure of an English colony resembles that of English society ; not from imitation, but because, in obedience to the same laws which developed the parent, the colony acts out, of itself and in its own way, the same principles to the same end. These expressions of social force are, therefore, one in nature and similar in form, and they would characterize the offspring were the parent stock to be blotted from the list of nations. But a French colony does not act in this way : it seems to look upon its fate as that of exile, of which the best is to be made, and solace is to be found only in adhering as closely as possible to the model of social life it left behind. The consequence is, that there is no self-dependence in a French colony ; no free, vigorous action, no life ; and a structure so hollow needs but a push to overturn it. Its happiness is complete when the strong arm of the government enforces such a sense of security that the process of imitation can go on without interruption ; but when the imitation is effected, the comparison it presents with the life of an English colony may be described as similar to that existing between a child and the portrait of its father : both resemble the person ; but one is a living being, and the other merely a likeness.

The reason, then, that the French did not retain their American possessions, but departed leaving scarcely a trace behind them worthy the notice of the political observer, is, that they lacked those institutions which take root and grow for themselves, even though dropped as seeds are by birds in their flight. Instead of relying on the inherent vitality of their people to secure what had been acquired, they depended only on the force of arms. So long, therefore, as their arms were successful, so long did they rest secure in their possessions ; but when disaster overtook their armaments, the prop which upheld the structure was knocked away, and the whole shell fell into ruins. In no instance was this so forcibly illustrated as by the issue of the battle fought under the walls of Quebec. While Montcalm lived, the French occupation lived ; but when he fell, the whole French power in America east of the Mississippi[1] fell with him. It absolutely vanished ; and, save the tongue, the religion, and those few institutions which are common to all peoples—for there is no civilized society without some institutions,—it left not a vestige behind. With the last breath of the French commander, the power of France in the West was transferred to England ; the colonists became British subjects, and the French settlements were restricted to the narrow territory they still occupy.

Not so the English, whose vitality depended upon the health of institutions and not upon the successes of arms. Disaster hardened them, and calamity lent force to their development. Bringing with them the institutions of the race, they grew of themselves, and it is a significant fact, that they never relied on the arms of the mother-country without loss, nor on their own without gain.[2] Self-dependence was a lesson early taught and soon learned. The colonies were young, but the institutions were old, and these were the ravens that fed them in the wilderness.

In nothing have the Europeans more persistently misconceived the character of American institutions, than in taking it for granted, that, because the country is "new" so are the institutions. So far from it, these are as old as the race itself, and it would be dif-

---

[1] Johnson *v.* M'Intosh, 8 Wheat. 543.

[2] On the one side, for examples, the capture of Louisburg and the never-ending frontier war ; on the other, Braddock's and Abercrombie's campaigns.

ficult for an Englishman, or a Teuton of any tribe, to lay his finger on one of our institutions which did not come out of the woods with the race. Even in those which may be called "new," the germs can be discovered among those of the early English. They are "new" only because ages have elapsed since the occasion has arisen for calling them into action, and, unused to the sight of them, the European naturally regards them as strange. One might as well assert the existence of a new language from the fact that the country is new, as, from the same fact, to assume the existence of new institutions. America is young in years, but in institutions it is old, very old.

The colonization of the English in North America was effected chiefly under the House of Stuart. These monarchs, at once arbitrary and impecunious, saw in the boundless plains of America and in the tide of emigration that was setting in thither, relief from two evils: the lack of money, and the fanaticism which, from day to day, was becoming more and more threatening to the peace of the kingdom and the stability of the throne. On one hand, land in another hemisphere was a ready substitute for money ; and, on the other, what could be better adapted for the crazy experiments of enthusiasts than remote deserts, or what location better for the overstock of London rufflers than that where gold might perhaps be found, and where tobacco was sure to grow? At one stroke both kingdom and exchequer would find relief. As men are lavish with what is not immediately before their eyes, and with what is apparently exhaustless in resources, so these monarchs were prodigal of a continent which lay beyond the ocean out of sight. What mode of paying an old debt could be easier than a deed of land in the Hesperides? What better way of getting rid of the pestering claims of ancient servants than a grant of franchises which could be effective only in a wilderness? It is this which accounts for the profuse dispensation of liberty beyond the seas, while, at the same time, it was grudgingly withheld at home. To this easy disposition of giving away what was worthless to the givers, as well as to the necessity of offering inducements for colonization, is to be ascribed the plantation of British colonies in America, and the broadcast scattering of franchises under which colonies and colonists multiplied as reeds by the water side. The heedlessness which bestowed these liberties was succeeded by an equally beneficent neglect, under which the institutions of the race developed unnoticed and without let or hindrance ; and when at last avarice disturbed the torpor of indifference, it was found that the colonies had not only acquired strength, but had concentrated it, and that, having grown to man's estate in undisturbed tranquillity, as far as the mother-country was concerned, they were ready and able to assert their existence as independent states.

The great distinguishing characteristic of the English colonies, from which springs the institutional character of which mention has been made, is that which distinguishes the English themselves from other peoples—their natural predisposition to govern themselves.   This also is a race characteristic, which showed itself in the earliest history of Britain, and to this inherent tribal law of self-government is due its character as a representative government, and, consequently, a limited monarchy, and, especially, the formation of counties and their division into parishes, hundreds, or townships.   Few have been the English-speaking men, since the final establishment of a parliamentary constitution, who have gone down to the grave without making themselves felt, to some extent, in the government of their land, be it where it might, or who have not actually taken part therein—if not in the government of the nation, in that of their province or colony ; if not in that, then in the administration of county affairs ; if not in the county, then in that of their parish or hundred : perhaps in all.   No matter how often, or by what means, the race has been pushed from its moorings, it has always returned to the anchorage of self-government at the very first opportunity.   It is the social force directly opposed to the centralization of the Latin or Gallican notions of government.   This latter looks on government as paternal, paramount, and as acting of its own motion ; the Englishman, on the contrary, regards it as vicarious, delegated, and representative. One considers the throne as the source of power ; the other, as the conduit through which the power of the body politic is conveyed to the object to be acted upon.   To one, the monarch is the absolute and unaccountable owner ; to the other, he is a trustee, and, as such, accountable for his exercise of the power entrusted.

No notions of government can be wider apart than those held by the Latin races and those held by the English. With the latter, the one solitary and natural idea of government is what is known as self-government. It springs from the love of the soil, so characteristic of the tribe ; an affection which makes the trespasser on one's field almost as great a wrong-doer as he who violates the sanctity of the person.[1] The race has always given the supremacy, in respect of property, to land, and has always girt it about with favoring laws no less marked than are the hedges and fences that surround it on the ground. Where this legislative expression appears, there the race displays its natural love of the soil ; where it does not appear, there, it is safe to say, this quality of the race is no longer uppermost, but has declined, or, perhaps, has never existed at all. No more significant sign of the decadence of race qualities can be given, than where the courts, who utter the voice of the state, enforce the doctrine that land shall be as easily transferable as personalty. It is the sacrifice of a race characteristic to present expediency, and if any thing which disturbs or destroys the natural action of the race is a wrong, then this doctrine is wrong and is sure to end in disaster. It becomes a precedent, to say the least, for further destruction of race characteristics, with which disappear the race notions of free government, and anti-race notions of despotic rule take their places as a matter of course.

It is to this love of the soil, this notion of personal independence, and to the sense of individual power which one has when standing in his own fields and on his own ground, that is to be attributed that freedom of action which is the true source of the institutions which mark the race.

The colonists brought with them this love of the soil, and the natural proclivity to self-government. From Virginia to Massachusetts Bay, no sooner was the land occupied than it was laid off in counties, and in hundreds, or townships. The very first thing the settlers did anywhere, was to betake themselves to the task of governing themselves ; and, forthwith, their natural institutions appear, as if they had been brought over in boxes which were the first to be unpacked. The little hives bestir themselves at once in the direction of social organization, and one invariable feature

---

[1] Chitty on " Pleading." Tit. Trespass.

of their labors is the provision made for the future expansion of
society.   Before the dwellings were built the governments were
erected.   Perhaps, like the dwellings, they were but temporary
shelters, to last only until houses took the place of sheds : but
there they were, and from the moment they appeared, they, and
the institutions they sheltered, went on developing without a
moment's retrogression.   If they were opposed, they were as
stubborn as the rocks ; if unopposed, they expanded with the
growth of their colonies.   Sometimes these governments were cut
and dried in the London office of "the Company" before the
colonists started ; sometimes they were outlined in their charters
by the imperial government ; and yet again, as in the cases of
Maryland, Pennsylvania, and Rhode Island, they were the results
of the direct action of the proprietary or the people.   But,
whether the work of cabinets, of proprietaries, of companies, or
of colonists, sooner or later, all had for their active, vital, controlling force, without which they would have been as nothing,
the people themselves.   They became, thanks to the remoteness
which thwarted the interference of the home government,
and to the indifference of that government, real examples
of popular sovereignty, no matter what might be the terms
of the charter, patent, or commissions of the governors.   They
made their own laws, laid their own taxes, fought their own
battles, and, in all respects, were their own men.   This was self-
government, local self-government ; for each colony looked out
for itself, and none so much as pretended to meddle with the
affairs of another, or to indulge in an interference which was sure
to be sharply resented.   Independent of each other and of the
world, with nothing to restrain them except the slight tie that
bound them to the mother-country, with the sense of power inherent in freemen, and with the love of adventure the ocean and
the wilderness alike fostered, it is no wonder that there arose, in
the course of time, that "fierce spirit of liberty," which filled, in
such large measure, the observant eye of Burke,—a spirit which
grew "with the growth of the people in the colonies, and increased
with the increase of their wealth."[1]

Foremost among the incentives of that fierce spirit of liberty
was the contemptuous regard for the colonies entertained by the

[1] Speech on Conciliation with America.

commercial classes of England, who looked upon them simply as so many institutions erected for the especial benefit of England; as, in short, so many sponges to be squeezed. These classes naturally had great influence with the legislature of a country given over to thrift, and they made their mark from time to time on the legislation, which, in turn, betrayed this notion. As these acts of Parliament were almost invariably encroachments in some shape or another on what the colonies deemed sacred rights, they were promptly resisted. The government, doubtful of enforcing success with bodies too important to be lost, yet not of too great importance to be imposed upon when the opportunity offered, would retire from the position adverse to colonial interests into which the greed of home commerce would at times thrust it, and thus, on its part, did its share in familiarizing the colonists with the belief that all that was necessary to make the government back down was to meet it with a bold front. This notion, which, it must be said, the facts warranted the colonists in adopting, was the first step on the road to independence; for those who saw that the colonies had sunk in the eyes of Englishmen to being mere commercial appendages to the empire, instead of being living parts and members of it, soon entertained the still further advanced idea, that, if the colonies were more important to England than England was to the colonies, they might be better off were they to cease being mere tributaries or feeders to the trade of London and Bristol. Hence arose the last notion of the series, that of independence, which, beaten down as fast as it raised its head, by the loyalty that bound the American heart to England, never ceased its struggles until it had asserted its existence, destroyed the bond of allegiance, and, carrying along with it the now enthusiastic masses of the colonies, had torn from the empire the best part of its continental possessions, and those, too, which were biggest with the promise of the future.

If we look at the career of this "fierce spirit of liberty," and observe its character, we shall not be astonished that it ends in independence of the mother-country. Little else, indeed, could be expected, if, from the plan of historical development, which, before the advent of the English in America had marked the different migrations of the race, inferences could be drawn upon which to forecast the colonial future. The colonists were of a people

whose whole career had been characterized by an insatiable craving after local self-government.   This kind of government they
brought along with them, and they were enjoying it to a much
greater extent where they were than they could have done had
they remained in England.   The appetite for personal influence
in the administration grew by what it fed upon, and caused the
colonists, when the pleasure of its enjoyment was interrupted, not
only to be galled in the most sensitive part of their nature, but to
regard the effort to curtail their liberties as downright robbery of
that self-government to which they had long before acquired the
actual right of possession.   Had the policy of George III. been
enforced by the house of Stuart, it is hardly probable that there
would have been any thing more than a murmur.   Men had not
yet grown up to liberty and the desire for independence, but in
the latter half of the eighteenth century, the spirit of liberty was
already more fierce, perhaps, than it had ever been before, and it
stood ready, if balked in its course, to hew its way with the sword
to the independence which suffered no questioning.   Hence we
see, that, at the bottom of this disruption, lay the determination to
keep inviolate the local self-government, to which, as living members of their race, they had the birthright, and of which they had
long had actual possession.   This it was that rode upon the
storm.

   The *forms of government* in the colonies having been considered,
and the effects of *descent and remoteness of situation* noticed, we
proceed with the analysis as given by Mr. Burke.

CHAPTER III.

IV.—*Religion in the Northern Provinces.*

PROCEEDING to the next cause mentioned by Mr. Burke which served to make liberty in the colonies fierce, namely, *Religion in the Northern Provinces*, we shall see that its striking feature was the principle of toleration, or, to use the broader expression, freedom of conscience ; and if we are to point out the localities where this principle appeared in its greatest vigor, we must name, above all other territories, Maryland, Pennsylvania, West Jersey, and Rhode Island.

Freedom in one thing is the natural progenitor and support of freedom in another, and it needs no argument to show that freedom of conscience was the natural forerunner and ally of freedom of the citizen. Inasmuch as free inquiry passed from religious to secular subjects in the colonies, just as it did in England, though without revolution and civil commotion, an inquiry into the causes of our political freedom must necessarily embrace the contemplation of what free inquiry did in America when it turned from religion to politics.

At the first glance, the colonies do not appear to be a chosen abiding-place of free inquiry in religious matters. Their foundations were laid when intolerance was still a sacred principle, and their structure betrays the characteristics of the age in which they rose. But, though intolerance came with the early colonists, it was the only thing they brought with them which did not display enduring vitality. Intolerance—practical, physical intolerance—was never more determinedly enforced than in the settlements around Massachusetts Bay ; yet, before one generation had passed away, we behold, in the settlement of Rhode Island by men of Massachusetts, the first example known to the world of a com-

monwealth founded on toleration as a principle of political constitution.   Intolerance, too, in the shape of a rigid establishment,
was a characteristic of Virginia, and one which she hugged to her
bosom with nervous tenacity ; yet we see arise alongside of her
the commonwealth of Maryland, which was the first to possess a
charter that guaranteed freedom of conscience.   When Pennsylvania, in her turn, took her place as a living expression and assertion of this great doctrine, the whole aspect of the colonies was
changed.   Toleration seemed the rightful lord, while intolerance
wore the air of an intruder.

To a right knowledge of those times, it must be clearly understood, that *dissent*, (which involved the notion of *separation* from
the Established Church), was a thing regarded by every one as
heretical, and that the state was the natural agent of its repression.   Thus, on the revolt of Henry the Eighth from the Papacy,
while the mass of Englishmen sustained and supported the king
in breaking down the old religion, it would have been, and was,
regarded on all sides as the rankest heresy, if not treason, to deny
the king's right and duty to impose a new religion on the country and to maintain it at all hazards.   In their eyes this duty of
the state was not in the least impugned by Henry's revolt.   That
meant merely independence of a foreign religion ; the duty of the
state to impose a home religion, and the duty of the subject to
maintain and obey it, were none the less.   There were few notions
of government—and a state religion was part and parcel of the
government—so stubbornly maintained as that one.   This is
shown with great clearness by the history of the times.   When
England broke from Rome, no one denied the right of the state
to impose upon the land the Established Church ; when the mass
of the Puritans broke from the Established Church, no one but
the handful of Brownists denied the right of the state to impose
the Presbyterian establishment, did the realm so desire it ; when
the Independents broke from the Presbyterians, eight out of ten
Englishmen were shocked beyond measure, that doctrines should
be recognized which practically left the country without a state
religion.   It is safe to say, that, in those times, ninety out of a
hundred Englishmen were born, lived, and went to their graves
with the conviction that it was the natural duty of the state to extirpate heresy ; or, in other words, that it was the natural duty of

the civil power to expel from the body politic those who did not conform to the national religion, be it what it might. So deeply was this notion rooted, and so effective an element was it in all ideas of government, that it was a long time before even the Independents themselves could be brought, as a body, to acknowledge the contrary. The Brownists, indeed, openly called themselves Separatists, and took the position that any religious establishment was contrary to the Word of God[1]; it was they who colonized Massachusetts; yet it was they who, as Independents or Congregationalists, withheld their censure at the expulsion of Roger Williams from, not only their communion, but their territory, for denying the authority of their establishment, for such it was; for asserting that thought should be as free in religious as in secular matters; that the Sunday laws were an abomination to the Lord; and that the magistrate had nothing whatever to do with the promulgation of the faith, the discipline of the church, or the extirpation of heresy. He was worthy of banishment, they said, who maintained that " the civil magistrate might not intermeddle even to stop a church from apostacy and heresy." [2] For asserting the right of free thought and free speech he was banished. Those who banished him acted according to their lights. They were born and bred in these notions, and were the mere agents of a tyranny which, at that time, was natural to all, was obeyed by all, and was enforced by all, except the great reformer himself and a few like unto him. If such were the ideas of the rightfulness of secular agency in ecclesiastical affairs among those who sought the wilds of America rather than bow the knee to Baal, how much more natural and forcible must they have been among those early English Puritans, to whom the very mention of reform smacked of heresy, and on whose minds dissent had not yet dawned. The religion of the land might be changed a hundred times, but, then, whatever the changes, all were alike bound by them, and one doctrine, one discipline, one religion in substance and in ceremony, could alone be tolerated.[3] This was intolerance, pure and simple, but in those

---

[1] But Brown himself relapsed, and accepted a living in the Established Church.

[2] According to the citations of Dexter in "As to Roger Williams," Brewster, and the other leaders of the Pilgrim Church at Plymouth, did any thing but remonstrate at this action of the Puritan churches.

[3] Barlow's "Sum and Substance of the Conference at Hampton Court," 71; Harrington's "Nugæ Antiquæ," I, 180, *et seq.*; Hallam, I, 404.

days intolerance was a fundamental maxim of all government. Personal persecution is not the only test of intolerance, but the true test is the question, *Was the civil power relied upon by the church, and recognized by the people, as the natural ally and agent of the ecclesiastical power in the prescription of faith, the control of religious opinion, and the extirpation of heresy?* If the answer is yes, then intolerance was a controlling maxim of government; if no, then toleration was. In those times the answer would invariably have been in the affirmative.

Looking, then, at the times in which the colonies were founded, it would be strange, indeed, if we did not find intolerance among the recognized principles of government brought over by the early colonists; but knowing what we now do of the men that brought these principles, and of the circumstances that effected their development, it would be stranger if we found intolerance display life and vigor. Acccordingly we look in vain for the evidences of a lasting vitality. The intolerance of the New England Puritans at last spent its force, and sunk down into dead ashes never to be revived; the intolerance of the Establishment never so much as called upon the state to prescribe a single article of belief, to regulate a single doctrine, or to extirpate a single heresy,—it was a legal fiction. Intolerance had, however, an existence which might have become life, had not the timely arrival of Pennsylvania upon the field forever turned the day against her, and established as the controlling force of the American people the common principle of George Calvert, Roger Williams, and William Penn. The career of intolerance in this country may be briefly described, so far as the Church of England is concerned, as decorous, harmless, and confined to the mere assertion of legal existence; outside of the Establishment, its action was sporadic, spasmodic, and indicative of the violence into which waning forces sometimes concentrate all their power.

Though, as has been said, the colonists brought with them intolerance, there are two notable exceptions to this statement: Maryland and Pennsylvania. These colonies secured to themselves freedom of conscience before they ever left England, one by direct grant and the other by implication; Lord Baltimore's colonists, indeed, making its possession a condition preliminary to their departure, and a part of the contract under which they were to extend the dominions of the crown in America. Such marked exceptions peremptorily arrest the eye, and the spectacle of the House of Stuart establishing and guaranteeing under the great seal freedom of conscience in one of its dominions, directs our observation upon the Maryland charter and the circumstances which called it into being.

But, before regarding the relations in which the credulity of Maryland stood toward freedom of conscience, let us first observe the effect upon its development produced by the mysticism of Pennsylvania and the rationalism of Rhode Island.

Quakerism.

The world is as much indebted to the mysticism of Pennsylvania and West Jersey for the assertion of freedom of conscience as a principle of political constitution, as it is to the unquestioning belief of Maryland, and the inquisitive rationalism of Rhode Island. What these planted, that saved; and, as Quakerism affords the latest and most complete development known to the colonies of the union of freedom of conscience and state, instead of the union of church and state, we shall now turn to its examination.

While the rising Independency of England, which had inscribed on its banner the device of free religion, was in the act of overthrowing intolerance in the persons of the Presbyterians, the enthusiastic nature of George Fox, the founder of the Society of Friends, was pushing his agonizing reflections and self-conviction toward a mysticism which, though it has failed to convert mankind, has indelibly stamped its mark upon the world. Quakerism, now a mere shell, and with hardly the appearance of life stirring in the void, was in its day one of the forces which deeply impressed American character; or, to speak with accuracy, its appearance at the time it made its advent, and its choice of the middle colonies as its abiding place, were events most fortunate for the establishment of freedom of conscience in America. Its coming unquestionably lent strength to a hard-pressed cause, and perhaps preserved it from total ruin.

It is needless to recount the rise of a sect, which demonstrates, for the hundredth time, that intellectual foresight, enthusiasm, tenacity of purpose, and fidelity to a noble cause, are qualities not

confined to the learned and powerful only of either a democracy
or aristocracy. This sect was plebeian in character,[1] and, in its
days of proselytism, fanatical ; yet it comprehended with remarkable clearness the virtue and beneficence of freedom of
conscience, and clung to it as a vital social element with heroic
tenacity. It was simply one of the innumerable forms of mysticism, which, for the first time since the days of Tutian, the En-
cratites, the Gnostics, the Nicolaitic heresy, and the Scholastics,
was organized into a permanent and proselytizing sect. Its distinguishing characteristic is, that it discards the Scriptures as the
one source of spiritual light, and refers the individual for illumina-
tion to his conscience, wherein exists what is styled the Inner
Light. "Oh, no," cried back Fox to the preacher who had taken
for his text the words, *We have also a more sure word of prophecy,*
"Oh, no ! it is not the Scriptures, it is the Spirit."[2] Chilling-
worth had not so ruthlessly swept away authority. This placing
the well-being of man in his conscience only, and under the
guardianship of the divine inspiration that illumined it, of
course presupposed that the conscience should be entirely free,
and thus the disciple of Fox, at the outset, demanded freedom of
conscience. The constant standard of truth and goodness,
says William Penn, is God in the conscience, and liberty of conscience is, therefore, the most sacred right, and the only avenue
to religion. To restrain it, is to invade the divine prerogative ;
to direct it, is to interfere between the Creator and the creature.[3]

This sect rose rapidly to its zenith, under the craving for new
religions to which the souls of those times were peculiarly subject, and under the attraction which the novelty of their doctrines
excited. These doctrines were all of the essence of passiveness,
and they were supplemented by certain peculiarities of address,
garb, and conversation, by which the eye and ear could distinguish
that they who affected them were separate and apart from the

[1] "I had the curiosity to visit some Quakers here [Ipswich] in prison ; a new
phanatic sect, of dangerous principles, who shew no respect to any man, magistrate, or other, and seeme a melancholy, proud sort of people, and exceedingly
ignorant."—Evelyn's "Diary," July 8, 1656.

[2] Barclay says, the Scriptures are a declaration of the fountain, and not the
fountain itself—a simile used likewise by Elias Hicks, a century and a half
later, to illustrate the same thing. "Letters," 228. And see Gurney's "Distinguishing Views and Practices of the Society of Friends," 58, 59, 76, 78.

[3] "Penn's Works," ii, 1, 2, 133.

world. The Quakers attempted, indeed, the hopeless task of uniting mysticism in spiritual life with formality in daily life. The attempt failed, and, as a sure result of time and human nature, the latter had so far absorbed the former, that, in our own century, when Elias Hicks sought to restore Quakerism to the point at which these two constituents had diverged, his opponents successfully claimed and have ever since maintained the appellation of "orthodox," while his followers have had to rest content with the name, hitherto unknown in the sect, of Hicksites.

The history of all religions displays an invariable yearning after something which cannot be defined, but which, for want of a better term, is universally recognized under the name of inspiration ; and of this yearning there is no more remarkable instance than that presented in the spiritual tribulations of George Fox, and the tacit submission of his followers. Rationalism of itself turned out to be inadequate ; formality in social life, like mere formality in spiritual life, proved to be dead : both together were but vanity. Something more was needed than the overthrow of the exclusive authority of the Scriptures : the great want became intolerable, and, rushing in where angels fear to tread, the Quaker rejected as authoritative what other men called inspired, and sought his revelation directly from God himself. He delivered himself over to an existence absolutely spiritual ; he looked at religion through the end of the glass other than that of the rationalist, and, ignoring the needs of the intellect as this one does of the emotions, he erred equally with him in discarding the composite nature of man, and with him inflicted injury upon a religion which covers the whole of man as with a garment. The intellect ignored, the emotions disdained, and formality having proved a badge indicating nothing, on what had the follower of Fox now to rest his feet? On nothing : he had placed himself outside the world designed for men. He was free to exercise his powers, but on what could he direct them except himself? Freedom was indeed his, absolute freedom ; but it was the freedom of a void.

It was not long before the law which directs the wandering course of bodies that, uncontrolled by judgment and unsteadied by system, would seek the sun, exerted its inexorable force, and

Quakerism, having rushed to its perihelion, obeyed the powers it had defied, and was soon lost in the outer darkness. It did what the spiritual part of man, unbalanced by his physical, his emotional, and his intellectual nature, has always done, when left to itself : it ran into mere mysticism. From the courses of the diverse societies of mystics which, from time to time, had risen and disappeared, its orbit might have been calculated with something like precision. Roger Williams seems to have had some notion of doing so. Be that as it may, in our day Quakerism appears as a star of exceedingly small magnitude. In fact, as a religious, moral, or social force, Quakerism, in the land where its greatest strength lay, America, had, even prior to the Revolution, outlived its day and spent its force. It is, however, only with its relations to freedom of conscience that we are called upon to notice it, and to those relations and the effect they produced on our character as a people, we shall now turn.

For the same reason that the Roman Catholics, the Brownists, and the Puritans crossed the Atlantic, came those dissenters from dissent, the Quakers. In England, they had been fined, whipt, pilloried, imprisoned, and executed. In New England, the same cup of bitterness had been presented to them, and the law was especially directed against a sect that was deemed peculiarly "accursed "; except in Rhode Island, where, let it be noted, in strict adherence to the principles of its founder, they had been met by only the natural antagonist of strange doctrines—discussion. Roger Williams himself had opened his batteries upon them in a work entitled, "George Fox, Digged out of his Burrowe," and though no persecution awaited them, and they could live there, if so minded, in harmony with God and man, yet little sympathy could be looked for, and it was evident, that, the ground being already occupied, the experiment of planting their principles in that soil would not be a work of great promise. The colony of New Amsterdam having been but lately transferred to the English rule under the name of New York, they would have been ground to dust between the upper millstone of the new Establishment and the lower one of the old Dutch Reformed Church[1] :

---

[1] As late as 1774, John Adams, then visiting New York, says in his Diary: " Mr. Livingston * * * says, they have never been able to obtain a charter for their burying-ground, or the ground on which their Presbyterian church

and the Swedish settlements on the Delaware having, likewise, yielded to England, a similar fate would have awaited them there.[1] Virginia was out of the question,[2] for nowhere in America was the Church Establishment so rigorously maintained as an exclusive element of political constitution ; and North Carolina, where they

---

stands. They have solicited their Governors, and have solicited at home without success."

In fact, New York, always intolerant, was more so than ever after the English occupation in 1664. " In an act passed in the beginning of the last century," says Story, "Constitution," i, ch. x, § 114, " it was declared that every Jesuit and Popish priest who should continue in the colony after a given day, should be condemned to *perpetual imprisonment ;* and if he broke prison or escaped, and was retaken, he was *to be put to death."* Half a century afterward, one of her historians, Smith, warmly praises this disgraceful enactment, and as late as 1777, the constitution was intended to exclude Romanists.

[1] During the Swedish supremacy, the worship of God was to be according to the Confession of Augsburg, the Council of Upsal, and the ceremonies of the Swedish church, though "the pretended reformed religion" might be allowed, provided its adherents abstained from dispute, scandal, and abuse." " Instructions to Gov. Printz ; Privileges granted to the Colony." Hazard. "Ann. Pennsyl.," 53, 67.

[2] " The first settlers in this country [Virginia] were emigrants from England, of the English church, just at a point of time when it was flushed with complete victory over the religions of all other persuasions. Possessed, as they became, of the powers of making, administering, and executing the laws, they showed equal intolerance in this country with their Presbyterian [Puritan ?] brethren, who had emigrated to the northern government. The poor Quakers were flying from persecution in England. They cast their eyes on these new countries as asylums of civil and religious freedom ; but they found them free only for the reigning sect. Several Acts of the Virginia Assembly of 1659, 1662, and 1693, had made it penal in parents to refuse to have their children baptized ; had prohibited the unlawful assembling of Quakers ; had made it penal for any master of a vessel to bring a Quaker into the State ; had ordered those already here, and such as should come thereafter, to be imprisoned till they should abjure the country ; provided a milder punishment for their first and second return, but death for their third ; had inhibited all persons from suffering their meetings in and near their houses, entertaining them individually, or disposing of books which supported their tenets. * * * At the common law, *heresy* was a capital offence, punishable by burning. Its definition was left to the ecclesiastical judges,before whom the conviction was, till the statute of 1 El. c. 1, circumscribed it, by declaring that nothing should be deemed heresy but what had been so determined by authority of the canonical Scriptures, or by one of the four first general councils, or by other council, having for the grounds of their declaration the express and plain words of the Scriptures. * * * By our own Act of Assembly of 1705, c. 30, if a person brought up in the Christian religion denies the being of a God, or the Trinity, or asserts there are more gods than one, or denies the Christian religion to be true, or the Scriptures to be of divine authority, he is punishable on the first offence by incapacity to hold any office or employment ecclesiastical. civil, or military ; on the second by disability to sue, to take any gift or legacy, to be guardian, executor, or administrator, and by three years' imprisonment without bail. A father's right to the custody of his own children being founded on his right of guardianship, this being taken away, they may of course be severed from him, and put by the authority of a court into more orthodox hands." Thomas Jefferson, in " *Notes on Virginia.*"

would, doubtless, have been hospitably received, was too far south for the inclination of the mass of them. They were, therefore, happily directed to the very part of the country, where, from the force of locality alone, the good example of their frugal and sober lives would be most apparent, and where their influence, exerted in behalf of freedom of conscience, would be of most avail. Fortunately, this did not take place until their demeanor had lost the peculiarities which had rendered them so offensive in their earliest days, nor until good sense, supported by self-control, had resumed its sway over them. Accordingly, they turned their faces toward what was afterward New Jersey, and, later still, when the Swedes had been rendered powerless to oppose them, to what is now Pennsylvania.

Their advent was most propitious for the cause of freedom of conscience. Massachusetts had intensified her intolerance by adopting a censorship of the press ; an innovation which derives its importance rather as an evidence of the spirit pervading the colony than from any practical result. In Virginia, where intolerance had entrenched herself, the forces of rationalism and mysticism would have had a weary and profitless contest. In Maryland, the Revolution had been felt, and the hands of the northern Puritans who had made their way into her bounds having been strengthened as those of the Roman Catholics had grown feeble, the former had lost no time in taking advantage of the change, to strike down toleration and raise the standard of intolerance. Cromwell, however, in whom the principles of the Independents were then uppermost, and who was not slow to perceive the political advantage of maintaining a tolerant commonwealth to counterbalance the intolerance of Virginia, had the proprietary's patent confirmed, and, after several fluctuations, this Palatine was reinstated in his rights, and with him the former principles of toleration, which, as it turned out, in a short time survived his own power. Still, though it had gained the ascendancy, the cause of conscience was not strong enough to maintain a defiant attitude. South of Virginia, the population was so thin and scattered, that its spiritual condition can hardly be described. The few people that were there, received with uniform kindness the representatives of any church or sect that happened to go that way, but freedom of conscience as a social force was unknown.

It was, then, in Rhode Island alone, that, about 1676, when Quakerism took possession of West New Jersey, the golden doctrine may be said to have existed in simplicity and purity ; for that colony then possessed a charter which, more liberal even than that of Maryland (inasmuch as it did not exact the oath of allegiance), gave every thing which freemen could desire. Charles II., in 1660, in answer to a petition of the colonists for a patent, which should enable them "to hold forth a lively experiment, that a most flourishing civil state may stand, and best be maintained, with a full liberty of religious concernments," granted a charter by which not only the independence of Rhode Island as to Massachusetts was recognized, but by which a democratic form of government was conceded, and full liberty granted the colonists to make their own laws ; the only stipulation being, that such laws should be in conformity with those of England, yet, nevertheless, "agreeable to the constitution of the place and the nature of the people." But by far the most important and beneficial clause in this benign charter was that which prescribed, that "No person within the said colony, at any time hereafter, shall be anywise molested, punished, disquieted, or called in question, for any difference in opinion in matters of religion ; every person may at all times freely and fully enjoy his own judgment and conscience in matters of religious concernments."

Thus it was, that in Rhode Island alone full liberty of conscience and of worship could be said to exist. The advent of the Society of Friends was now, however, to give it the impulse necessary to the enlargement and establishment of its domain. This impulse was due to four things : to the time when West Jersey and Pennsylvania were settled ; to the central position occupied by these two colonies, Pennsylvania, at a later day, indeed, from its topographical relations to the other colonies, being styled, the Keystone of the arch ; to the accession of adherents thus brought to the cause ; and to the judgment and prudence with which the Quakers advocated their principles and the fidelity to them they displayed.

The first Quaker settlement in West Jersey was planted, in 1675, at Salem, on the Delaware, and, to those who emigrated, the Proprietaries gave this remarkable assurance : " We lay a foundation for after ages to understand their liberty as Christians and as men, that they may not be brought into bondage, but by their own consent; for we put *the power in the people.*" This is the most striking instance of a purely popular government being resolved upon in England, and being freely granted therefrom to a colony, and justifies the assertion, that the Quakers did not content themselves with seeking greater freedom in religion, but aspired to a form of government more popular in its constitution than any then existing. The fact may be explained by the natural indisposition of the colonists, who were all of the same social class, and that a humble one, to open the door to the ascendency of any ambitious men the ignorance and inexperience of the colony might tempt thither, or who, under the unequal favors of fortune, might rise out of their own midst. Were such the motive, it was a wise one, but, be it what it may, the interest of this surprising step is heightened by the consideration that it was first taken by a people who make it a part of their creed to uphold and maintain the existing government, whatever it be, so long as it is not hostile to the laws of God, and who profess to abhor change in political rule.[1]

The laws enacted under the guaranty of the Proprietaries at once showed the existing desire for a government by the people, and the lofty principle which the colonists meant to enforce on the banks of the Delaware. The very first enactment made by these rustics was as follows: *No man, nor any number of men, hath power over conscience. No person shall at any time, in any ways, or on any pretence, be called in question, or in the least punished or hurt for opinion in religion.* Then followed the clauses relating to the legislature, the elective franchise, the executive and the judicial branches of the government. The general assembly was to be chosen, not by the confused way of cries and voices, but by the balloting-box, and every man was to be capable of choosing and being chosen. The electors were to instruct the deputies, and, in return, the deputies were to bind themselves, by indentures under hand and seal, to obey the instructions. Were the deputy disobedient or unfaithful, he could be questioned before the legislature by any one of his electors, and "that he may be known as the servant of the people," one shilling was to be paid him daily by his constituents, in satisfaction of his trouble and outlay.

As for the executive power, it lay in ten commissioners appointed

---

[1] Penn's Preamble to his "Frame of Government."

by the legislature ; and, with respect to the judiciary, the judges were likewise appointed by the same body, and, holding their offices for a term of two years only, sat merely as assistants to the jury, which, as in England, consisted of twelve men. No attorneys or counsellors were permitted to practise ; no one could be imprisoned for debt, and the penalty of death could be inflicted only for murder.

This constitution, if so it can be called, is a medley of golden principles and inefficient mechanism. The head is the head of a god, but the limbs are those of a paralytic. Here are a people, who, of a truth, love justice and hate iniquity ; a people, whose humble pride is to order their ways by those of experience ; whose cardinal doctrine in the pursuit of truth is absolute freedom of investigation and discussion, and who, be they ever so hard pressed, scorn any other weapon in its defence ; whose sense of order and attachment to freedom of action lead them to abhor the confusion of mob rule or the oppression of oligarchies, and whose maintenance of the doctrine of equal rights to all, is known of men ; yet, we behold this people, when they come together to organize a body politic which shall have these matchless principles for social forces, cast to the winds the teachings of experience and common-sense, and the same voice which startles a world by its crying in the wilderness, forbids the existence of an independent judiciary, takes away from the accused his right to thorough investigation, shuts the mouth of the patriot against discussion, deprives the legislator of the noble character of representative, fetters his action, and hands over the commonwealth to as real a Council of Ten as ever whispered its decrees in the chambers of the Doge's Palace.

This constitution might exist for a while among a scanty, simple, and agricultural people, whose wants were few, whose ideas were narrow, and whose moderate ambition offered no field to conflicting interests : but it could never endure in any ordinary community, and, in fact, it savors more of the government of a sect, or order, than of a people. But, on account of the popularity of government which it exposes, it should be held in the greatest importance by the historian and the political philosopher. . No matter how defective the machinery these clumsy hands put together, one thing appears—that its force was deliberately intended to maintain a democracy. It is not, however, the merits or demerits of this constitution, as a work of state-craft, with which we have to do, but the spirit which gave it being, and the results it produced. What was its motive, what its tendency, and what were its effects upon American character? Its motive, undoubtedly, was the desire of the individual for greater freedom of political action than any he had hitherto enjoyed—its intention was to organize a democracy; as the work of those who had bargained it out of the lords of the soil, its tendency was, by showing those who came after them that they could obtain the same liberties if they pursued a like course, to broaden the area of popular government; and its result was, to plant a democracy on American soil and to foster the notions of self-government.

That such were the effects, was soon shown in the fruit of the tree; for, a few years afterwards, in 1682, Pennsylvania was founded. There can be no question of the settlement of Pennsylvania being a result of that of West Jersey. The attention of Penn, the great founder, had been attracted to the territory west of the Delaware, by the success of the West Jersey colony, of whose progress he kept himself informed through his connection with the estate of Byllinge, the proprietor. The patent issued by James the Second, in 1681, makes no mention of toleration, nor does the "Frame of Government," composed by Penn and published in 1682; but as, in the "Laws Agreed upon in England," in 1681, toleration in matters of religion was broadly asserted, in a way that leaves no doubt of its recognition as a social force, and as afterward, in the "Great Act," passed at Chester, it was emphatically made the law of the land, in almost the very words of the "Laws Agreed upon in England"; and, moreover, what is of still greater importance, as both Proprietary and people held themselves out to the world as the guardians of toleration, and not only enacted statutes to protect it, but obeyed them in spirit and in truth, the Quakers of Pennsylvania have ever been regarded, the world over, as the devoted advocates and supporters of freedom of conscience, and the settlement of the province as one of the greatest events in the annals of that doctrine. It would, in fact, under the principle of the Inner Light, so fondly cherished by them, have been impossible for the Quakers to be any thing else; and the prominence attained by them at the time is mostly due to the tenacity with which they clung to liberty of conscience, the earnestness with which they advocated its extension, and to the good-fortune which transferred to their hands the destiny of this doctrine, in a locality where there were none to oppose it, and in days when the encouragement of the sovereign was augmented by the necessity he was under of courting the good-will of the Dissenters.

Though their history, like that of every other religion, is disfigured, at times, particularly at the outset, by the marks of sectarianism and fanaticism, they were never unfaithful to this principle, and their unwavering fidelity has won from all creeds the respect and gratitude which have been ungrudgingly accorded it.

The times, and the relations existing between the Penns and the royal family, were propitious to the undertaking that William, the son, resolved upon. The services of the late Admiral, in the war against the Dutch, and a debt due to him from the crown, smoothed the way to a successful negotiation, and Penn soon found himself in possession of a charter, which gave him all he desired—the title to a seigniory, to be styled Pennsylvania,[1] of vast extent, lying in a temperate and fruitful region, easily accessible by water, clothed with dense forests, and, above all, unoccupied by Europeans. The soil and climate offered every thing requisite to the rapid and healthy growth of a sturdy people, and the solitude opposed nothing to the free exercise of their principles, except the physical limitations imposed everywhere by the seasons' difference. The woods were more free from peril than the envious court.

This charter, as expressed in the preamble, was granted to Penn, "out of a commendable desire to enlarge our British empire, and promote such useful commodities as may be of benefit to us and our dominions, as also to reduce the savage natives, by just and gentle manners, to the love of civil society and Christian religion "; and having described the boundaries and defined the tenure, which was " to be holden of us, our heirs and successors, kings of Eng-

[1] "I proposed * * *Sylvania*, and they added *Penn* to it, and though I much opposed it, and went to the king to have it struck out and altered, he said it was past, and would take it upon him. * * * I feared lest it should be looked on as a vanity in me, and not as a respect in the king, as it truly was, to my father." "Letter to Rob. Turner." Hazard's "Annals," 500. "Reg. Penns.," I, 297. "Memoirs, Penn. Hist. Soc."

land, as of our castle of Windsor, in the county of Berks, in free and common socage, by fealty only, for all services, and not *in capite* or by knight service, yielding and paying therefor to us * * * two beaver skins, to be delivered at our castle of Windsor, on the first day of January in every year," it granted to Penn, among many franchises, the right of making the laws "with the advice, assent, and approbation of the freemen of the said country, or the greater part of them, or of their delegates or deputies," so long as they should not be repugnant to those of England; but the right was reserved to appoint, on the petition of twenty inhabitants, "preachers" approved by the Bishop of London.[1]

Thus, while the people were assured of their liberties by the safeguard which a personal share in the government alone secures, a saving clause retained the right to the enjoyment of the Church of England's services, upon the demand of a number of inhabitants sufficient to warrant the procedure. It will be observed, that this charter, which breaks the silence respecting religion to display a qualified preference for that which was established in the mother-country, cannot be ranked in the same category with that of Rhode Island, which placed no limitation whatever on conscience; or with that of Maryland, which imposed but one; nor, on the other hand, can it be classed with those which directly recognized the establishment of the Church of England, as did those of New York and Virginia. In respect to religion, it was silent; it permitted, indeed, freedom of conscience by implication, but the enforcement of this freedom, which brought such glory to Pennsylvania, was due to the devotion and determination of the Founder and his people only: in no respect was toleration a gift of the crown, which regarded the grant of a desert in the other hemisphere simply as a new way of paying old debts.

Penn sent out a deputy to take possession, who likewise bore a letter to those who had already gone before, in which he tells them, that they are now fixed at the mercy of no governor that comes to make his fortunes great, but that they shall be governed by laws of their own making, and live a free, and, if they will, a sober and industrious people.[2] He himself remained in England,

---

[1] See preamble to the charter, and sections I, III, IV, V, and XXII. Hazard's "Annals," 488, *et seq.*

[2] "Letter for the Inhabitants of Pennsylvania, to be read by my Deputy." *Ibid.*, 502.

for the time being, for he knew well that the foundations of an English colony were, first of all, to be laid there,[1] and that it would only entail on Pennsylvania the evils which other colonies had been called on to endure, were he, like their leaders, to first plant the colony, and then secure the privileges. Accordingly, profiting by their experience, he delayed his departure in order to oversee for himself the organization of what he firmly believed was to become a great State,[2] and it was thence that he issued his "Letter to the Inhabitants of Pennsylvania,"[3] his "Argument in favor of Colonies,"[4] the "Conditions and Concessions"[5] agreed upon between himself and the purchasers, the "Instructions to his Commissioners,"[6] in which he first exposes his admirable policy respecting the Indians, his "Letter to the Indians"[7] themselves, the "Charter for the Free Society of Traders,"[8] the "Frame of Government,"[9] which is preceded by an essay setting forth his views of government and civil society, and, especially, the "Laws Agreed upon in England,"[10] which were intended to be altered or amended by the colonial assembly, if needs be, and which was afterward done. Then, having thus made straight his paths beforehand, he bade farewell to England, and, on the 27th day of October, 1682, arrived before the town of New Castle, in what is now Delaware.

The political principles and method of organization which were to direct the colony, are to be found in the "Frame of Government," but it is in the "Laws Agreed upon in England" that we are to seek for the first proclamation of religious liberty in Pennsylvania. It is as follows: "That all persons living in this province who confess and acknowledge the one Almighty and Eternal God to be the Creator, Upholder, and Ruler of the world, and that hold themselves obliged in conscience to live

---

[1] "I shall have a tender care to the government, that it will be well laid at first."—"Letter to R. Turner," Hazard, 500.

[2] There are many instances of this hopeful anticipation on his part. I will cite, however, only the earliest one I have at hand ; it is contained in the letter to Robert Turner, previously referred to, and written before he set foot in America: "It is a clear and just thing, and my God, that has given it me through many difficulties, will, I believe, bless and make it *the seed of a nation*."

[3] Hazard, 502-3.

[4] *Ibid.*, 505, *et seq.*

[5] *Ibid.*, 510, 516, *et seq.*

[6] *Ibid.*, 527, 528, 529, 530.

[7] *Ibid.*, 532, 533.

[8] *Ibid.*, 541, *et seq.*

[9] *Ibid.*, 558, *et seq.*

[10] *Ibid.*, 568, *et seq.*

peaceably and justly in civil society, shall in noways be molested
or prejudiced for their religious persuasion or practice in matters
of faith and worship ; nor shall they be compelled at any time to
frequent or maintain any religious worship, place, or ministry
whatever." Thus, Jew or Gentile was to be protected both in his
faith and in the observance of it, and could live on the shores of
the Delaware unmolested and unprejudiced on account of conscience, so long as the existence of God was acknowledged. If
freedom of conscience was not asserted, toleration was. Atheists
and polytheists were alone debarred, and with the same breath
there was erected a barrier against the establishment of any church
as a political institution.

It must be confessed, however, that the broad principle thus
laid down was not maintained in the legislation that followed.
Hardly had Penn taken the repose necessary after a long voyage,
and one which was rendered doubly trying by the presence of an
epidemic on board ship, than he called together a General Assembly of the colony (which at that time embraced what is now the
State of Delaware as well as that of Pennsylvania), at Upland, or,
as it is at present styled, Chester, in order that the colonists might
begin for themselves the legislation needful to the well-ordering
of their affairs. The constitution, as it may be called, of the colony, was, until then, to be gathered only from the royal letters
patent, the "Frame of Government," and the "Laws Agreed
upon in England." The colonists were now, however, to take
care of themselves, and their first duty was, evidently, to ratify
by their own legislation the principles contained in the organic
law, and to enact a body of laws which, dispensing with those
agreed upon in England, should derive their force and virtue
solely from the action of those who were to obey them. This
they promptly did, and, after settling the affairs which were most
pressing, they gave to the inhabitants what has since been known
as the "Great Law of Chester" ; a code to this day held in reverence by the people of Delaware and Pennsylvania, who regard it
as the source of some of their most cherished institutions.[1] In
this law the different branches of the government were defined,

---

[1] Particularly those which prescribe the registry of deeds, etc.; the distribution
of intestates' estates ; the power to make wills ; the liability of lands to be taken
in execution and sold for the payment of debts ; prisons to be workhouses,
etc.

and their limits prescribed.[1]   The Governor, as Proprietary, of course derived his powers from the Charter, which expressly enumerated them ; but the limitations on the legislature and the judiciary, and the qualifications of the officers, representatives, and electors, could, under the letters patent, be determined only by the Governor, as Proprietary or lord of the seigniory, by and with the advice, assent, and approbation of the people themselves in general council assembled.   It was on the qualifications of these officers, representatives, and electors, that the emphatic assertion of religious liberty, so broadly laid down in " the Laws Agreed upon in England," first received a check.   The religious liberty there described and pledged, was, in the very first section, made to read *Christian* liberty ; an ominous modification which was speedily amplified in the second section into the provision, that all officers employed in the service of the government, and all members elected to serve in the Assembly, with those who had the right to elect them, should be such as professed and declared that they believed Jesus Christ to be the Son of God.[2]   Thus, no Jew or freethinker (atheists and those equally heretical having been excluded already from the shelter of toleration) could be either an elector, a deputy, or an officer of government ; though there was nothing to prevent his being a resident, and, as such, claiming the protection of the administration, so long as he behaved himself well and paid scot and lot to the governor.

To this qualification for freemen was added still another, by section sixty-fifth, which required them to be landholders, or, in default of realty, to pay certain taxes.   Between these two sections, the latter of which makes no mention whatever of faith or creed, there seems to be a conflict ; as the sixty-fifth expressly says, that any "other resident in the said province [than a landholder], that pays scot and lot to the governor, shall be deemed and accounted a freeman of this province and territory thereof ; and such only shall have right of election, or being elected to any service in the government thereof."   Thus, there is an obvious

---

[1] " I took a trip once with Penn to his colony of Pennsylvania.   The laws there are contained in a small volume, and are so extremely good that there has been no alteration wanted in any of them.   *   *   *   There are four persons as judges on the bench ; and, after the case has been fairly laid down on both sides, all the four draw lots, and upon whom the lot falls decides the question." —Spence's " Anecdotes."

[2] See Appendix B

difference ; for, if the freemen were to be such as are thus described, and those who were freemen were to be electors, then, no religious restriction herein appearing, any one, be his belief what it may, was a freeman, and could vote and be voted for ; and section sixty-fifth must conflict with section second, wherein the right to elect and to hold office is restricted to Christians only. But, inasmuch as these two sections are part and parcel of the same instrument, are of equal weight, and refer to the same things, the conclusion is irresistible, that they must be construed together, and that, by the "Great Law of Chester," the freedom of the colony belonged of right only to the Christian landholders and the taxpaying Christians of the province.

It can hardly escape the notice of the observer, that where the doctrine of toleration was set forth with no limitation except that of a belief in God, was in England and previous to Penn's departure ; and that where the restriction concerning Christianity was imposed upon it, was in America where the people had a voice.   It is impossible to forego the conclusion, that the former was the doctrine of Penn,[1] and the latter that of his followers ; and that the Proprietor was compelled to accept the qualification in order to save what he could of the principle.   As a body, the Quakers, evidently, were not yet abreast of their leader's standard. However, the " Great Law of Chester " reduces Pennsylvania to the plane of Maryland, elevated though that be in the list in which the historian of religious liberty must to-day class its strongholds, and both these colonies must yield to Rhode Island the distinction of being the only one, as yet, whose head rose above the clouds.

One cannot refrain from admiring the order, system, and prudence which characterized the settlement of Maryland and Pennsylvania.   What can be said of Maryland may also be said of Pennsylvania, where as little as possible was left to chance, and where common-sense governed the enterprise from first to last. The distinguishing fact has already been remarked, that the Proprietary used his experience of courts and high places to the ben-

---

[1] " I went thither to lay the foundation of a *free* colony *for all mankind that should go thither*, more especially those of my own profession ; not that I would lessen the civil liberties of others because of their persuasion, but screen and defend our own from any infringement on that account."—" Letter to Mompesson," " Mems., Hist. Soc. of Pa.," ix, 373.

efit of his people, in this respect : that he obtained his franchises and privileges *before* he planted his colony. The same prudence dictated the ensuing measures. Instead of casting shiploads of helpless enthusiasts into a wilderness without provisions, without shelter, or even the resources to supply the ordinary wants of human beings, the proper seasons for making voyages were chosen, the nature of the ground had been thoroughly ascertained beforehand, shelter and comfort awaited those coming, and, in fact, every thing was conducted, from the first step to the last, with a systematic ordering, which looked, not to the temporary seclusion of a sect, but to the foundation of a State for all time and for all people. First went the surveyors to lay off the land ; then followed the artisans to build the tenements, which enabled the colonists, immediately upon their arrival, to enjoy the repose needed after a wave-tossed voyage ; and, last of all, came the men, women, and children. Gardens were planted, fields tilled, towns laid off, and houses erected, before the mass of emigrants arrived. The new sect, in its increase, now embraced members of the higher classes, and, as these colonists were of a station in society which implied ownership of goods, they naturally brought with them considerable wealth, and it may be truly said, that Penn's colonists simply transferred themselves and their belongings from homes in England to homes in Pennsylvania. The letters of the settlers to their friends and relatives, previous to leaving the old country, afford abundant evidence of the deliberate and orderly way in which the removal of their household goods to America was regarded by those among them who were best off, and it is not an uncommon thing to meet with paragraphs imparting the information, that, as soon as the dwelling in Pennsylvania should be finished—generally by the ensuing spring,—the family expected to sail, and to find, on its arrival, the garden planted, the farm stocked, and the house provided with the furniture already shipped under the care of servants.[1] The shifts for lodging which the first builders of Philadelphia were put to, were merely those that are incident to the building of any frontier village. It is yet

---

[1] In order to induce servants to go to the colony, fifty acres each are promised, and that this class became at once sufficiently numerous to justify the especial attention of the administration, is shown by the references to it in the "Conditions and Concessions," sect. vii ; Penn's "Charter to the People," sect. xxiii ; and in the "Great Law of Chester," sects. 25, 56, 65. Of course, they indicate also the prosperous condition of their superiors.

a daily occurrence of border life, that the mechanics and their families, if there be any, must "camp out" until the roofs which are to cover them, are constructed ; and so it was with these. The solid, substantial growth of Philadelphia, indeed, can only be accounted for by the wealth the colonists brought with them, by its steady increase, by the orderly, careful, and thorough way in which they set about building their city, and by the determination of every family which had come, to stay.[1] At a very early period we find the more opulent families in possession of country houses,[2] to which they retired during the heats of summer, as well as of town houses, where they passed the winter ; and to this day the neighborhood of Philadelphia is dotted over with antiquated residences, or with modern mansions which have taken their places, whose well-trimmed lawns and hedges, old though they be, are not as ancient as their names, which perpetuate the early settler's fond remembrance of the home he left behind him in England.

Nor are the physical features which distinguish this colony from the others, more marked than those which characterize it socially, religiously, and politically. The anomaly presented by a people professing the doctrine of passive obedience, and whose grateful regard for the intolerant House of Stuart never grew cold, actually stipulating for the free exercise of political principles which were sure to modify the form of government they were born under, has been already pointed out ; but it is as remarkable as it was when Maryland and Rhode Island returned the world good for evil, that a people whose existence had always been at the mercy of intolerance, should be foremost in the establishment of toleration, and that those who had scarcely known any thing else than to be smitten on the one cheek, should make a political principle of the sacred injunction to turn the other. This passiveness, indeed, has been, at once, the glory and the bane of the Quakers. It has achieved for them some of the most splendid conquests ever gained by man over himself : but, then, by inces-

---

[1] Taylor, afterward the Surveyor-General, in lines expressing the result of his astrological computations respecting Philadelphia, thus breaks forth :
     " A city built with such propitious rays,
       Will stand to see old walls and happy days."—(1705.)

[2] The Proprietary had his country house at Pennsbury. The Logans, Norrises, etc., contemporaries of William Penn, all retired in summer to their country-seats. Southwark, Spring Garden, Stenton, Germantown, Springettsbury, etc., were chosen places.

santly repressing the most active forces of social life, it has cramped some of the best qualities of human nature, it has forced the currents of existence into narrow channels, and has stinted society in the rich variety of personal characteristics which is the most pleasing feature of our race. The sworn foe of individuality, and chilling in the uniformity with which it has covered the Society of Friends, it is a poor compensation for the multiform variety which inventive nature is constantly asserting its right to produce.

Immobility is not a heroic quality : nevertheless, *vis inertiæ* has more than once shown the world how effectually evil can be resisted by refusing to get out of its way. There are times, when, to resist evil, the most active assault is necessary ; there are others, when the necessity is to be met by a vigorous defence ; and there are yet others, where the end is gained by sheer immobility. Of these last were those in Pennsylvania which embraced the reign of James the Second, and which succeeded the Revolution of 1688, until terminated by the accession of the present reigning House. Every attempt to inoculate the body politic with the distemper of intolerance was resisted by the indisposition of the system to take the disease. As Quakerism embraced the majority of the people and most of the wealth, and, politically, was conservative, it acted as a restraint upon innovation, and became a corrective of notions which would tend to subvert established principles. Before this passive exertion of power, the attempts of intolerance were bootless, and every gale was ridden out in safety by the bark which held the treasure simply holding on to its anchor.

Thus, next in point of time after Rhode Island and Maryland, we are indebted for freedom of conscience to the Quakers. In Rhode Island, a purely democratic colony was established, after persecution and exile, by the efforts of the colonists. In Maryland, New Jersey, and Pennsylvania, which were seignoral colonies, and where what democracy existed, existed by the bounty or sufferance of the Palatine, we see popular government placed firmly on its feet by the enlightenment or judgment of the founders. In New England, then, it was wrung from society ; but on the Delaware, society accepted it from the hand of the philanthropist ; and on the Potomac, from that of the courtier.

CHAPTER IV.

Religion in the Northern Provinces—Continued.

Rationalism of New England.

WE are now to witness freedom of conscience rising from the bosom of society instead of descending upon it, and to behold this social force asserting its existence by its own endeavor, unaided by the generosity of philanthropy or the exercise of authority.

The Great Movement, which closed its grand era of destruction with the investiture of the Protector, so affected the people of England, that henceforth they appear in a new character, and then began a period in their career which still continues. The history of England in those times is our history. We were subjects of the English crown or citizens of the Commonwealth, and, being Englishmen, any thing that affected England was not foreign to us, but affected us as it did those in the old country.[1] In fact, the very settlement of some portions of our land, and notably of New England, was by no means an indication of sympathy with that great movement, but was a direct expression, a very part of that movement itself. The colonization of New England, then, occurring when it did, is of the highest historical importance, as it was one of the earliest manifestations of the spirit of revolution,

[1] "Old England, dear England still * * * left indeed by us in our persons, but never yet forsaken in our affections. * * * There is no land that claims our name but England ; * * * there is no name that calls us countrymen but the English. Brethren, did we not there draw in our first breath ? Did not the sun first shine there upon our heads ? Did not that land first bear us, even that pleasant island, * * * that garden of the Lord, that paradise ?"—William Hooke's "New England's Tears for Old England's Fears."

and the most decided and practical indication of the leavening then going on which had so far been given.

It was, indeed, the most positive and emphatic expression of insubordination possible at that time for Englishmen to enunciate. The mass of the colonists came to New England during a period when the old order of things at home was still too strong to be successfully resisted, and the true colonization of those wilds began with Winthrop's expedition in 1630.

When the Parliament of 1629 was dissolved, the hopes of rising Puritanism were stricken to the ground : henceforth the Puritan saw no chance for him or his in Old England. The crown was fully committed to the support of the Church, which, under the leadership of Laud, had, on laying aside the conservative policy of Parker and Whitgift, adopted the most radical form of intolerance, and the complete union of the powers of Church and State in an active and aggressive policy. Resistance was apparently hopeless. In times not much later, and when revolution was boldly cleaving its way, the men that now fled would have resisted to the death. Some of them actually did so ; they recrossed the Atlantic and joined their forces to a warfare which resulted in the downfall of Church and State ; but in 1630 the mind had not yet cast off its old fetters, and, apparently, there was nothing else to do but escape. This they did, and thus Puritanism became American as well as English. The same Puritanism which, unopposed, developed quietly in Massachusetts, opposed brought on the struggle in England that terminated only with the Commonwealth. The Puritanism of America sympathized with and countenanced that of England. It did more : it gave physical aid toward the accomplishment of Puritan ends at home. It did not make itself one with it, for it was already and ever had been one and the same thing, and hence it is necessary to a knowledge of Puritanism in New England to know what it was in Old England— the more so, as, from the opposition it there met, its characteristics were more clearly brought before the world, and its nature can be more easily and fully determined, while the very freedom of its course in New England prevented the most active and interesting qualities of its nature from making themselves conspicuous.

That the motive which led to the colonization of New England was one in nature with that which brought about the Puritan revolution in Old England, needs no argument. Religion was the inciting cause of both ; though the remote cause, as we have seen, is to be found in the necessity of supplying the new wants which resulted from an antecedent expansion of intellectual action. The historical importance of this identity is strikingly shown by the epoch of the Puritan colonization, by the duration of emigration, by the sudden cessation of that emigration, and by the history of its activity as a social force on American soil.

The way for emigration had already been pointed out by several feeble bands of Brownists or Separatists, who had sought shelter in Holland, and had thence betaken themselves to America. The first of these (who have since been exalted by the appellation of "Pilgrims") had directed their course to the Hudson, but had been compelled to land in Massachusetts Bay. Their numbers were sufficient only to augment their misery and to disclose the impotence of efforts to colonize where means, influence, supplies, and even ordinary foresight were lacking.[1]

The dropping of their anchor was the signal for a compact, which was intended to be the first step toward organization. It was as follows :

"In the name of God, amen. We, whose names are underwritten, the loyal subjects of our dread Sovereign Lord King James, etc., etc., having undertaken for the glory of God and the advancement of the Christian Faith, and the honor of our King and Country, a voyage to plant the first colony in the northern parts of Virginia, we do by these presents solemnly and mutually, in the presence of God and one another, covenant and combine ourselves together into a civil body politick, for our better ordering and preservation, and furtherance of the ends aforesaid : and by virtue hereof do enact, constitute, and frame such just and equal laws, ordinances, acts, constitutions, and offices, from time to time, as shall be thought most meet and convenient for the general good of the colony : unto which we promise all due submission and obedience."

---

[1] Their improvidence and helplessness are shown by the facts, that, for four years after their arrival, their chief dependence was on the corn purchased from the Indians. They did not even have nets to catch the fish, with which the waters teemed, nor salt to preserve them, had they been caught. In 1623, all they could set before the third arrival of colonists were a lobster, a piece of fish, and a cup of water. Bread there was none. Yet these people had contracted to pay forty-five per cent. interest per annum on loans. This and community of property repressed energy and fairly choked the enterprise from the start.

This, the whole of the compact, was signed by forty-one persons. It has been greatly lauded, and this laudation may be summed up in the assertion of a writer of great weight,[1] that the compact "was in its very essence a pure democracy."

This emphatic and sweeping assertion cannot maintain itself against scrutiny; for a democracy is not *expressly stated* in the instrument, it does not appear *by implication*, nor is it warranted *by the condition of the parties.*

I. In respect to *the condition of those who signed it:* that all were of one class, and of the class of commoners, no more affects, of itself, the nature of the instrument, and what flowed from it, than if all had been lords. They were citizens of a monarchical and aristocratic State, engaged in a voluntary undertaking, and they must be taken as representatives of such a State, and of no other. There is, then, nothing in the condition of those who signed the compact to warrant the assertion that their covenant was in its essence a pure democracy, or the outcome of one.

Such a conclusion, therefore, can be justified only by express terms or by reasonable implication.

II. The *terms* speak for themselves, and they express nothing of the kind. They are worthy of analysis. The compact is composed: first, of a Preamble; second, of a Covenant; and, third, of a Provision for Autonomy.

The *preamble* contains (1) the *style* under which the signers act: it is "the loyal subjects of our dread Sovereign Lord King James"; and (2) the *objects* of the undertaking, which are (*a*) "the glory of God and the advancement of the Christian faith," and (*b*) "the honor of our king and country."

Then follows the *covenant,* which has for its object their combination "together into a civil body politick," and which expresses one other purpose in addition to the two specified in the preamble; namely, (*c*) "our better ordering and preservation."

Further than these there is no assertion whatever except this, "and by virtue hereof [we] do enact, constitute, and frame such just and equal laws, ordinances, acts, constitutions, and offices, from time to time, as shall be thought most meet and convenient for the general good of the colony : unto which we promise all due submission and obedience." This last clause may be re-

[1] Mr. Justice Story, "Commentaries on the Constitution," ch. iii, sect. 55.

garded as an assertion of autonomy ; but whether that autonomy is to be aristocratic, oligarchical, democratic, or composite, is not disclosed.

Here, then, we have the subjects of a monarch undertaking the planting of a colony for (*a*) the glory of God and the advancement of the Christian faith ; (*b*) the honor of king and country ; and (*c*) their own better ordering and preservation.

III. Is a democracy to be deduced by *reasonable implication?* The tenor of the whole instrument taken together does not convey such implication. Certainly, a declaration beginning with a solemn assertion that the parties to it are subjects of a certain king, and ending with the equally solemn avowal that the enterprise is undertaken for the honor of that king and country, contains nothing from which a democracy can be deduced. The presumption that it means what it says must prevail—that a band of monarchists are engaged in an undertaking by which they hope and intend to enlarge the dominion and power of their monarchy. This conclusion established, the subsequent clauses must be interpreted by it. These clauses, however, contain nothing but the ordinary language which any body of men, whether from an autocracy, a monarchy, or a republic, would use when taking the first step toward organization in a desert, where neither civilization, its laws, nor the machinery to enforce order exist. The natural interpretation, therefore, gives place to no other, and, as organic law, the compact must be regarded as simply a first step to order, and one which serves equally to the establishment of a republic, a monarchy, or a despotism.

This compact is justly considered of the highest importance from its assertion of autonomy. Farther than this, however, it demands no especial regard from the student of political history. It does not define what the nature of this autonomy is to be ; indeed, it could not well do so, and, in order to ascertain that nature, we are left to the time, when, under the force of self-development, the character of the autonomy becomes fixed and manifest. This is soon effected, and the result is any thing but a democracy. The state consisted of the freemen ; the freemen were the adult male members of the church [1]; the legislature consisted of the

---

[1] " Not a fourth part of the adult population were ever members." Hildreth, " Hist. U. S.," rev. ed., I, chap. vii.

whole body of freemen, and these chose the governor. Thus the autonomy was built upon the church as the foundation. In spirit it was a theocracy, and every theocracy is of the essence of despotism : in the flesh it was an oligarchy whose invisible Head and Ruler was God, who spake by the prophets, and whose vicarious executive force in the commonwealth was the clergy.[1] A despotic government, it was soon rent by dissension ; an intolerant government, its arrogance disappeared before the first rays of freedom of conscience ; an ideal government, it was merely that dream of the enthusiast, well known to history, of which in our times no illustration exists, unless it be found in the Church of Latter Day Saints, or Mormonism.

Thus it is seen, that, instead of being of the essence of a pure democracy, the compact was the natural expression of law and order simply, and that the autonomy revealed in it developed into an oligarchy. This it did with startling rapidity ; and, if a tree is to be known by its fruits, we cannot with truth apply to the seedling planted by the Pilgrims any democratic attributes whatever.

At first the progress of the colony was slow ; few reinforcements arrived, dissension agitated it, and its foothold was in every way precarious. Help, however, came from an unexpected quarter. Laud, the very antichrist himself, unwittingly did for the colony what it could not do for itself : he strengthened it with numbers and respectability. The Pilgrims had been poor and of small account, but a different class of men was now to shape the destinies of the settlements. Laud undertook the reactionary work of bringing back the religion of the kingdom to the point whence Puritanism had pushed it. This brought on the crisis, and those who could not maintain their footing against the combined forces of Church and State, fled across the waters. Hence, the Puritan emigration, which sought Boston and the northern shore of Massa-

---

[1] Forty years afterward, Stuyvesant thus writes : " The colony of Boston remains constant to its old maxim of a free state, dependent on none but God." " Albany Records," xviii, 124.

" According to the system established in Massachusetts, the Church and State were most intimately blended. The magistrates and General Court, aided by the advice of the elders, claimed and exercised a supreme control in spiritual as well as temporal matters ; while even in matters purely temporal, the elders were consulted on all important questions." Hild., " Hist. U. S.," I, chap. vii.

chusetts Bay. The Pilgrim or Plymouth settlement, in familiar language became "the Old Colony."[1]

The emigrants were of a class superior to their predecessors in the *Mayflower*. Like them they were God-fearing, but socially they were of "only the best" among the farmers of the eastern counties and Lincolnshire. Some of them were large land-owners, others were professional men from the Inns of Court and the offices of physicians. There were clergymen of renown, like Cotton ; and many, very many, were university men. Members of the highest classes, foreseeing a storm, provided themselves with places of refuge in New England, should events compel their flight. Lord Say and Sele, and Lord Brooke, at one time contemplated removal to the colony ; Hampden made a purchase on the Narragansett, and Lord Warwick another in the valley of the Connecticut, while Sir Harry Vane actually came over. Winthrop's party was shortly followed by eight hundred souls more, and in one year three thousand colonists arrived from England. Between the sailing of Winthrop's expedition and the assembling of the Long Parliament, in the space, that is, of less than eleven years, two hundred emigrant ships had crossed the Atlantic, and more than twenty thousand English people had found a refuge in New England.[2]

As the mass of the colonists was intelligent, sober, and industrious, so, many of the leaders were men of ability and learning. In the schools and universities of England they had acquired a familiarity with history and the classics, and a fondness for inquiry and disputation ; and, from the start, they brought along with them their private collections of books, which the impulse of the true scholar, to impart to others the knowledge he has gained, afterward united in foundations whence have since arisen the splendid libraries of Yale and Harvard. Nor was this disposition confined to the passive acquisition of knowledge. Their resolution and the activity of their intellect conquered the dialects of

---

[1] "The people at Plymouth were generally Brownists, or of the more rigid separatists from the Church of England ; but those who afterward settled at Boston, like the other Puritans, lived in communion with the Church, though they scrupled conformity to several of the ceremonies."—Neal's "Hist. New England," etc., i, 130.

[2] Johnson, b. i, c. xiv ; Josselyn's "New England," 258 ; Dummer's "Defence of New England Charters" ; Hutchinson, i, 91 ; "Massachusetts Hist. Coll.," i, xxiii ; "British Empire in America," i, 372.

the savages that surrounded them, and lighted up the dark recesses of the forest with rays which had first beamed in the cloisters of Magdalen and Trinity.

The manners and habits of the early Puritans fully sustain the assertion that they then belonged to those who were simply "Reformers." They were thoroughly English and churchmanlike, and bore no more resemblance to the habits and manners of the later Puritans than the ruddy faces and genial countenances of those whose laces and flowing locks might well cause them to pass for cavaliers of the days of Rupert, do to the pinched and sour visages that stare from the ungainly portraits of the Barebones and Hasleriggs. The gorgeous colors of the Elizabethan age had given way to the quiet and autumnal tints which steal over the scene when glowing fancy yields to sober meditation. The light and airy conceits of poetry, the magnificent creations of the drama, the bold adventure of the mariner, the courtly delicacy of intrigue, all had given place to a life even more personal and emotional, yet marked by an abiding sense of duty, by the gravity of reflection, the tranquillity of self-control, and the quiet dignity of thoroughly felt and thoroughly appreciated manhood. The heroic age was at hand, but had not yet come : still the Renaissance had done its work, and, in the pursuit of perfect truth, men now turned from the cold contemplation of perfect beauty to the soul-absorbing contemplation of God in self.

An unutterable dislike of the Church of Rome pervaded all classes of Protestant England. Clergy and laity alike showed their repugnance to those usages which, having descended from the Roman Church, savored of Romish superstition.[1] The country gentlemen, with Burleigh at their head, remonstrated against the measures which expelled from their charges those clergymen who declined to subscribe the Three Articles, and showed their restiveness on the subject by a protest, in Parliament, which had the approval of a number of the Queen's own Councillors. But, on the other hand, while the same men so far supported reform, as to indulge a sympathy which raised the Presbyterians from an obscure sect to a party, they by no means nourished an antagonism to the Established Church. They welcomed the appearance of the "Ecclesiastical Polity," wherein the judicious Hooker ap-

---

[1] Strype's " Whitgift," 157.

pealed to the common-sense and loyalty of Englishmen against
the gloomy and despotic theology of Cartwright ; they even approved of the latter's expulsion from his chair in Cambridge, and
placidly acquiesced in the expedients which checked the Presbyterian movement.   At that time Puritan and Presbyterian were
two wholly different beings, though, unquestionably, the Presbyterian had more or less of the Puritan's sympathy.   The latter
lent his countenance, if he did not his support, and, under the
influence of a sympathy rather felt than seen the cause of Presbyterianism was strengthened, and ·a new sect, called the Independents, moreover, rose into existence.   These Independents
were the outgrowth of a handful of zealots, called Brownists,
and who were unconnected with the Puritans or the Presbyterians.   For a time they were called Separatists, from their
absenting themselves from public worship on the ground that
any national church was contrary to the Word of God.   It
was this sect that sought a refuge in Holland, and which afterward founded the colony of Plymouth in New England.   At the
period of their leaving England, religious opinion, outside of the
Roman Church, might thus be classified :—High Church, Puritan
òr Low Church, Presbyterian, and Independent.   Of these, the
last-named was the one whose hand was against every one, and
against whom the hand of every one was raised.   It is a common
error to class " the Pilgrim Fathers " with " the Puritan Fathers " ;
but it is none the less an error, for when the Independents left
home, the Puritans were still within the limits of the Church cf
England, while the Independents, or Brownists, were outside of
and hostile to it.   The Puritans were not, at that time, a sect, nor
were they much more than a class.   They were members of the
Established Church, and they regarded the Independents as so
many contumacious sectaries, in respect to whom the country was
better off without than with them.   In after times, Puritanism
supplied New England with colonists ; but "the Pilgrim Fathers "
were not Puritans, and it is a violation of historical truth to so call
them.

   The Puritan of the days of James the First was a man who
looked with horror on the Church of Rome, and with contempt
on the Brownists.   The sectaries were, to him, a tribe of fanatics,
whose only business in life was to deny the rightfulness of every

thing which preceding generations had established, and which he himself was glad to swear he would maintain ; they were, in short, almost as bad as atheists, and, moreover, were of such low extraction, and of such offensive manners, as to shock every instinct that an educated and well-bred Englishman could fall heir to. As for the Church of Rome, it was the scarlet woman ; the embodiment of every superstition ; the impersonation of every thing hostile to freedom of intellect and purity of soul. For the High Churchman, indeed, the early Puritan had the contemptuous pity of one who sees an erring comrade approach, in spite of every warning, too near the practices of the enemy ; and for the Latitudinarian, he had the same sympathetic solicitude which one has for a brother, who, heedless of the recalling voice, is wandering too far from the paternal standard. But from neither the High Churchman nor from the Latitudinarian was he yet estranged. He was a member of the same body with themselves, and, in respect to that body, no notion of dissent had yet crossed his mind. With him reformation preceded dissent ; he was first a Reformer, then a Dissenter. It was only when, long afterward, his efforts toward ecclesiastical perfecting were thwarted, and he himself proscribed by the one brother, that he followed the other, and that both joined company with the heretical Independents, whose native antagonism at last showed itself in a hostility which culminated in the downfall of both Puritan and Presbyterian.

Coming hither when and as it did, the result of this later emigration was Puritanism in all its simplicity, and as a distinct sect in doctrine, though politically subordinate to the Establishment. The royalists and churchmen had no motive to emigrate, and, therefore, stayed at home ; but the Puritans had such a motive, and hence it was they who came over. Had the Puritans not regarded England as the dominions of Giant Grim, had they not looked upon the ocean as a highway of escape, and the possessions in America as places of refuge, and, above all, had they not been actuated by the motive of getting somewhere where they would be let alone, they would have stayed where they were, and America would have remained a wilderness until commercial adventure, or some other equally exciting cause, had peopled its deserts. Or, while yet in England, had the Puritans been strong in numbers and in organization, and had they, at that time, been able to display their strength sufficiently to excite in their adversaries any more unfriendly disposition than a desire to simply be rid of them, then, in that event, in order to achieve their design of colonization, they might have been forced into a bargain with the crown, which would have precluded the establishment of Puritanism pure and simple in the West, even were the Church debarred from molesting it.   But the fact is, the colonization of New England is due to these facts : first, the Puritans beheld there the peace which at home was neither afforded by the present nor promised by the future ; and, second, the State, which, for awhile hesitating, was at last glad to get rid of them, and, by so doing, to extend her dominion in the new commonwealths they were certain to erect.   The voluntary exile of one of the parties thus gratified both.

It was thus, that, upon the dissolution of the Parliament of 1629, the real Puritan emigration began, and, though composed of a class much more respectable in the social scale, was impelled hither by the same motive that had urged the Brownists or Pilgrims—namely, the desire to be where they would be let alone.

A notion exists in these times, that the Puritans came to America for the purpose of founding free states for posterity, of establishing religious freedom for all, and of opening the gates of the New World to the oppressed of every people.   This, however, is but the offspring of the same pious delusion which led the Greeks to see demigods in their ancestors, and the Romans to deduce their lineage from heroes.   A few expressions, scattered here and there, may countenance the supposition that the most sanguine among them indulged the thought that posterity might regard them as founders of states, but there is nothing to indicate that they landed with the avowed purpose of building another Troy in Latium. They builded better than they knew, and there is nothing whatever to show that they were animated by any higher impulse than the desire to get away from human society ; a motive hardly to be classed as heroic.   The more remote and secluded the retreat, the less inviting and accessible it was to the ungodly, the better it was for the saints.   Such disposition to seclusion might be pardoned as a consequence of persecution, were it not that the intention to exclude the rest of the world betrays itself at the first opportunity in full force and vigor. This unsocial spirit is shown, not only by their express avowals, but by their legislation, which had for one of its chief objects the exclusion of all who did not think as they thought, nor do as they did, and the expulsion of any backslider who presumed to differ from or even doubt their tenets as a peculiar people.   In fact they held themselves out to the world as a close corporation, which under no circumstances would tolerate the intrusion of others or the presence of the dis-affected.[1]   What, moreover, disproves any intention on the part of the mass of the colonists to act the part of founders of new states, is the fact that, before Strafford's head was fairly off his shoulders, the moment the Puritans obtained the upper hand in England and could make their neighbors feel the intolerance they themselves had been protesting against, from that moment (1640) the colony was left to its natural increase, emigration ceased, and, worse still, the colonists began to return to the mother-country. The heroic work of founding states for posterity was dropped for that of uprooting the one which had come down to them from their fathers.

Nor do the character of the colonists and the conditions under which they sailed lead to the conclusion that they came with the purpose of planting anew the tree of liberty, which, under their culture, was to blossom as it never had done before.   They were monarchists, from Winthrop, who was moreover a conformist, down to the humblest follower.   They were members of a corpo-ration emanating, like all others, from the throne, and which, like every other corporation, was amenable to the laws of England. Their charter did not grant religious toleration, nor a jot of civil liberty beyond what existed at home, and as the emigrants sailed under its solemnly accepted provisions, civil tyranny could scarce-ly have become intolerable, nor could the sacred fire of liberty have burned very fiercely in the breasts of those who subscribed it.   In fact, for years their condition was too feeble to permit

---

[1] Bancroft well says : "The emigrants were not so much a body politic as a church in the wilderness."—"Hist. U. S.," i, 348.   Roger Williams was the twentieth person ordered out of Massachusetts within the first seven years of its existence.—Dexter, "As to Roger Williams," 17 ; and further respecting exclu-sion, see *id.*, 139, 140, and "Lowell Lectures (Joel Parker) Mass. Hist. Soc.," 418 ; also "Home" Poetical Works of Ray Palmer, 138.   For list of New England officers that served under the Parliament and Cromwell, see Halibur-ton's "Rule and Misrule of the English in America."

their indulging dreams of a freedom, of which, moreover, their
acts and utterances show they had not the faintest idea.[1]

Freedom, and the notions of it, came to the colonies, as it comes
to all bodies politic ; that is to say, by the process of natural development.   It is the product of necessity rather than of the
dreams of enthusiasts.   When the colony had so waxed in strength
and stature as to be conscious of its ability to take care of itself,
then only, and not till then, do we hear voices declaring the goodness of liberty, and a determination to have it ; but even then,
these notions of liberty seemed to be confined entirely to the preservation of the liberties specified in their charter, and the idea of
independence to be satisfied by less interference on the part of
the home government in their domestic affairs.   It was not until
after the cessation of immigration, not until the colony had the
assurance of experience that it could stand alone, and not
until the Parliament was so hampered by civil discord that it
could not resent assumption,—it was not till then that we hear any
thing like independence.   Then, indeed, following out the natural
law of development, the General Court, or Legislature, summoned
up enough resolution to declare[2] that "plantations are above the
rank of an ordinary corporation," and that "colonies are the
foundations of great commonwealths"; but down to that time
(1646), all utterance is limited by thankfulness for their happy
escape from religious oppression, of joy at being able at last to
worship God in their own way and free from intrusion, and of
reverence for a charter which had made them, to their great content, members of an "ordinary corporation" indeed.   In short,
there is nothing to indicate that they came over with any loftier
purpose than to get away from the world and to find an asylum
where their peculiar tenets could have free scope and action ; and
the thought of assuming a nobler political character than the one
they had always borne, or of securing civil liberty for future generations, does not seem to have crossed their minds, nor to have
interrupted for a moment the play of the fanaticism they had
braved the dangers of the ocean to enjoy.   If there were any

---

[1] "A royal donation under the great seal is the greatest security that may be
had in human affairs.   *   *   *   God knows our greatest ambition is to live a
quiet life in a corner of the world.   We came not into this wilderness to seek
great things to ourselves."—Address to Charles II, A.D. 1644.

[2] See "Remonstrance to the Long Parliament," and note *supra.*

thing of the kind, they left it for those to accomplish who had stayed behind, and it was with shrewd delight that they accepted a charter, which, while it allowed freedom of worship to themselves, permitted them, nevertheless, to exclude the ungodly from their midst, and with them all their unhallowed joys. It was not civil liberty they sought, but full play of their religious notions.[1]

It is well for a people when they can show that they have transmitted in purity the social forces of the vigorous and sensible race from which they sprung, and that they have faithfully pursued the plan of development imposed upon them by natural law. No people can do better than to live naturally, and they who have done this, the hardest of all things for men or states, are entitled to the praise of mankind, be the motives of their origin what they may—whether they were led to found the new state from the necessity of escaping from slavery, like the Israelites ; from the need of defensive combination, like the Romans ; from the crowding of excessive population, like the Franks ; from the desire to worship God in their own way, like the Roman Catholics of Maryland and the Puritans of Massachusetts; or even by the lust of conquest or the dread of their fellow-creatures, like the Spaniards in Central America or the mutineers of the *Bounty*.

It is certainly pleasing to liken the rise of our own people to that of the sun, who, by his rays, chases away the darkness which covered the land, and warms into activity the teeming life, which unto his coming had lain dormant. The fancy glows with the colors of the new-born day. But, after all, the pleasure is as fleeting as the hues of morning, and the mind receives greater satisfaction in comparing the growth of the state with that of the oak, which, growing with its growth and strengthening with its strength, at last, "moored in the rifted rock," spreads abroad its arms in hospitable shelter, and raises its head alike careless of the summer's gust or the winter's storm. No one, looking at it, asks

---

[1] "We now enjoy God and Jesus Christ, and is not that enough ?"—Winthrop. "I shall call that my country where I may most glorify God and enjoy the presence of my dearest friends."—*Id.* "New England was a religious plantation, not a plantation for trade." * * * "We all came into these parts of America to enjoy the liberties of the Gospel in purity and peace." * * * "New England was the colony of conscience."—Extracts from Puritan authorities, cited in Bancroft, i, 464 ; see further, *sparsim,* "As to Roger Williams."

where it is, or how it got there, so long as the glorious object confronts the gaze. It may have been planted by a king from the acorns of Boscobel, or dropped by a quarry as he turned from the eagle's stroke. There, however, it stands ; it is enough that it is one of the perfect works of nature, and that, as such, men turn to it with pleasure and take delight in its perfection.

So with the rise and growth of peoples ; and the only mode of ascertaining the true greatness and well-being of a people, is not by observing the circumstances of its origin, but by observing its growth. If a people has steadily developed according to the laws of nature, then it may be taken for granted, that it has been worthily fulfilling the purpose for which it was created. It has been doing good to its neighbors as well as to itself, and in fulfilling this double object consists the true well-being of nations. But if it has not developed according to natural law, then it may be as safely assumed, that it has not been subserving the purposes of its being, and that it has not achieved true greatness. And so sure as the individual betrays upon his person the scarred protests of outraged nature, so sure do states display in their condition the revenge of natural law violated. It is, then, from understanding distinctly that states are planted and grow by a natural law which cannot be evaded with impunity, that we are to start on an investigation which is to lead us to a true conclusion respecting them. That law being clearly understood, we can easily judge of the true character of a people, by observing whether they have obeyed or resisted its authority ; for, where it has freedom of action, compliance or non-compliance with it will indicate a healthy or unhealthy condition of the state.

Thus, we see that the real greatness and well-being of a people is affected neither one way or the other by the motives or circumstances of that people's origin, but that it depends solely and entirely on their conformity or nonconformity with the natural law of development. This law acts in the same way everywhere— as well among the Esquimaux as among the English, as well among the Patagonians as among the French. Its operation is affected only by influences with which the God of Law has surrounded it, as those of climate in one place, soil in another, race everywhere, or of all three combined. If its effects are not so apparent in Terra del Fuego as in Burgundy, it is because in the former region it is met and overcome by other forces which the plan of nature has designed should limit its action in that locality. If its effects are more apparent in England than in Labrador, it is because that same controlling power of nature has lessened opposition to it, and has assigned that locality as one of the theatres of its greatest activity. No one will dispute that the force which expands the Victoria Regia on the Senegambia is the same as that which covers the rocks of Greenland with lichen. It is the same force in both places, acting in the same way, but varying in results as the conditions differ under which it exerts its powers.

Viewing this law of development, then, in its actual operation on the Caucasian race, and particularly on our own tribe, our history shows that it is slow of action; that at times it acts spasmodically; but that, taking one century with another, its advance is startlingly marked, and that, so far, it has always been progressive among the English-speaking societies. If we go no further back than strictly historical times, and see how England was peopled, and if we observe the subsequent development of the English, it will be seen at a glance that the great question is not how they were planted, but how they have developed. What have they become, what have they done, and what are they doing? Apart from the consideration of race, the circumstances attending their settlement, and the conditions under which it was accomplished, have nothing to do with our estimate of them as a people.

Taking the English for an example, we see them developing sometimes rapidly, sometimes slowly, but still steadily developing. When they stand still, we observe that it is from such reason as the exhaustion caused by conquest or civil strife, the operation of bad principles in Church and State, or the destruction caused by pestilence or famine; and when they progress, we conclude, what investigation shows us to be the case, that the conquest is over, the civil war ended, the bad principles are eradicated, and the ravages of the plagues are repaired. Sooner or later, the losses are made good, and the people take another step forward. But, under this law of development, even in its best estate, the growth of a great principle is at first very slow. If, for instance, we follow the course taken by the principle of Freedom of Conscience, we shall see, that, though it made its appearance in the history of England as far back as the twelfth century, it, even now, has not attained its full development. At first, those who broached it did not know what they were doing. Their view was bounded by the walls within which they were born, and their aim extended no farther than a reformation of the evils before their eyes. Following it along, and noting only the most striking features of its growth, we next observe that this principle had developed to a remarkable degree, when the Reformation, which was its first great result, occurred ; but that even then, though there were those who recognized it as a principle and a vital social force, and not only advocated but died for it, the mass of Englishmen were blind to its very existence, and that, to them, the Reformation was but the mere throwing off of a foreign yoke. After that event, however, and as a consequence of it, its development is exceedingly rapid, and we observe that it has extended the domain of its struggle to secular affairs, and that its progress is attended by convulsions which not only rent England in twain, but which ultimately shook the whole of Europe, and peopled a continent beyond the ocean. But we see, too, that, though by this time the church was standing on its defence against it, though the state was attacking it with all its might, and though society was stirred by it to its deepest depths, it was, nevertheless, but half understood. Men had still no broader notion of freedom of conscience than as it affected them individually, and it on its side had so little influence over men that it was powerless to compel them to share with their fellows that which they selfishly sought the solitude of deserts to enjoy. The people evidently had not yet taken it home to their hearts, and were not yet ready to assert it as a principle ; it was still nothing more than the meagre doctrine of religious toleration, and so little was it a social force, that as sect after sect raised its head under the encouraging help it extended to all, no sooner did these sects get a footing than each outvied its predecessors in intolerance. It is evident, then, that religious toleration is not yet become an accepted principle, and still less is that great force, of which it is the offspring, freedom of conscience, under which term is to be included also freedom of thought. But to complete our observation, we next behold it in an aggressive attitude, and religious toleration not only asserts its existence, but, upon its imperious demand, obtains recognition. Henceforth its career is that of conquest.

The development of New England character is due, first, to the
original vigor and expansive force of the race blood ; and, second,
to the impulses that blood received from the new conditions under
which it has since acted.   There can be no question, that to the
civil and religious development of the race given by the great
strifes of the seventeenth century, is due much of the expansive
force since so marvellously brought into action, and that the Puritanism which started the England of to-day on her career, started
also the northern colonies of this country on theirs, and is actuat-
ing the States which succeeded them at this very hour.   The earlier stage of development gave the force necessary to the existence
of the later.   Its nature has already been discussed, and how the
Puritanism of New England was one and the same with that of
Old England, has already been disclosed.   Such it was, though in
the different countries it met with different fates.   In one country
it rushed into civil strife, and though, after apparently burning
itself out in the flames of discord, it sank into the ashes of a cold
and icy despotism, it yet left its spirit so indissolubly connected
with the body politic as to forever change the character of the
people and of the state.   In the other, unopposed by obstacles,
its career has been one of peace ; for the conflict of the colonists
with the natives neither retarded its advance nor affected its character.   In one, its history was eventful ; in the other it was uneventful.   Here it had nothing to contend with but itself. as,
progressing under the inevitable law of historical development, it
continued to grow, and to produce from time to time new sects
and new ideas, which, struggling for existence with those from
which they sprung and with each other, in their turn produced
others, and all united in hurrying it along to still further advances.

The early history of Puritanism in this country, therefore, is uneventful, and of interest to him only who seeks history in results
rather than in a present warfare of polemics.   He who wades
through the dreary annals of our early Puritanical history has little
for his pains but the husks of hard, dry, and abstruse disputations,
and the worm-eaten leaves of theological controversaries now un-
readable.   Mute records of a psychological condition long since
passed away, they are impotent to excite any emotion more moving than regret that intellectual energy so great should ever have

been wasted on subjects so insignificant, and the sole interest they possess is that which draws the antiquary to even the most worthless palimpsest, or to hieroglyphics absolutely undecipherable. These piles of dust and ashes serve no longer any purpose but to show us how unsubstantial were the phantoms over which conflicting sects once tore each other to pieces.

The virulence of theological strife in those days is almost incredible. Still it is accounted for when we reflect, that, constituted as society was, and cut off as it was from ordinary subjects of contemplation and exercise, the mind had little else upon which it could exert its powers than the hair-splitting distinctions of theology. Of politics, history-making, and philosophy there was little ; of tradition and romance there was nothing. The novelist and the poet[1] of later days have beheld in the quaint and stilted manners of those times, in the armed worshippers, and in the migrations of resolute enthusiasts forcing their way through tangled forests, the dreamy beauty half revealed through the mist that always rises from the distant past ; but the historic picturesqueness bestowed by marching armies, contending hosts, dethroned kings, scattered Parliaments and stern dictators, is altogether wanting. All is a dead level of polemics unrelieved by art, by song, by literature, or by war. Even of architectural monuments—the first expressions of new civilization, and of which there were examples for emulation, few and scattered though they were, in the solid ruins left by a mysterious race that preceded them—none have come down worthy of the name.

Such an element as a class that creates solid and enduring literature, is out of the question in a community hardly strong enough to stand alone ; and even an educated *class* is not to be expected. We are not surprised, then, at the absence of a literary class, but certainly there is ground for astonishment when it appears that the mass of this singular people was so highly educated that no distinction on the score of education can be drawn. There doubtless was an uneducated class, but it is too insignificant to be noticed, and the remarkable phenomenon exists of society consisting entirely of the learned and having the wilderness for its habitation. After the Winthrop immigration, it may be said, that for two gen-

---

[1] Hawthorne, Longfellow, and imaginative writers of New England.

erations there were few men in New England who were not educated ; for, as a late writer remarks,[1] "it is probable that between
the years 1630 and 1690, there were in New England as many
graduates of Cambridge and Oxford as could be found in any
population of similar size in the mother-country. At one time,
during the first part of that period, there was in Massachusetts
and Connecticut, a Cambridge graduate for every two hundred and
fifty inhabitants, besides sons of Oxford not a few." Such being
the case, the colonists were probably the most educated body of
people ever beheld, and not the least singular element of the singular spectacle they presented to the world, was the extremely
flourishing condition of classical knowledge in what was in reality
a howling wilderness. Greek, though cultivated, was less known
than Latin, but Latin was there, as in the Old World, the language
of the learned. Hebrew was diligently studied. Of course divinity flourished, and that was the great difficulty of the day and of
the people—it flourished too much. The State being an oligarchy,
of which the clergy formed the ruling class, every energy was bent
to secure a position in that class, and there was not a matron but
hoped to live long enough to see her favorite son "wag his pow
in the pulpit." That pious spectacle enjoyed, earth had no greater bliss, and the happy mother could die content. As the clergy
absorbed every aspiration and every energy of the better sort, it
is natural that the feeble attempts at literature which expressed
the independence of a few resolute minds, should be drowned in
the deluge of profitless and windy disputation which marked the
sacred rage of the day. Moreover, there, as everywhere else
where priestcraft has had its way, the clergy were averse to a literature which did not emanate from themselves : it was they, and
no others, who were to feed the lambs, and the bold layman who
raised his voice was eyed askance as one who infringed upon their
sacred rights, then, as an intruder, he was made to feel that he
was not at home, and, lastly, as an enemy he was stifled or expelled. The clerical odium of freedom of conscience has always
been extremely hostile to literature, whose greatest achievements,
since the decline of monachism, when it escaped from the mon-
asteries into the world, have been in spite of the clergy and not
with their concurrence. The gloomy despotism of the New Eng-

[1] Tyler, "Hist. Am. Lit.," i, 98.

land oligarchy did not belie this universal disposition, and the independence of thought essential to healthy literature, when not plucked up by the roots, attained, to say the most, a precarious existence under its dark shadow. Accordingly, we find hardly any thing worthy the name of literature, and, of a consequence, where there was no literature there could be no literary class. The description that may be given of the Puritanical literature of Old England applies with redoubled force to that of the New. It constitutes a weary, hopeless desert, in which the few stunted growths that raise their heads, serve only to render more dismal the dreary waste around them.

But, in the steadfast search after results, we cannot rest contented with showing what this general love and exercise of disputation did not do. It is not enough to note that it smothered any rising efforts toward profane literature, or that it failed to yield, on the instant, good fruits. In fact, even had it not possessed the land to the exclusion of every thing else intellectual, it is hardly probable that a people, few in number, widely scattered, and whose days were devoted to a conflict with the elements for mere existence, could have given the world any literature worth speaking of, be the other circumstances of their condition what they might. There is nothing in the intellectual life of man unworthy of observation ; nothing, indeed, that should not be the subject of profound study. And so with this century of disputation. The deserts have their uses, and this apparently intellectual waste, on its part, effectually served great ends. If we regard, as we should, the growth of a people as a composite fact, in which one of the details is but a step to something better, we must accept, without cavil, the conclusion, that in the plan of historical development, every phenomenon is a natural expression of design ; has, or has had, its uses ; and is, or has been, necessary to the fulness of that growth. In thus regarding the intellectual life of these colonies, the eye is at once arrested by the continued and long-sustained epoch of religious disputation, and, as the beholder stands amazed at the marvel of a wilderness resounding with the accents of what would be foreign to any place but the Sorbonne, the Synod, or at least the schools ; as he gazes in bewilderment at the spectacle of men, who, carrying their lives in their hands, seek refreshment, after the labor of subduing savages and breaking the stubborn soil, in acrimonious debate on the doctrine of original sin, he naturally inquires, on gaining breath, For what good purpose can all this be ? The question would have been difficult to answer in those days, but with the results before us, the place this era of disputation filled in the formation of American character, is readily seen—it did for New England what the disputation of the schoolmen did for western Europe. In the days of inexorable physical toil, it served to render men's minds acute ; it kept alive the learning they brought with them, and it stimulated the love of letters in a people who, cast upon a rocky coast, might, otherwise, have been called upon to witness their intellectual life hopelessly sinking under the unequal contest it was compelled to wage with the hard and brutalizing forces of nature. It helped to conquer those forces, and was the only discipline which, under the peculiar constitution of this branch of society, the public mind could receive. It is true, that the first thing these people did, was to organize a system of schools, with a college for its head ; but a little reflection will show us, what the recorded facts do, that, from the force of circumstances, many years must have elapsed before this system could become a self-sustaining, active, vitalizing social force. For a long time, in fact, those who could afford it, sent their sons back to England to be educated. In the meantime, what other field had this strange community to exercise its intellect upon ? It was a colony of religious enthusiasts ; its government was that of a religious oligarchy ; its State-house was the meeting-house ; religion was what brought them to that desert, and religion it was that was the very marrow of their bones. Cut off such a community from the world ; put it on the island of Juan Fernandez, and what would be the natural field of its public life ? The answer is to be found in what actually occurred in the New England colonies. The intellectual life of the public expressed itself solely on religious subjects, the only ones it had at hand ; and, where no hierarchical organization exists, no liturgy, no ecclesiastical system, in a word, no church, but merely a band of religious enthusiasts, the intellectual life of religion universally expresses itself in long prayers, long sermons, and tedious disputations in the shape of debates in synod, in tracts, in essays,

and in books.[1]   So with the colonists, and, in the plan of historical development, we must ascribe this sway of the dialecticians to
the thirst a youthful society felt for an outward expression of
their intellectual life, the necessity of substituting the best make-
shift for the means of education which were wanting, and the
desire of stimulating the love of learning.   That this was the part
performed, is shown by the fact, that as society advanced and
the means of education became abundant and of easy application,
theological disputation faded away ; the meeting-house, as a place
of assembly, was dropped for the school-house ; the lawyers
pushed aside the preachers, and the conflicts of the pulpit gave
way to those of the courts and of the debating society—an institution, for such it is, which, having its origin in those disputatious
days, still keeps its place with tenacity in every school-house of
the North, and to which, far more than has been attributed to it,
are due some of the most peculiar traits of our people.

Were we to confine ourselves to noticing the effects of this
wordy theology on the study of divinity and metaphysics in New
England, we should find ample excuse for its existence in the
known influence exerted by it in the discipline it wrought on the
great mind of Jonathan Edwards.[2]   But its effects have reached
further, and have been more broadly extended, than can be displayed in the works of one man.   They extend to the present

---

[1] The prayers were hours long. See instance of one of two hours' length,
quoted from Sibley's " Harv. Grad." in Tyler, i, 189, 190. The sermons were
longer still. *Id., id.* As to books, essays, etc., the fecundity was simply won-
derful.   John Cotton wrote books by the dozen. Tyler gives some of their
names, from which I extract a few : " Of the Holiness of Church Members " ;
" The Keys of the Kingdom of Heaven " ; " A Modest and Clear Answer to
Mr. Ball's Discourse of Set Forms of Prayer " ; " Spiritual Milk for Babes " ;
" A Treatise of the Covenant of Grace as it is Dispensed to the Elect Seed."
Roger Williams wrote a book, the title of which was, " The Bloody Tenet of
Persecution for cause of Conscience," which Cotton answered with, " The
Bloody Tenet washed and made white in the Blood of the Lamb " ; to which
Williams rejoined, " The Bloody Tenet yet more Bloody, by Mr. Cotton's En-
deavor to wash it white in the Blood of the Lamb." This apparently silenced
Cotton.   Another Williams' title is, " George Fox digged out of his Burrowe "
—disputing Quakerism. But, in fecundity, the ineffectual stars of these
worthies pale before that of Cotton's grandson, Cotton Mather. This man
actually wrote more than *three hundred and eighty* separate works (Tyler, ii,
79). In one year, besides doing the work of his pastorate, keeping sixty fasts
and twenty vigils, he published *fourteen* books. The fasts, vigils, and the
books, all told, surpass any thing the monks can show.

[2] From a single one of Thomas Shepard's books, Jonathan Edwards, it is
said, drew nearly a hundred citations for his celebrated " Treatise concerning
Religious Affections."—Tyler, i, 207.

day, and their influence is now felt by millions. The secession, or rather the expulsion, of Roger Williams let loose the floodgates of controversy, and turned the attention of the colonists from mere theological questions to those which savored of the secular. The tide once turned, it pursued its course, and as dialectics subsided, reflections on the abstract principles of liberty, the fondness for discussing which is so prominent a feature of the Northerner, usurped their places. The science of politics is a practical one, and none have applied the principles of liberty more practically than the New Englander. But, on the other hand, while he acts practically, no one delights more in the abstractions of that subject than he. When the disputation of the pulpit died away, secular debate took its place, and, without yielding their love of abstractions, the theories of political life took the place of theological dogmas. Every American can recall the time, when, a beardless boy, he harangued his debating-society on the exceeding great glory of liberty, the different modes of government, the distinction between the several kinds of law, as, for example, the moral and the municipal ; and can remember, as of but yesterday, when he discussed, with the ease which only the assurance of youth can give, questions before which Plato and Machiavel gave up the ghost in despair. The effect of such discussions on the youth of a republic is simply incalculable. Though it may be adverse to depth and thoroughness, it certainly produces familiarity with the subject, and a confidence which is of all importance to one who, from the mere fact that he is a voter, is, in a certain sense, a legislator. Without laying this national tendency entirely at the door of a Massachusetts conventicle, it is nevertheless the fact, that this latent tendency was, as far as New England is concerned, warmed into life by it, and that these discussions can be followed back in an unbroken stream to the times when secular and forensic debate rose on the ruins of its progenitor, the theological disputation of the Puritan divines.

Such was one of the effects of the early controversial theology of New England. It intensified in the breasts of one of the most practical people on earth a love of abstraction, and aroused a fondness for discussing the abstract principles of liberty, which might have been often tempered by them to their benefit, but which has never left them.

The pent-up enthusiasm and mental activity of the colonists had not long to wait before the sluices were opened, and the life-giving flood was suffered to pour over the fields. It was in the earliest days of the Boston settlement that there appeared a man about whom his fellow-colonists had much to say, and in whom posterity still takes the deepest interest. This interest is not misplaced, and the character and the career of Roger Williams merit all the attention given them ; for, before Richelieu had laid the axe to the root of intolerance in France by making the church secondary to the state ; before Descartes had parted his lips with the utterance *Cogito, ergo sum,* which prepared the way for freedom of thought by recognizing the importance of the individual ; before the Baconian philosophy had given new direction to inquiry, this man had maintained that free religion and freedom of thought were essential elements of the body politic ; and while Europe was yet the battlefield where contending creeds strove for mastery, and while Protestantism, dead to noble impulses, was sunk into drivelling disputation, and faith everywhere betrayed no force other than what lay in the gripe of intolerance, then it was that the voice of Roger Williams was heard in the wilderness crying truths which were to be thenceforth accepted by the world as vital forces of social, religious, and political life.

Freedom of conscience, until his time, had been regarded as a dream, or entertained only as a theory ; after his time it was a positive, substantial fact. His work in life seems to have been that of transforming this sentiment into a living force, and to him is due the honor of being the first who recognized it as a constitutional principle, and who actually erected a polity that had it for a foundation-stone. The effect of this action is incalculable ; but it is enough to say, that, from that moment, a new force was infused into American life, and that the Americans then began to assume the character which distinguishes them to-day. The establishment of freedom of conscience as a constitutional element of the body politic effected, sooner or later, a total change in the character of American society. The Englishmen in America began to cease being such, and to put on new armor that had been welded on the spot, and, after the lapse of two centuries and more, it is no exaggeration to style the man who brought this transformation to pass, the First of the Americans.

Roger Williams was probably a Welchman, who had drifted to London, where he attracted the attention of no less a person than Sir Edward Coke. There must have been something powerfully attractive in him to kindle the sympathy of that dry and crabbed lawyer, but so it was, and Coke's interest being happily of the practical sort, exercised itself in giving the lad an education. He first procured him admission to what is now known as the Charterhouse, or Blue Coat School, and afterward had him entered at Pembroke College, Cambridge. The world has never been in haste to ascribe excessive goodness of heart to Coke, and it may be that to his sagacity rather than to sympathy, is due the foresight which detected greatness in Williams, and the kindness that fostered him : but whatever the motive, it was a good one, and to Coke must be assigned the credit of having given to the world one of its foremost men.

After he had taken orders in the Church of England, his whole view of religion, and particularly, of the relations which religion ought to hold toward the conscience of the individual and the powers of the State, underwent a radical change. He could no longer subscribe the Articles of Faith, and, cutting loose from the Church, he became a Puritan, or rather, as the term meant in those early days, a Reformer ; and a reformer he certainly was in every sense of the word that is good and noble. At last, his safety being threatened, flight was the only thing left him, and so, without having time to say farewell to his benefactor, he shook the dust of England from off his feet, and bent his way toward Massachusetts.

When he reached America he was about thirty years of age. His mind was active and clear, and he reasoned well ; he had studied hard, and was learned ; he had thought much, and was a man of opinions ; he had sought light, and had convictions ; he was ambitious, resolute, courageous, and of inflexible will ; he had winning manners,[1] and being of an amiable, sociable disposition, was born to persuade men—yet the first thing he did was to set them against him.

Much has been said of the short career which terminated in

---

[1] "A man lovely in his carriage."—Edward Winslow, " Hypocrisy Unmasked," 65. The New England literature of the time teems with Roger Williams ; but for a modern view of him, and for citation of authorities, consult Dexter's " As to Roger Williams," though not written in a very friendly spirit.

the expulsion of Williams from the infant settlements of Massachusetts Bay, and the agitation caused by his abrupt departure does not seem even yet to have entirely subsided. It has not in itself, however, greater importance than any event has which may be regarded as the first step from which great results have flowed, and it may be dismissed after a brief consideration.

The facts of the case are few and simple, and the affair may be summarily described as follows :—Roger Williams, a licensed member of a hierarchy, and an accepted member of an oligarchy, conscientiously made use of his position to preach doctrines which were viewed by the hierarchy as heretical, and by the oligarchy as seditious. For such offence he was conscientiously tried, convicted, and sentenced. Before the sentence was executed, and while it was yet held in suspense, he contumaciously repeated the offence, and the indignation of the authorities being thus excited, he deemed it best to flee the colony ; and this he did.

The part performed by those who sat in judgment on him is perfectly intelligible. The colonists had sought seclusion for the very purpose of enjoying their peculiar tenets unmolested, and to effect this purpose the corporation of which they were members was rendered a close one to those outside and a disciplinary body to those within. From circumstances and from the charter, civil power was lodged almost exclusively in the hands of the members, and from their character and disposition this power was allied with, and was made subservient to the ecclesiastical power. There being but one creed the result was an oligarchy. Those were the days when the union of Church and State seemed natural, and, in this respect, if the colonists were no better they were not much worse than the most civilized communities of their day. By the standard of their times must they be judged, for it would be unreasonable to exact of a community that it should reflect greater light than what was shed upon it. If, then, the Puritans are to be censured, they must be so for the oligarchy which they erected, and for exacting and excessive exercise of a principle at that time universally admitted to be true ; but for the principle itself they cannot be held responsible, however false it may be, inasmuch as it was not in their power to know better. No Roger Williams had yet taught them better things ; for his ideas, still confused, half-formed, and urged with hysterical energy, had not

assumed the harmonious and systematic shape in which we behold them, nor were they presented as those which had been tried
by experience ; and they lacked the self-asserting force that time
only can give to doctrine. The admitted fact, that Williams was
in advance of the age, blunts of itself the edge of censure, which
must be reserved for the descendants of these Puritans, who
maintained this principle long after Williams and his disciples
had exposed its fallacy, and long after freedom of conscience had
displayed its surpassing worth and set them a bright example in
other communities. It is not strange that, wanting the power of
vision to discern in the new light which broke so abruptly upon
their eye the dawn of a brighter and better day than that in which
they were groping, the colonists should behold in a rising sun
only another of the many false lights which had already to their
sorrow gone out in utter darkness. To us their error may be
plain enough, but it must be admitted, that, from their standpoint,
and it was the only one they had, they acted rationally and displayed a sense of duty in promptly resisting innovations which
threatened to unsettle their faith and to disturb the repose they
were bound as trustees to do their utmost to maintain. To a
people who regarded reverence for the king as a virtue second
only to reverence for God, and to whose existence it was essential
that the ground they stood upon should be theirs,—to such a
people, the assertion that the appellation of " most Christian king "
conveyed a falsehood, and the denial of their patent's validity
implied in the proposition that the Indian title never had been
and never could be divested by an alien, even though he were the
King of England, were serious and shocking things which combined within them disloyalty to the crown and hostility to the
settlement : and what could be more abominable and monstrous
to those to whom the union of Church and State seemed natural,
and who were themselves oligarchists, than the denial that the
Establishment was a church, and that the civil power had nothing
to do with executing its decrees, even if it were ? In fact, when
we consider what the age was, and how far Williams was in
advance of it, we have no right to be astonished at the course
taken by the colonists in his case, nor is there ground for censur-
ing them ; the less so, as the more conscientious they were, the
more relentless they had to be, their principles being accepted as

true. In this matter of the trial of Roger Williams, the party really deserving censure seems rather to be the one that displayed so little tact and judgment as to force food upon those whose stomachs were not strong enough to bear it, and to be he who showed so little knowledge of mankind as to attempt by assault the demolition of prejudices which can be dislodged only by gradual and persistent approach.[1] In the moral order of things, nothing, except truth itself, has such vitality as prejudice or is so tenacious : it appears in the same guise, it flies the same banner, it wears the same armor, it contends for the same ground, it is nerved by the same conscientiousness, and all it lacks of being the same thing is having the same soul.

The trial of Roger Williams will ever retain its deep significance from the fact, that one of the charges against him was, that he maintained "that the civil Magistrates' power extends only to the Bodies and Goods, and outward State of men." It may be, as Cotton says, that this, though charged, was not one of the reasons for Williams' banishment ; but the fact that at this time, and in this place, the subject was a point of such variance between the parties as to be made by one of them a charge against the other more than smacking of criminality, has a significance which the reasons Cotton assigns for its not being a cause of expulsion only emphasize : "There are many known to hold both these opinions [one of these is that here given], * * * and yet they are tolerated not only to live in the Commonwealth, but also in the fellowship of the Churches" ; which is not a denial that such charge was made, but an argument that it could not have affected the verdict.

Such being the case, several things are evident : (1) That toleration, though not accepted by the community as such, was entertained by "many" members of that community ; (2) that it seems to have so far made its way, that its existence in the breasts of individuals was "tolerated" by the Commonwealth and the Churches ; and (3) that it had assumed such proportions and had become so formidable in the eyes of the Commonwealth and Churches as to justify the censure and the attitude of hostility to it involved in so solemn an act as an indictment, or what was equivalent to one.

[1] For a different view of this subject, see Appendix C.

These facts being apparent, it is manifest that this event did involve the principle of intolerance, and thereby the union of Church and State (for the term "Commonwealth and Churches" is but another way of saying "Church and State"), and that Williams' preaching had struck at its root. For, otherwise, wherefore the necessity of contradiction, which the trial itself on such a charge implies, or of evasion, which the denial of its being a cause of banishment is after it was officially stated to be such during the sentence?

It has been already laid down in another part of this work,[1] as a rule whereby to ascertain the existence of toleration or intolerance, that, *where the civil power is made subservient to the ecclesiastical in the prescription of doctrine, the maintenance of discipline, or the extirpation of heresy, there is intolerance; where it is not so subservient, there is toleration.* Judged by this rule, the Puritan oligarchy, like many a better organization of its day, was intolerant. But the limitation of the civil power to "the outward State of men," so insisted upon by Williams, does not suffer that power to reach their inward state, or conscience, and deprives the church of the power to regulate faith by corporal force. This is toleration, the first and great step to freedom of conscience. Toleration and intolerance, then, met each other at this trial face to face. That toleration was resisted by the court, or evaded by others as interested, shows with equal conclusiveness that it was involved in the issue before the court; that Williams then fought, or stood ready to fight, for the cause of Cotton's "many known to hold [this] opinion"; and that the trial is justly, as it is generally, considered to be the point whence freedom of conscience in America started on its career as a vital and aggressive force.

This trial, then, is important in showing that the doctrine of freedom of conscience was strong and bold enough in the settlements of Massachusetts Bay, in the year 1635, to struggle for a foothold and assert its existence as a social force, and that it then had vitality enough when worsted in one locality to plant itself successfully in another. It has an additional value to the observer in this, that it affords a historical date whence the career of that force in this country can be pursued, and that it offers a standard whereby its attempts and success in other communities can be measured.

---

[1] Page 62.

The doctrines set forth by Williams at Plymouth and Salem were but rudimental. They did not assume the form of a system until after his departure from Massachusetts, and until he had a community all to himself upon which to experiment. His progress of thought is defaced by the contradictions, the inconsistencies, the impetuosity, the extravagance, and the errors to which all human action is incident : but he held steadily on his way, having been taught the bitter lesson, that, no matter how great the inspiration of the prophet, truth can be planted in the hearts of men only by patience in well-doing. Like those of other great thinkers, his steps at first were slow and halting ; he himself was restless and wayward ; but as experience lent him confidence, he walked more and more erect, until at last, when he felt the ground solid beneath his tread, he bounded eagerly forward into the newly discovered realms that teemed with glorious visions, and where truths, like Alp on Alp, rose before him.

Roger Williams' whole being was possessed by the one great principle that the soul should be free, and he was wont to express his heart's aspiration by the term "soul-liberty." He boldly threw down the gauntlet to the world, by announcing that soul-liberty was of God, that conscience was by nature free, and that it was the duty of human society to preserve intact that freedom, whereof the least violation was invariably but the first step to soul-bondage. The conscience, the soul of man, being free, no limits bounded that freedom but those set by the Creator. Of a consequence, any limitation imposed on the conscience of one man by another, was an interference between the Creator and the created ; it was intolerance, a thing altogether abhorred by God and unjust to man. Religion being a relation that existed solely between the Creator and the created, God was the only judge of the latter. No religious organization, then, had a shadow of right to dictate what one should think or what one should do in matters religious. As a necessary deduction from this conclusion, no such right existing, there were no need of agents to enforce the observance of faith, nor any right to use them. Consequently, the use of the civil jurisdiction by the ecclesiastical, and the subordination of the former to the latter, had no justification, and was, in fact, a monstrous perversion of truth, which called for immediate reformation.

Thus, at one blow, Williams would have cloven the Church and

State asunder, and sponged from the statute-roll the very mention of conformity or non-conformity. Heresy, with him, had no existence, and, carrying his doctrine to its conclusion, he fearlessly asserted that compulsory worship of God was an abomination ; that, where the spirit was not a willing one, worship compelled was an offence to the Deity ; that if one would not worship, he should not be made to do so ; and that no man should be compelled to support any religion whatever, least of all one in which he had no faith.[1]

This doctrine overturned the intolerance whereby the civil power is made the agent of the ecclesiastical in the prescription of faith and the extirpation of heresy, and left error at the mercy of the only power that can combat it—truth. It was the sentence of divorce between Church and State, and it ordained that neither should have any thing to do with the other, further than extending the protection under which the latter is bound to shelter every element of society ; yet this protection was to be given, not so much to the institution, as to the worshipper, in whom lay the natural right to freedom of conscience, and, consequently, the inherent right to freedom of worship. No man has ever had a clearer view of the true relations existing between the civil and ecclesiastical powers. The civil magistrate, he says, may not intermeddle even to stop a church from apostasy and heresy * * * his power extends only to the bodies and goods and outward estate of men.[2] But if the power to impose a style of worship on the individual was denied, nothing could be more positive, nor more catholic, than the emphasis with which he asserted the duty of society to protect the consciences of its members, be who and what they may. Jew or Gentile, Christian, Turk, or Pagan, all were, as the children of God, alike to this apostle of liberty,[3] who would have men learn that one poor lesson of setting

---

[1] Bancroft, i, chap. ix : " No one should be bound. to worship, or to maintain a worship against his consent." " Queries of Highest Consideration ": " We query where you now find one footstep, print, or pattern, in this doctrine of the Son of God, for a national church." Again : " A tenet that fights against the common principles of all civility, and the very civil being and combinations of men * * * by commixing * * * a spiritual and civil state together."

[2] Quoted from a rare tract in Bancroft, i, chap. ix.

[3] " It is the will and command of God, that * * * a permission of the most Paganish, Turkish, or anti-Christian consciences and worships be granted to all men, in all nations and countries ; and they are only to be fought against with that sword which is, in soul-matters, able to conquer, to wit, the sword of God's Spirit, the word of God." Quoted in Tyler, i, 254.

absolutely the consciences of all men free,[1] and who would have lifted his fellows to that sublime height, where charity forbids persecution, and where common-sense disdains it as a confession by error of the truth it cannot overcome.[2]

This assertion of a doctrine which placed the civil and ecclesiastical jurisdictions, each on its own ground, naturally drew attention to the nature of each, and the just relations they bore one another. Heretofore, men had contemplated them in unison, but now they were called on to observe them separately, and as, to the mind's eye, the State now stood by itself, a secular tone henceforward characterized the discussions of the colonists. What the true nature of government was, contested the ground with questions relating, for example, to the efficacy of infant baptism, and the mind broadened with the new field it was called upon to explore. Williams himself profited by his own doctrine, to which he was ever faithful, and as he ascended height after height of the elevation whither it led him, his vision became clearer and more far-reaching, until at last the ever-receding horizon embraced results, of which, in his earlier writings, the existence does not seem to be suspected. Doubtless, at first, his conception of his great doctrine was limited to its effects upon the moral and mental condition of the individual only, and then it embraced the religious condition of society, by a short and easily taken step. But his mind expanded with the glowing years, and at last he views its effects on the social and political condition of the State, and of the whole world. To us, who have been born long since intolerance ceased to be formidable north of the Alps and of the Rio Grande, and to whom the effects of this doctrine are more familiar in the constitution of the State than of the Church, it seems strange that his ever-pushing intellect should have been so slow in foreseeing its mightiest conquests. But such has been, almost always, the lot of those from whose brain great ideas

---

[1] " The Bloody Tenet yet more Bloody, by Mr. Cotton's Endeavor," etc.

[2] " For me, I must profess, while heaven and earth lasts, that no one tenet that either London, England, or the world doth harbor, is so heretical, blasphemous, seditious, and dangerous to the corporal, to the spiritual, to the present, to the eternal good of men, as the bloody tenet * * * of persecution for cause of conscience."—*Id.* "—a monstrous paradox, that God's children should persecute God's children," " Narr. Club Pub.," i, 319. " Persecutors of men's bodies, seldom or never do these men's souls good." *Ibid.*, 327-328.

have sprung ; they have had to live up to them, and, though their
force has been instantly felt, it has almost invariably taken years
for their creators to appreciate their compass. It is not, therefore, until 1652, that we have from him the evidence of a foresight
embracing the last measure to be meted out by the doctrine of
freedom of conscience—*to be,* for a glance shows us that the world
is still far from the point his vision reached. "The removal of
the yoke of soul-oppression,"[1] he says, " as it will prove an act of
mercy and righteousness to the enslaved nations, so it is of binding force to engage the whole and every interest and conscience
to preserve the common liberty and peace."[2] Thus from a free
conscience he advanced to a state of society where peace and
good-will should dwell among men.

He was no dreamer, but a doer of his word. He was thorough,
and when a principle once rose from the depths of his mind, he
made no toy of it, but, fixing it immovably in his heart, made it
part and parcel of his being, and straightway sought the means of
putting it in force. Thus, he had not been long in the land,
before the condition of the Indians having excited his benevo-

---

[1] " The Hireling Ministry none of Christ's," 29.

[2] Here may be given his admirable description of a commonwealth, wherein
the distinction of Church and State is observed, and the true relations they bear
to one another are set forth. It contains, *in petto,* his whole doctrine, and is
taken from his " Letter to the People of Providence," A. D., 1655.

" There goes many a ship to sea, with many hundred souls in one ship,
whose weal and woe is common, and is a true picture of a commonwealth or a
human combination or society. It hath fallen out sometimes that both Papists
and Protestants, Jews and Turks, may be embarked in one ship ; upon which
supposal I affirm, that all the liberty of conscience that ever I pleaded for,
turns upon these two hinges—that none of the Papists, Protestants, Jews, or
Turks, be forced to come to the ship's prayers or worship, nor compelled from
their particular prayers or worship, if they practise any. I further add, that I
never denied that, notwithstanding this liberty, the commander of this ship
ought to command the ship's course, yea, and also command that justice, peace,
and sobriety be kept and practised, both among the seamen and all the passengers. If any of the seamen refuse to perform their services, or passengers
to pay their freight ; if any refuse to help, in person or purse, toward the common charges or defence ; if any refuse to obey the common laws and orders of
the ship, concerning their common peace or preservation ; if any shall mutiny
and rise up against their commanders and officers ; if any should preach or
write that there ought to be no commanders or officers, because all are equal in
Christ, therefore no masters, nor officers, nor laws, nor orders, nor corrections,
nor punishments ;—I say, I never denied, but in such cases, whatever is pretended, the commander or commanders may judge, resist, compel, and punish
such transgressors, according to their deserts and merits. This, if seriously and
honestly minded, may, if it so please the Father of Lights, let in some light to
such as willingly shut not their eyes."

lence, he gave himself to a consideration of the relations in which they stood to the colonists, their rights, their wrongs, their perils, and their safeguards. The result of it was, that he came to the same conclusion which afterward placed William Penn among the benefactors of mankind :—that whatever rights civilization possessed, *ipso facto*, over the unsettled and barbaric parts of the earth, it had no right, however nomadic or savage they might be, to divest the title to the soil from the aborigines. This doctrine, it may easily be imagined, gained him little credit with his neighbors, whose self-interest took alarm at what seemed to strike at the vitality of the patent, to their lands, and the vitality of their political constitution. But the good-will he lost among those of his own race was compensated by that of the race to be benefited, and when he was flying from the intolerance of one, he was hospitably received by the other. To his dying day he never ceased to be grateful for the help then extended, and in his later years, he tenderly referred to it by saying, "The ravens fed me in the wilderness." Nor did he content himself with this expression of gratitude. He made the cause of the Indians his own ; he advocated it in high places, and, like Eliot, betaking himself to the study of their language, he ministered unto them in their own tongue. He, on his part, had little cause to accuse them of ingratitude.

Roger Williams was the man for the times and for the place. A genius, with an intellect as clear as it was fervid ; with convictions so intense as to make him dare all to enforce them ; with those convictions broadened by great knowledge and experience, tempered by never-failing benevolence, and adapted, as the growth of surrounding circumstances, to the needs of the community ; with a courage that laughed at wounds, a resolution which never faltered, an enthusiasm which never failed, a good-nature which softened the hearts of savages, and a sincerity which retained for him the respect of such men as Winthrop; with untiring energy and a robust constitution, he was, of all men, the man best fitted for breaking down a despotism, establishing a principle, or founding a State. He would have been great anywhere. He would have made a name for himself equally in London, as in Providence, but such a fame as he deserves, is due only to one who, like him, has not only planted a State, but, who has forever stamped the millions that populate the other common-wealths of his race, with an impress all his own. He was impulsive, rugged, earnest, and thorough. Had any other sort of man than the one he was, ventured to do what he did, it is hardly probable, that the work of his lifetime had ever been accomplished. The iron despotism which chilled Massachusetts might be making itself felt to-day; the colony, as it increased in numbers, would have gone on from bad to worse, and, instead of a commonwealth whose name is synonymous with all that is good, intelligent, charitable, and wise, we might be contemplating a community, the very name of which would strike our hearts with the chill which creeps over us at the recollection of Rochelle, Drogheda, Geneva, the Cevennes, and Piedmont. Worse than this : had America, instead of being inspired by this noble impulse, been indoctrinated with the absolutism, almost Venetian, then existing, she might never have been blessed by the light which now illuminates her path ; and freedom of conscience and the liberty of the citizen, the two kindred principles which have made us what we are, might have shaken our dust from off their feet, or passed us by as unworthy of their presence.

The doctrines of Williams, in the course of events, returned to the land which had borne him, and leavened there, also, the lump. Although Williams does not seem to have produced much effect on the public by his tracts and essays, there is no question that the advanced position taken by his friends Vane and the poet Milton was owing in a great measure to his personal influence over them while on a visit to England. The part taken by both these friends in behalf of freedom of conscience is too well known to be repeated. They not only brought the doctrine before the people and advocated it, but they rendered the subject a familiar one, and, having paved the way to its accomplishment by their speeches and writings, trod it themselves.

Faith of Maryland.

At the same time that the Brownists, or Pilgrims, and, after them, the Puritans, were turning their eyes toward the West in wistful search of a place of shelter, another body of religionists, from the same cause, and with the same object, were doing the same thing. The Roman Catholics, persecuted during four reigns, were also looking across the Atlantic for a haven of rest. It must be said to their praise that the modes by which they sought to effect their ends have shed upon the colony of Maryland a distinction which increases with the augmenting appreciation of the principle of freedom of conscience, which everywhere marks the progress of modern enlightenment.

George Calvert, a friend of Sir Robert Cecil, was a native of Yorkshire, and of a good family. Educated at Oxford, he was advanced by Cecil in public life, was knighted, and became one of the secretaries of state ; in which position he gained reputation with the people, and favor with the king. As a member of Parliament, he was thrown into the whirlpool of the rising discussion of the times, but being a thorough adherent of stability in matters of religion and state, the stronger the tempest blew, the more tenaciously he clung to principles that were defined, and to institutions that were old and rooted. He was a man of great capacity for business, of a clear and broad intellect, with reflective habits, and of a warm and benevolent disposition. He was also a man of resolution. Aristocratic, courtly, urbane, and withal just ; while, in common with Roger Williams, he loved truth and hated iniquity, no two men could be more unlike. They sought their ends at opposite poles—one left the Church of England for Independency, or rationalism ; the other for Roman Catholicism, or credulity unqualified : both share the glory of giving freedom of conscience to America.

Under the law, Calvert, on his conversion, had to resign his place, which, with its great emoluments, was cheerfully abandoned by one to whom the free exercise of his convictions offered greater wealth ; but James the First, always kind to those who supported the royal prerogatives, as the Catholics unhesitatingly did, retained him in the privy council, and, as a mark of his esteem, and as a reward for faithful service, created him an Irish peer, under the title of Lord Baltimore. For many years the attention of Baltimore had been directed toward America—he had been a member of the Virginia company,—and he had gone so far as to secure a patent for a portion of Newfoundland.[1] The poverty of the soil, however, and the severity of the climate had no compensation,

[1] It is narrated that he twice visited that coast.—Bancroft, i, chap. vii.

now that the freedom of the fisheries was established, and he
abandoned the hopes of a settlement in those parts, and at last
gave up the territory itself, and turned his eyes toward Virginia.

At that time the condition of the Roman Catholics in England
was as burdensome as intolerance could make it. It was hardly
possible for one of that belief to conform to the rules of his church ;
much less to worship God in his own way. If the attempt was
made, it was at the risk of the pains of *præmunire.* This offence
took its name from the words of the writ preparatory to the prosecution thereof,[1] which warned the accused to appear to answer
the contempt charged ; which contempt was recited in the preamble. It took its original from the exorbitant power formerly
claimed and exercised in England by the pope, and was, in the
time of Lord Baltimore, almost altogether directed against the vio-
lations of the statutes against Papists. When we learn what
some of those statutes were, the condition of a Romanist in
England, and what Calvert had to face in order to become one,
may be easily comprehended.

To refuse the oath of supremacy incurred the penalty of *præmunire*[2]*;* to defend the jurisdiction of the pope within the realm
was a *præmunire* for the first offence, and high treason for the
second[3] ; to import any *agnus Dei*, crosses, beads, or other super-
stitious things pretended to be hallowed by the bishop of Rome,
or to tender the same, or to receive them without discovering the
offender, and, if a justice of the peace, not to declare the offence
within fourteen days to a privy counsellor,—all these things incurred a *præmunire.*[4] Importing or selling mass-books, *or other
popish books*, incurred the liability to a fine.[5] To contribute to the
maintenance of any popish seminary whatever, beyond sea, or any
person in the same, or any jesuit or popish priest in England, was
made liable to the pains of *præmunire.*[6] To sue to Rome for any
license or dispensation, or to obey any process from thence, was
to incur a *præmunire.*[7] These are only some of the statutes enacted for the abolition of a certain religion. The Romanists were
also in jeopardy, moreover, under the statutes against heresy, and
to effect this end, we see that one result is to create, and set apart

[1] 4 Blackstone's "Comm.," 103. [2] 5 Eliz., cap. 1. [3] *Ibid.*
[4] 13 Eliz., cap. 2. [5] 3 Jac. I, cap. 5, § 25. [6] 27 Eliz., cap. 2.
[7] 24 Hen. VIII, cap. 12 ; and 25 Hen. VIII, cap. 19 and 21.

for persecution, a special class—to wit, the adherents of that religion.   Nothing more forcibly illustrates the spirit of intolerance
than the legislation of England against the Romanists, unless it
be the course of the Roman church itself against heretics, and
the laws and deeds of the Puritans against everybody but themselves.   Under these statutes an English Roman Catholic was
practically debarred from the enjoyment of any of the ministra-
tions of his religion ; for he was forbidden so much as to give
a farthing to the maintenance of the only one at whose hands he
would receive such ministration ; he could not console himself in
the absence of the priest with the ordinary aids to devotion, for it
was a crime to sell him the books he required, and he could import
none himself, and for doing what every Protestant matron who
visits the Vatican gladly does for the humblest Catholic domestic
—bring back a rosary blessed by the pope—any one, Protestant
or Catholic, was liable to the pains of *præmunire.* What those
pains were, may now be seen :—"that from the conviction, the de-
fendant shall be *out of the king's protection, and his lands and tenements, goods and chattels, forfeited to the king ;* and that his body
shall remain in prison *at the king's pleasure,* or (as other authorities have it) *during life."* [1]

If the Brownists, who were simply harried by the government,
sought to escape, it is not surprising that the Roman Catholics,
who were thus born to be criminals by statute, and whose hereditary reward for devotion was imprisonment, for life, or, at the
least, proscription as a class,[2] should eagerly strain their eyes in
the direction of the West for a city of refuge.

---

[1] Coke, 1 "Inst.," 129.

[2] The following letter from Sir Maurice Fortescue to the Earl of Chesterfield
conveys an idea of the situation in which the Romanists found themselves in
Ireland so late as the last century. [No date is given.]   "The Catholics being
thus peaceable and well-disposed, I pray you, my Lord, consider the many disabilities and misfortunes of our condition.   A Catholic has every worldly advantage to gain by changing his faith.   For a Catholic cannot buy land nor lease
it for longer than 31 years, nor loan money on mortgage ; if, by his industry,
he makes more than a third penny profit, any Protestant who may choose to
denounce him may take his land for the trouble ; he cannot educate his children save as Protestants or beyond the seas, and if he dies while they are yet of
tender years, they may be taken from their Catholic kindred and reared among
Protestant strangers ; he cannot become a lawyer or a soldier, nor occupy any
public office, not so much as that of a constable, or tithe collector, nor to speak
of a justice or member of Parliament ; if he be a tradesman, his trade is hampered by all kinds of quarterage ; if a gentleman, he may not carry a gun, nor
wear a sword, nor own a horse valued above 5 guineas ; and yet he that is thus
excluded from all management of public affairs, and from all opportunity of

Foremost among those who sought to deliver his people from the bondage of this death, was Lord Baltimore, who went in person to Virginia with the purpose of effecting there the settlement of his followers. But Virginia was the stronghold of conformity; it especially avowed the exclusion of Romanists from its territory, and, as an earnest expression of this avowal, it tendered Baltimore an oath, which no one of his faith could take, and which it was not expected he would subscribe. He proposed, as a compromise, a form of his own, which, happily for our country, was obstinately rejected, and he was forced to seek a soil as yet unencumbered by the stumbling-blocks of intolerance.[1] This he did, and in gratitude for the royal favor, which gave him a charter on his own terms, he named it after the queen, Maryland.

There is this difference between the New England charters and one such as that of Maryland—the former were given to companies; they were really nothing but franchises granted for the purpose of trade, through which the colonists, by their own exertions, acquired from time to time, such liberties as were not theirs by the mere fact of being British subjects. But the charters, such as that of Lord Baltimore, were very different affairs. In them the royal franchises were deliberately and solemnly parted with by the throne, and vested in the grantee, who thus became a Proprietary, or Lord Palatine, and who was thus constituted the guardian of the liberties of the colonists, as well as their governor. These liberties the proprietary colonists brought with them; those, the company colonists had to acquire as best they could. Where, as was commonly the case, the grantee was a favorite of the king,

---

pleading his own cause, is taxed more heavily than any other to support Church and State.

"My Lord, I am sensible that many of the most galling of these laws are softened by the good-nature of Protestants, but I would most respectfully ask your Lordship to consider what tremendous temptations are offered to men of indifferent virtue to profess a religion which they do not in their souls believe. And * * * I would beg you to reflect whether men that resist such temptation have not at least one merit, and should be utterly crushed and subjugated."—*Lippincott's Magaz.*, May, 1879, 569. For such class-oppression, the only remedy is that prescribed by Defoe for the plague—to fly from it. This writer gives likewise the date when emigration from Ireland began. He attributes it to "the killing of the wool manufacture by the Act of 1699 [probably 10 and 11 William III, c. 3, ed. of Article], * * * and from that time began the mortal drain on our population, which takes from 3,000 to 5,000 yearly to the West Indies or the American colonies, and these not belonging to the miserably poor, but to the better sort."

[1] Hazard, i, 72; "Notes on Virginia."

the crown was not niggardly as to the conditions of the grant, and to the credit of the Proprietaries, it must be said, that they never failed to make the best terms possible for the future colonists. None made better use of the favorable disposition of the crown, nor turned it to greater advantage for his people, than Lord Baltimore. His quick eye at once detected the opportunity of serving the interests of his followers, and of conferring a great boon upon mankind ; and his generous spirit and shrewd judgment rushed to embrace it ; for there is no doubt that he himself penned the charter which it was the honor of England to give, and the blessing of America to enjoy.

In this charter the prince reserved absolutely nothing but the evidence of feudal tenure ; he gave away every thing else a free people deems worth having. The tenure of fealty, of itself, reserved the final authority to the crown ; but this charter, the first of the kind ever known to be given, granted to the colonists independent legislation, a representative government of their own creation, exemption from taxation by any but themselves, a limitation that the authority of the proprietary should not extend to the life, freehold, or estate of the citizen, and, above all, not only equality in religious rights was guaranteed, but preference to any sect was forbidden, and protection was assured alike to all who believed in Christ. There was, in fact, no limitation whatever on the freedom of conscience, save that Christianity was made the law of the land ; a limitation, which, by no means implying the right to persecute for opinion's sake, became in effect innocuous.[1]

Such were the provisions of a charter which caused a great advance in civilization, and which relieves the dark record of the House of Stuart by the honor of being the first to have inscribed upon it, toleration in religion. This is not the only instance where a tyrant in one hemisphere has been a liberator in the other: a despot heedlessly tosses to a favorite what he holds back from

---

[1] "I will not," was part of the oath administered to the Governor of Maryland, "by myself, or any other, directly or indirectly, molest any person professing to believe in Jesus Christ, for or in respect of religion."

"And whereas the enforcing of the conscience in matters of religion hath frequently fallen out to be of dangerous consequences in those commonwealths where it has been practised, and for the more quiet and peaceable government of this province, and the better to preserve mutual love and amity among the inhabitants, no person within this province, professing to believe in Jesus Christ, shall be anyways troubled, molested, or discountenanced for his or her religion, or in the free exercise thereof."—*Charter.*

his people, and generation after generation rises up and calls him blessed.

Before the charter had passed the great seal, Lord Baltimore died ; but his mantle fell upon worthy shoulders. The patent issued to his son, who earnestly took up the work left undone by his father. Unable to go in person to overlook the foundation of the colony, he sent his brother, who, with a following of over a hundred gentlemen and their servants, successfully accomplished the task ; and thus, while democracy and rationalism, in the person of Roger Williams, were preaching freedom of conscience in the North, aristocracy and faith, embodied in a handful of Roman Catholics, were laying deep its foundations in the South. The career of this principle in Maryland and Rhode Island, though not exempt from the fluctuation incident to the action of every great social force, proved so fortunate, as not only to vindicate the faith of the Americans in its truth, but to justify the assertion, that, without it, the dozens of prosperous States which have made it a corner-stone, would not be what they now are, nor American character be what it now is.

CHAPTER V.

v.—*Southern Life and Manners : Manners of the Frontier.*

Manners in the Southern Provinces.

FROM his treatment of the subject, *Manners in the Southern Provinces*, it is evident that Mr. Burke meant to give full effect to the haughtiness that distinguishes an aristocratic constitution of society, and especially one where there are but two classes, the owners and the owned. He confines his remarks, however, to the influence of the spirit of liberty which emanates from slavery itself. While he is careful not to express commendation, he asserts very positively the fact, that such a social condition renders fierce and stubborn the spirit of liberty that possesses the owners. But the subject is regarded in this work not so much respecting the effect which the personal relations of slave-owner and slave have upon the owner, as the effect which an aristocratic and dispersed condition of society exerts upon the upper class, and this, too, where the element of slavery is superadded.

Although the manners of New England are not dwelt upon in his remarks, it is evident that the contrast between them and the manners of the South, and the further contrast afforded by the social constitutions of these distinct localities, are present to his mind. These contrasts are set forth in the ensuing chapter, and are still further to be disclosed in that relating to *Education*, and particularly in what is therein said concerning the *Township*. Thus the manners of the North and the South are more or less described. But, as the Middle Provinces, at the time of the Revolution, comprised the most dense population, and the locality where wealth was most widely distributed, it is thought that their conservatism, which tempered the fierceness of colonial liberty without weakening it, should not go unheeded ; and as Pennsylvania, from the force of locality and circumstance, exerted the predominating influence in this respect, her social constitution and the manners of her people, have been taken as illustrations of the force which affected greatly the spirit of liberty on her right hand and on her left.

As a direct force in rendering the spirit of liberty fierce, the *Manners of the Frontier* are also considered.

1. The manners of the Southern Provinces differed from those of the Northern, as much as did the soil, climate, social life, and political principles and organization. The manners of Virginia and Maryland exerted the greatest influence on manners and upon the development of personal, social, and political freedom in the South, and may be considered as the patterns after which those of the other Southern colonies followed. It will be enough, then, to observe these.

And, first, if the topography of Maryland and Virginia be remarked, as well as the equable and temperate climate which these colonies enjoyed, it will not fail to strike the observer, that soil, climate, and distribution of land and water, are admirably adapted to the unrestrained action of an athletic, hardy, and active people, and, consequently, to the development of the social and political forms natural to them.[1] Their winters are long and severe enough to confine the inhabitants within doors, and thus subject them to those influences, which, springing from the hearth, tend to the expansion of the domestic virtues that lie at the very foundation of free States and animate the character of free citizens ; while their summers and autumns are sufficiently warm and prolonged to tempt out of doors, for the rest of the year, a race which has always loved the open air. The land divided, in its eastern portion, by a great bay, is penetrated by the arms of this inland sea in every direction, and pours into it the fresh waters, which, taking their rise in the great Apalachian chain, and descending in falls and rapids over the rim which marks the boundary between the Piedmont or uplands and the alluvial plain or sea-board, at last debouche in the form of great rivers or streams, up which the

---

[1] "The Present State of Virginia," etc., 1, 2.

tide forces its way for many miles. These waters and the territory they drain, not only tempt the venturesome to bold explora-
tion, but by their exhaustless treasures of food and of game,
supply the whole population with healthy and delicate sustenance,
and afford an illimitable field for the exercise of manly sports.
The bays are ribbed with beds of delicious oysters ; the tide
waters teem, in their seasons, with countless schools of shad and
rockfish [1] ; the running brooks are stocked with trout ; and stream
and river, in the late autumns and the winters, are covered with
vast flocks of teal, of red-head, and black ducks, and the peerless
canvas-back. On shore, the pheasant, the quail, the woodcock,
the wild pigeon, and, chief among them, the wild turkey, abounded
in profusion, while the forests of the uplands and the mountain
ranges were roamed over by deer, and by the coarser animals,
whose chase demanded every exertion that tests the endurance or
the cunning of man. In the fields the crops were bounteous and
reasonably certain, and when, with these natural advantages for
comfort, and the liberation of the mind from care, the hospitable
disposition of the race from which the inhabitants sprung is considered, their love of field sports and adventure, and the facilities
given to the development of these qualities by that peculiarity of
social organization which divides the soil into large estates producing great incomes, it will easily be conceived, that the manners
of the people were characterized by a love of manly, open-air
adventure and daring, and by a free-handed hospitality which
took its character of heartiness from the elevated class that
peopled the land, and from the abundance which supplied its
bounty.

The distribution of population throughout this pleasant land
was on a plan directly in contrast with that of New England, and
had no parallel in America, save that which appeared on the
banks of the Hudson, under the rule of the Dutch Patroons.
The first immigration of Virginia, like that of New England,
was composed of the ruder classes, but the after-immigration of
both was of a very different sort ; and that of Maryland was,

[1] "These waters are stored with incredible quantities of fish, such as sheeps-
heads, rockfish, drums, white perch, herrings, oysters, crabs, and several other
sorts. Sturgeon and shad are in prodigious numbers ; of the latter 5,000 have
been caught at one single haul of the seine."—Burnaby's "Travels," 1759–60,
15, 16 ; the Abbé Raynal, "Hist. Brit. Settlements in America," i, 195.

from the beginning, thoroughly aristocratic. As that of New England embraced the best of the middle classes, being men of substance and learning, so that of Virginia was in a great measure drawn from the aristocracy or squirearchy. Some of the best names of England were there represented, and were augmented during the civil wars by royalists like themselves, and on the Restoration by Dissenters, generally Presbyterians, of the most respectable though not uniformly of the highest classes. These latter located themselves chiefly in the Western settlements, or in the interior valleys of Maryland, Virginia, and the Carolinas, while the aristocratic class remained where it was first established, on the sea-board. After the influence of class which controlled the tide-water planters, it is to this distribution of population that is chiefly due the peculiar manners of Maryland and Virginia.

In New England the tendency of population was toward cities and towns. Peopled by the middle classes, those classes, true to the instincts of tribal development, acted out in America the plan of life to which those instincts had of old subordinated them in England. They congregated ; and the individuality of the citizen became secondary to that of the community of which he was a member. He was but a subordinate part of the state while, in the South he was a pillar, without which the structure would tumble into ruins. There, the citizen was made for the state ; but here, the state was made for the citizen. Around the Massachusetts Bay, society was concentrated, and the country depended on the town ; around the Chesapeake Bay, on the other hand, it was dispersed, and the town depended on the country. In New England we hear of villages and towns before we hear of farms ; in Maryland and Virginia we hear of plantations before we hear of boroughs, and, in fact, throughout the South, we are familiar with the names of plantations long before the handful of dwellings at the cross-roads, or even the county capitals, are so distinguished. In Massachusetts the court-house followed the litigants, and was placed in the middle of the most populous or accessible town ; in Virginia it was placed in the fields, and the town gradually clustered around it. In a word, society was concentrated in the North, but in the South it was dispersed.[1]

---

[1] "Our country being much intersected with navigable waters, and trade brought generally to our doors, instead of our being obliged to go in quest of it,

This difference in distribution of population was caused by difference in soil, class, and character, and it directed the industry of the people toward opposite ends. In Maryland and Virginia, the social structure was built upon agriculture—that universal support of aristocracy,—and to this pursuit every thing else gave way ; but in New England, the activity of the people was directed to commerce, and to trade, shipping, and the fisheries, all other occupations were subordinated. In this part of the colonies, society was composed entirely of what in England was the middle class : in that portion, no middle class worth mentioning appeared ; society there was made up of owners and owned, masters and slaves, and so insignificant was any class between them, that, in the early days, there were even no middle-men to receive and distribute the crop, but the planter shipped his produce to England from his own wharf, and dealt directly with his factor in London or Bristol. In New England, society was democratic and progressive, and legislation acted upon the people in its entirety ; but in the South, society was aristocratic and conservative, and the laws, which recognized the division of society into two classes, asserted the superiority of one of those classes over the other. Thus was inculcated and maintained in the breast of the Southerner, from his earliest days, that sense of personal superiority which possesses those only whom the laws distinguish as a class for whose benefit the rest of society is born to toil. This very sense of superiority, so irritable upon the slightest injury, or even neglect, will not brook for an instant the infringement of a privilege, but will expend its whole strength to preserve a right or redress a wrong, and hence it is, of itself, a powerful incentive to render the spirit of liberty a fierce one.

As in New England the individuals congregated, in Virginia and Maryland they dispersed, and isolation was as striking a characteristic of society in the South as association was in the North. The peculiar topography of the country favored the tendency to isolation quite as much as the magnitude of the estates did by placing the mansions far apart. The rivers were navigable,

has probably been one of the causes why we have no towns of any consequence. Williamsburgh, which, till the year 1780, was the seat of our government, never contained above 1,800 inhabitants; and Norfolk, the most populous town we ever had, contained but 6,000."—" Notes on Virginia," Query xii ; " Present State of Virginia," etc., 2. Edenton, the capital of North Carolina, in 1729, had but forty houses." Burnaby's " Travels," 6.

and, in selecting the site of a plantation, it was as much the object of the planter to obtain a place on such waters, as it is that of the Western settler to-day to be within reach of a railway. The wharf was even a greater necessity than the barn. Transportation by water was easy and cheap, and being the best there was, and by far the best in point of comfort, the streams naturally became the real highways of the lowlands. As travel and transportation, then, sought the avenues which were ready at hand and cost nothing, there was not the same necessity for a road system as existed in the North, and the 'cross-country roads were neglected both in construction and repair. Travel was thus confined chiefly to the rivers which permitted access to the interior, and to the Bay which allowed passage north and south, and intercourse was restricted mainly to the shore which bounded them. The space devoted to locomotion being in this way contracted, the distribution of land and water exerted for several generations (until, at least, the habits of the people had become formed) a strong influence on the distribution of population, and favored the isolation to which the planter found it necessary to conform.

This isolation, relieved only by the daily duties of the estate, the observances of social intercourse, the sports in the open field, the recurring election of delegates, or the annual visit to the colonial capital, had a powerful influence on the modes of thought and on social life. It certainly tended to make the planter a reflective being to an extraordinary degree, and, though it narrowed the horizon of his experience, it preserved the simplicity of domestic habits, and, turning the mind back upon itself for aliment, contributed its force toward impressing that synthetical cast of thought and expression on the people, which their descendants in that part of America retain in greater or less degree to the present day.

It preserved, too, the simplicity of a language, which was brought over in the days of its greatest purity ; when the predominance of its Gothic element made it at once forcible and picturesque, and when the admixture of the Latin element had reached the point at which it rendered the tongue copious without enfeebling it. This distinction—for distinction it must ever be, to speak one's language purely and correctly—has, for many years past, been undergoing obliteration before the corrupting encroachments brought upon it by the unrestrained intercourse of modern times, by the flood of immigration, and, not least, by the late Civil War. But, even to-day, it still lingers, as if loath to depart from the hearths at which it for so long found shelter ; and in regions, like that of the Eastern Shore, which are yet remote from the contamination of a dialect which has sacrificed purity to copiousness, and rustic force to fluency, one's ear is even now occasionally refreshed by household words and forms of expression, which mark, at once, the unalloyed descent of the speaker from those who used the tongue in its purity, and the isolation of the generations who handed it down to him. Indeed, at the time when the fraternal strife of the Parliamentary wars was turning its honey into gall, and the cant of the Puritans was changing its wine to vinegar ; when, still later, the vices of the Restoration and the dilettanteism of Queen Anne's reign were either polluting its being or sapping its strength, during all that time our language was being spoken in its by-gone purity and comeliness around the hearths of Maryland and Virginia.

It was exposed to three extraneous influences—the dialect of the negroes, the language of the Indians, and the debilitation of the tongue which became apparent in the reigns of the last Stuart and the two succeeding monarchs. Of these, the first, happily, affected the accent only, but did not reach the body of the language ; the second proved actually beneficial, by relieving the nomenclature, servilely imitative of that of England, with the beauty of the Indian names, which added a charm to the tongue without assimilating with it ; and the third, never extending to customary discourse, had only the exceedingly scanty literature of the colonies to affect, and that it vitiated but slightly. Thus the language, if not invigorated, was, at least, not impaired. Down to the reign of Queen Anne, Virginia was preserved from the influences that corrupted the language in England, at first by the remoteness of situation and by her indisposition to cross the ocean only to land on a field of civil strife ; and later by the inability of the incomplete fortunes of the planters to meet the heavy expenses which a journey to Europe at that time imposed upon tourists of their social position. When, however, the magnitude of their incomes represented that of their estates, and coincided, as it did at the beginning of that reign, with the established tranquillity of the kingdom, the situation changed. Then the colonist could afford to gratify his desire to see the world, to renew the ties which, though weakened by lapse of time, still bound him to his English kin, and to refresh his own civilization by contact with the old. The custom arose among the rich, of sending their sons abroad for a university education, to study a profession, or to make the grand tour ; and then, and, especially, afterward it was, that it became the mode, *de rigueur*, for the young Virginians to ruffle at Tunbridge Wells, to have a glimpse of the great Doctor Johnson as their fathers had had of the great Mr. Pope, to dance a minuet at Holland House, to visit the play and see Macklin or Garrick, and to lose a few hundreds at White's or the Cocoa, before settling down to marriage and the staid and homely duties of Virginia squires. These were they, who, to dissipate the dulness of plantation life, brought back boxes filled with the literature of the day, or even went so far as to try their own hands at an occasional epigram. But, as their efforts generally ended there, or expressed themselves only on some political or other practical question, which scouted at stilts and exacted common-sense and homely language, no great harm was done ; and the dilettanteism or foppery, which spread itself, like a mist, around the shores of Chesapeake Bay, was thus restricted to the few subjects which presented themselves for its display, and, at last, cleared away before the breezy vigor which the stirring times of the Stamp Act again freshened into life. It did not corrupt the tongue.[1]

This isolation, or, rather, the interruption of it, produced still another effect on the Southerner, which was enhanced by the preservation of the language in its purity. When the placidity of rural life was disturbed by the exigencies of politics, as the county election of delegates, for example, the work in hand was not undertaken heedlessly or without due consideration. Whether the question underlying the election was some impending encroachment of the crown (the only quarter from which attack was to be feared), an affair of colonial administration, the rectification of an Indian frontier, or something affecting the planter's pocket, it had been, long before the eventful day which settled it, thorough-

---

[1] The absence of printing facilities—for there was but one printing-house in Virginia—proved, in this respect, a godsend.

ly, not to say solemnly, discussed. Where the ground was first broken was at the dinner-table. As the importance of the measure loomed up and filled the heavens, the gentlemen of the county, one after another, bade their neighbors to a feast, and, on the withdrawal of the ladies, and with the advent of pipes[1] and a fresh supply of port or claret, the question was there broached, and the *pros* and *cons* were discussed with an ardor characteristic of the disputants, and with an earnestness which betokened their responsibility as law-makers. Before the party broke up, it was generally understood who should represent them as candidates at the ensuing election, and the guests went home to turn the whole thing over in their minds when unclouded by wine and unbiassed by the accents of allies or opponents.

When the day for the county or parish meeting arrived,[2] the planter issued forth to help along the plan previously agreed upon with his neighbors. As we have seen, he went not blindly nor unprepared : discussion had made him familiar with the features of the measure, and observation had enabled him to take its bearings. On reaching the appointed place, he found himself one of an assemblage, of which each member was on an equality with the rest, and where every one was free to speak his mind on what concerned all. If he were prompted to address the meeting, he did so with a fearlessness which sprung from his familiarity with his subject and his hearers, and he betrayed none of the hesitancy of a stranger to either. He presented his views with the zeal of a propagandist, and with a positiveness enforced by the earnestness of his straightforward nature and his simple habits of life ; and, as the question on the carpet was always one which touched his principles, his position, or his pocket, he treated it in the most business-like manner, and always spoke directly to the point. Government, with him, was a practical and homely art, and he applied it in a practical and homely way. His sense of equality with

[1] Cigars were not in use until the very close of the last century—in Philadelphia, not until after 1798.—1 Wats. An. 98, n.

[2] " The State, by another division, is formed into parishes, many of which are commensurate with the counties ; but sometimes a county comprehends more than one parish, and sometimes a parish more than one county. This division had relation to the religion of the State. * * * We have no townships."— " Notes on Virginia," Query xii. " —the house of delegates [is] composed of two members from each county, chosen annually by the citizens possessing an estate for life in 100 acres of uninhabited land, or twenty-five acres with a house on it, or in a house or lot in some town."—*Id.*, Query xiii.

those of his own class and the community of interest he had with them, intensified as they were by his sense of superiority to the only other portion of the society in which he lived, emboldened him to every accent of persuasion possible, and tempted him to discussion and party action that were characterized by perfect freedom. From such sources flowed that readiness in oratory, that fondness for debate, that familiarity with the principles of government, that aptness for administration, and that sense of political responsibility, which have always characterized these people.

On the day of election, the voters that were not actually bed-ridden turned out to a man ; and when the votes had been duly cast, and the clerks had righteously counted them and declared officially the result, then ensued a scene of joviality which made the country-side ring. The newly elected members were chaired, and the victorious party celebrated its triumph, while the defeated drowned its sorrow, in brimming bowls of rum and arrack punch.

A form of society in which there was no political centralization worthy of the name, and where the only centralization that existed was domestic, and had the lord of the fields for its object, naturally heightened the self-esteem of the planter, as his membership of a privileged class also increased his self-respect ; and a life broken in upon only by the duties of citizenship, or the claims of neighborly intercourse, left him who led it pretty much the absolute master of his own actions. Such a life, therefore, tended to great individuality of character and freedom of action, two things highly conducive to the growth of a free spirit, while its quality of isolation, by inducing reflective habits of thought, gave to the Southern temperament a meditative cast, which found its contrast in the more active and acute mind of the North. In the Southern colonies, as has been said, society was dispersed, while, on the contrary, the life of the individual was exceedingly concentrated ; but in the Northern colonies society was concentrated while individuality was dispersed, or, rather, merged and diffused in the body politic. This individuality, so markedly a Southern characteristic, manifested itself in various ways, but in none more conspicuously than in the boldness with which the measures of government were met and criticized, and in the fertility of resources which the people displayed in matters of government. As class is one of the offsprings of individuality among free people, it may be said that this latter aided the natural superiority of race in limiting the law-making power to the minority, and in the restriction of its action to the almost exclusive benefit of this class.[1]

It is natural that a people living apart from each other, and dependent almost entirely for society on their own families, should make much of their homes. Accordingly in Maryland and Virginia, we find, universally, not only a strong and fond attachment, for the fireside, but a development of domestic life to which the history of the race affords few parallels. If the individual at the North was absorbed in the general mass of society, in the South whatever individuality departed from him was lost in the family. This, not the person, was the unit of society. Each family, with its dependents, was a distinct social organization of which the great house was the centre. To this abode, as the capital of the little province, all roads led, and from it all life went forth. What was done in the field was done for the house, and the head of it was a patriarch for whom the crops grew, the herds browsed, and the bondsmen toiled. The family it was, on which was built the whole social structure of the State. As the agricultural character of society compelled its existence; as the pride of class stimulated its creation ; and as the highest enjoyment of life was to be found only within its precincts, interest, pride, and the pursuit of happiness all combined to establish it, to maintain it, and to enlarge its importance. Hence, marriages were early and prolific, and if there was any one feeling stronger than the

---

[1] "The public or political character of the Virginians corresponds with their private one ; they are haughty and jealous of their liberties, impatient of restraint, and can scarcely bear the thought of being controlled by any superior power. Many of them consider the colonies as independent states, not connected with Great Britain otherwise than having the same common king, and being bound to her with natural affection. * * * In matters of commerce they are ignorant of the necessary principles that must prevail between a colony and the mother-country ; they think it a hardship not to have an unlimited trade to every part of the world. They consider the duties upon their staple only as injurious to themselves, and it is utterly impossible to persuade them that they affect the consumer also. Upon the whole, however, to do them justice, the same spirit of generosity prevails here which does in their private character ; they never refuse any necessary supplies for the support of government when called upon, and are a generous and loyal people." Burnaby's "Travels,": 1759–60, 34, 35.

ambition to found a family, it was the desire, on the part of
those who formed one, to perpetuate what already existed. The
ties of blood were very strong, and reached to a point so much
further than what was ever before attained, that the term "Virginia cousin" includes that extremely remote kinship which,
among other people, is scarcely ever recognized. Domesticity
was thus the most positive fact of this patriarchal existence, and
to its advancement and preservation every energy was bent. The
household gods were never held in greater reverence than on
the banks of the Patapsco and the James.

The magnitude of the estates and of the incomes derived from
them, the absence of any preponderating middle class, the fact
that the labor was actually owned by the planter, that the making
of the laws was in his own hands, and that these laws were made
for his benefit, the lofty sense of social position, the pride of race
and of class,—all these combined in making him content to live on
his own ground, and in giving him the position of an autocrat
among his own people.   Hence that haughtiness and self-esteem
in the land and slave-owner, which, as it has been remarked, was
easily irritated and which chafed at restraint.   His vices were few
and rare, and, except the excesses of the table, in which, however,
he did not begin to equal his cousin of Yorkshire, his habits were
marked by simplicity aud dignity.[1]   He was remarkably free from
avarice, and delighted in the possession of money, not for itself,
but for what it would bring : yet, though lavish in hospitality and
family state, he had a cautious eye to the future, and a prudence
which led him to seize every advantage of the present.   Land was
the one standard of wealth and influence, and as the expansion of
his estate increased his weight in society, he was ever seeking to
enlarge it, and thus was often led to fall into the prevailing vice of
the day, greed of land, and to become the victim of what was in
those times called "land hunger."[2]   When this species of famine
had once taken hold of him, he seemed incapable of throwing it
off.   He frequently kept himself poor, and would even go so far
as to impoverish himself in the attempt to extend his estate ; and

[1] " I will do justice to this country. I have observed here less swearing and
prophaneness, less drunkenness and debauchery, less uncharitable feuds and ani-
mosities, and less knavery and villianys, than in any part of the world where
my lot has been."—Spotswood's " Letter to the Bishop of London."
[2] Davenant, "On Plantn. Trade," Pol. and Com. Works, ii, 27, 28.

he was often loaded down with vast tracts of wild lands purchased from the crown, which rivalled dukedoms in extent, but which were as barrren of income as they were of crops. Sometimes the taxes on these expanses of rock and forest ate up his substance long before the wilderness, of which they were a part, was sufficiently rid of savages to command a market, and his descendants, in the bitterness of their poverty, had reason to curse the imprudent accumulation of acres, which, never having even reached their hands, bore no other evidence of his foresight than the repetition of his name on the surveyors' maps. Generally, his land speculations were founded on the assumption, that before the debt, which was contracted in the purchase, was due, it could be paid from the rise in value consequent upon the increased demand of an inflowing population, and yet leave him a handsome surplus. The failure of such schemes beggared hundreds, but where sufficient money was in hand, the home or tide-water plantation free from debt, and the income certain, the wild lands were held without risk, and these purchases accomplishing their object, posterity in time found its hands strengthened by the bounty which flowed in from the ancestor's foresight. The chief object of the planter's life seemed to be attained when he was able to give a plantation to each child, with prospective estates for the grandchildren, yet to be carved out of the western wilderness when their time came.

In the halcyon days of these colonies, before the fields were run down, and when the tobacco crop was still certain and valuable, the style of domestic life along the sea-board was very great. The planters were given to field sports, and every county had its meet of fox-hunters, who, with the belles of the neighborhood, swept over the fields in a way which in these days would do honor to Melton Mowbray. Kennels were as much a part of the plantation's equipment as the stables, and a knowledge of dog-breaking was as necessary a branch of domestic learning as that of horse-training. In the spring and early summer the rods were out, and much sport was had in taking the rockfish or striped bass. The low-lying thickets of bushes and brush afforded woodcock in summer, and autumn, of course, called into exercise every kind and shade of field and upland shooting. But in duck-shooting none equalled the dweller on the banks of the Chesapeake waters, and he braved the early days of winter with a zest the elements could not chill, and displayed skill and quickness which would have mortified with envy the soul of a Lincolnshire fen-hunter. The Virginian was half his time on horseback, and, to gratify his passion for equitation, he imported blooded stock and improved the breed of horses.[1] If he went to overlook his laborers in the field, he rode ; if he visited a neighbor, he rode ; and, if he had nothing else to do, he mounted his horse, and, often accompanied by his daughters, cantered along the banks of the river, or through the quiet woods. Nothing was more common than riding parties ; they broke the monotony of house life, and when there were guests, saddle-horses always stood ready before the door.

The circumstances of the planter's condition led, too, to a freedom of manners, which, however, was any thing but adverse to the development of the domestic virtues that shone so brightly among them. Nowhere has the world seen greater freedom of intercourse between the sexes, and nowhere greater purity of morals. To such an extent was this association carried, that the women shared, as far as possible, the open-air life of the men, riding with them over the country, following the hounds, and braving together the roughness of the rivers and the bay. Nor did this sympathy stop with the pursuit of pleasure ; for, during the illness or absence of their lords, they looked after the affairs of the estate, and saw for themselves that every thing went on as it should do. Notable housewives, these helpmeets were famed as the very divinities of good housekeeping, and the cuisine, which, at this hour, makes that portion of the country synonymous with good living, had its origin in their taste and in their kitchens. Their whole aim in life was to make themselves and home pleasing, and the undiminished fame of matron and maid proclaim to this generation the success they attained.

In return for this sympathy in matters of interest and pleasure, the men yielded an affection and respect to the women, which, without exaggeration of sentimentality, may be characterized as something which in those days might have been sought for in vain as a prevailing characteristic of the corresponding class of English and French society. The vicious tone which followed the Restoration was utterly lost on the pure relations that existed between the men and women of the colonies.

---

[1] Jones, " Present State of Virginia," 44.

Much of this free association of the sexes was undoubtedly compelled by the want of society which the isolation and loneliness of their lives occasioned, but, whatever the cause, it existed, and existed in a purity to which their descendants can recur with proud satisfaction. Nor will it be denied, that the liberty of a freedom-loving race derives great ardor from the flame that lights a pure and spotless hearth.

To this isolation of their estates, and to their own isolation on their estates—for so great was the gulf fixed between the planter and his slaves, that the family was entirely dependent on itself for society—to this isolation was due, in a great measure, the free hospitality which has come down to us as a golden legend. For, when the monotony and irksomeness of the daily life on a plantation was once broken in upon by an arrival from the world outside, the contrast which at once presented itself to the dulness of the ordinary routine was amazing. Nothing was too costly or too good to compensate fortune for that greatest of blessings among a dispersed society—the companionship of friends. The planter delayed not in showing his appreciation of the godsend thus vouchsafed. As the heavy coaches and six lumbered up to the door amid the barking of dogs, the cracking of whips, and the delight of the negroes, the lord of the manor stood ready to receive them with open arms, supported by his wife and family, and surrounded by an army of servants. The whole crowd of idlers, which seems to have been a necessary pest on every plantation, was at once in motion. As the postilions flung themselves to the ground, grooms sprang from the earth to care for the equipages and horses, and the dignified but hearty welcome was witnessed by awe-struck groups of negroes, whose heads protruded from around the corners of the great house. A dozen hands contested the honor of helping the ladies to unmantle, and when these had retired to their rooms, and their escorts had rejoined their host, the loving cup, in the shape of mint juleps in summer, and, in winter, punch or egg nog, speedily went round among the gentlemen. The kitchen fires blazed like beacons, and, from cooks to scullions, all, in this part of the mansion, strained every nerve to outdo their past triumphs of the table.[1] The oyster beds had

---

[1] " The gentry pretend to have their victuals drest and served up as nicely as the best tables in London."—Beverly, " Hist. of Va."

been raked, the seine hauled, the fields and woods scoured for game. Riding, fishing, strolling, reading aloud the last batch of *Spectators* or *Gentleman's Magazines*, and dozing, was the order of the day, and, after the grand dinner, the card party, and the minuet, or Virginia reel, the whole household, guests, family, and servants, gathered together in the library to close the evening with a service read by the master of the house from the Book of Common Prayer. Happy was the host who saw his stables filled with his neighbors' horses, his coach-house crowded with their carriages, and his fields torn up by the cobs of the merry hunters ; nor did he hesitate when he and his had to turn out of their quarters to make room for the crowd of friends and kin. The departure was even more impressive than the arrival, for, grudging every instant of his friends' society, loath to say good-by, and anxious to postpone the moment when his hospitable attentions must terminate, the head of the house mounted his horse, and, attended by his sons, escorted the cavalcade and train of coaches, until the next cross-roads, by separating the party, broke it up. Then they pulled bridle, and, when the last farewells were said, rode quietly back home, and the plantation subsided into its wonted monotony.

Nor was this freehandedness lacking in refinement. At the time when the squirearchy of England was marring its hospitality with the coarseness of mere profusion, and with a more obnoxious coarseness of speech, and was finding its highest pleasure in drenching its neighbors with seas of brown October, the squirearchy of the South was gracing its social intercourse with manners acquired in the most polite circles of Europe, and was setting before its guests wines, which were taken with the same gusto they would have commanded had they been sipped among the vineyards of the Garonne.

As winter is the season of repose for the agriculturist, so was it with the planter. The crops sent to market, and the shooting season over for the year, there was nothing to pin him down to the plantation, while, on the other hand, there was the annually recurring desire of change of scene to induce him to leave home for a time. The natural object of this erratic inclination was the capital of his province. Then it was that Annapolis and Williamsburg appeared in all their glory. The family sloop conveyed the household to its destination, or the family coach, with the arms of the house emblazoned on its panels, and with its negro postillions and six, toiled through the mire, loaded down with the wife and daughters, while the august head followed after in a gig, or, on horseback, accompanied by his sons and servants, rode by the side of the coach conversing with the ladies,[1] or scoured ahead to order refreshments on the arrival of the carriage at the inns, or lingered in the rear to urge on the baggage.   Once at the capital, no lord at Bath could have assumed grander state, and cards, routs, balls, dinners, and suppers were the order of the day and night.   The House of Delegates in the morning, the ordinary at noon for punch and politics, a grand dinner in the evening, and a ball at the government house, or an assembly, as it was called, at night,—such was the daily round.   The society was unexceptionable, the manners were courtly, and the habits, though much wine was drunk, immeasurably better than those of the same class in the British isles or on the continent.   With the adjournment of the Legislature, or even before, but not until the fashions of the year had arrived out from London, the family returned to the plantation in the same style in which they had left it, and, tired with gayety, settled contentedly down to what it deemed its real life, that is to say, life on the plantation.

As a boy, the Virginian or Marylander, when not in the school-room with his tutor, roamed the fields with his gun, attended by his negro, who was at once his servant and companion, or spurred his horse through the lonely woods.   As a youth he went to England for his university education,[2] and when, after this had been completed, and it had been polished with all the accomplishments he could pick up during a season of London society, or by the grand tour, he returned to the barbarism of America, it was to a great wide-spreading house,[3] built, probably, in the days of his grandfather, of bricks brought from England, and which, posted on an eminence commanding a charming view, and with lawns stretching down to the water, was embosomed in trees, was stocked with books, family pictures, and old plate, and was flanked by

---

[1] Randall's "Life of Jefferson," i, chap. 1.
[2] Jones, "Present State of Va."
[3] Beverly, "Hist. of Va."

rows of negro quarters where dwelt a multitude to wait on him of those whom he could call his own. He raised his crops, bought land—he never sold any unless compelled,—bred stock, chased foxes, hunted game, fished the rivers, entertained his neighbors, talked politics, cared kindly for his servants, was attached to his church,[1] loved his wife and children, and when all this was over, his bones were laid away to rest in the soil he had been so fond of, and in sight of the home that had sheltered him.

After all, this life was a simple one, and was invested with the dignity which always accompanies simplicity. Its constitution was patriarchal, and the manners that expressed it were as simple and unaffected as itself. The very element of trade that was in it, insignificant as it was, was characterized by a directness which is refreshing to look back upon. Every tide-water plantation had a wharf at which there touched, once a year, a vessel from London or Bristol, owned in part or wholly by the planter, and which, having made the outward-bound voyage by way of the West Indies, at last landed his supplies for the year before the door. On its arrival, the negroes would empty the storehouse of its contents, and rolling the hogsheads down to the ship, would put them on board. Its freight taken, the vessel would then set sail ; often with the planter himself or some of his family, as passengers, going out to visit their English relations or to travel on the continent. When it reached its destination, the factor, or consignee, would sell the cargo, and remit the proceeds, less the amount required for the next year's supplies, which were sent back by the vessel on her return. This purchase of supplies was rendered necessary by the fact of their being no manufactures in the Southern colonies, the most common utensils having to be bought in England.[2]

Such was the extent to which commerce was carried on the plantations, or, such at least it was in the palmy days of tobacco culture ; for, as that declined, and the exactions of the Acts of Trade increased, so declined the fortunes of the planter, until the English factor, by advancing money to supply the recurring deficits, stood in the position of creditor, and thus the servant became greater than the master. At the time of the Revo-

---

[1] "Virginia may be justly esteemed the happy retreat of true Britons and true Churchmen."—Jones, "Present State of Va.," 48.

[2] Beverly, iv, 58 ; Abbé Raynal, "Hist. Brit. Settlements," etc., i, 198.

lution, the indebtedness of the planters to the London and Bristol merchants had become burdensome, and being attributed, as in part it was, to the onerous taxation imposed by the Navigation Act and the Acts of Trade, it incited the disposition of these colonists toward independence.[1]

The colonial squirearchy of the South was evidently similar to that from which it sprung, and illustrates what has already been said[2] concerning the spirit of English colonization. The branch cut from the stock in England, and planted in America, grew right on perfectly independent of the parent, and developed the same form, modified only by difference of conditions, simply because, under the exercise of free action, the same principles were brought into play in Virginia as in England, and expressed themselves in the same way.

The squirearchy of the south had, for example and support, that of England in its brightest days. It was the squires who constituted the bone and sinew of England, from the time of the Restoration down to that period, when, weakened by the brilliant but undermining policy of Chatham, they succumbed to the aggrandizement of the lords on the one hand and the encroachments of the commercial classes on the other. During all this time they supplied the administration of the kingdom with conservatism, and its armies and navies with men and money. Their influence in Parliament, during this period, was paramount, and, as in Parliament, so in the Cabinet. The English squire was rough, homely, attached to Church and State, was fond of field sports, and was the very incarnation of conservatism. He was tenacious of custom, slow to move, and was absolutely immovable when a personal right was at stake, and his love of country was of a healthy, stubborn sort. He stood between the aristocracy and the yeomanry, with qualities and habits derived from each ; but, with two classes, or, rather, divisions of society above him, he centred in himself all the political forces which could be expressed by the term " commons," save what the rapidly growing commercial classes kept constantly taking from him more and more. He became a great man under Walpole and Marlborough, and held his own until the lords and merchants, through the tongue of the

---

[1] "Hist. Brit. Settlements," etc., *id., id.*   [2] Page 49.

first Pitt, sounded the hour of his decay; then he gradually declined, and went out in glory at Waterloo. He was no longer needed. An era which had no use for him had dawned on England; an era which saw his acres swallowed up in the already overgrown estate of his neighbor and kinsman, the lord, and which turned the old hall into a tenant house. From before the insatiable baron, on the one hand, and the hostile genius of Threadneedle street on the other, his estate disappeared; and, with the disappearance of his manor, he, too, vanished.

It was from the ranks of the squirearchy that the sea-board planters of Maryland and Virginia were chiefly recruited, and it was from the English squire that they inherited their principles and instincts. But in America there was much to modify and elevate the characteristics which in England maintained their footing with rustic obstinacy. Here the planter had no class whatever above him. Lords, there were none; and as for king, he was too remote to be any thing but a sentiment. There were no commercial classes worth mentioning; and as for the laboring classes, they were his slaves, he carried them in his pocket. He was, in fact, sole lord of these realms, and his position was, in reality, the most exclusively aristocratic of any this side of the religious aristocracy of India, on which he looked with the contempt of a conqueror, or of Japan, of which he knew nothing. Socially, on his own plantation, he was an autocrat. This monopoly of political power, combined with the exclusive occupancy of the social heights, profoundly modified his relations to society, and gave him an aristocratic cast his cousin of England did not possess. The latter was only partly aristocratic; his head was indeed of brass, but his feet were of clay. Not so the Virginian. The whole constitution of the society in which he lived tended more and more toward an aristocracy pure and simple, and the man was wholly an aristocrat. With him class instinct had only to concern itself with keeping his class inviolate, while with the Englishman, it looked toward the enlargement of the commons' rights, and, under the influence of trade, the aggrandizement of the nation. It modified, too, the Southerner's personal characteristics, and rendered haughty him, who, in England, would have been simply exclusive. Moreover, one lived in isolation, the other in society; so that while the Englishman had ever before him the

repressing presence of his superiors, the Virginian was accountable to no one for his actions, and his conduct was uninfluenced
by any but his equals.   As tenacious of his rights as the Englishman, and as obstinate in maintaining them, his sense of freedom from restraint made him more sociable and accessible, his
manners were more cultivated, and travel being a part of his education in the days when the young squires never went abroad,
he was thus earlier open to foreign influences than one living in
the heart of England, and more expansive than he whose vision
was bounded by the waves which begirt his island.[1]   Thus, equally
attached to freedom, he was broader in his views of it, and more
haughty in its assertion, and, being quick to take offence, he was
more alert in guarding it, and more ready in its defence.   With
him the spirit of liberty naturally became fierce.

Such was the colonial squirearchy, such the constitution of
society on the sea-board of Maryland and Virginia, and such the
manners that affected the growth of liberty in that part of our
country.   The piedmont, or that portion lying between the lowlands and the Blue Ridge, was gradually overspread by this class,
though in this region it received an infusion of population not so
intensely aristocratic.   On the downfall of the Commonwealth,
and upon the Restoration, numbers of those not in communion
with the Church of England made Pennsylvania, Virginia, and the
Carolinas their abiding-place.   As the territory of the lowlands
was mostly at that time already occupied, necessity compelled the
immigrants to go further west, and thus the Valley of Virginia, as
it is called, or that part of the colony lying between the Blue
Ridge and the Alleghenies, received an influx of population.
Even here large bodies of land had been taken up and held by
the wealthy of both America and England, but the mass of soil
still remained to the crown, and that possessed by subjects was,
sooner or later, thrown on the market created by this and ensuing
immigration.   Among this population, which, the stirring times
it had passed through had rendered somewhat restive and intrac-

---

[1] "The manners of the English gentry in this age were in a great measure
purely national ; and, except at Court, had received from foreign nations neither
polish nor corruption.   To travel had not yet grown to be a very common practice.   It was not yet that a visit to more genial climes, or more lovely land-
scapes, was the best preparation for afterward living happy and contented in
our own." Lord Mahon, " Hist. Eng.," cap. i.

table, sprung up an opposition, which, on the organization of the State government, culminated in the downfall of the Church Establishment. These people, as regards religion, were mixed, but in respect to race, they were at first as homogeneous as those of the sea-board, though afterward they became infused with Scotch, Scotch-Irish, and even continental blood. The political constitution of the colony, therefore, while more freely criticised perhaps than by the lowland planters, was not molested by them ; but with the growing influx of Dissenters the tide naturally continued to rise against the Church. Those who had been provoked, if not actually moved, to emigrate from England by reason of the limitations there imposed on the enjoyment of their faith, chafed at finding, on their arrival, the very same bonds the Parliaments of the Commonwealth had unloosed. The new-comers had not come over with any disposition toward paying tithes to what they had once humbled in the dust, nor, by so doing, to acknowledge the supremacy of an Establishment which had kept its footing in spite of them, and which boasted, that on that soil its flag had never been struck ; and they fretted at the thought of subjection to the intolerance they had once protested against, but which they themselves had, in the day of their power, inflicted on their countrymen. But there was no help for it. The country, long before their coming, had been laid off according to the ecclesiastical division of parishes, where the ministers of the Church of England were entitled to glebe, house and land, and whence they drew salaries for which all alike were tithed. This division of the territory was firmly established, it had become familiar to the people, and time was already bringing to the support of the wealthy planters, who upheld it as the work of their own hands, the disinclination to disturb an accepted system, and that dread of innovation which always overhangs a conservative community. Any system which compels a man to pay for another's enjoyment, is wrong on the face of it ; and if the wrong is aggravating when that enjoyment is exercised at the cost of those to whom it is actually repulsive, much more is it so, when those who enjoy are in the minority, and those who suffer are in the majority.[1] But freedom of conscience was not one of

---

[1] " Autobiog. Memoir of Jefferson," ed. 1829, pp. 31, 32 ; " Notes on Virginia," Query xvii. " Two thirds of the people had become Dissenters at the commencement of the Revolution." The proportion was much greater in the frontier countries where there were hardly any Churchmen.—Girardin, 181.

the shining qualities of Virginia ; the Church members, though a minority of the population, constituted the majority of the Legislature, and, being human, acted on the rule that they should keep who have the power ; and, besides, they were indisposed to accord to Dissenters in America the religious freedom they had abused in Europe.   They accordingly turned a deaf ear to complaint, and the Establishment, with its obnoxious parishes, remained until 1776, when the first republican Legislature was crowded with petitions to abolish this "spiritual tyranny."   "These," said Thomas Jefferson, "brought on the severest contests in which I have ever been engaged."   The struggle ended in the subversion of the Establishment, and, in the end, freedom of conscience (though with limitations) maintained its sway in Virginia ; not, as far as it appears, from any great motive of reform, but from the circumstances which gave the control of the Legislature to those who were no longer disposed to pay for what they did not get, nor to accept what their consciences rejected, and who resented what, assuredly, was an imposition on personal rights.

Except the more progressive cast the discussion of this subject betrayed in this portion of the population, it cannot be said that their institutions and manners differed so greatly from those of the sea-board as to demand especial observation.   There was apparently greater mental activity and acuteness ; domestic life was more homely and with less state than that maintained on the great plantations of the lowlands; but there was the same lack of a middle class, though a tendency toward one manifested itself more speedily ; there was the same agricultural basis of society, and the same distinction between owners and slaves.   Two differences, however, existed, which may be noticed.   One of these, the lack of navigable waters, forced on the population a road-system, which, compelling united exertion, to some degree, broke in upon the isolation of plantation life, and paved the way to greater association.   The other was the nature of the crops, which were composed of the cereals.   On the sea-board, from the very beginning, tobacco was the favored crop, and the sole one which in America then conferred distinction.   It was also the most valuable, and, in colonial days, the tobacco-planter was thus invested with the special dignity and importance, which in our own times we have seen distinguish the cotton lord.   West of the Blue

Ridge, however, the productions of the soil conveyed no such distinction. What the farm produced there could be produced almost everywhere else. The agriculturist was no longer a planter, he was a farmer; although his "farm" might be greater than a lowland plantation. The valley was but an extension of the one which crossed southeastern Pennsylvania, and the crops were altogether the same as those raised by the peasantry which they looked down upon, and which to this day are called the "Pennsylvania Dutch." Thus the aristocracy of the valley was not supported by the agricultural distinction, nor, indeed, by the wealth which invigorated so strongly the class feeling of the seaboard. The dweller between the Apalachian ranges, from the force of the system under which he lived, was an aristocrat, but, as his aristocratic feelings had not so great a number of subjects to display itself upon as had those of the lowlander, they were not so often called into play, and they were neither so intense nor so symmetrically developed.

2. Beyond the Blue Ridge and the Alleghenies, north and south, from the Hudson to the Chattahoochee, a fringe of population was displayed, which effected the double purpose of protecting that to which it was attached, and of forming a warp from which a closer woof was to be made. These sojourners in the wilderness were known as frontier settlers or backwoodsmen. Here society bordered, in nature as well as in location, on savage life. It was dispersed, and those who composed it were isolated to the last degree. It constituted an advance guard of civilization —it served, in fact, as a picket to the army in its rear—and was the rudimental form of social crystallization. It was made up, for the most part, from the humbler classes of society, from those adventurous spirits who were too restive to endure the restraints imposed by order, and from those who, destitute of the means to locate themselves where land had a marketable value, were constrained to seek the parts where it was to be purchased at the cost of the comforts of civilization. Indeed, none had it in their power to pay this price but the hardy, the athletic, and the adventurous, or those who had been previously inured to the hardships awaiting them by a mode of life which rendered them indifferent to what a higher class would deem necessities. These people,

therefore, started into the woods a hardy, athletic, and adventurous race, and their life, when on the ground, developed to an incredible degree physical endurance, acuteness of observation, rapidity of action, fertility of resources, and the faculty of making a little go a great way. They went, rifle in hand, and, with the tomahawk constantly before their eyes, sought in the solitudes of the forest the sustenance which the patch of ground, still encumbered with stumps, was not yet fully able to yield. These hunting and trapping expeditions were prolonged for months, and often extended miles into a country swarming with hostile Indians, and where it was death to set up a shelter, to build a fire, or to use any more audible weapon than the bow and arrow, or the spear. Such an ever-present mistrust of the very ground he trod upon made the frontiersman extremely cautious and observant. But he had to take his natural rest, during which he was helpless, and he would have been more than human had not familiarity with danger sometimes thrown him off his guard. Often, therefore, he went forth never to return, and it was not until long after all danger had passed away, and another generation had taken his place, that the startled farmer or sportsman would stumble upon his remains, where a hollow skull, dented by a hatchet, a little heap of bones, and a few shreds of clothing, with an arrow sticking in a neighboring tree, told his story but too well. Then the elders of the vicinage had their recollections stirred to the point of remembering, that before they had settled in that locality, they had heard that such-a-one had declared his intention of hunting in that region and had departed, but that he had never come back. Where all trace of the missing was lost, his fate was certain, and easily described: he had been taken captive, tortured, and burned at the stake.

These were the men who, pushing ahead of civilization, hewed out the way for its advance into the valley of the Ohio. Led on by the excitement of the hunt and the love of adventure, they spread over the prairies north of the river, and, south of it, drove the Indian from the buffalo-haunted meadows of the "dark and bloody ground." The fury of the elements could not make them pause, nor could any danger deter them. They loved the solitude of the wilderness, and so much were they a part of it, and so estranged did they become from society, that no denizen of the woods fled sooner at the approach of civilization than they. But, though thus shunning the proximity of neighbors, they, nevertheless, considered themselves the guardians of their kind, and, at the appearance of danger, turned on their tracks, and braving every storm, swam rivers, crossed mountains, traversed forests, and ran the gauntlet of enemies, to warn a young settlement of its approach, and to lend a hand in warding it off. In respect to physical wants, they were as independent of the world as ever a Diogenes or an Epictetus could wish. Their bed was the ground, their drink was water, their fuel was at hand, their game afforded them food and clothing, and their rifles supplied them with what the elements did not. They could drive a nail with a bullet at forty paces, bark a squirrel at fifty, and snuff a candle as far as the wick could be discerned.[1] Danger had a fascination for them, and they delighted in matching their cunning with that of the Indian, and their endurance with his. They surpassed the savage in his peculiar skill, they outwitted him on his own ground, and, of course, were richer in the resources of civilization ; yet, as the same life compelled the same habits, they did not disdain the wild appearance such life brought with it, but were delighted beyond measure when, on their rare visits to the settlement, they were told that they looked like Indians ; and when the children mistook them for such it was homage to their adaptability to nature.[2] Like the Indian they became taciturn among strangers, and like him, too, their one vice was inebriety. Otherwise their lives were pure ; from necessity it may be, but still the modern vices of the frontier were almost unknown to them. Sometimes they married squaws, and reared a family of half-breeds, and there are instances even of their joining tribes of Indians. Though first on the ground, and with every facility of choice, they rarely acquired land. Stability was not in their nature, and they were indifferent to possessions which might have been purchased with the proceeds of a season's hunt, and were content to "squat" without inquiring into the title to the ground, or even if there were one. All they asked of life was plenty of game, plenty of adventure, and no civilized neighbors.

At the first notes of a war between England and France, they

---

[1] Audubon's "Travels."

[2] Darby's letter to *The Republic.*

busied themselves in observing the attitude of the Indians, and in inducing them to side with the former power. Whether successful in this object or not, they soon appeared at headquarters with their budget of information, and with whatever allies their persuasion had gained ; and, at all events, offered their own services as scouts or rangers. In this capacity they were invaluable. Their primitive habits dispensed with the necessity of supply trains, for they were content with what could be carried in their pockets, and, moreover, they needed no shelter. They covered the column's front and flanks, and taking to the brush with the readiness of savages, they rendered it impossible for an attack to occur without warning. Luxury being unknown to them was not missed. They never indulged even in the soldier's privilege of grumbling, but, disdaining it as a mark of incapacity, endured extreme fatigue without a murmur. Such were the men who covered the frontiers.

The part enacted by these men in the civilization of the country was no mean one ; they paved the way for its advance. Preceded by the Leatherstockings, and under their protection, our frontier constantly advanced, and, like the god Boundary of the Romans, it never stopped to rest. The establishment of well-ordered society in the interior was the same everywhere along the border, and the formation of one community illustrates all. The first on the ground were, of course, the rangers, who, according to the plan of historical development, led the way, and performed the task of spying out the land, of getting a proper knowledge of its geography and resources, and of securing the friendship of the aborigines who were inclined to peace, or of driving out those who were hostile. These rangers were the Leatherstockings, and they were succeeded by the pioneers, who usually appeared in small bands, numbering from half a dozen to a couple of scores, and whose first business was the erection of a stockade or rude fort at the junction of two streams, or at some other point which equally united convenience with capacity of defence. These bands would fell the timber necessary for the block-houses and dwellings of the fortifications, dig a well, plant some corn, and make all the preparation they could for the shelter of the women and children, who, if they had not already appeared, were the next to come.[1] The

---

[1] The men went in the spring, the families followed in autumn.—Otzinachson.

little community having got its habitation, and a name, which, if
not Indian, at least savored of the wildness of the woods, proceeded to break the ground of the vicinity, and to till the land.
The men worked ordinarily in gangs, carried their rifles with
them to the field, and, with an eye to security, returned at night-
fall to their families within the stockade. But, for the first season,
by reason of there being no provisions except the little they
brought along with them, and for many seasons afterward, from the
insufficiency of the crops on account of the slow destruction by
fire or frost of the stumps which cumbered the ground, the men
were driven to eke out an existence by hunting. The order of
nature so established it, that the game lasted until the fields became
sufficiently productive, and thus the settlement was sustained.

The next step forward in the development of society was taken
after the great Indian fight, which, occurring with invariable regularity, gave the rude flourish which really rung up the curtain of
this little theatre. For, so long as the savages were in the neighborhood, expansion was difficult and dangerous, immigration was
deterred, and the settlement was confined within sight or sound of
the block-houses. With the defeat of the Indians, however, the
vicinity was cleared of danger, and the families, glad to be re-
leased from their narrow confines, ventured to build cabins on
the adjacent tracts of land from which each had made its selection. The stockade, being still maintained in the midst of the
settlement as a rallying point in case of alarm, naturally became
the resort of the settlers for supplies, and when the clearings had
become farms, and the population had multiplied by natural increase and immigration, it is to be observed, that it too has burst
its bonds. The breastwork and log cabins have disappeared, frame
or brick houses have been erected, the road has become a street,
and stores and shops have taken the place of the common magazine. In a word, a village, with its schools and churches, has
grown up amid a farming community. One change, however, is
to be noticed with regret ; the beautiful Indian name is gone, and
in its stead there flaunts some high-sounding title such as Athens,
Rome, or, perhaps, Baalbec.[1] Before this, the frontier had long

---

[1] Any one glancing at the map of our then Western, but now Eastern regions,
might suppose that the demon of nomenclature, before smiting the door-posts
of their towns, had just emerged from the index of some ancient history. In
fact, it did, and this botch of the pedagogues, I regret to say, has been imitated
all over the West.

ago followed the sun westward, and, departing, carried with it all trace of border life. The principles of law and order which are henceforth to control it now govern society.

But one step more is certain; the erection of a county. On that event, a court-house takes its place among the schools and churches; the village becomes a borough, the borough a county town, and all the first steps of civilization have been taken ; it is now in full march. Perhaps the future will make a city of the borough, but, should that happen, society will only be an expansion of what already exists, and the course of civilization present a higher tide only than that which now flows.

Familiarity with the principles of government is not to be looked for among these simple settlers and hunters. They organized society from instinct, not from induction, and freedom of individual action was its animating principle, not from philosophical forecast, but because nature had ordained it to be the soul of their social life. These children of nature acted naturally, and therefore their development of society is in every respect as worthy of observation as was that of their ancestors, ruder even than themselves, the Angles and Saxons. Local self-government was the direct outgrowth of their blood, and was as natural to them as the surrounding forests were to the soil on which they stood. We, consequently, find it to be the beginning and the end of their organization. Whatever affected that, affected them ; and, inversely, for what did not concern them, they did not care. Of the imperial government they knew almost nothing ; it scarcely reached them : and if even to the cultivated Virginian, royalty was but a sentiment, what a mere abstraction must it have been to those to whom the most positive evidence of civilization was a piece of calico, who laughed at writs, and whose notions of coercion were limited by the number of rifles which could be brought to bear on an offender. Until the court-house appears, then, the influence of the central government may be entirely left out in considering their social development, and that of the colonial taken into but little account ; for they looked to this only in distress, and turned their backs on it the moment they no longer needed its help.[1] The restraints of order in a dispersed society

[1] This independence of the remote governments, imperial and colonial, is

were little needed, and what were necessary, difficult to impose : administration was therefore slighted, and its cares sat lightly on authority. Personal liberty was the soul of the settlement, and every thing like government was measured by the rule that alone laid down. That their ideas of freedom were limited to the person of the citizen, is to be expected when we observe, that they were a migrating people, whose roaming had a continent for its field, and was restricted only by the opposition of savages or by the forces of nature. It is natural, therefore, that among those whose notions of personal freedom were bounded only by the moral law, the spirit of liberty would be very arrogant, not to say fierce, and that their sense of allegiance, from the nature of things exceedingly weak, would be easily extinguished. So it was, and when the troubles concerning the Stamp Act arose, what affection these people had for the crown became in an instant alienated forever. Not that they were moved by the principle underlying a taxation their mode of life would rarely call on them to pay, but because their personal feelings outweighed their sense of political responsibility, at the recollection of the slights which had been put upon them during the French wars by the king's troops, the/ only representatives of royalty they had ever seen, and because they resented the arrogance which regarded them as fit only to be hewers of wood and drawers of water for those who sprang from the same loins and were no better than themselves.

---

shown by the fact, that, with an utter disregard for authority of any kind, settlements were frequently pushed far beyond the reach of civilization, and on disputed territory where accountability to either power was denied. Yet the process of social organization went on precisely as it did where the claims of government were recognized, and the remote governments were not submitted to, until civilization had reached that point where it always imposes central control on its children.

CHAPTER VI.

Manners in the Middle Provinces.

3. Between the Susquehanna and the Hudson, the manners of the people differed much from those of the Southern and the Northern colonies. In the agricultural portion of the Middle colonies we come to farms, and these were greater than the farms of New England, but were smaller than the plantations of Virginia and the South. On the seaboard we behold commerce in its best estate, and Philadelphia, the largest and most populous city in British America, outshines all others in trade, wealth, hospitality, politeness, and culture, and in every thing which gives a capital its peculiar features. It was a large and flourishing city when Boston was still fearing the rivalry of Salem,[1] when New York had barely crossed Wall street, when Annapolis, Williamsburg, and Charleston were yet mere villages, and before Albany, Pittsburg, Baltimore and New Orleans had crept beyond their stockades or had any greater distinction than what their names could give them. It was essentially English, though the most cosmopolitan of American capitals in aspect and character. It had been founded by the Friends or Quakers, who, for a long time, kept the lead in wealth and influence ; but the inflowing population had brought hither a class which soon surpassed all others in culture and the higher forms of education, and to whom the colonial reputation of Philadelphia for refinement was mostly due. This class belonged, for the greater part, to the Church of England, and was that which built the now venerable and historic piles of Christ Church and St. Peter's, and the one whose tombstones, with their quaint inscriptions, still fill these church-yards. The

---

[1] "Fam. Letters," John Adams, No. 5.

spirit of opposition to Quakerism [1] aided its natural tendency to a mode of life very different from that of the followers of Fox, and broadly marked the contrast it made with the manners and doctrines of the Quakers. It constituted the progressive party in Philadelphia, and was liberal and expansive in its views of life. Coming over, when, even in England, the hereditary intolerance of its Church had wellnigh disappeared, and at a time when it had neither the opportunity nor the disposition to display any of the qualities which had made that Church obnoxious to the Dissenters, its career, as far as religion is concerned, was on the whole a tranquil one, and, as far as regards social life, was invested with elegance and dignity which it delights its successors to look back upon. As a party it was strengthened by the sympathy of the ever-increasing immigration, which, as fast as it became settled, arrayed itself in opposition to the Quaker government, and thus its influence was extended far beyond the city and its neighborhood, and expanded constantly from day to day, as the frontier kept advancing. [2] It need hardly be said, that its spirit was naturally sympathethic with that of Maryland and Virginia on the one hand, and with New York on the other.

It was this class, likewise, which, even before the Revolution, bestowed on the city its reputation for excellence in law and medicine.

As the great and constantly growing commerce of Philadelphia broadened, there was to be seen there a greater diversity of nationalities than in any other city in America ; and, consequently, a greater diversity of manners, and not a little of the refinement of its highest classes, were due to the immigration it welcomed, when, in consequence of the insurrections in the West Indies and the religious troubles in Europe, it became the refuge of many foreign families. These, in general, were French by birth or descent, and Protestant in religion, and being of the upper classes, affected

---

[1] " As the chief part of the inhabitants were Quakers, they with others were and are concerned in acts of government ; but as the province increased and prospered in every respect, many of other persuasions came and settled here with worldly views, who have formerly attempted to wrest the civil power out of the Quakers' hands, as it is very probable they may and will do again."— Fishbourn MS.; Penn and Logan Corresp., " Mem. Hist. Soc. of Pa.," *sparsim.*

[2] The Germans, however, co-operated with the Quakers, through sympathy with the doctrines of peace maintained by the latter. See *sparsim,* Logan's Letters in Penn and Logan Corresp., " Mem. Hist. Soc. Pa."

the manners of society by adding a sprightliness and vivacity not hitherto possessed.

This, by far the most important of the colonial cities, was, too, the most stately. From the earliest period of its existence, life assumed there a dignified as well as genial aspect. The houses of the rich were spacious, comfortable, luxurious. The trade with Europe and the West Indies, and even from far-off China and Bengal, brought to its doors every luxury known to man ; its household comforts were supplied in profusion by the fertile regions surrounding it, and its markets were filled with what land, air, and water could furnish, in such abundance and excellence, as to excite the admiration and wonder of the stranger, come from where he might.[1] Its merchants displayed their taste and riches in town-houses whose gardens stretched down to the water-side, and in country-houses surrounded by lawns and groves, from whose broad verandas the eye took in scenes which might charm the wanderer from Hampshire or Devon. Agriculture filled its bins with plenty, and trade poured opulence upon its wharves.

Nor were there lacking incentives to intellectual exertion and the means of mental culture. Not only the questions of local interest called into activity the faculties for disputation, but from a remote period of colonial existence, the mind of this capital was reaching forth to meet that of Europe in fields common to both. The men for intellectual work, and the souls with lofty aspirations were there. To say nothing of those who, in the course of time, made the name of Philadelphia synonymous with all that is excellent in law and medicine, there were Godfrey, who invented the quadrant ; the astronomer Rittenhouse, who constructed the famous orrery ; and Franklin, who discovered the transmitability of electricity, and whose works on the practical philosophy of life belong to the world. In the earliest days of the colony, James Logan brought over with his books a love of them, and to his latest day never ceased those graceful pursuits which drew to his seat of Stenton the companionship of the rising intellect of America and the sympathetic correspondence of the cultured abroad. It was he who, dying, bequeathed to the public the literary accumulations of a lifetime, and who left behind him the

---

[1] "——it is allow'd by Foreigners to be the best of its bigness in the known world, and undoubtedly the largest in America."—Black's "Journal," *Pa. Mag.,* etc., i, 405.

Loganian collection,[1] which to this day remains the pride of that splendid depository of thought, the Philadelphia Library. This cultivated man had Pastorius, Kelpius, Lloyd, Thomas, Aquila Rose, and Story for his companions, and graced in scholarly retirement the declining years of his life by translating for the benefit of his fellow men the " De Senectute" of Cicero. It was after him that Shikellamy named his son, the future great chief, Logan, in grateful recollection of the just dealings of this good man with the Indians.[2]

The love of books and literature breathed into the colony by these men was not lost. After them came Smith, the first master of what is now the University of Pennsylvania, an institution which, from that time to this, has maintained its reputation undiminished, and Shippen, Webb, Godfrey, and a horde of lesser lights, to whom literature owes no debt, it is true, but whose names recall an intellectual activity not to be despised. Nor is it to be forgotten, that here was the abode of him to whom David Hume thus wrote : "America has sent us many good things, * * * but you are the first philosopher, and indeed the first great man of letters, for whom we are beholden to her." The genius of Franklin not only revivified the love of science and literature, of which Logan in his day had set the good example, but stimulated and developed it, and it is to him we owe such institutions as the Philadelphia Library, the American Philosophical Society,[3] and the Society for the Diffusion of Useful Knowledge, with which it combined.

---

[1] " After the Tea Table was remov'd, we were going to take leave, but it appear'd we must first view his Library, which was Customary with him, to any Persons of Account. He had really a very fine Collection of Books, both Ancient and Modern, he seemed to Regrate that none of his Sons knew how to use them, and that he design'd them as a Legacy to the City when he Died."— Journal of William Black, *Pa. Mag. of Hist.* etc., vol. i, No. 4, 407. It, with the Union Library, was combined with the Philadelphia Library in 1792.

[2] " We got to Mr. Logan's, a few minutes after 3, and found him hid in the Bushes, an expression the Indians used when Treating with the Province at Philadelphia, in July, 1742, saying, ' They were sorry to find their Good Friend James Logan hid in the Bushes,' Meaning, it gave them concern their Friend was so much Oppress'd with Sickness as to be Oblig'd to live a Life Retir'd from Public affairs: he had been a very great Benefactor to the Indians, and conducted several Treaties with them, and they having always found him true to them, had an Extraordinary Regard for him : The Commissioners * * * told him, his Advice would be of the last Consequence to them in Conducting the Treaty."—*Id., ibid.*, 406-7.

[3] " This last institution is erected upon an admirable plan, and is by far the

Of the social life of Philadelphia during its colonial days, there are many records and traditions. But there are none more valuable and interesting than the " Journal of William Black,"[1] a Virginian, who recorded the events and the impressions made upon him during a visit to that city in May and June, 1744. Black was a native of Scotland, and accompanied, in the character of secretary, the commissioners sent by Virginia to unite with the commissioners from Pennsylvania and Maryland in a treaty with the Iroquois, or Six Nations, having reference to lands west of the Alleghenies. This record is in the shape of a Diary, which opens with the departure of the yacht *Margaret* from Stratford, a plantation on the James River, entertains us with the reception of his party at Annapolis, in Maryland, and finally brings us to Philadelphia, after the Virginians had been met, at the Blue Bell Tavern, near Darby, by a deputation of officials and private citizens appointed to conduct them to the Governor's house. His official position brought him in daily contact with the governing element, and opened to him the hospitable doors of the highest classes. As his diary was jotted down without a thought of publication, the facts noted are to be relied on implicitly.

From the few pages of this Journal alone—to say nothing of other authorities—it is to be gathered, that the society of Philadelphia, in that day, was extensive, wealthy, educated, and courteous, and that it presented the characteristics of one founded on professional pursuits, and upon trade in its most elevated condition. There hangs about it an air of stateliness, which, as we descend the social grades, mellows into ease and comfort. Among the higher classes, there was a ceremoniousness which regulated rather than interfered with sociability, and the style of conversation among the young—for Black was then a young man and naturally sought the companionship of youth—was carried to a degree of sentimentality which, in our days, we should consider stilted. When young ladies were present, the discourse invariably turned on love and the emotions, and these subjects were discussed in a style that would have done honor to Miss Lydia Languish,

---

best school for learning throughout America."—Burnaby's " Travels," 85 ; " Works of Franklin," vi, 194. " They have societies, the Philosophical Society particularly, which excites a scientific emulation, and propagates their fame."—John Adams, " Familiar Letters," No. 125.

[1] *The Pennsylvania Magazine* etc. (Hist. Soc. of Pa.), vols. 1 and 2.

and with a pertinacity and a particularity which would have stirred the soul of Clarissa Harlowe. It was, to tell the truth, somewhat lackadaisical, and was varied, if monotony is ever varied, by excursions into the domain of criticism, where the beauties of Addison, Prior, Otway, Congreve, or Dryden, were set off against the polished satires of the heartless Mr. Pope. Its fault was, that it was too sentimental; it smacked too much of the fine writing of the age, and it can be easily imagined that, to one listening to it with his eyes shut, it would sound as if some one were reading a poor imitation of the *Tatler* and *Guardian*, or, at best, of the *Spectator*. The taste of the day mercilessly exacted that young ladies should grow lachrymose over the wrongs of the distressed heroines—for distressed they always were—and that their beaux should wax indignant at the ruffianly Lovelaces who scandalized innocence on every page of fiction.[1]

From many sources we know the habits and manners of colonial society in Philadelphia, and we know that it was characterized by a remarkable degree of elegance and display, when it is considered that, at that time, it was the growth of but three generations. The accumulation of wealth had been exceedingly rapid, and doubtless would have brought with it the evil that almost invariably attends the hasty acquisition of riches, had it not, after all, been a natural and healthy result of circumstances, and had not its use been regulated by a moderation and sobriety admirable to look back upon. That society was pure, every record we have of it clearly testifies. It was moral, religious, and, on the whole, cultivated.

Pennsylvania and its capital were, in many respects, far in advance of the rest of colonial organizations. In agriculture, it reached the highest point then attained in America[2]; in com-

---

[1] "The women are exceedingly handsome and polite; they are naturally sprightly and fond of pleasure; * * * without flattery, many of them would not make bad figures even in the first assemblies in Europe."—Burnaby's "Travels," 86, 87.

[2] Philadelphia was "well lighted at night and patrolled."—Burnaby's "Travels," 76.

"For nearly four miles the road is as straight as the streets of Philadelphia. On each side are beautiful rows of trees, buttonwoods, oaks, walnuts, cherries, and willows, especially down toward the banks of the river. The meadows, pastures, and grass-plots are as green as leeks. There are many fruit-trees and fine orchards set with the nicest regularity. But the fields of grain, the rye and wheat, exceed all description. These fields are all sown in ridges, and the fur-

merce, it was unquestionably pre-eminent ; the commonwealth displayed in its government the principle of representation in greater activity than was seen anywhere else ; and, from the very first day of its existence, freedom of conscience, the mother of every kind and degree of liberty, was established as the foundation on which the whole structure rested ; moreover, her geographical position, between the North and South (there was then no West known to American civilization), gave her natural advantages which her sisters on either hand could not possess. Philadelphia thus became metropolitan : it was the centre, to which every impulse, intellectual or physical, made its way, and from which it again went forth. Here were not only the libraries, but the printing presses which the Bradfords and Franklin made famous, and as most of the colonies were lamentably deficient in this respect, and some altogether destitute, the printers of this city naturally monopolized that industry, so far as the Middle and Southern colonies were concerned. It is evidence at once of no little intellectual activity, and of considerable industrial energy, that of works printed before the Revolution, in Philadelphia, there are in the City Library alone four hundred and fifty-nine books and pamphlets.[1]

Every where in America there was little or no poverty, and in Philadelphia and its vicinity there was less even than the density of

---

row between each couple of ridges is as plainly to be seen as if a swath had been mown along. Yet it is no wider than a ploughshare, and it is as straight as an arrow. It looks as if the sower had gone along the furrow with his spectacles, to pick up every grain that should accidentally fall into it. The corn is just coming out of the ground. The furrows struck out for the hills to be planted in are each way as straight as mathematical right lines ; and the squares between every four hills as exact as they could be done by plumb and line, or scale and compass. I am ashamed of our farmers. They are a lazy, ignorant set, in husbandry I mean ; for they know infinitely more of every thing else than these."—" Familiar Letters " of John Adams, No. 185 (Phila., May, 1777).

[1] Thomas I. Wharton, " Prov. Lit. of Pa.," " Mem. Hist. Soc'y. of Pa.," i, 156. The taste for reading was general. " You would be astonished," says Duché, in his " Observations," etc., p. 11, quoted in Wharton's " Essay," " at the general taste for books which prevails among all orders and ranks of people in this city. The Librarian (of the City Library) assured me, that for one person of distinction and fortune, there were twenty tradesmen that frequented this library." Again, *id.*, p. 30, " Literary accomplishments here meet with deserved applause. Such is the prevailing taste for books of every kind, that almost every man is a reader ; and by pronouncing sentences right or wrong, upon the various publications that come in his way, puts himself upon a level, in point of knowledge, with these several authors." * * * " Many excellent productions in the literary way have been published here. *That spirit of freedom*, which I have already mentioned, has given birth even to orators and poets, many of whose performances I have heard and read with the highest satisfaction."—*Id.*, 150.

population would lead one to reasonably expect. The mechanics, for whom it was then as noted as it is now, and the tradesmen, were, as a class, well off, and many were wealthy. Hospitals and benevolent institutions of one kind or another were established, encouragement was given liberally and practically to apprentices, the schools enjoyed a reputation that extended throughout the land, and, in short, during her colonial existence, Philadelphia displayed a lofty condition of civilization. Education was not confined to the city. At Bethlehem the Moravians were annually sending forth educated youth from the same school they are conducting to-day ; and at Ephrata, in Lancaster County, a community of Dunkers relieved the tedium of a cloistered life by composing and publishing works on religion and morality.[1] Lindley Murray, who was a native of that county, was at that time, too, engaged in those studies which eventually produced his works on the English language.

Pennsylvania, during her colonial existence, owed much to the German element of her population. The Mennonites, from the Palatinate, settled Germantown, and a general immigration from other parts of Germany diffused itself through the rich valley which extends on the south of the Blue Mountains, from the Delaware to the Susquehanna, and thence, southwardly through the land. Their knowledge of agriculture, their sagacity, and their patient toil and love of labor, made this valley a garden. For some time, indeed, the influx of these immigrants was so great, that a wide-spread alarm possessed the English-speaking colonists lest the Germans might get the ascendancy in government as well as in numbers, and thus transform Pennsylvania from an English into a German colony.[2] But this fear gradually disappeared before the natural increase and the immigration of the former, and vanished entirely on the arrival of great numbers of Irish, Welch, Scotch, and Scotch-Irish. These last, for the most part, went directly to the frontier, which was not long in crossing the Susquehanna and advancing beyond the rich valleys of the interior. There the struggles of border life at once de-

---

[1] See Israel Acrelius' visits to Bethlehem and Ephrata in " Mems. Hist. Socy. Pa.," and Watson's " Annals " ; also John Adams, " Fam. Letters," No. 155.

[2] See, *sparsim*, Logan's Letters in Penn and Logan Corresp. As late as 1755, Sam'l Wharton expresses his fears in this respect. MS. 198–202 ; Watson's "Annals," 256, 257.

veloped the hardy population heretofore described. To the north of the Blue Mountains, in the valley of the upper Susquehanna, and in what is the northeastern part of the territory, an immigration from New England, chiefly from Connecticut, had set in, which, claiming the soil under the Connecticut charter, led to long and sanguinary broils with those who attempted to head them off, or to expel them, under color of the charter granted to Penn. This conflict of tenure was suspended by the common necessity which compelled the contestants to take part in the Revolution, and it was not until after the return of peace that the strife was settled by the decision of the federal court, sitting at Trenton, invalidating the Connecticut title, or, to speak accurately, confirming that of Pennsylvania. Beginning, then, at the southeast, and advancing north and westwardly, we find that the population of Pennsylvania contained, first, Swedes, next English, then Germans, and lastly New Englanders ; while the whole front of this mass, from the west branch of the Susquehanna southward, was covered by one consisting of Irish, Welch, Scotch, and Scotch-Irish, as the Protestant immigrants from the north of Ireland were called.

Thus Pennsylvania had a greater diversity of nationalities than any other colony, and offered, consequently, a greater variety of character. While agriculture drew to itself the largest number of people, the commercial class, from its greater concentration and wealth, exercised the weightiest influence, and the timidity of trade uniting itself with the natural tenacity of the farming class to ancient institutions, rendered this colony to a high degree conservative. As far as the ancient institutions of the race were concerned, the progressive party was as conservative as any other. It aimed principally at a modification of manners and a change of the ruling element ; at a more active development of natural resources and greater facilities for commerce. Its strongest ally within the city was the industrial classes, and, in the country, the immigration that was not Quaker was on its side. This was the class, which, once moved to act, carried the colony into rebellion.

Looking at the whole of Pennsylvania at once, it cannot be said that its spirit of liberty was a fierce one. The frontier population, of course, brooked no restraint,[1] but the natural placidity of the German farmers did not give way to an aggressive character, and the English counties were under the influence of the mercantile caution of Philadelphia, and of the deliberation natural to the Quakers and the wealthy class there gathered together. But the placidity of the Pennsylvania German is not to be taken for indifference : his emotional character is undemonstrative and expends its force in simple tenacity.[2] The stubborn, resisting quality of the English blood need hardly be mentioned. It takes much, yields little, and, when under such personal control as that maintained by the Quakers, is as little ostentatious as the phlegmatic temperament of the Germans.

Thus the Spirit of Liberty does not assume in Pennsylvania the aspect of defiance so familiar in the Northern and Southern colonies. It is tempered by gravity, and is stubborn rather than fierce.

---

[1] On the 4th July, 1776, the settlers on Pine Creek met and resolved that they were independent of Great Britain—and this without the knowledge, of course, of what was at that hour going on in Philadelphia.—M'Ginnes' " Otzinachson," 192.

[2] John Adams thus conveys the impressions he received of this people. It must be remembered, however, that he was then a fugitive at York, where, with Congress, he was constantly threatened by Howe—circumstances not calculated to favorably impress a man impatient of the delay, then being experienced, in resisting the enemy, and irritated by the patience he mistook for want of spirit. Moreover, his remarks are directed against those who, removed from the theatre of war, had not yet been excited by the spectacle of it :—" The people of this country are chiefly Germans, who have schools in their own language, as well as prayers, psalms, and sermons, so that multitudes are born, grow up, and die here without ever learning the English. In politics they are a breed of mongrels or neutrals, and benumbed with a general torpor." " Fam. Letts.," No. 223, Oct., 1777.
Burnaby, whose judgment is entitled to great respect, says of the Pennsy vanians in 1759–60: "They are great republicans, and have fallen into the same errors in their ideas of independency as most of the other colonies have." —' Travels," 86.

CHAPTER VII.

New England's Five Advantages as enumerated by John Adams; and herein of Education.

ACCORDING to the order adopted, the remaining reason for the spirit of liberty being fierce in the colonies, given in Mr. Burke's analysis, namely *Education*, is now to be considered, and in connection with it the advantages mentioned by John Adams[1] which New England possessed "over every colony in America, and, indeed, of every other part of the world," may be reviewed with profit.

These advantages are thus enumerated :

"1. The people are purer English blood ; less mixed with Scotch, Irish, Dutch, French, Danish, Swedish, etc., than any other ; and descended from Englishmen, too, who left Europe in purer times than the present, and less tainted with corruption than those they left behind them.

"2. The institutions in New England for the support of religion, morals, and decency exceed any other ; obliging every parish to have a minister, and every person to go to meeting, etc.

"3. The public institutions in New England for the education of youth, supporting colleges at the public expense, and obliging towns to maintain grammar schools, are not equalled and never were, in any part of the world.

"4. The division of our territory, that is, our counties, into townships ; empowering towns to assemble, choose officers, make laws, mend roads, and twenty other things, gives every man an opportunity of showing and improving that education which he received at college or at school, and makes knowledge and dexterity at public business common.

---

[1] "Familiar Letters," 120, No. 75.

"5. Our law for the distribution of intestate estates occasions a frequent division of landed property, and prevents monopolies of land.

"But in opposition to these we have labored under many disadvantages : the exorbitant prerogative of our Governors, etc., which would have overborne our liberties if it had not been opposed by the five preceding particulars."

There can be little question, that, had not the inflexibility of these free institutions and the stubborness of blood withstood the encroachments of the crown, liberty in these colonies would have been ground to dust under the crushing pressure of royal prerogative. They are therefore worthy of thoughtful consideration, and shall be noticed in the order enumerated.

1. The first advantage set forth by Mr. Adams might not meet the assent of those theorists in ethnology who maintain that tribal mixture increases the vigor of race. But accepting as a fact the implication deducible from his proposition, that the purer the blood the better the race, it is to be observed that this advantage is not one peculiar to New England. The governing class in the Southern colonies, by whom alone resistance was made, was equally pure in blood with the people of New England, and we have seen that in Pennsylvania, where fully as high a pitch of civilization was reached, this eminence was greatly due to the admixture of nationalities. Nevertheless the advantage possessed by New England in this respect is not thereby lessened, though it be not one in which that region surpasses " every colony in America."

That the times in which the colonists left England were purer than those in which the new-born states assumed their manhood, and that those who came over were less tainted with corruption than those that were left behind, are facts which cannot be emphatically asserted, because they cannot be definitely ascertained. Granting, however, that such were the cases, and that thence descended an untainted race, the Quakers of Pennsylvania, the Roman Catholics of Maryland, and the later immigration of Virginia can all claim with justice the same hereditary purity. It cannot be denied that to this purity of race and character the colonists owed much of the resolution and endurance which distinguished them, and that in these noble qualities the New England people were not outshone by their fellows.

2. That the institutions of New England exceeded those of the other colonies in the support they gave to religion, morals, and decency, is an assertion likewise open to dissent; for, where was there a more religious people than those of Pennsylvania and Maryland, a more moral people than that of the South, and in what respect did New England excel in that general decency which everywhere alike pervaded the simple manners of the colonists? The reasons given for such superiority, namely, the imposition of clergy upon communities, and Sunday laws, have demonstrated their insufficiency by ceasing to exist in the New England to which they are asserted to give such great advantages; nor could their existence even be excused, unless it be granted that there can be no public worship without an Establishment, no religion without intolerance, nor any morality and decency without both. But among free peoples, though religion sustains morality and decency with the sympathy of a kindred spirit, it is the arm of the municipal law that enforces their observance, and though the State regards religion as one of the institutions of society it is bound to protect, it by no means follows that such institution has actual control of the manners and conscience of the community for weal or woe. It certainly did not in New York and Virginia where Establishment was the law of the land, nor was its rule effective or perpetual in the days of the Massachusetts oligarchy. It is difficult, then, to see the extraordinary advantages conferred by such relics of intolerance as the forced imposition of clergy and compulsory attendance upon public worship. As parts of political constitution the enlightened now regard them as so many weaknesses of the body politic, and even as so many hindrances to the development of purity in morals and religion, and the observer is, therefore, apt to conclude that New England was religious, moral, and decent, not on account of these irrational institutions, but in spite of them.[1]

---

[1] How tenaciously Massachusetts clung to these twin relics of intolerance may be seen from the following account of an interview which took place as late as 1774.
"* * * Some gentlemen in Philadelphia * * * wished to communicate to us a little business, and wished we would meet them at six in the evening at Carpenters' Hall. * * * We all went at the hour, and to my great surprise found the hall almost full of people, and a great number of Quakers seated at the long table with their broad-brimmed beavers on their heads. We were invited to seats among them, and informed that they had received complaints, from some Anabaptists and some Friends in Massachusetts, against certain laws of that Province, restrictive of the liberty of conscience, and some

3. But whatever doubt may hover over the first two assertions of this great statesman, none clouds the rest. Political science affords no greater verities than those contained in the ensuing paragraphs, and the school, the township, and the equability of intestate distribution did exert a notable influence over New England character, and served to render her spirit of liberty exceedingly bold.

The establishment of the school system of New England was aided by the concentration of population, to which the climate, the distribution of soil, the theocratic constitution of society, the

---

instances were mentioned, in the General Court, and in the courts of justice, in which Friends and Baptists had been grievously oppressed. * * *

"Israel Pemberton, a Quaker of large property and more intrigue, began to speak, and said that Congress were here endeavoring to form a union of the Colonies ; but there were difficulties in the way, and *none of more importance than liberty of conscience. The laws of New England, and particularly of Massachusetts, were inconsistent with it, for they not only compelled men to pay to the building of churches and support of ministers, but to go to some known religious assembly on first days, etc. ;* and that he and his friends were desirous of engaging us to assure them that our State would repeal all those laws, and place things as they were in Pennsylvania.

"A suspicion instantly arose in my mind, which I have ever believed to have been well founded, that this artful Jesuit, for I had been before apprized of his character, was endeavoring to avail himself of this opportunity to break up the Congress, or at least to withdraw the Quakers and the governing part of Pennsylvania from us ; for, at that time, by means of a most unequal representation, the Quakers had a majority in their House of Assembly, and, by consequence, the whole power of the State in their hands. I arose, and spoke in answer to him. The substance of what I said was, that we had no authority to bind our constituents to any such proposals ; that the laws of Massachusetts were the most mild and equitable establishment of religion that was known in the world, if indeed they could be called an establishment ; that it would be in vain for us to enter into any conferences on such a subject, for we knew beforehand our constituents would disavow all we could do or say for the satisfaction of those who invited us to this meeting. That the people of Massachusetts were as religious and conscientious as the people of Pennsylvania ; that their consciences dictated to them that it was their duty to support those laws, and therefore the very liberty of conscience, which Mr. Pemberton invoked, would demand indulgence for the tender consciences of the people of Massachusetts, and allow them to preserve their laws ; that it might be depended on, this was a point that could not be carried ; that I would not deceive them by insinuating the faintest hope, *for I knew they might as well turn the heavenly bodies out of their annual and diurnal courses, as the people of Massachusetts at the present day from their meeting-house and Sunday laws.* Pemberton made no reply but this : 'Oh ! sir, pray don't urge liberty of conscience in favor of such laws !' If I had known the particular complaints which were to be alleged, and if Pemberton had not broken irregularly into the midst of things, it might have been better, perhaps, to have postponed this declaration."—"Life and Works of John Adams," Diary, ii, 398, 399.

Better ! It would have been best had this declaration never offended the ear of freedom of conscience ! John Adams was ahead of his times in every thing except toleration ; in that respect Israel Pemberton was in advance of Adams.

disposition of character, and the habits of class all contributed. This concentration made practicable what the dispersion of Southern society rendered impracticable, and in every Northern neighborhood a number of children sufficient to warrant the existence of a school was always at hand, while in Southern localities the scholars were scattered over territory too great to permit their daily assemblage. As we go far South, and the population becomes more and more scanty, this obstacle to the formation of common schools becomes greater and greater. That a disposition favorable to education existed in the South, as well as in the North, is shown by the fact, that where the density of population permitted the support of schools they appeared ; where it was insufficient they did not appear. Fortunately, the absence of public schools does not always imply want of education, inasmuch as from the constitution of modern civilization, a dispersed society is generally accompanied with wealth sufficient to make up the deficiencies incident to isolation. In fact, in the Southern colonies, education made its way by adopting a mode of dissemination different from that of the Northern, but nevertheless efficacious. Here society gathered to receive it,[1] but there it had to seek society, and its agents were as dispersed as the families. Instead of public there was home instruction, and the children were taught by tutors who were members of the household. Often these were the neighboring parsons, curates, or students of theology, or, where such could not be had, young graduates of the universities lately come out from England. Still, though education in the South is thus shown to have been steadily cared for, it was nevertheless imperfect. Every form of solitary instruction is defective, and to this the instruction on the plantations was no exception ; for it was confined to one class of society only, and, so great was the dispersion, it could not reach all the children even in that class. Education, therefore, was not so much diffused

---

[1] So early was this tendency to concentration, that, in 1636, a law was enacted in Massachusetts which prohibited the erection of dwelling-houses in any new township, at a greater distance from the meeting-house than half a mile. Lands were sold or granted only to companies associated together for the purposes of settlement. This regulation was based on religious more than on social or political motives, and it was a provision by which two birds were killed with one stone :—for, none but church members being allowed to vote in township affairs, the theocratic oligarchy was strengthened the more the land was peopled.—Hildreth, i, chap. ix.

in the South as in the North. Again, the one teacher had to instruct in all branches, and as the men are rare who are good at teaching every thing, learning was infected with the inequality of excellence which naturally results from that of capacity ; and, lastly, from the paucity of pupils competition was rare, and thus a highly effective force was almost wanting. These defects, lack of diffusion, inequality of excellence, and feebleness of competition, placed the education of the South in an unfavorable contrast with that of the North. Good in one thing, it was deficient in another, and it thus betrayed irregularity and shortcoming. The want of competition was, next to the actual paucity of numbers (and the blacks are out of the question), in a great measure owing to the absence of the middle class, which ordinarily fills the benches of Northern school-rooms, where to this competition is chiefly due the excellence of the schools embraced in the communal system. Then, too, the social concentration which the South lacked, was able, in the North, to supply several teachers to one school, and as each of these instructed in the subject for which he was best fitted by taste and acquirements, the pupils thus enjoyed the best instruction in all branches that the locality afforded, and their knowledge became more completely rounded and filled out than that of the Southern youth. In a word, as the education of a community is a communal affair, the education of the North enjoyed the advantages to be derived from the cooperation and concentration of all the social forces that can be brought to bear upon the subject. That there was no positive want of education among the wealthy class in the South, is shown by the early foundation of William and Mary College, which could not have come into existence, had not the need of higher instruction than what the plantation could give, been felt by a class who stood ready to receive it.

But there can be no doubt, that, during our colonial existence, the love of learning was more general in the North than in the South. We have seen the pre-eminence of the schools in Pennsylvania, where the Quakers provided education as soon as they were able to furnish shelter for the scholars, and where they set up printing-presses to diffuse knowledge, while the forest trees were still standing at their doors.[1] The New Englanders did the same

---

[1] " It is believed that no one of the States of this Union can exhibit so early, so continued, and so successful a cultivation of letters as Pennsylvania. Hardly

for their children, with the exception of the printing-press, for which they long manifested an aversion.[1]   One of their first enactments was, " that every township, after the Lord hath increased them to the number of fifty householders, shall appoint one to teach *all* children to write and read ; and where any town shall increase to the number of one hundred families, they shall set up a grammar school ; the masters thereof being able to instruct youth so far as they may be fitted for the university."[2]   This was done, " to the end that learning may not be buried in the graves of our forefathers," and for the purpose of baffling " that old deluder Sathan," who would "keep men from the knowledge of the Scriptures."[3]   It would hardly have been accomplished had there not been a thirst for knowledge common to the people, and this was the beginning of that communal system of education, which, in the last century, caused learning to be more generally diffused throughout New England than it was anywhere else. Learning, with the New Englanders, was not a distinction, but ignorance was a badge of unpardonable inferiority—it was the mark of the Beast.[4]

Nor was this avidity for knowledge confined to the rudiments of education, or to that which simply facilitates the business of daily life.   One might naturally suppose that those whose business was to subdue nature, people solitudes, and found States, would be so occupied as to have time for nothing but the performance of these duties, and the cultivation of those powers which were essential to the work in hand.   But to the undying honor of these people, it must be said, that they sought the object of their culture not so much in their newly broken fields as in themselves.

had the emigrants sheltered themselves in their huts,—the forest trees were still standing at their doors,—when they established schools and a printing-press, to teach and to be enlightened ; literally *inter silvas querere verum.*   Within four years from the time that our ancestors landed in the wilderness, a printing-press was at work in Philadelphia   *   *   *   and only a few months after the arrival of William Penn, public education was attainable at a small expense."—Wharton's " Prov. Lit. of Pa.," " Mems. Hist. Socy. of Pa.," i, 100, 110.

   [1] " In the leading colony of New England legal restraints upon printing were not entirely removed until about twenty-one years before the Declaration of Independence."—Tyler's " Hist. of Am. Lit.," i, 112, 113 ; Thomas' " Hist. of Print. in America," i, 58, 59, etc.

   [2] " Col. Laws," 74, 186, A. D. 1647 ; Hildreth, " Hist. U. S.," i, 370, 371 ; Bancroft, *id.*, chap. x.

   [3] Hildreth, *id.*, 370, 371.

   [4] De Tocqueville, tom., i, chap. xvii.

They were content with no provision for the future that did not contemplate the highest possible cultivation of their minds. The significance of this last step in the plan of public education is not lessened by the fact that the colleges were the work of individual instead of the common energy. Such has been the history of the early universities the world over, and it is so universal that it must be accepted as a step of the natural development of culture. The individual founds what the State is often glad to assist, and what the community always sustains. So it was in the New England colonies. In the colony of Massachusetts, John Harvard, who, unfortunately, did not live to see the fulness of his work, founded the institution, to which his grateful fellow-laborers in the field of education gave his name,—an institution which, taking the lead, has not had its supremacy in learning disputed from that day to this, save by its splendid rival, to whom the learned of Connecticut, inspired by the same generous emotion as that which stirred the bosoms of those of Massachusetts, gave the name of Yale. These two great universities have always borne toward each other somewhat the same relation as that existing from time immemorial between Oxford and Cambridge, in England, or, rather between those of England and those of Germany. That has been pre-eminent in elegance of culture ; the flame of this has steadily shed a light which has illuminated the path trodden by six generations of seekers after useful and solid learning. They have not sought it in vain, and perhaps no institution in the world has, in the same duration of time, and from the same number of students, given to society so many useful citizens, and, certainly, none in America has exerted so great an influence on the fortunes of the country as Yale. The effect of both these universities on the character and manners of the Americans is incalculable. Harvard has probably exerted its greatest influence on literature ; Yale on public affairs, particularly law, the administration of justice, and the administration of government. Before the year 1765, seven colleges had been established in the British colonies : William and Mary in Virginia ; Philadelphia, now the University of Pennsylvania ; the college of New Jersey, now Princeton College ; King's in New York, now Columbia ; Yale, at New Haven ; the University of . Rhode Island, now Brown University ; and Harvard University, in Cambridge, Massachusetts. Of these, all but one were north of Mason and Dixon's line. South of Virginia the small and greatly dispersed population scarcely warranted the existence of such institutions. It was easier and better to send the few aspirants for the highest grade of education to the North or to Europe.

It needs no argument to prove how great the effect of learning must have been on those already possessed with the spirit of liberty. Learning of itself does not produce freedom, as we see from the examples of those people who, though very learned, are yet not free. Freedom is the result of race instinct, stimulated by circumstances, and mere culture of manners does little to aid it, while, by diverting vigilance, it may prove to be the means of positive injury. In fact, the most cultivated people have often been the least free, and the freest nations are, as a rule, the least polite. Freedom, though favoring education, has not a softening effect on manners ; excessive amelioration of manners arouses its sense of insecurity, by exciting its instinctive jealousy and dread of enervation. Mere book-learning, however, has no such softening effect on manners as to tend toward enervation, while, as knowledge, it increases the security of freedom. Therefore, freedom favors learning, but does not favor culture where manners are more the objects of its attention than knowledge. While knowledge, then, cannot of itself bring forth freedom, it may be the helping ally to that which already exists. It gives those who have it the means of cultivating the spirit of liberty intelligently ; it assists them to reason concerning its nature, broadens the view of it, shows them what it is, enhances its value in their eyes, and a knowledge of how others have dealt with it makes it clear to them how to deal with it themselves. Above all, by showing how it is lost, how easy it is to lose it, and how dreadful are the consequences of its loss, knowledge impresses upon them the necessity of preserving their liberties, and stimulates the constant exercise of the one sole means of preservation, vigilance. Of course, the greater the number so instructed, the greater the number of guardians, and the more secure is freedom.

The most marked effect upon the notions of government in the Northern colonies, was that by which the common learning relaxed the rigid utilitarianism that characterized its application, and invested this practical art with an air of theoretical speculation. Every thing on the subject of government, the relations between the ruler and the ruled, and the rights and responsibilities of the subject and the citizen, was read with avidity and discussed with unflagging interest. The debating societies teemed with such subjects, propounded in the form of questions containing an alternative, and the clergy, always ready to take part in secular affairs, were not slow to put in their oar from the pulpit. The consequence was, that when the practical knowledge of the art of government displayed by the South was augmented by the familiarity with theory and principle which the North held in reserve, the statesmen of the old world were completely dumbfounded at the spectacle. They beheld statesmen among people whom they had deceived themselves into believing were little better than barbarians, and saw institutions where they least expected to find them, but where Montesquieu had already told them their own had originated, in the woods.

The concentration of society enabled the New Englanders to support a common-school system. That concentration was due, as has been said, to the distribution of soil, to the climate, and above all, to the constitution and instincts of the class from which the population sprung. Society had but one class, that class was invested with self-government, and being that which, in England, represented the democratic element, was, under the full play of action permitted it in America, entirely democratic, and naturally made so the colonies it established. They may, in brief, be styled the democratic colonies. One effect, then, of this common-school system, was the powerful support it contributed to democratic notions. Where the child goes to the town school, is put on a perfect equality with his comrades, has to compete with him for reward, and has to share the same punishment, and this in a community where he cannot help seeing that all are alike, and that none stand higher than another, unless it be the minister, and he only one day out of seven; when, beside this, he is positively instructed, that all men are equal before God, it naturally results, that he grows up with the conviction, fixed in his mind, that all are really equal, socially as well as politically, even though there be lords across the water. The condition of society being democratic, the instruction such society gave was naturally in favor of a democracy, which was thus powerfully supported by the schools. In this manner, too, they emboldened the spirit of liberty; for, in a democracy, the existence of liberty is attributed to that democracy, and whatever supports that consequently invigorates freedom.

4.   But the education which most affected the spirit of liberty in New England was not that of the schools, but of experience. The art of government is essentially a practical one, and, though it has its theories, it acts only upon solid ground.   The tendency to abstractions, so characteristic of the New England mind, was, as it is still, powerfully counteracted by an institution which is to be found in its highest form of development in that part of the country.   That institution was the township, which was to the society of Massachusetts and Connecticut what the family was in Maryland, Virginia, and the Carolinas, namely, the unit of social organization.   There local self-government found its natural habitation, and one that was all its own ; thence it set forth, and thither it returned.

From the very beginning of New England colonization, the township appears as the most prominent feature of political organization, and so close does it come to the hearth that it may almost be called a division of society, using the term "society" in its limited sense of neighborly association.   It is the smallest territorial, autonomic division of the commonwealth, and may be described, in a word, as a neighborhood.   Having its limits defined by law, being in jurisdiction set off separate and apart from the rest of the community, and invested with self-government, it is an autonomy, and, as it comes nearest home to the citizen, is constantly before his eyes, and is, moreover, that which he himself governs ; it has a reality of existence which nothing but what directly affects the citizen's interests can give, and is the most important factor by far of the political distribution of social forces. It embodies two things which constitute the very soul of a free community—independence and individual authority. The administration of the township is perfectly independent of that of the State ; its authority within its limits is as absolute, and as a form of social organization it ranks higher ; for it possesses to a greater degree the elements of vitality, its constitution is as varied and more complete, it reaches more interests, it can use the whole force of the State to compel the execution of its lawful mandates, and when the source of life is destroyed, so great is its vitality, that, though the State lie in ruins, the township will yet survive in full force and vigor. It is the germ which contains the whole of social life, and from which grow the other forms of political development. The State is not the mother of the townships, but it is the townships or aggregations of neighborhoods which bring forth States.[1] The business of the commonwealth is conducted by representatives of the neighborhoods.[2]

From its smallness of size and numbers the township can hardly contain any great conflicting ideas, classes, or interests, and the work to be performed is almost entirely of an executive nature : there is, therefore, no necessity for a purely representative government, which, moreover, would be too cumbersome and expensive. The representative and executive forces are consequently merged into one, and the exertion of power thus becomes direct and immediate. This power is vested in a body numbering from three to a dozen persons, who are styled "the select-men." These are elected by the town meeting, and bear a composite character, for they represent the persons of the voters, and are the agents to execute their will. Their duties lie in administering the affairs of the township, and these are prescribed by custom,

---

[1] " In this part of the Union political life had its origin in the townships, and it may almost be said that each of them originally formed an independent nation. When the kings of England afterward asserted their supremacy, they were content to assume the central power of the State. They left the townships where they were before ; and although they are now subject to the State, they were not at first, or were hardly so. They did not receive their powers from the central authority, but, on the contrary, they gave up a portion of their independence to the State. This is an important distinction, and one which the reader must constantly recollect. The townships are generally subordinate to the State only in those interests which I shall term *social*, as they are common to all others. They are independent in all that concerns themselves alone ; and amongst the inhabitants of New England, I believe that not a man is to be found who would acknowledge that the State has any right to interfere in their town affairs."—De Tocqueville, Bowen's Transl., i, chap. v., which see for general view of *Townships*. *Cf.* also Goodwin's " Town Officer," the Statutes of the New England States, and the " Law Reports " of the same. The character of the township is the least mutable of all forms of polity, and was the same in colonial times as it is to-day. " Each settlement at once assumed that township authority which has ever formed so marked a feature in the political structure of N. E. The people assembled in town meeting, voted taxes for local purposes, and chose three, five, or seven of the principal inhabitants, at first under other names, but early known as ' select-men,' who had the expenditure of this money, and the executive management of town affairs. * * * Each town constituted, in fact, a little republic, almost complete in itself."—Hildreth, i, chap. vii. See on the subject of the township the valuable paper of Joel Parker, entitled " The Origin, Organization, and Influence of the Towns of New England," Mass. Hist. Soc., 1866-7.

[2] The government of France sends its agents to the *commune ;* in America the township sends its agents to the government.—De Tocqueville, *id., id.*

enjoined by law, or created by unforeseen emergencies. The select-men have also duties that are imposed upon them by the general statutes of the commonwealth, and which relate to interests that are common to all the townships concerned ; but as in these instances they are constituted the agents of the whole community (from motives of public economy and convenience), and are thus *dehors* the township, they do not require our consideration in such capacities. They enjoy freedom of action, but it is universally limited, and they must refer to the source of power for authority to do any thing which, for example, would change the established order of things, or introduce innovation. The people vote as well as pay the taxes, and the select-men under their direction expend them. The select-men, likewise, call the town meeting, and there receive the instructions which they are afterward to fulfil.[1] They see to the building of schools, the employment of teachers, and, having a general supervision of affairs, are a little council of governors, whose masters are veritable despots, holding them to strict accountability, and swift to mete out the punishment of removal. Besides the select-men there are numerous officers. There are assessors to rate the taxes, collectors to receive them, a treasurer to keep the funds, and a town-clerk who has the custody of the records ; there are constables to keep the peace and execute the laws, overseers to look after the poor, committee-men to visit the schools and see that the standard of

---

[1] As in the South, so in New England, matters were well talked over before being broached publicly, and in the large boroughs, if not in the rural districts, the "caucus" was early recognized as the preliminary step to the town meeting. The following is an extract from the " Diary of John Adams," the entry being " Boston, February " [1763]. The ensuing extract from " Gordon," is taken from a note to the first extract in the " Life and Works of John Adams." " This day learned that the Caucus Club meets, at certain times, in the garret of Tom Dawes, the adjutant of the Boston regiment. * * * There they choose a Moderator, who puts questions to the vote regularly ; and select-men, assessors, collectors, wardens, fire-wards, and representatives, *are regularly chosen before they are chosen in the town.*"

" More than fifty years ago," (from 1774) " Mr. Samuel Adams' father and twenty others, one or two from the north end of the town, where all the ship business is carried on, used to meet, make a caucus, and lay their plan for introducing certain persons into places of trust and power. When they had settled it, they separated, and used each their particular influence within his own circle. He and his friends would furnish themselves with ballots, including the names of the parties fixed upon, which they distributed on the days of election. By acting in concert, together with a careful and extensive distribution of ballots, they generally carried the elections to their own mind. In like manner it was, that Mr. Samuel Adams first became a representative for Boston."—" History of the American Revolution," i, 365, *n.*

instruction and the attendance of scholars are maintained, path-masters to look after the laying-out, making, and repairing of roads, firemen, hog-reeves, fence-viewers, timber-measurers, sealers of weights and measures,—in short, such a little army, that, in the smaller townships, it would seem impossible for any voter to escape conscription : and, in fact, hardly does it happen to a respectable New Englander, anywhere, to pass through life without having actually administered township government in some of these particulars.

It must be evident, that the township affords the best field known to the Teutonic race for the play of those incentives which develop its highest forms of citizenship. In the first place, the administration of its affairs concerns the soil, of which the citizen is generally an owner, and to which he is always attached, and it thus addresses his instincts ; secondly, it directly concerns the things which affect his daily life, and it thus touches his interests ; next, it gratifies his sense of self-esteem, and thus arouses his pride ; and, lastly, it gives the opportunities for cultivating popularity, and thus it develops his ambition. It is not large enough, however, to afford scope to the inordinate ambition of the individual, neither is the body of townsmen sufficiently great to threaten by combined action the tranquillity of the commonwealth, while at the same time the interests of the townships being similar, they would readily unite against the encroachment of the State. Power is divided at its source, yet it can be readily concentrated for action, and thus the forces of society are decentralized in their inception, and combined only on what is remote. The authority is divided, but the power is concentrated in action. There can be no such thing as a despot in the township, for there is no consolidation of authority, no hierarchy of office-holders, and no personal transmission of power ; and mis-government, cannot be enduring, for it can be terminated at the next annual election. It is this instinct of decentralization, or dispersion of force and authority, which multiplies the town officers. Liberty is timorous and jealous: it eyes askance the consolidation of any force that may prove too strong for it, and the presence of any power that rivals it is offensive. It is itself a despot, and follows the despotic maxim of ruling by dividing.

The township, moreover, is purely a local self-government, in which every citizen has a part. It thus fosters the pride of citizenship, and stimulates its exercise ; and as the questions to be decided, the means to be used, and the objects to be attained, are of the most homely and practical sort, practical citizenship is developed to a remarkable degree. No matter how many theories a New Englander may have on the subject of government, no matter how many vagaries he may indulge, or how many abstractions he may pore over, the questions, how much he must pay for a school-house, whether a new road is needed or not, and where the fire-engine is to be housed, are such as come right home to his experience and common-sense only, and such as are to be answered by common-sense and experience alone. He may be the veriest of theorists by his fireside, an enthusiast and a Don Quixote in politics, but before he goes to the town-meeting he lays all this aside and puts on the armor of common-sense.

Once there the whole character of the man is changed. He no longer dreams of Toboso, no longer tilts at windmills. He revels in the prosaic. If he charges at a gang of rogues, it is not to release those worthy men, but to set them to breaking stones on the highway. The chairman is the only one to whom he looks up, and he yields undue consideration to none, unless, in his secret heart, he stands in awe of the town-clerk as the power behind the throne. His fingers hold the pencil, his features are rigid in the absorption of calculation, he scrutinizes every item of the accounts, he allows, he objects, he resists, he haggles. In one respect he is unlike the knight and very like the squire,—he sees things as they are, and mistakes not the scent of garlic for the breath of roses. He goes further. His candor gives way to suspicion, he assumes that mankind are more intelligent than honest, and he pauses at every measure, not to weigh its merits, for that is an after-step, but to be certain that there is no lurking evil. His reticence vanishes before a volubility to which the members of his family are totally unused, and he talks by the half hour on a matter which at home he would settle with ten words. One thing he repeats incessantly and with tireless persistence, that, as practical men, they must look at the question in a practical way, and from a business point of view. When he has talked himself out, has satisfied himself as to the accounts, and has voted what money he thinks he ought to pay, he returns home, rests himself

in his easy chair, and resumes his perusal of Malthus " On Population " or Adam Smith's " Wealth of Nations." Thus the township
corrects his natural tendency to abstractions and makes a practical
citizen of him : his interests make him an earnest one, and his
sense of rulership a proud one.   It is no wonder that, under such
an institution, popular sovereignty passed from the ideal to the
actual, and became a reality, even though a king sat upon the
throne.

The attachment of the New Englander for his township could
be surpassed only by that of a Virginian for his homestead.
What touched the township, touched him.   Its citizens were his
neighbors, connections, relatives, and fellow-rulers.   All their
interests were his, and his were theirs.   There it was where
he was born, brought up, had lived, and there was where
he expected to die and be buried.   There, above all, was
where his manhood displayed its highest and best form of
development, and where those rights, which came to him
from his father, and which it was his determination should go
down unimpaired to his son, were recognized and respected.
There was only one thing dearer to him than his township—his
hearth.   The "town" was as ancient as the neighborhood, and
older than the county ; his great grandson knows that it is much
older than the State, or the union of the States.   Of the political
divisions of which he was a constituent none had so great a share
of his veneration as the township.   He loved it as men always
love their homes, but he venerated it for its age.   As a neighborhood with a name and a positive existence, it was more ancient
than the county, and was old before the settlers had crossed the
Connecticut.   If it was venerable from its age, and beloved for its
associations, it was none the less respected for its stability.   The
commonwealth had changed, and might change again, but the
township had not changed and would not change.   It had seen
the oligarchy of the commonwealth pass away and a democracy
take its place, and yet it remained.   It had seen the absolutism of
the Stuarts come and go, and yet it was the same.   What would be
the outcome of the troubles now existing between the home government and the colonial, he could not tell.   The result was doubtful, society was already turned upside down, but of one thing,
and one thing only, he was certain : come what might, the town-

ship would endure. All the kings in the world could not destroy the neighborhood, unless they tore it up by the roots and flung it into the sea ; and that no civilized being would be guilty of.

It is not surprising, then, that this real world of the New Englander, the township, figures so prominently in his life, and that, when any great question arose, which affected either his own or all the colonies alike, his first thought was, what will " the town " do ? This positiveness, this reality of existence, this ever-present being, manifests itself constantly in all the laws of the New Englanders, their writings,[1] public and private, and in their conversation. Every man is proud of his township, and between the different neighborhoods there was an honorable rivalry in social matters.

It is impossible not to see that the township imparts a disposition to be free, and discloses the art of being free. The love of freedom grows by what it feeds upon, and the aliment supplied by self-government is as boundless in quantity and variety as human action itself. The practical education it gives in the art of government is that which comes from experience only. All the theorizing and all the book-learning in the world, can no more give the education in the art of government supplied by the experience of one year's administration of a township, than speculation and mere learning can supply that which is necessary to the practice of law or medicine. The distinction between science and art is nowhere greater than in government. How to manage the affairs of a community can be learned from practice alone. As the township teaches this lesson, and as this education is diffused among the whole body of citizens, it is not too much to say, that the New Englanders are, and were, a people accomplished in the art of self-government. Now self-government is the direct complement of liberty, and, reciprocally, they support each other.

---

[1] In the letters of Mrs. Adams to her husband, John Adams, when he was at Philadelphia, constant mention is made of their town—what "the town" was doing, what "the town" contemplated doing, and what the "town spirit" was, etc., etc. This "town" was a township, and when it is remembered that it is a woman who speaks, and at a time when a great family affliction, the presence of the enemy in Boston, the battle of Bunker Hill, etc., naturally filled the correspondence of the day with any thing but what was local, this constant reference to "the town" as the one political unit, is strikingly significant. Particularly is this the case, when contrasted with the little mention of the commonwealth, of which her husband, too, was then Chief Justice. While this was almost in ruins, that was more vigorous than ever.

They are indissolubly joined together, and, among the free tribes, the condition of one denotes the condition of the other. The greater the self-government, the greater the liberty of the citizen, and as the former was almost entire in a country where monarchy was little more than a figure of speech, and where popular sovereignty was the reality, it follows that the spirit of liberty in New England was an exceedingly lofty one. That it was fierce, to use again the term employed by Mr. Burke, is natural, when we consider how full was the play of action enjoyed by the fierce blood of the race, and when we remember its characteristic restiveness under restraint, and the delight it takes in leaping all bounds which it has not itself set up.

5. The natural disposition of a people expresses itself in their laws, and the laws thus expressed, adapting themselves to the needs of circumstance and locality, develop, in their turn, their institutions, and impress upon them the popular characteristics. Thus, in different localities, different branches of the same people display different characteristics, and the philosophical mind, at the sight of these different effects, naturally seeks their causes. In the New England part of the colonies we see no great estates, no vast establishments. The people live upon small pieces of ground, for the most part owned by themselves, and the middle class predominates over the others in number and importance. In the valley of the Hudson, with its Dutch manors, and in the Southern colonies, the establishments are great, the estates vast, while particularly in the latter, the almost total absence of a great middle class is to be noticed. Indeed, as one advances southward, this class becomes of less and less importance, until in the extreme South it fades almost entirely from the sight. Immense estates meet the eye, upon which are to be seen but two forms of society, the owner and the owned. The former are few in number, and are proud, jealous, and arrogant; while the latter are so numerous as to comprise the great mass of the population, and are timorous, cringing, and servile.[1]

At once the distinction forces itself upon the eye, that the constitution of the Northern society is democratic, that of the Southern aristocratic; a distinction the history of the country has, ever since, emphasized at every step. The causes of this distinction,

---

[1] Burke's Speech on " Conciliation with America."

so far as the difference in character of the settlers bears upon it, have already been considered, but there remains to be shown the divergence which the natural expression of these characters, the laws, reciprocally produced. This divergence is to be traced, in a great measure, to the course of descents and distribution of intestate estates, and to the establishment of the legal principle, in the greater part of the colonies, that lands were assets for the payment of debts.[1] These rules, though silent in their operation, acted as irresistibly upon the structure of society, as the secret but evermoving forces of nature act on the fabric of the globe.

Where the tendency of the colonies was to a democracy, there the rule of partible inheritance is invariably to be found. Where, on the contrary, the tendency was to an aristocracy, there, on the other hand, an adherence to the course of descents at the common law is seen. Thus it was, that, in the Northern or democratic colonies, where the rule of dividing the inheritance equally among the children or next of kin prevailed, a few generations saw the large farms parcelled out into small ones, and the social equality which the operation of this rule of law brought with it, produced at last that democratic form of government which remains to the present day; while, in the Southern or aristocratic colonies, where the estates, already great, still further increased under the accumulative effect of the course of descents at common law, the social disparity, which this principle brought with it, developed those aristocratic features which are still to be traced in the constitutions which have succeeded the ancient charters.[2]

Let it not be considered an anomaly, that, in both the Northern and Southern colonies, these totally diverse constitutions of society united in the endeavor to found a common republic. It is not the first time that history records the meeting of extremes in a common cause. Indeed, such a concurrence is not unusual, and has its explanation in natural and logical causes. The Northern or democratic colonies sought, in an independent republic, the natural field for the exercise of those principles of social and political equality which animated them, while the very haughti-

---

[1] Story " On the Constitution," chap. xvii, § 179, *et seq.*

[2] Virginia would not even permit the barring of entails by fine and recovery, except by special act of the legislature. See Act 1705.

ness and sense of power which made the Southern colonies chafe
at the mere display of imperial authority, impelled them to seek
relief in independence of that restraint, and greater aggrandizement in a form of government which their assumption of superiority flattered them they would control. Both, then, desired and
sought a republic ; the difference between them being, that one
desired a democratic, the other an aristocratic republic.

The second powerful incentive to a democratic constitution of
society, was the disposition to make lands liable for the payment
of debts. In England, lands were liable only to what in law par-
lance is called an *extent upon an elegit ;* whereby a moiety of the
lands was held by writ until the debt was paid, when it was re-
leased. But, in a great number of the colonies, lands were liable
to be set off upon appraisement, or sold for the payment of debts.
In a country where there was little money but much land, the
latter was naturally substituted for the former, and hence it was,
that the principle of making lands assets came to be asserted and
established even in the administration of decedents' estates. It is
impossible here to set forth fully the effects of this principle upon
the structure of American society. These effects may be described, on one hand as moral, and, on the other, as physical.
The physical effects were, to divide and cut up the land into small
portions ; to make farms instead of plantations, and to create a
great middle class. The moral effects were, to impair the Gothic
reverence for the soil ; to encourage a migratory spirit by detach-
ing the affection of the people from the land, and to throw the
balance of power into the hands of the very class this principle
had itself created. These effects, it may be added, have grown
in magnitude until the present day, when, by the operation of
time and the downfall of the aristocratic States, we behold them in
full possession of the country. The Gothic attachment to the
soil itself has almost died away, and that mysterious instinct
which has so often invigorated the fainting energies of the Teutonic race, seems to have wellnigh disappeared before an impulse
which finds expression in the judicial assertion, that realty shall
be as easily transferred as personalty. When to these are added
the curtailment of entails, the abolition of the right of primogeniture, the repugnance to long trusts, and the facilities given to the
alienation of estates by public registry and simplicity in the forms

of conveyance, it is not surprising, that, in the words of Daniel Webster, there "has been a great subdivision of the soil and a great equality of condition,—the true basis, most certainly, of a popular government."

We have now completed our consideration of Mr. Burke's six capital sources whence the spirit of Liberty in the colonies derived its intractability or fierceness ; and we have discussed such other elements as are allied or of kindred with these, and without which their full force could not be appreciated. This consideration, it has doubtless been observed, has really embraced the development of those race or tribal qualities essential to the existence of defiant and aggressive liberty among free peoples. These qualities are shown to be the same as those in the parent stock from which they sprung, but modified by change of physical conditions, and enriched by characteristics drawn from the soil into which they had been transplanted. We have seen, too, that the peculiar circumstances of the colonies developed an exceedingly great individuality ; that predisposition to local self-government expanded without let or hindrance ; and that this individuality, or sense of personal importance and responsibility in matters political, combined with this predisposition, naturally tended to render the spirit of liberty bold. We shall yet see, so self-reliant had it become, that it was intractable when opposed, and, when assailed, fierce.

Not the least influence toward this result was exerted by a cause which, though an indirect one, is of the highest importance, and which is next to be considered : a cause which, springing from relations to the mother-country created by an artificial system, and securing material prosperity to the colonists, at the same time favored the growth of self-government by making it the compensation for the enjoyment by the parent of a monopoly of colonial trade. Conditions which permitted local self-government to root itself and develop without interference, while they were simultaneously strengthening the colonies with wealth, deserve the thoughtful consideration now to be given them.

CHAPTER VIII.

The Commercial Relations of the Colonies.

THE annihilation of French power in America was the sig-- nal to put in force, with exasperating exaction, those Acts of Trade which related to colonial commerce with foreign peoples alien to the British crown.[1] The destruction of the French power had several important results : the northern colonies were relieved from a pressure which had cemented their connection with England ; the part their troops had taken had taught them their capacity for self-defence, and the immigration that came with peace was rapidly augmenting the natural increase of population everywhere.[2] As these results of the war made themselves felt, the importance of the colonies became greater, the people

---

[1] " It was hard parting with a free open trade to all parts of the world which the Massachusetts carried on before the present charter. The principal Acts of Parliament were made many years before, but there was no custom-house established in the colonies, nor any authority anxious for carrying those acts into execution. It was several years after the new charter before they were generally observed." Hutch., " Hist. Prov. of Mass. Bay," ed. 1767, ii, 447. The first charter was from Charles I. The " present charter," here alluded to, was that of William and Mary, 1691. See note, this chapter, *post*.

[2] " Dans les guerres dont nous venons de parler, les hommes de colonies et d' opinions différentes combattirent souvent côte à côte, oubliant à l' heure du péril toute haine ou jalousie anciennes. Ils connurent leur force en convoquant des assemblées, en levant et en entretenant des troupes. Ne recevant ni secours, ni conseils de l' Angleterre aux moments les plus difficiles, ils apprirent ainsi à penser et à agir en dehors de la tutelle de la mère-patrie. Par la connaissance de leurs droits, les idées démocratiques prirent racine chez eux et ils apirerent à la liberté.

" La manière dont les officiers anglais se conduisaient envers les troupes coloniales, se moquant ouvertement de la tournure gauche et embarrassée des recrues, contribua aussi à affermer l' union des colons. Beaucoup d' officiers américains expérimentés avaient été remplacés par de jeunes subalternes anglais, mais cela ne put empêcher Washington, Gates, Montgomery, Stark, Arnold, Morgan, Putnam, et une foule d' autres, de faire leur education militaire, et d' apprendre même, ainsi qu' ils le montrèrent lorsque le temps en fut venu, à

were emboldened to assert rights heretofore unrecognized, and their air of self-reliance strengthened the suspicion, which had always existed at home,[1] that they were ready to demand their independence as soon as the natural course of development, now no longer to be ignored, would enable them to do so. So long as the presence of the French overawed the frontier, so long these colonies were unable to set up for themselves ; but, that compression removed, and with their hands strengthened by immigration, the danger of insubordination became manifest to England, and she determined to forestall such a catastrophe by clipping the wings that seemed to her already fluttering for flight. To do this, no expedient appeared so effectual as one which would strengthen the home government at the same time that it weakened the colonies. Were, however, a law enacted for that purpose, its antagonism to colonial interests would be so apparent that resistance might be provoked by the very act, and the government might thus find on its hands the worst of all evils, a rebellion, which would not only withhold what was expected to be gained, but which would risk the enjoyment of what was already in possession. Nothing, on the contrary, could be more reasonable than that existing laws should be enforced, and these, happily, were at hand.

As early as the time of Richard II., in order to foster the creation and maintenance of a navy, it had been enacted by Parliament, that "none of the king's liege people should ship any merchandise out of or into the realm, except in the ships of the king's ligeance, on pain of forfeiture." This act was afterward repealed, or became obsolete, and, though one or two attempts were made to establish it, it was not until the time of the Commonwealth, that the policy of England concerning the carrying-trade of the ocean was settled and distinctly proclaimed in what are known as *the Navigation Acts* and *the Acts of Trade.* These embodied a policy which had for its object the supremacy of the British flag on the high seas, the aggrandizement of the carrying-

---

combattre les reguliers anglais." Nolte, "Hist. des États-Unis d' Amérique," chap. xix, 216.

"The treatment of the provincial officers and soldiers by the British officers during that war made the blood boil in my veins." "Life and Works of John Adams," ix, 592.

[1] See Appendix D.

trade by England, and the absolute control and direction of the commerce of her colonies. The Navigation Acts were intended to regulate the commerce of Great Britain with foreign peoples, while the Acts of Trade were designed more particularly for the regulation of the internal and colonial trade : both together constituted the system by which England, as a commercial power, sought her prosperity

The discovery of America and the doubling of the Cape of Good Hope gave the signal to the great powers to scramble for the rest of the globe. The scene presented was like that at the loot of a Chinese palace. All had but one object, booty : the rights of the weak were disregarded, every one looked out for himself, and, even when so loaded down with spoil as to be incapable of grasping more, each quarrelled with his neighbor about what he had. Spain and Portugal, with their inherent greed of territory, acquired the greatest share of land, but Holland, whose spirit was a commercial one, contented herself with what in the end proved to be still more valuable, the trade. The Dutch went everywhere, and spurred by the lust of gain, pushed their voyages into every sea and anchored in every port. Their commerce grew so rapidly and to such an extent, that they secured a proportion of the carrying trade as never before had been concentrated in the hands of one people, and soon became to the whole world what the Venetians had been to the Mediterranean. Antwerp took the place of Venice, and as commerce went on gathering in their hands, the Dutch continued to thrive as their neighbors declined. France had no merchant service worth mentioning. Spain and Portugal saw their commerce shrink, not by reason of the fierceness of Dutch competition only, but in consequence of their overweening disposition toward adventure instead of trade, and from the restrictions by which they themselves hampered their colonial traffic. The Thames was nearly bare of merchantmen, the galleons deserted the Adriatic, whose ports harbored nothing greater than feluccas, and from the Scheldt to the Hudson, and from the Hudson to Java and Japan, the lugger ploughed the waves unchallenged. To extend her trade, to protect her convoys, to keep what she had, to get more, to expel intruders, and to drive off her rivals, Holland created and kept afloat a navy which soon became the terror of the seas, not so much for what it actually did (for instinct, interest, and circumstance all disposed the Dutch toward peace), but for what it could do, and what the least provocation might incite it to do. All nations in this way became tributary to her, and the wealth of Holland rose with her tides.

With those tides it also ebbed. Of all the people that brought tribute to this little publican, none approached the receipt of customs with so bad a grace as England. Her territory consisted of islands, and inasmuch as she could neither come nor go unless upon the ocean, she was absolutely dependent upon the waves. In them was her sustenance and her wealth, upon them she beheld her natural field of action, and there, to say the least, she should meet the other maritime powers upon an equality. Yet, for generation after generation, she was compelled to sit with folded hands and see, passing her very doors, the wealth of the world on its way to pay toll to a handful of people who lived in a swamp, and whom she could crush could she only have the opportunity. That opportunity, however, rarely presented itself, and when it did come, it came at such times and in such shapes that she could never take advantage of it. Sometimes it was her own dissensions, sometimes her lack of means, sometimes the popular indisposition to weaken a Protestant power, but, be it what it may, there was always something which prevented her profiting by the occasion. In the meantime Holland grew richer and richer. At last, when England was rent by civil strife and in a predicament so sorry as to render her an object of insult to the domineering Dutch ; just at the time when it could be least expected of her to rise and resent affront, and when, perhaps, she herself did not seriously contemplate such an act, just at that time she took the step which henceforth wrought such a wonderful change in the destiny of herself and of her rival. In a few years the carrying-trade of Holland declined, her magnificent fleet was brought to its destruction, the commerce of the world was transferred from the Dutch to the English shipping, the supremacy of the ocean was shifted from the decks of Van Tromp to those of Blake, and England was started upon a career of prosperity which at last made her mistress of the seas.

All this was accomplished by an act of Parliament, which,

passed during the Commonwealth, was re-enacted and continuously enforced after the Restoration.[1] It provided simply, that thenceforward no goods, the produce of Asia, Africa, or America, should be imported into England or exported out of it, but in vessels belonging to the people of England, and that no goods, the produce or manufacture of any part of Europe, should be imported unless in English ships, or ships of the country where such goods were produced or manufactured, and that, of these English ships, the master and three fourths of the mariners should be English, under penalty of forfeiture of ship and cargo.

This, the old act of Richard II. in spirit, was enlarged and strengthened from time to time by others having the same object.

The effect of these Navigation Acts was, to place the commerce of England in English ships, to call back English mariners from foreign decks to their own, to give English capital employment in English bottoms, and to make England the sole staple, or distributing centre, of the colonies. Thus nothing could be brought to England by foreigners, except what she herself could not supply, and as nothing could go to the colonies unless from or through English hands, so neither could any thing be exported thence but through the same channel. The absolute control of her colonial commerce being taken by England into her own hands, the supply of her markets by foreign vessels was cut down to the root, and the world was given to understand that what England wished of its traffic she would take, but what she could or would not have, it might keep. Inasmuch as, at that time, the Dutch were almost the sole carriers, they were the ones most to be injured, and the English Navigation Act was naturally interpreted by them to mean the sheer annihilation of Holland as a great maritime power. They therefore struggled hard before submitting to the inevitable effect of this legislation, but the English held the line firmly, and the prize of maritime supremacy was at last landed upon their decks.

What led the English to take this sudden step after waiting motionless so long, is doubtful. Some say that a disposition to

---

[1] The acts passed by the legislature of the Commonwealth were not recognized as laws after the Restoration, inasmuch as they had not the assent of the crown. "Where is Downing's statute? British policy has suppressed all the laws of England, from 1648 to 1660. The statute book contains not one line."—John Adams, " Life and Works," x, 330.

punish certain colonies for lukewarmness toward the Commonwealth produced it[1]; others, the necessity of strengthening the fleet to a pitch where it could counteract the efforts of the army to dissolve Parliament[2]; and others, again, attribute it to a desire to punish the Dutch for harboring the royal family and the disaffected, and to the revengeful spirit of St. John, who more than once during his embassy received the attentions of Dutch mobs, and to whom the most sensitive reminiscence of his sojourn in Holland was that of being thrashed there by the Duke of York, afterward James II.[3] None of these reasons is sufficient. If it were passed in order to punish certain colonies, why did it not discriminate between the friendly and the unfriendly, as, for example, between Barbadoes and Connecticut; or, if it were at all intended for punishment, how is it that Massachusetts, friendly to the Commonwealth, adopted it of her own motion? The reason that it was intended to offset the army by a fleet, fares no better; for, though impending dissolution stared Parliament in the face, it is impossible to suppose that the legislature looked for immediate help from a marine which the most favorable conditions would require years to develop. As for the remaining reasons, while they may account for the readiness of individuals to approve it, they fail to offer motives for public action. Anger, resentment and desire for revenge on personal enemies, are not causes which usually control the actions of people, least of all of one so deliberate as the English, or of one which, like them, is governed by interest. If such, however, were the motives, why is it that this policy was made definitive and enduring under the reigns of those who had been the objects of this anger and resentment, and who, moreover, owed Holland gratitude for shelter when proscribed? We must look to other reasons than those given for the origin of the Navigation Act, and we naturally turn to the most general motives of national action—

---

[1] Eccleston's "Engl. Antiq.," vi, chap. v, sec. 2; Hildreth, i, 355.

[2] Green, "Short Hist.," etc., chap. viii.

[3] "The famous Navigation Act * * * arose from a personal affront offered to one of our republican ambassadors." Lord Campbell, "Lives of the Chief Justices," *tit.* St. John. Whitelocke, 487, 491; "New Parl. Hist.," III, 364; Ludlow's "Mems.," 133, 250. But John Adams says, that the Act was proposed, under resentment for ill-treatment, too, by George Downing, a native of New England, who was sent to Holland, as ambassador, by Cromwell. —"Life and Works," x, 329.

self-interest and necessity. In these, it is conceived, the true reasons for this Act are to be found. The cramped powers of England struggled to be free, and to develop themselves naturally. This could take place only on the field in which nature had placed her, but from which she was debarred by the possession of Holland. Her first step then was to gain a footing of equality on the ground already appropriated by her neighbor; that done, the law of competition would do the rest. As every thing depended solely upon herself, it was to her own resources that she had to look. This Act made use of all her forces, and was naturally adopted by a power conscious of the necessity of self-development, and of the fact, that, unless she was as free upon her natural field of action, the ocean, as her rivals, she never could develop. The destruction of the Armada, and many a naval victory since then, had rightly given the English a firm reliance upon their powers to maintain their footing by the force of arms, but these same victories had also taught them that the force of arms merely will never command substantial trade. This is a victory with which force has nothing to do except to render sure its fruits, and it is to be achieved only by the wisdom and energy which know how to make the most of favorable conditions. It was, then, strictly according to natural law, that a maritime people conscious of the physical ability to maintain their footing upon the waves, should take the second step, and seek to share the wealth of the sea by making use of every resource that nature and social development had given them.

It was the clear head of St. John that, enlightened by what he observed in Holland, found England's remedy in a policy which, while of little benefit to those powers that looked solely to territory, brought great gain to those that sought prosperity in trade ; and it was the same shrewdness which saw England's opportunity in the Parliament's necessities. However, whether smarting under resentment or not, St. John penned the statute, Whitelocke had it passed,[1] and the House of Stuart afterward adopted it.

Its results far transcended the wildest dreams of Lombard and Venetian avarice, or the grandest schemes of Spanish and Portuguese conquest. It not only secured to the people who enacted it the greatest share of the world's carrying trade, but, at a stroke,

---

[1] It was passed October 9, 1651. Scobell, ii, 176.

it changed the character of the English colonies, and for the first time made them available to England. Trade knew its master, and at once followed with becoming servility.[1] But its effects reached further than the traffic which was its immediate object. It put into the hands of England the means of sustaining itself as the greatest of the Protestant powers. Dutch Protestantism had been any thing but aggressive, or even propagandist. English Protestantism, on the other hand, was of a totally different stamp ; it was captious, intolerant, and aggressive, and as soon as it felt the support of the greatest naval power, and had the comfort and assistance of the greatest merchant-service in existence, it assumed a stubborn and dictatorial tone at home, and pushed its way into unknown lands abroad, with the force and rudeness of a conqueror. Its effect in this respect was immediately seen in the religious turbulence which extended from Virginia to Massachusetts. Down to the time when this Act was passed, England could hardly be said to have absolute control of those who could seek what markets they chose. This Act gave her that control by placing the fortunes of her colonists entirely in her hands. With such a rein they could be driven wherever she would have them. At the time the Act was passed, the Independents, the most turbulent, radical, aggressive, and violent party and sect that England has ever seen, were the dominant party. Just at that instant they had not possession of Parliament, but before the Act was felt they had every thing. Party and sect being combined in them, every thing political which they did savored of religion, and every thing religious smacked of politics. It is natural, that being at the time the head and front of English Protestantism, such Protestantism should reflect the character of its leaders. It did so, and so effectively that there was not a colony, even the most conservative, like Virginia and Maryland, that did not henceforth carry with it the marks stamped by this new-born spirit of aggression. Never before could England wield over the colonies the influence which

---

[1] See for increase of trade, Eccleston's "Engl. Antiq.," vi, chap. v. He tells us that the mercantile shipping in 1688 was nearly double in tonnage what it had been in 1666, though the Plague of 1665 and the Great Fire of 1666 must have checked the increase. DeWitt's "Interest of Holland" also expressed the liveliest apprehensions, in 1669, of the "great navigation" of the English. In 1676, the East India Company doubled its capital out of the accumulated profits of sixteen years only, and the stock rose to 245 per cent. See Macpherson's "Annals of Commerce."

a control of their supplies and productions now gave her : never before was Protestantism led by so aggressive a party as the Independents. It is not to be wondered at, then, that, during this period, Protestantism in America took upon itself a character whose aggressiveness differed from that of Protestantism in England only as the conditions of the two countries differed.

Such was its effect upon Protestantism, and especially upon Protestantism in America. Its effect upon the commerce of England in respect of monopoly was, however, more remarkable :— it took monopoly from the hands of individuals and transferred it to all the people of Great Britain. It will be observed, that the principle was not abrogated nor denied : this remained as firmly established as ever. The parties alone were changed, and the subjects of the monopoly. Instead of guilds and courtiers, the whole people of Great Britain were to be the monopolists ; and instead of certain articles, the whole colonial trade was to be monopolized.

The growth of English trade had been injuriously affected by a fungus growth of monopolies, which, from time to time, and notably during the reign of Elizabeth, had threatened to completely sap the vitality of commercial life. It is singular now to look back upon the mushroom appearance traffic then presented ; and when we consider the extent of the evil and the grievous injury it wrought, the patience and long-suffering of the people is incredible. " Is bread in ?" exclaimed a member of the Commons in Elizabeth's time, when a monopoly act was presented. "Bread ! " echoed the astonished mover of the measure. "Yes." retorted the questioner, "for, if it is not, it is the only thing left out." The aristocracy demanded monopolies as the readiest means of filling the pockets of its needy members ; the monarch granted them as the shortest and easiest way of enriching favorites ; and trade in general insisted on them as inducements to remote ventures. The guilds, one and all, true to the instincts of corporations, clamored for monopolies. A new trade could not be started unless it was fostered by monopoly ; an old one could not be sustained without the help of exclusion. There was a monopoly in hides, another in wool, another in salt ; in gold thread, in silver thread, in flax, in hemp. Competition was discouraged, and no one dreamed of disputing the prerogative of the crown to grant as privileges what are now regarded as of common right. All that was done by way of correction was, to clip off or pinch the twigs; no one dared to lay the axe to the root. At times those who had to do the paying would shear down this parasitic growth, but nevertheless the poison of monopoly still remained in the bone and marrow of trade.

In all this the Navigation Act effected a great change. When, under its influence, the greatest share of the carrying-trade betook itself to English ships, and the whole colonial traffic was poured upon English wharves, trade began to assume a different aspect in the eyes of British merchants. What was the colonial trade but monopoly on a scale hitherto undreamed of? Here were the exports and imports of numbers of far-off countries concentrated under the control of a single people. It was monopoly on a gigantic scale, beside which the monopoly of separate articles, like hides or hemp, shrunk into insignificance. Moreover, the wealth that flowed into the country by this system was so great, that the necessity for the former system no longer pressed heavily, and besides, the people at large being benefited in common now began to look with jealous eye upon the monopolies which favored individuals at the expense of the community. Hence the old system made way for the new. First the monopolies in favor of courtiers dropped off, then the guilds began to lose their character of pure monopolists, and, finally, nothing of the old system remained but a few survivors who claimed a right to exist by the force of vested rights. Even these came to an end, and the new system was in full possession of the field. Monopoly, as a principle, was seemingly as strong and as vigorous as ever, but, evidently, it had submitted to a change—it had passed from individuals to the people at large, and this change is extremely significant.

To the Act of Navigation is due this great change in monopoly, whereby the demand and the supply of a score of active communities were placed under the control of one people. To this Act, therefore, is due the changed relations of the colonies to the mother-country. Henceforth they were regarded mainly as feeders to its carrying-trade, as consumers of its manufactures, as factories for the distribution of its capital, and, in a word, as mere commercial appendages of what was now the great commercial power. Dominion became subordinate to trade.[1]

I.—*The Legislation concerning Trade and Navigation.*

That such was the effect upon the relations of the British colonies toward the mother-country, is disclosed by a brief consideration of the imperial *legislation* which followed the Act, of Navigation, and of *the treatises having the colonial trade* for their subjects, written from time to time by Englishmen, after the passage of the Act, and before the passage of the Stamp Act. From both these sources we can clearly discern the view taken of the colonies by the government and the commercial world of England, and as clearly ascertain the spirit which animated the intercourse of the mother-country with her offspring, and which inspired the enactments of Parliament and the writings of political economists.

a. The Three Acts.

Beginning, then, with the re-enactment of the Navigation Act after the Restoration, we find that the new system which is to regulate colonial trade and define the relations of the colonies to the parent, is contained in three Acts of Parliament.[2] *First*, in the re-enactment itself of the Act of Navigation in 1660 ; *secondly*, in an act, passed in 1663, entitled " an Act for the encouragement of trade"; and, *thirdly*, in an act, passed in 1672, and entitled "an Act for the encouragement of the Greenland and Eastland fisheries, and for the better securing the plantation trade."

In these three acts is to be found the system. Many others sprung from these and followed them, but as they only enlarge, extend, or render more effective the acts mentioned, they may be regarded merely as modifications, in one form or another, of the

---

[1] "A great empire has been established for the sole purpose of raising up a nation of customers who should be obliged to buy from the shops of our different producers all the goods with which those could supply them."—Adam Smith, " Inquiry into the Nature and Causes of the Wealth of Nations," ii, 517.

" Si cette nation envoyait au loin des colonies, elle le ferait plus pour étendre son commerce que sa domination."—Montesquieu, "Esprit des Lois," liv. xix, chap. 27.

[2] Stat. 12, Car. II., c. 18 ; stat. 15, Car. II., c. 7 ; stat. 25, Car. II., c. 7. For these acts, see Appendix E.

" Let me, however, say in my own name, *if any man wishes to investigate thoroughly the causes, feelings, and principles of the Revolution, he must study this Act of Navigation, and the Acts of Trade, as a philosopher, a politician, and a philanthropist.*"—" Life and Works of John Adams," x, 320.

already established system. To this supplementary legislation the term Acts of Trade may be appropriately confined, though all are frequently comprehended under the generic name, Acts of Trade and Navigation. The three acts which created the system, were all passed in the reign of Charles II.; the others followed rapidly, and in great numbers, for a century, until they were checked by the attempt to transform this system of trade into a system of trade and revenue, by means of what is known as the Stamp Act, shortly after which they terminated with the downfall of the British dominion in thirteen of the colonies

St. John's Navigation Act was re-enacted in 1660, under Charles II., as the first-fruits of the Restoration. This act forbade importation into or exportation out of the colonies, save what came and went in English ships, and its object was, to shut the doors of the colonies against foreign trade.

In 1663 another step was taken, and an act was passed with the object, openly avowed in its fifth section, of keeping the colonies in "a firmer dependence" upon England, and of making *that kingdom* the staple, or place of distribution, not only of colonial produce, "but also of the commodities of *other countries and places, for the supplying of them.*" To effect this, the Act of 1663 went beyond that of 1660, and exacted, that no supplies should be imported into any colony, except what had been *actually shipped in an English port*, and carried "directly thence" to the importing colony. This act forced the colonists to get what supplies they could not themselves furnish in England only, and thus not only could none but Englishmen transport merchandise to and from the colonies, but the colonists were not suffered to go anywhere but to England for what they could not get at home. If, for instance, any thing were exported from Rhode Island to France, or from France to Rhode Island, it could not go directly from one of these countries to the other, but, come from which it might, it had first to be landed on an English wharf, and to pay toll to English trade and English revenue. The goods were stopped *in transitu*, and the transaction was shorn of any characteristic belonging to traffic between France and Rhode Island, and forced to assume, first, one of trade between France and England, and then one of trade between England and Rhode Island, or *vice versa.* Come from what quarter it might, it was prerequisite to any exchange whatever of productions, that England should be the go-between or factor.

This position of factor between the colonies and foreign markets was a lucrative one. But the spirit of trade is such, that it regards much as only a stepping-stone to more, and the next enactment concerning colonial trade, or that of 1672, betrays this characteristic. The existing factorage was maintained only between the colonial and foreign trade ; it had no place in intercolonial traffic, and there was nothing to prevent Rhode Island from transporting her produce to the Carolinas, or the Carolinas from laying down their produce in Rhode Island. Of this traffic the colonies took advantage, and their coasting trade grew rapidly in importance. From her situation, her resources, and the peculiar aptitude of her people for this trade, New England took the leadership, and was rapidly becoming toward the other colonies what England had already become to the world, the common carrier. As this intercolonial trade developed, it attracted the observation of the English merchants, who at last demanded the control of it. In compliance with this demand, an act was passed in 1672 subjecting any enumerated commodity (such commodity being, of course, one she could herself supply) to a duty equivalent to that imposed on the consumption of it in England—and thus was destroyed the freedom, and, to a great extent, the incentive of intercolonial traffic. This act was well entitled "an Act for the encouragement of the Greenland and Eastland fisheries, and for *the better securing the plantation trade.*" History is silent respecting the fisheries, but it has been very outspoken concerning its effect on the plantations. The effect was this : if Rhode Island wished to be supplied by Massachusetts with fish, for example, and Massachusetts desired to furnish Rhode Island with that commodity, the delivery of the goods could not be made by the producer to the consumer, but the fish would first have to be sent to England, and landed there, and then be sent back from England to Rhode Island before the consumer could touch them. A line drawn from Boston, in Massachusetts, to Bristol, in England, and thence back to Newport, in Rhode Island, will show the course which a barrel of fish must take, if sold by Massachusetts to Rhode Island, before the demands of English commerce were satisfied ; it will in all probability likewise show the least angle with the longest sides ever subtended on the chart of trade. Should, however, the parties to the transaction desire to avoid the risk and delay incident to this phenomenal voyage, they could do so by paying England the difference between the cost incurred in delivering the goods by the base of the triangle, and that incurred in delivering them by the two sides. Without this there could be no such thing as Rhode Island buying directly of Massachusetts, or of Massachusetts selling directly to Rhode Island. In this problem the value of the angle was made entirely dependent on the length of the sides ; and the longer, the better.[1]

b. The System embodied in the Three Acts.

Such were the provisions of the Three Acts enacted in the reign of Charles II., and which acquired the name of The Restrictive System. It was purely a system of trade, and as such was accepted by the colonists without cavil, who found no fault with it until the design of diverting it from trade to revenue became manifest. A great deal has been said of its being dead letter, and there is no question of its being much and systematically evaded, particularly by the generation that resisted the Stamp Act ; but the constant references to it here and abroad, and the continued legislation respecting it by Parliament, show clearly that it maintained its position effectively, and that, both in America and in England, it was regarded as the very foundation upon which colonial social life was built. That its integrity was so little impaired as to render it, a century after its adoption, the means whereby the administration of George III. sought its ends, and that during its whole existence it determined the relations existing between England and America, are reasons sufficient for here making it the subject of earnest consideration. One thing is certain—without a knowledge of this system and the effects it produced, the relations between the mother-country and the colonies cannot be explained, nor the American Revolution be accounted for.

---

[1] " Shall none visit the sea-coast for fishing ? " said Coke in 1624. " This is to make a monopoly upon the seas, which are wont to be free. If you alone are to pack and dry fish, you attempt a monopoly of the wind and the sun." " Deb. of Commons," i. The monopoly James I. refused was thus accomplished by the Navigation Act.

The system created by the Three Acts was actually this : of the two parties which it immediately concerned, one was the sole Manufacturer for the other, who was not even permitted to make a hob-nail for itself ; this sole manufacturer was also the sole Carrier for the other ; and this sole carrier was likewise the sole Middleman between this other and the world.

Trade never ran in more restricted channels, and obviously monopoly was the mother of this invention. There was, first, a monopoly of the manufactures required by the colonists ; secondly, a monopoly of their exports and imports ; and, thirdly, a monopoly of their transportation. The old English notion of monoply pervades the entire scheme, and it is seen that this is the controlling principle which made the system of colonial trade regulation such as to deserve the name of The Restrictive System.

At first blush we are struck with the apparent selfishness and injustice of a spirit which fostered communities who were to exist solely for the benefit of others ; but our wonder becomes amazement when we behold these communities satisfied with their lot, and so content with it that they defend it as eagerly, though not altogether for the same reasons, as the English themselves do ; and, in fact, begin to decry it only when they suspect that it may be diverted from the purposes of its creation. Some great cause must exist for such placid contentment and satisfaction ; there must be a valuable consideration somewhere for what seems so one-sided a bargain. What is it? The answer discloses the whole social and political constitution of American colonial life, and we now turn to its consideration.

Briefly, the answer is, that there *is* compensation ; and that this compensation is of twofold nature. First, there is *a pecuniary or material compensation*, and, secondly, there is *a political or moral compensation.*

1.—*The* PECUNIARY OR MATERIAL COMPENSATION *derived by the colonies from the Restrictive System created by the Acts of Navigation and Trade.*

Notwithstanding the existing system of commercial restriction, our ancestors who sought America after the establishment of this system, sought it with the hope of gain. Their steady development of internal and external trade, the continued inflow of English capital, the rapid and great accumulation of wealth, and the universal prosperity which characterized the colonies, prove that the hope was not delusive and that there was an incentive which had not failed them.

In the first place, the conditions of colonial life ensured that freedom of personal action and those rights of property, without which material prosperity is impossible anywhere, no matter how favorable the remaining conditions, but with which trade will thrive even in the face of meddlesome regulation and restriction. These elements of safety and stability are to be found, first, in the Charters, which guaranteed personal rights as well as bestowed franchises; and, second, in the open and avowed policy of the home government, that it was not to the interest of the mother-country that any relations should exist between her and her colonies, save those of a purely commercial character on the one hand, and of simple crown dependencies on the other. Where there were no charters, the absence of these guaranties was supplied, as has been seen,[1] by the terms of the commissions issued to the royal governors; a custom to which time lent the force of solemn grants under the great seal. Thus grants, custom, and the self-interest of the strong party to the contract, assured safe and quiet enjoyment to the party that was weak in a manner than which nothing could be better in the eyes of commerce. In a political aspect, this assurance lacked only constitutional guaranty to make it perfect. While, therefore, the energies of the American were restricted by this system to two things, trade and agriculture, there was no restraint placed upon him within those pursuits, other than that imposed upon the members of all well-ordered societies, and he could enjoy the fruits of his labor in perfect security.

Looking at him in the commercial character with which this system invested him, it is to be observed that he found his greatest benefit in this very factorage which the Acts of Navigation created.

The emigrants who streamed to America, though not paupers, were not capitalists. They were of the classes which, in respect of birth, were below the highest; in respect of means were below the rich; but which, in respect of position, were above the lowest.

[1] See p. 39.

They came with the avowed object of bettering their condition, of getting in America the ready money they lacked in England, and of establishing in a new country the positions and fortunes the old was powerless to create, and for which, indeed, society there afforded no room. To get money, however, money or credit is requisite, and where could these be obtained outside of Britain and the British possessions? The Dutch, who, alone of foreign nations, had capital sufficient for the cultivation of so vast a desert, could not be expected, without enormous insurance, to part with what, once gone into foreign hands beyond the Atlantic, was also beyond the reach of recall ; and the other peoples of Europe were so deficient in available funds, or so little commercial in disposition, as to render recourse to them out of the .question. In the English, on the contrary, all the qualities and conditions for developing the new country united. They had the capital ; they had an incentive for loaning it, in the enormous gain the expanding commerce of a continent would be sure to yield ; and they had the dominion and the power to maintain the security of their outlay. These people naturally became the money-lenders to the Americans, who, in return, became to the English in reality, as they generally were in name, their factors as well as their customers.

It was on English capital that the Americans traded, navigated, cultivated, and reaped their crops ; with it life and activity filled their coasts, but without it their seaboards and their valleys would have remained solitudes.

Being factors, they shared in the profits of the ventures ; they became rich along with the English, and, so long as their right to partition in the common profits was acknowledged, so long as their existence as part and parcel of the system was recognized, this system, so far from being considered an unmitigated evil, was regarded as something highly advantageous. To factors there could be nothing objectionable in investing the colonies with the attributes of factories.

While it must be constantly borne in mind that it was this political and actual control of America which caused the outflow of loanable capital to be abundant and unintermitting, and that it was this outflow which attracted an immigration naturally commercial in character, it must be observed, too, that the multiform

interests of to-day had no existence in those times, and that, consequently, there was not the material to be raised in opposition to
the system then as there would be now.   Trade and agriculture
were the only features of colonial business, and in the Southern
colonies these were so blended together, that, so far as commerce
was concerned, they may be regarded as one and the same thing :
the planter sold his crop directly to England, and to him were
consigned the manufactured articles in return, which he himself
distributed among the consumers.   There was no mining, and
but little manufacture ; trade absorbed nearly every thing, and,
the interests of the colonies being thus commercial, their placidity
under such restrictions, as that on manufactures, for example, is
readily accounted for.   So long as this restraint conduced to the
advantage of the commercial monopoly of which they shared the
gain, they were not only content, but satisfied :   when, however,
the grasp of the lion in this partnership was laid on their share,
the instinct of self-preservation, uniting with the avidity for fur-
thur trade in what they were loath to part with, called forth a
resistance which proved as effectual as it was prompt.

Thus it will be seen, that the colonists were compensated in
actual wealth, for what, at this distance, looks like a shocking
want of commercial freedom. As this privation was acquiesced in
by those who voluntarily placed themselves under it ; was accepted by those born and bred on the soil, as they accepted the
air they breathed and the bread they ate ; and was actually advocated by those who shared the gain it brought, it must be admitted, that, to a certain extent, it existed more in appearance
than in reality — particularly as, in reliance on the Charters,
there was widespread disregard of the Acts,[1] and as the systematic evasion of these Acts was always winked at by those
capitalists in England, who, when embarking their capital in
colonial commerce, saw to it, that the restrictions intended for

[1] " Notwithstanding the acts of Parliament for regulating and restraining the
plantation trade, a constant trade was carried on with foreign countries for con-
traband and enumerated commodities.   This gave great offence.   There was
no custom house.   The Governor was the Naval Officer * * * and being annually elected by the people was the more easily disposed to comply with popular opinions.   It seems to have been a general opinion that all acts of Parliament had no other force, than what they derived from acts made by the General
Court to establish or confirm them."   Hutch. " Hist. of Prov. of Mass. Bay,"
ii, 4.   In this last sentence we have the reason for the enactment of the Navigation Act by the General Court or Legislature of Massachusetts.

others should not come home to themselves. Indeed, it may be asserted, that the monopoly existed more in the system's principle than in its practice. That oppression cannot be said to be intolerable which is sanctioned by the indifference or acquiescence of the oppressed, nor that restriction destructive to prosperity under which poor and feeble communities became in a century marvels of thrift in the eyes of old Europe.[1] The colonies were compensated, and, in fact, were compensated so well, that, until interruption of that compensation was threatened, not a thought of revolt entered their minds.

2.—*The* POLITICAL OR MORAL COMPENSATION *enjoyed by the colonies in return for the restriction upon their commerce.*

Were this compensation, however, merely pecuniary, it is hardly to be conceived that it had been deemed sufficient : but there was added one quite as effective, one which gratified the highest aspirations of manhood and of citizenship, and which was a political compensation. The colonists were self-governed. When we consider that the same people who ruled themselves in America would have had no place in the actual government of Great Britain ; that they would have been represented by men in whose election they would have taken no part ; that they would have been directly ruled by a crown whose awful distance from them would have intensified their sensibility of having no share whatever in the administration ; that the revenue derived from their taxation would have been disbursed by those who sought not their counsel and who were beyond their control ; that the defence of their homes even would have been made without their acting any other part than that of him to whom it is said go, and he goeth, come, and he cometh, and that, in short, they would have had no vote nor voice in public affairs ; to such a people— especially when it is remembered, that, as Britons, a love of self-government was their natural, tribal characteristic—to such a people, the exercise of self-government must have proved a very

---

[1] Nothing in the history of mankind is like their progress. For my part, I never cast an eye on their flourishing commerce, and their cultivated and commodious life, but they seem to me rather ancient nations grown to perfection through a long series of fortunate events, and a train of successful industry, accumulating wealth in many centuries, than the colonies of yesterday." Burke, " Speech on American Taxation."

blessing, and a compensation far outweighing any mere restriction of traffic. That it was so esteemed by them appears at every turn.

This political compensation was not the result of remoteness merely from the seat of government : it sprung from their nature as commercial dependencies. Of course from the very constitution of a simply commercial, non-political connection, no such thing as American representation in the imperial Parliament could occur. But then, on the other hand, neither did those responsibilities and burdens exist which a strictly political connection would exact. For example, while the colonists, as subjects owing allegiance, could demand protection of the mother-country against that country's enemies, that country could not directly exact revenue for the protection already compensated for by allegiance, nor levy troops in a colony against a power unprovoked by a dependency. These consequences flowed from the fact, that the colonies were not part of the realm of England, nor of the other realms embraced in the Act of Union, but were mere dependencies of the crown. to which they owed personal allegiance. Under this system the crown owed them protection from attack, come from what quarter it might ; but the colonists owed the crown the defence only of their colony—they could not be ordered across seas, as in a war against France or Spain, and in case a colony did go beyond its borders, in an offensive campaign, as when the New Englanders attacked Nova Scotia, it was entirely from its own volition, and was regarded by the imperial government as an aid to the king, which was to be reimbursed and satisfied from the royal treasury. Thus from their nature as simple crown dependencies, they were exempt from the most oppressive service incident to society, while the operation of the fundamental maxim, no taxation without representation, preserved them from even being called upon to commute that service by the payment of money. No wonder a revolt marked the termination of such halcyon days, and no wonder that colonial opinion rejected the notion of representation in the imperial Parliament, even were it practicable.

Their internal affairs being thus left to their own management, their legislatures were chosen by themselves from their own people. These assemblies had the common good for their object, and they amply sufficed the purposes of their creation. The judiciary, though appointed by the crown, was of their own selection, and no courts except those of the land were open to their conviction. In every thing, too, which concerned the daily life of their neighborhoods, they were lords. Moreover, no standing army was quartered upon them, nor were they burdened with the care of a navy. They paid no taxes to the empire, they were constrained to no service save that of the common defence, and thus, without imperial taxation, without the care of an army and navy, yet under the protection of both, filling their own jury boxes, masters of their own affairs, and in the enjoyment of rapidly accumulating wealth, having, in fact, the advantages without the burdens of Britons, they basked in the sunshine of political freedom, and revelled in plenty such as has rarely been vouchsafed to human kind.

Add to this the gratification the colonist felt in conducing to the welfare and glory of the splendid empire of which he was a part, and it will be seen, that, as far as his interests were concerned, his bargain was any thing but a hard one.

We have now seen in what lay the colonist's compensation for commercial restriction. He was compensated, first, in the actual pecuniary profits resulting from the loan of English capital this very restriction placed in his hands ; next, in the greater political freedom he enjoyed here than what could possibly be his in England ; again, in exemption from imperial taxation and service ; and lastly, in the gratification his pride of blood received at the sight of the increase in power, wealth and honor, which his hands had brought to his race.

II.—*The Treatises having the colonial trade for their subject, and the significance of them.*

There was nothing to disturb the enjoyment of this happy condition but the fear of those changes to which even the most stable of human devices are liable. Legislation and policy, though the practice of generations, may be changed by the force of the public opinion that created them, and this is itself in a state of constant change. We must look, therefore, to the expressions of public opinion, wherever we can find them, in order to ascertain the

spirit which actuates a people, and for the signs of the changes
that come over it. Nowhere are these to be found more clearly
and with greater significance than in those writings which, taking
such facts for their texts as existing systems and statistics, argue in
favor of a new state of affairs, or, at least, a modification of the
old. They express the spirit and designs of the far-reaching and
earnest men who direct public opinion, and in an age when, Parliament being closed, the projects of such could reach the popular
mind only through the printed page, the treatises they put forth
are of the greatest importance to us. It will be well, then, to observe the drift of public opinion in England respecting the nature
and uses of the colonies, as it is disclosed in the peculiar literature to which the Restrictive System gave birth.

The expansion of trade produced by the Navigation Act
brought to the light in England the science to which the name of
Political Economy has been given. Forthwith had risen two
theories, one of which was designated as the Mercantile, the other
as the Manufacturing system. The first was founded on the assumption that nothing but gold and silver was wealth, and therefore, that the test of prosperity is whether trade brings more money
into the country than it takes out. If more, then trade is prosperous ; and the degree of prosperity is measured by the answer
to the question, How much more ? The other theory, which may
also be called the Monopoly theory, assumed that trade is prosperous only when it can be made profitable ; and that when it is
not profitable, it should be made so by means of exclusive privileges in favor of the seller. The first class of economists recognized the consumer as a factor in the problem to be solved ; the
second was blind to his existence ; for, whereas the former took
trade as it found it, the latter said : We leave trade different from
what we found it, and where there is no trade we force one.

From these two crude theories have arisen the great schools of
Free Trade and Protection, which, to-day, the world over, are
dividing administrative political economy into two parties.

The early English writers upon this subject were Thomas Mun,
Sir Josiah Child, Sir William Petty, Charles Davenant, Joshua
Gee, John Ashley, and others of less note, all of whom display
the spirit of the English commercial classes toward colonies in
general in discussions more or less extended. Their conclusions,

according to John Adams, may be summed up in the one principle : that earth, air, and sea, all colonies, and all weaker nations
were to be made subservient to the growth of the British navy
and marine, which, in turn, were to be instruments for the enlargement of British wealth, British commerce, British power, and
British domination, as much so as all nations and things were, in
time past, to be sacrificed to the grandeur of Rome.[1]

It is natural, with the record of their country's prosperity being
the record of monopoly, and with the East India Company in a
flourishing condition then before their eyes, that the Act of Navigation should appear the best, as it was the latest, monument to
British thrift and foresight, and that these men should look at
trade and human rights from the standpoint of monopolists.
Such is the case.

Child's work was written about the year 1677, when strict execution of the Act of Navigation was being urged and insisted
upon, and only a year after the stock of the East India Company
had been doubled. He had two objects in view: the defence and
eulogy of corporate monopoly, and the defence and eulogy of national monopoly. In short, he wrote for the purpose of defending the East India Company, and of urging the enforcement of
the Act of Navigation. In doing so he treats of the relations
existing between the mother-country and her colonies in general,
and also of those between the government and the colonies which
he specifically mentions. No writer displays a greater appreciation of the Navigation Act than Sir Josiah, nor a clearer comprehension of its scope and design. He discloses with perfect
sincerity the motives which actuated England in adopting this
measure, and as, at the same time, he exposes with ingenuous
simplicity the view taken of the colonies and the colonists by the
commercial classes of England, his work may be safely accepted as
truthfully exhibiting the spirit and designs of those classes, at the
time when the benefits of the new system were making themselves
felt, and when the merits of the colonies as dominions had already
made way for their value as feeders of trade.

The title of this work is, "A New Discourse of Trade"; its
fourth chapter is "Concerning the Act of Navigation," and its
tenth "Concerning Plantations." In this latter chapter the knight

---

[1] " Life and Works," x, 330, 340.

lays down as a fundamental proposition, that "all colonies and plantations do endamage their mother kingdoms, whereof the trades of such plantations are not confined by severe laws, and good executions of those laws, to the mother kingdom." The minor premise, "that New England is the most prejudicial plantation to the kingdom of England," follows on the next page, and the *sequitur* is left to the inference of the reader. How that inference was supplied by the New Englanders, may be seen from the one attributed to James Otis by John Adams: "And those views, designs, and objects were, to annul all the New England charters, and they were but three, Massachusetts, Rhode Island, and Connecticut; to reduce all the colonies to royal governments, to subject them all to the supreme domination of Parliament, who were to tax us without limitation, who would tax us whenever the crown would recommend it, which crown would recommend it whenever the ministry for the time being should please, and which ministry would please as often as the West India planters and North American governors, crown officers, and naval commanders, should solicit more fees, salaries, penalties, and forfeitures."[1]

That this inference was justifiable, so far as the reduction of the New England colonies to the condition of mere Parliamentary dependencies is concerned, appears from the work itself. In his chapter "Concerning Plantations," Childs institutes the inquiry, what kind of people they were that transported themselves to the colonies. The answer is not flattering to the family pride of the Americans. New England, he says, owed its population to "a sort of people called Puritans" who, wearied with church censures and persecutions, would in any event have deserted their country, and would have gone to Holland and Germany had there not been a New England found for them. As for Virginia and Barbadoes, they were peopled at first by a sort of loose, vagrant people, vicious and destitute of means to live at home, gathered up about the streets of London or other places, and who, had there been no English foreign plantation in the world, could probably never have lived at home, but must have come to be hanged, or starved, or died untimely of those miserable diseases that proceed from want and vice, or have sold themselves as soldiers to be knocked on the head, or, at best, by begging or stealing two

[1] "Life and Works of John Adams," x, 330.

shillings and sixpence, have made their way to Holland to become servants to the Dutch, "who refuse none." These colonists, worthy of the chain-gang, the galleys, or of Botany Bay, were reinforced during the Parliamentary war by the worsted party who "wanted means to maintain them all abroad with his Majesty," and great numbers of Scotch soldiers after Worcester fight. "Another great swarm" followed "when, the former prevailing party being by a divine hand of Providence brought under, the army disbanded." "The constant supply," continues Child, "that the said plantations have since had, hath been such vagrant, loose people as I have before mentioned, picked up especially about the streets of London and Westminster, and malefactors condemned for crimes, for which, by the law, they deserved to die; and some of those people called Quakers, banished for meeting on pretence of religious worship.

"Now, if from the premises it be duly considered what kind of persons those have been, by whom our plantations have at all times been replenished, I suppose it will appear, that such they have been, and under such circumstances, that if his Majesty had had no foreign plantations, to which they might have resorted, England, however, must have lost them."

The knight certainly renders it very plain, if the truth of his premises be granted, that the plantations were chiefly instrumental in saving to English society flocks of jailbirds, who, like the Don's "honest and worthy gentlemen," were on the road to the gallows; but he does not make it appear so clearly why England should emulate the moral obliquity of her outcasts by treating them as they had already treated their fellows. His effort to do so involves him in a labyrinthine tangle of logic, at which the colonists might well have afforded to smile, had it not been made the basis of legislation so adverse to their interests and their rights as to render serious what otherwise would have been accounted merely fantastic. The following is his style of ratiocination, and, as the after enactments of Parliament showed, that, too, of England.

Having noticed the colonies of Virginia and Barbadoes in the manner we have just seen, he thus proceeds: "I am now to write of a people whose frugality, industry, and temperance, and the happiness of whose laws and institutions, do promise to themselves long life, with a wonderful increase of people, riches, and power ; and although no men ought to envy that virtue and wisdom in others, which themselves either cannot or will not practise, but rather to commend and admire it, yet I think it is the duty of every good man primarily to respect the welfare of his native country.   And, therefore, though I may offend some whom I would not willingly displease, I cannot omit, in the progress of this discourse, to take notice of some particulars, wherein Old England suffers diminution by the growth of those colonies settled in New England, and how that plantation differs from those more southerly, with respect to the gain or loss of this kingdom ; —namely ": 1. All the American plantations, except New England, produced commodities of different natures from those of England, whereas New England produced generally the same. These also took some fish, which was prejudicial to the English Newfoundland trade ; they traded their produce with the British West Indian colonies "to the diminution of the vent of those commodities from this kingdom ; the great expanse whereof in our West India plantations would soon be found in the advance of the value of our lands in England, were it not for the vast and almost incredible supplies those colonies have from New England.' 2. The people of New England, *by virtue of their primitive charters,*' being not so strictly tied to the observation of the laws of this kingdom, do sometimes assume a liberty of trading contrary to the act of navigation, by reason whereof many of our American commodities, especially tobacco and sugar, are transported in New England shipping, directly into Spain and other

---

¹ How tenacious this notion was in the English mind, is shown by its incorporation into the preamble of the Act of 10 and 11 W. III., c. x.   The idea, that colonial industry meant depression of English real estate, was almost ineradicable.

² The passages in these charters operative hereon are recited in that of William and Mary, 1691, as follows :—" Whereas King James I. * * * did grant to the Council at Plymouth, for the planting and governing of New England, all that part of America, from the 40th to the 48th degree of latitude, and from sea to sea, together with all lands, waters, fishings, and all and singular other commodities, *jurisdictions*, royalties, privileges, franchises and pre-eminences, both within the said tract of land upon the main, and also within the islands and seas adjoining, to have and hold all * * * yielding to the king a fifth part of the ore of gold and silver, *for and in respect of all and all manner of duties, demands, and services whatsoever.*"   By this charter, Massachusetts, New Plymouth, the Province of Maine and Nova Scotia were united in one province.   A proviso withheld the erection of any colonial court of admiralty, but detailed at large the fishing rights.

foreign countries, *without being landed in England, or paying any duty to his Majesty,* which is not only loss to the king, and a prejudice to the navigation of Old England, but also *a total exclusion of the Old English merchant* from the vent of those commodities in those ports where the New English vessels trade, because there being no custom paid on those commodities in New England, and a great custom paid upon them in Old England, it must necessarily follow that the New English merchant will be able to afford his commodity much cheaper at the market than the Old English merchant; and those that can sell cheapest, will infallibly engross the whole trade, sooner or later. 3. Of all the American plantations, his Majesty hath none so apt for the building of shipping as New England, nor none comparably so qualified for breeding of seamen, not only by reason of the natural industry of that people, but principally by reason of their cod and mackerel fisheries; and, in my poor opinion, *there is nothing more prejudicial, and in prospect more dangerous to any mother kingdom, than the increase of shipping in her colonies, plantations, and provinces.*

"To conclude this chapter and to do right to that most industrious English colony, I must confess, that though we lose by their unlimited trade with our foreign plantations, yet we are very great gainers by their direct trade to and from Old England; our yearly exportations of English manufactures, malt, and other goods, from hence thither, amounting, in my opinion, to *ten times*[1] the value of what is imported from thence; which calculation I do not make at random, but upon mature consideration, and, peradventure, upon as much experience in this very trade as any other person will pretend to; and, therefore, whenever a reformation of our correspondency in trade with that people shall be thought on, it will, in my poor judgment, require great tenderness and very serious circumspection."

Thus the knight, who, as the mouth-piece of the classes which, even then, under the operation of the Navigation Act, had risen to the control of the legislation of Parliament and the policy of the government, gives us plainly to understand what the disposi-

---

[1] Nearly a century later, Burke said: "Are not these schemists well apprised, that the colonists, particularly those of the Northern provinces, import from Great Britain, ten times more than they send in return to us?" "Observ. on the Present State of the Nation."

tion of those classes toward the colonies is. It is true that no hint of the colonies as sources of revenue is given, and that the light in which they are placed is purely a commercial one. He has a grievance, and this grievance is, that there still remains to the colonies some direct trade with foreign nations, which England has not secured. His efforts are directed solely to answering the double question : How shall this be prevented, and England make all that there is to be made out of her dependencies? and so long as the discussion is kept subordinate to this question, and the spirit which prompts it is confined within bounds which do not encroach upon personal rights, the colonists need be apprehensive of few evil results. But an argument which makes the alleged debased origin of a people and the present good qualities of that people equally detrimental to the welfare of those from whom they sprung is so singularly illogical as to arouse the suspicion that it contains a hidden meaning. That there may be no mistake as to the conclusions, an analysis of this argument is here presented. It is as follows :—

Competition injures us ; New England offers competition ; therefore, Old England suffers diminution by the growth of New England.

The people of New England undersell us in the British West Indies ; by this underselling there is a diminution of the vent at home : therefore, New England must be prevented from selling.

By virtue of their charters, the New Englanders sell to Spain, which is a foreign nation, without paying tribute to the Old British merchant ; from the force of circumstances the New England merchant sells to foreign nations cheaper than the Old British merchant can : therefore, take from the New Englander this advantage by making him pay the Old British merchant, under the Navigation Act and in spite of the charters, the difference between their prices.

So far, it must be conceded that the inexorable logic of trade supports Sir Josiah, and that he strictly pursues it. His position, indeed, is nothing more than this—by the Navigation Act and the legislation supplementary to it, England has converted her colonies into communities of consumers of English manufactures. This she has a right to do, and, now that she has done it, any other character than this her interest cannot permit them to assume. She alone of the British family is to.trade with her colonies and the world, and any competition with her on the part of any member of the family, shall not be tolerated.[1]

With this position, which is strictly a logical result of the Act of Navigation, the colonies could find little fault. It does not encroach upon their rights as dominions, and it leaves their character as commercial dependencies as they themselves had accepted it ; only more strictly defined, and that is all. Unfortunately, however, Child goes further, and puts forth two propositions, in one of which, it may be said, he sets up virtue against itself, and in the other, leaves open to inference the possibility of the colonies being deprived of any other character than that of bare dominions. His disregard of charters as barriers to the advance of trade must already have struck the observer, but, to complete the analysis, the following are the two propositions here alluded to :—

Frugality, temperance, and industry strengthen a competitor ; New England is a competitor having these virtues : therefore, "a reformation of our correspondency in trade with that people [is to be] thought on."

No plantations are so apt for ship-building and breeding of seamen as New England ; nothing is more prejudicial to a mother-kingdom than a ship-building and seamen-breeding plantation : therefore—what ? Destroy these plantations, if necessary ? The knight left his *sequitur* open, but Otis seemed to think this inference a natural one ; though the most charitable deduction would be, the repression, by some means or other, of New England's ship-building and marine.

These propositions go too far ; and one of them, at least, steps beyond the proper limits of the subject to enter a field dangerous to public morality. Assuredly that spirit is subject to condemnation which makes the virtues of frugality, temperance, and in-

[1] " Trade is our object with them, and they should be encouraged. * * * If they will not be subject to the laws of this country ; especially if they would withdraw themselves from the laws of trade and navigation. of which I see too many symptoms, as much of an American as I am, they have not a more determined opposer than they will find in me. They must be subordinate. In all laws relating to trade and navigation especially, this is the mother country, they are the children ; they must obey and we prescribe. It is necessary ; for in these cases between two countries so circumstanced as these two are, there must be obedience, there must be dependence. And if you do not make laws for them, let me tell you, my lords, they do, they will, they must make laws for you." Lord Chatham in 1770.

dustry, reasons for changing the relations of the offspring with its
parent in a manner detrimental to the former ; and it is not saying too much, that the mind that can see in honest thrift and prosperity elements hostile to the well-being of the family to which
their possessors belong, is already prepared to view with calm-
ness the extinction of this thrift and prosperity. If New England was to be crippled for being frugal, temperate, and industrious, are we to conclude that the other colonies, who are represented as vicious, should be encouraged in prodigality, debauchery and laziness ?   Virtue is thus set up against herself.

It is not within the purpose of this work to discuss the principles expounded in Child's treatise, nor to criticize theories, many
of which time and experience have long since buried out of sight.
We have only to extract from its pages the drift of public opinion
disclosed by them, the disposition toward the colonies entertained
by the commercial classes of England, the designs of these classes
upon colonial trade, and the spirit which animated the imperial
legislature in its treatment of colonial affairs.   By doing so, we
do what the observing colonist did : we note the same evidences
of change in public opinion which struck him, and, by subjecting
ourselves to the impressions he received, we render clear what
otherwise might appear doubtful in the measures he adopted for
the security of his interests.

When, then, we observe persistent defamation of the colonists,
and the suggestion that their territories be made receptacles of
the outcast of British society[1] ; when we behold virtues themselves made use of as reasons for repressing colonial prosperity ;
and when we see contemptuous disregard of the charters, we
have seen enough to warrant the conclusion that the treatise was
not written in a spirit friendly to the colonies, but that it disclosed designs as threatening to the stability of their institutions
as they were to their trade.   In short, we are brought to the un-
welcome conclusion, that, under the effect of the Navigation Act,
the colonies already existed for no other purpose, in the eyes of
Englishmen, than as conveniences whose well-being depended solely
upon the manner in which they effected the purposes of commerce,
—a conclusion which hands over colonial prosperity to the doubt-

---

[1] This work advocated the enforced emigration of paupers and convicts to the
colonies.

ful chances of a trade over which it has no direction, and colonial institutions to the mercy of men whose notions of freedom are measured by the effect it produces upon the balances of their accounts.

The colonists did not exaggerate the importance of Child's discourse. His position as an East India Company director warranted the inference that the sentiments he uttered were those of the monopolists and of the trading classes. They certainly must have been those of the government; for, to mark approval of them, Child was knighted the year after the publication of his book, and henceforth all doubt was dissipated by Parliamentary enactments conforming to his assertion—that colonies endamaged the mother-country, unless their trade was "confined by severe laws and good execution of those laws."

Child's book has the merit of giving the public the first exposition it had of the Restrictive System, of which the Navigation Act was the foundation; its mischief lay in the acrimonious disposition it bears toward the colonies, in inoculating the commercial classes with the notion that the colonies were feeders to British commerce and nothing more, and in spreading throughout all ranks an indifference to, if not a contempt of, colonial rights. Being the first work of the kind that appeared, it had the unfortunate effect of setting the note which those who came after were to take up and prolong. It gave direction to the drift of public opinion, which was to find expression in the works of Gee and Ashley. It did not, however, consider the colonies in any other light than that of commerce.

The next generation produced *Joshua Gee,* the man upon whom fell Child's mantle. Sir Josiah's fondest hopes had been more than realized by the Acts of Trade and Navigation, and the righteousness of the Restrictive System had been demonstrated by success. The country had become wealthy. Gee thought nothing could be more natural and appropriate than the "principles" of Child, and he warmly coincided with him in his view of colonial population; for he quotes with approbation the latter's scurrility concerning the people of Virginia and Barbadoes. This book, which was entitled: "The Trade and Navigation of Great Britain Considered,"[1] takes up

---

[1] Fourth Edition, London, **1738**.

the thread where Child dropped it, and pursues the same course. Gee is the disciple, and Child the master ; but Gee outruns his leader in one respect, and has thereby attained the notoriety of being the first author of repute who considered the colonies *sources of revenue* as well as of private gain. This is a step forward, and since the importance of it cannot be exaggerated, it may be well at this point to set forth the reasons why such importance is so great.

Under the influence of the Act of Navigation, as we have seen, the colonies had had added to their condition or character of *dominions* that of *communities for the consumption of British manufactures and the feeding of British trade.* It was in this twofold character that they now stood before the world, and this character had been fully accepted by them as the true one. As the Restrictive System expanded and filled the field of trade, its augmenting importance dwarfed every thing with which it was contrasted. For the nurture and expansion of this system Parliament sat, and armies and fleets marched and sailed, and England itself assumed a commercial character such as no other people, but the Venetians and the Dutch, had ever taken upon themselves. Every thing was regarded from the standpoint of trade, and it is not surprising that in the eyes of a people who subordinated the energies of their own government to the requirements of thrift, the political character of their dependencies should be lost in their commercial character ; that their quality of dominions served no other purpose than to make them more subsidiary to the uses of trade, and that, indeed, the colonies were factories and nothing more. We have also seen, however, that, though this notion might possess the English people, it could not, from the nature of things, be altogether true ; and that the view taken of colonial relations and colonial constitution by the colonists themselves, gave the first and all-important place to their character of dominions. In fact, there had grown up in the colonies a positive, free, local self-government which had every element of stability in it save one—the element of constitutional guaranty. This local self-government, we have further seen, had been a very great inducement to colonization, and was regarded by the colonists as the most important compensation they had for the restriction of their trade. It was deemed by them amply sufficient,

and of such value, indeed, that, upon any question arising between these characters, further restriction was at once accepted
as the price for the continuance of the right to govern themselves.

It will be observed, that between the character of factory and
the character of self-governing dominion there is so great a difference that they have really nothing in common. The latter was
dependent upon the former in the same way that the compensation depends upon the thing to be compensated for ; the colonist's freedom as a citizen depended upon his subjection as a
trader, inasmuch as this was the price he paid for that, and that
was the compensation he received for this. Nothing, however, in
the two characters was of the same nature. They were absolutely
separate and distinct, and one was purely economical while the
other was purely political. Now, imposts for revenue is taxation,
and taxation is a thing political. It is an essential of direct
government, and, where not imposed by a people upon itself, admits a right in a superior to exact it of an inferior. Such an
admission once made, the character of dominion would be at an
end ; for the term dominion implies autonomy, and autonomy
has no existence where one people is governed by another, as is
the case where taxation is ordained by others than those from
whom it is to be collected.[1] Not one of the thirteen colonies was
attached to either of the three realms of England, Scotland, or
Ireland, for whom, under the Act of Union, the British Parliament
made laws : their legislation, therefore, had to be enacted by
themselves, and this was being their own masters. Any attempt,
therefore, to make the colonies sources of revenue was an invasion

---

[1] " The Commons of America, represented in their several assemblies, have
ever been in possession of the exercise of this, their constitutional right, of giving
and granting their own money. They would have been slaves if they had not
enjoyed it. At the same time, this kingdom, as the supreme governing and
legislative power, has always bound the colonies by her laws, by her regulations and restrictions in trade, in navigation, in manufactures, in every thing,
except that of taking their money out of their pockets without their consent.
Here I would draw the line. *Quam ultra citraque nequit consistere rectum.*"—
Pitt "On Stamp Act." Polit. Deb. 7.

" —— we may bind their *trade*, confine their *manufactures*, and exercise
every *power* whatsoever, except that of taking their money out of their pockets
without their consent."—*Ibid.*, 18.

" The authority of Parliament was allowed to be valid in all laws, except such
as should lay internal taxes. It was never disputed in laying duties to regulate commerce."—Benjamin Franklin, " Ex. Com. on Repeal of Stamp Act."

of their political condition and an attempt upon their existence as dominions ; and the destruction of this character would involve the destruction of their right to local self-government, a right which, they maintained, was theirs by the force of circumstance and solemn grant, and one now confirmed by the operation of time and by the uninterrupted recognition of the grantor.

The mere facts, that the colonists assumed such a right, and that any proposition to consider their provinces as sources of revenue touched the vitality of their autonomy, are enough to explain their alarm at the bare suggestion of such a thing.

This alarming proposition is the one made by Joshua Gee, and the colonists would have been blind indeed, if they had not accepted it as evidence of a disposition on the part of public opinion in England to take an aggressive attitude toward the colonies. As the government had shown its approval of Child's principles by knighting the author, so this work received the marked testimony of its appreciation ; for, when the second attempt to force a revenue system upon the colonies was made, and the government was ransacking archives and libraries for justification, a second edition was put into the market, bearing the timely date of 1767. If, as it was openly asserted at the time, this was done by certain friends and members of the administration, the conclusion is a strong one, that the government had at least adopted Gee's suggestion, if it had not, in the first instance, inspired it.

Any doubts of the suggestion being acceptable to the British public are sought to be dispelled by the editor, who informs us that "this valuable treatise has for many years been scarce, though strongly recommended by the best judges and writers on trade." That "the principles upon which it was written continue with little variation," there is hardly need of asserting. The eagerness with which the public caught at the suggestion, betrayed its readiness to make it an accomplished fact, and the multiplication of the Acts of Trade and the occupation of every foot of colonial ground by their provisions, showed that Parliament was ready to burst through the bounds set by its own Act of Navigation. Since then there had been nothing done to counteract the poison, and the conclusion is forcible, that the principles upon which this book was written had continued with little variation to affect public opinion.

Thus these two writers betray the spirit which actuated the British public in its dealings with the colonies, and foreshadow the great change which was at last attempted by the Stamp Act. This spirit shows itself persistent and aggressive, and never more so than in the writings of *John Ashley.*

This writer came to the front during the reign of George II., in a work entitled "Memoirs and Considerations concerning the Trade and Revenues of the British Colonies in America, with Proposals for rendering those Colonies more Beneficial to Great Britain." It will not fail to catch the notice of the reader that the word Revenue is here boldly connected with the word Trade ; its connection with the latter part of this ominous title conveys a still more sinister disposition. The great point, in fact, in Ashley's treatise is *the advisability of colonial taxation for revenue*, and he dwells with ungracious energy upon the manner and the means by which it can be effected.[1] He is not one of those who sit down and cry out for Hercules to come and help them. He disdains the entangled logic of Child, and accepting that master's *ipse-dixits* as proven, busies himself only with their application. For him, as with Sir Josiah, charters are no barriers to the enforcement of Parliamentary enactments, and statutes being all-sufficient, there is nothing to be done but to execute them.

Here, in the literature bearing upon this subject from 1677 to 1767, a period of ninety years, we have the feelings and motives which actuated three generations of Englishmen, and the principles which governed them in their dealings with their colonies. In a word, we find disclosed in the writings of the times the public opinion of England respecting the nature of the colonies and their relations to the mother-country ; and we find them, too, set forth in such a way that there can be no mistaking the drift of that opinion. There can be no exaggeration, then, in saying that the sentiment which slighted the justly acquired franchises of generations and the sanctity of charters, was not friendly to the political constitution of the American dependencies.[2]

---

[1] See *post*.

[2] "If any man of the present age can read these authors and not feel his feelings, manners, and principles shocked and insulted, I know not of what stuff he is made. All I can say is, that I read them all in my youth, and that I never read one of them without being set on fire."—John Adams, "Life and Works," x, 336. And see "The Political and Commercial Works of Charles Davenant," ii, Discourse 3, "On the Plantation Trade."

It is not to be expected that the policy of mother-countries toward their colonies should be generous, but only that it should be just. In order to ensure that justice, and to define the relations existing between the parties with clearness and distinctness, are two great reasons why charters are given by the parent state to its offspring. These charters define the rights secured thereby to the colonists, and they bind the mother-country to observe them. As it is the interest of the latter to extend her possessions, the franchises are construed as inducements to emigration, which, it is therefore presumed, would not occur without them. Hence it is that, although the enlargement of the kingdom's bounds and the enhancement of its welfare are natural obligations under which the subject rests, the learned consider the charters to be contracts, notwithstanding no such naked contract can be technically said to exist between the sovereign and the subject.[1] Practically, how-

[1] *a.* "This pretended *grant* is but an acknowledgment of your antecedent right by nature and English liberty. You have no power or authority to alienate it. It was granted, or rather acknowledged, to your successors and posterity as well as to you, and any cessions you could make would be null and void in the sight of God and all reasonable men."—"Life and Works of John Adams," x, 355.

b. "Although the crown might not have a right to grant such exclusive privileges, yet the grants having once been made, and the colonists having settled upon the faith of them, they doubtless thereby acquire a sanction and an authority which nothing but the most urgent Necessity can justly alter. Though wrongly given, they are rightly established, and it would be much more wrong to take them away."—"A Short View of the New England Colonies," by Israel Mauduit, 4th ed., 7. Mauduit wrote in defence of the government's conduct toward Massachusetts: his testimony, therefore, to the contract nature of the charters, being in spite of his feelings, acquires extraordinary weight.

c. "I think it is plain, if the crown resumes the charters, it will take away the whole it gave, and deprive the patentees of the only recompense they were to have for their toil and fatigue, which they thought to have conveyed safe to their posterity. Could they have imagined this, could they have foreseen that their privileges were such transitory things as to last no longer than their work should be done and their settlement completed, they had never engaged in so hazardous and difficult an enterprise. They would never have departed from their native land, being neither criminals nor necessitous; and those countries which have since added so much to the wealth and greatness of the crown, might have been a barren wilderness to this day; or what is worse, and more probable, might have been filled with French colonies, whereby France would have reigned sole mistress of North America."—Dummer's "Defence of the New England Charters," 20, 21.

d. "The original contract between the king and the first planters there, was a royal promise in behalf of the nation, and which till lately it was never questioned but the king had a power to make, that, if the adventurers would at their own cost and charge, and at the hazard of their lives and every thing dear to them, purchase a new world, subdue a wilderness, and thereby enlarge the king's dominions, they and their posterity should enjoy all the rights, liberties, and privileges of his Majesty's natural born subjects within the realm."—Extract from a "Letter of the House of Representatives of Mass. Bay to their Agent, Dennys de Berdt." 4, 5. Lond. 1770.

ever, they are so far contracts that even men like Child admitted their existence as such, and one would naturally expect from an element so dependent upon contracts as trade is, some respect for them. Not a trace of it, however, is to be found in the works discussed ; and it is only too apparent that the British merchant, for whose interest the Restrictive System was created, looked upon a colony with no more humane feeling than that with which Le Sage's grandee looked upon Mexico.

Before proceeding to the legislation of Parliament, to which our next steps should naturally incline us, it may be well, at this point, to revert to the system which has already been unveiled by the enactments and the treatises just discussed, and draw therefrom some further considerations, especially such as affect the colonial relations with the mother-country and the policy it imposed upon the government.

The growth, then, of English commerce and the encouragement of English manufacture, was the avowed object of the colonial policy of Great Britain. The whole aim and scope of her legislation, as it was the first and last aim of her government, was to make the colonies feeders to British trade. It was for this, that, coeval with the re-enactment of the Navigation Act, a Board of Trade for the colonies was established, and it was for this that the Acts of Trade followed thick and fast ; and so emphatically was this the end and being of the colonies, that Lord Chatham, than whom none knew better the commercial nature and policy of Great Britain, declared in Parliament, that, were he to have his way, he would not permit them to manufacture so much as a hob-nail.

Trade being the motive, the Act of Navigation was the cornerstone upon which was built the whole policy of Great Britain toward her colonies. Indeed, it may be said, that the policy consisted in nothing else than what would give effect to this enact-

---

e. " The American charters are of a higher nature, and stand on a better foot, than the corporations in England. For these latter were granted on improvements already made, and therefore were acts of mere grace and favor in the crown ; whereas the former were given as premiums for services to be performed, and therefore are to be considered as grants upon a valuable consideration, which adds weight and strength to their title. To increase the nation's commerce and enlarge her dominions, must be allowed a work of no little merit, if we consider the hardships to which the adventurers were exposed ; or the expense in making their settlements : or, lastly, the great advantages thence accruing to the crown and nation."—Dummer's " Defence," etc., 11, 12.

ment, and that it was contained in the simple term, the Restrictive
System.   This system was purely artificial.   It contemplated that
all American products were to go to England in the first state, or
raw, and that nothing was to return thence but what was in the
last state, or finished.   This was the controlling principle which
made the entire system of colonial regulation restrictive.   The
government was not slow in reflecting popular desire, and the
cabinets, seeking popularity where it could easiest be found,
were, one after another, so possessed with the rage for regulation,
that it would seem as if no minister could come into office or go
out of it, without adding something to the existing restriction.
This principle of commercial monopoly, says Edmund Burke, runs
through no less than twenty-nine acts of Parliament, during the
period which, beginning in 1660, terminated in the unhappy year
of 1764[1]: the period heretofore referred to as the one in which
monopoly had passed from private hands to the public, from courtiers to the people.

Whatever the motive, then, which founded these colonies, the
enlargement of English trade and manufacture was what changed
the relations of the colonies to the mother-country and imposed a
new character upon them ; and it was this, too, which directed
the imperial policy in the control of them.   Massachusetts may
have owed its existence to motives purely religious, Georgia to
those purely humane, Rhode Island and Pennsylvania to those
both religious and humane ; nevertheless, be the sentiments that
brought them into life what they may, those sentiments were confined entirely within the bosoms of their founders and the members of the colonies.   They had no place anywhere else ; they
had no force to increase or decrease their political credit with
their rulers ; they were not such as relaxed their duty of allegiance, nor such as entitled them to the greater regard of the
crown ; and, in brief, they were not such political forces as should
modify in any respect the natural relations existing between all
colonies alike and the parent.   By their natural submission to
parental control and their dependence on the imperial power for
protection, the colonists admitted to the world their existence
as English colonies, their territories to be parts of the British
empire, and themselves to be British subjects.   This done, ac-

---

[1] "Speech on American Taxation."

quiescence to British rule became a duty which could not be absolved by mere whim or caprice, or by the simple fact that it had become onerous. Nothing but a violation by the parent of the original compact could justify a revolt,—a violation such as making the Restrictive System so exacting as to render life burdensome, or threatening the vitality of the local self-government. In either of these cases the consideration of the contract would be destroyed, and the resistance of the injured party even to revolt would be justified. But, before that stage is reached, it must be conceded, that the parent has a right, nay, that it is her solemn duty to regard her interests as the chief object of her policy, and that it is the duty of her offspring not only to acquiesce in such action but to further it : the more so, as in a natural and healthy state of society, what is the interest of one is likewise the interest of the other. So far these rules of action apply to the case in hand in purity and simplicity, but beyond this point they do not ; for growth and development affect the relations of colonies to the mother-country as growth and development modify those existing between the parent and child, and time inexorably brings along with it the changes which divide the responsibility between those, for one of whom it restricts the exercise of control, while for the other it enlarges the enjoyment of independence.

But, while in the condition of childhood, of pupilage, it is undeniable that the protected should yield acquiescence to her whose protection is still invoked ; and, as the parent has a perfect right to plant colonies for commerce, for defence, for relief from redundant population, in short, from any proper motive, and even change that motive as the contingencies of existence may demand, England cannot justly be censured for fostering colonial growth in the interest of what was her very life, her commerce. All censure must be reserved for the way in which this policy was enforced, and the excess to which it was carried.

Nor can it be urged that the colonists were compelled to settlement by force, or were entrapped therein by false pretences. As has already been seen, the English colonies were not directly planted by the government, like the ancient colonies, or those of France ; and, notwithstanding the lugubrious description of Child and the vagabondizing schemes of Gee, the mass of colonists gathered together on these shores, were not so much expelled by outraged society as they were attracted by the hope of gain.[1] Even the Puritans who sought New England, and the Catholics who founded Maryland, were not ejected from their native land. The settlers, therefore, who established these colonies cannot be said to have done so under compulsion, and, if they were exercising volition in this respect, much more were those who, inspired by the hope of bettering their condition, continued the unbroken stream of immigration long after this policy had been proclaimed to the world. These came from choice, with their eyes open, with a perfect knowledge of the policy which actuated the government toward its colonies, with a full comprehension of the Navigation Act, and with enduring loyalty in their hearts. It was, in fact, this very power of volition that so effectively enabled them to enjoy and express a contentment which, to us, to whom commercial freedom has become natural, is amazing. They came expecting to be in a condition of pupilage; they were by no means shocked at meeting what they anticipated and what they had deliberately sought, but were content. The shock came after they had proved their ability to take care of themselves, and when, in spite of the proofs they had given that their adolescence was terminated, the parent announced, that, now that they were able to live for themselves, they should live solely for her.

As for those who were born and bred in America, it is enough to simply state the fact of their being so born and bred, to account for their acquiescence in a system which must have seemed as natural to them as the air they breathed.

The inherent defect of the Restrictive System was, that it was artificial. The consequence was, that its existence and application depended upon Parliamentary enactments instead of upon natural laws. Nothing stood between the colonist and the ever augmenting demands of commerce but the wisdom of Parliament and the prudence of the administration. But inasmuch as Parliament represented the very people from whom the exactions came, it is evident that little dependence could be placed upon

---

[1] "The convicts were so few in comparative numbers as to exercise little or no tainting influence on the mass of the population." Ld. Mahon, "Hist. Engld." v, chap. xliii.

the self-control of that body, and that what protection the colonists could claim, must come from the throne and the administration. To whatever extent the opinions of the individuals which composed the different cabinets may have been affected by the demands of the commercial classes, it must nevertheless be acknowledged, that, down to the time of the Grenville administration, the attitude of that branch of the government was commendable ; and that, whatever the public opinion of England respecting the colonies might be, it respected their autonomies too much ever to lay its hand upon them, and appreciated their importance to British commerce too highly ever to assist in the work of over-exaction.

So impressed, indeed, was the government with the importance of the colonies to the commercial welfare of England, that it used every exertion to prevent the least disturbance of these harmonious relations. The *laissez-faire* policy, which, begot of indifference, had arisen of itself, and which, from necessity, was confirmed during the civil wars, was now maintained by the government as the best principle that could be devised for the conduct of its colonial relations, and the one to be applied without question to the political administration of the British possessions. No doubt of its being the true policy can now possibly exist. The prosperity of the colonies speaks for itself, and, in speaking for itself, emphatically commends that policy which left an energetic people to work out its own way.

Thus it will be seen, that, toward the American colonies, the conduct of the government was of a twofold character : in respect to commerce it was active, but in respect to politics it was passive. In the light of factories, the British possessions were constantly being " regulated." The activity of the government in this respect was as amazing as it was persistent : it could not do enough to satisfy the mercantile interest at home, though in the eyes of the colonists it was always doing too much. On the other hand, in the light of dominions, the action of the government toward the British possessions was altogether another affair. It was, indeed, hardly action at all. " Hands off ! " was its cry. " Let them alone ; no meddling ; they are doing better than we can do for them." In this the government took the broad ground that, politically, the colonies were mere dependencies, of whom the crown would exact no token of subordination, but allegiance, and to whom it would accord no right but that of protection.

It was the wisest colonial policy ever known unto men. It was the very same to which England, scarred by the loss the downfall of this policy inflicted, has since reverted with honor; the same for which Burke, Chatham, and Camden pleaded with the earnestness of fervid patriotism; the same which has since covered the northern shores of our great lakes with a contented, prosperous, and happy people, and dotted the huge globe itself with rising empires. Interest, of course, dictated this policy, which, happily, accorded with what was right, and prosperity flowed from a union blessed of God and man, until the subjection of right by interest tore asunder the bond that united them, and peace and good-will gave way to discord and hatred.

The happy condition of the colonies during the first era of their existence, and the tranquillity of their relations with the mother-country, were due entirely to this policy, which, by recognizing the superiority of self-directed forces, and by leaving them to find out their own way, acknowledged the natural relation of a Gothic offshoot to its stem. The fruits of this intuition were healthy and abundant, and the government was not blind to the fact. Not only did it recognize and advocate the *laissez-faire* policy, so far as the political administration of the colonies was concerned, but it went further, and resisted at the outset every attempt to substitute another. From time to time demands like those of Gee and Ashley, looking to the colonies as sources of revenue, were made, only to fall upon deaf ears. No matter what the party in power, the administration acted on the accepted maxim, that, though colonial *commerce* should be regulated, colonial *politics* were to be left to themselves. The Childs, the Gees, the Ashleys, screamed in vain for revenue, but the baneful influence of Lombard Street and the Treasury was of no avail; the caution of the crown resisted innovation,[1] and the government, keeping its eye

---

[1] As far as George II. was concerned, "although he consented to the statute and others which he thought sanctioned by his predecessors, especially King William, yet it was reported and understood that he had uniformly resisted the importunities of ministers, governors, planters, and projectors, to induce him to extend the system of taxation and revenue in America, by saying ' that he did not understand the colonies; he wished their prosperity. They appeared to be happy at present, and he would not consent to any innovations, the consequences of which he could not foresee.' Solomon in all his glory could not have said a wiser thing."—John Adams, " Life and Corresp.," x, 347.

steadily fixed on the one object for which the colonies were maintained, moved not an inch toward revenue, and was deaf to importunity. Of all the acts of trade, but one only was conceived
in the terms of a revenue act, and the haste with which the
government disavowed any political motive and explained away
the offensive terminology, lent emphasis to the purely commercial
character of its policy. The legislation, it is true, displayed the
influence of the wharves, but the merchants were consulted so
far only as commerce was concerned, and no further : the politicians were not even listened to with patience. "What," exclaimed
Sir Robert Walpole to Keith, lately Governor of Pennsylvania,
who was submitting a plan for raising revenue from the colonies,
" what ! I have Old England set against me, and do you think I
will have New England likewise ! " Walpole but echoed the fixed
maxim of Whitehall, " Let colonial politics alone ! " and no truer
thing was ever said, than that Mr. Grenville lost America by doing
what no other minister had ever done—reading the American
dispatches.[1]

The evil day fell upon Great Britain, when, tempted by the
rapidly increasing wealth of her American possessions, irritated
by the expressions of a desire for independence on the part of a
few politicians, and urged by the needs of an exchequer inadequate to her suddenly augmented armament, she first listened to
suggestions for making the provinces sources of revenue, and
then adopted them. It was a step which indicated the ascendancy of prerogative over chartered liberties, of absolutism over
the rights of kindred people, of centralization over local self-
government, of a policy, in a word, which was to annihilate their
local self-government, and place the fortunes of the colonies at
the mercy of the necessities of a fluctuating Treasury.[2]

For a moment the undisturbed tranquillity may have led the
government to suppose the measure unobjectionable, and to consider acquiescence as granted. But the unruffled calm was only
the silence of amazement, or of want of comprehension. Fixed
and rooted systems of administration are not torn up in a day,

---

[1] Ld. Orford's "Mems.," n. by Sir Denis le Marchant, ii, 69. Laboulaye,
" Hist. des Etats-Unis," ii, 32.

[2] " —— a resolution," said Lord Chatham afterward, in speaking of the Declaratory Act, " for England's right to do what the Treasury pleased with three
millions of freemen."—" Correspondence," ii, 365.

nor are they changed ordinarily from whim or fancy. In this case, as it will be seen, the first step was a modest one, its effect was not immediately appreciated, and it was not followed by any significant response. When, however, emboldened by the success of the first, the government announced its determination to take the second step, long, loud, and piercing was the cry that protested against its advance. At once this conduct was regarded as evidence of a total change of policy, whereby the compensation for commercial restriction was to be withdrawn and their local self-government extirpated ; the result of which would be, that, in the end, the colonies would remain the uncompensated feeders of British trade, and the colonists would become the unrequited bondsmen of British revenue and imperial power. Were such a policy to gain a foothold, two things, either of them intolerable, would ensue : on one hand, the colonists would be driven from the lofty position of self-government in which they took such pride, they would, in fact, be set back to the condition in which they were previous to leaving the old country, and would thus lose the headway made by more than four generations ; and, on the other, their obedience would be enforced to pecuniary exaction which would have no limits but those set by the forbearance which refrains from killing only so long as the eggs are laid. This touched their fortune ; that, their self-respect. If the right to raise money from them for imperial purposes were once conceded without limitation, as submission to unconstitutional legislation would imply, then their property lay at the mercy of the growing necessities of the empire ; if the right to intrusion in their affairs, such as would necessarily follow the enforcement of revenue acts, were granted, they would no longer possess the power of governing themselves. Tax-collectors, not their own, would swarm through the land ; courts, over which they had no control, would be established in their midst ; troops, to compel the execution of process issuing from these obnoxious tribunals, would be quartered among them ; and the provincial assemblies, overawed by the presence of organized force, would be dumb in their behalf, and would be powerless to resent insult ; or, worse than all, might actually be servile in lending help to oppression. Already their excited imagination pictured a monstrous growth, rising out of their very midst, under whose weight they would be helpless, and they saw themselves exposed to the burden of an establishment which, foreign to their tastes and sentiments, and hostile to their interests, would bring along with it all the enginery needful to the injury of those for whose benefit it ought only to exist. The right of self-government, without its enjoyment, would be but a mockery, and liberty, shaking the dust from off its feet against them, would fly their coasts.

Thus it was, that, before the wooden horse had fairly left the beach on its way toward the walls, before the first halt was over, and before the order for its further advance had died away, our ancestors broke forth into frantic clamor. What caused them to do so, can be gathered from what has been said heretofore, but the exposition will not be complete without first considering the legislation which reflected the sentiments that characterized the literature to which we have just given our attention.

PART III.

THE ERA OF CONSTITUTIONAL DEVELOPMENT IN AMERICA.

—— "*les révolutions que forme la liberté ne sont qu' une confir-mation de la liberté.*"

Esprit des Lois, liv. xix, chap. xxvii.

CHAPTER IX.

The Wooden Horse.

IT is unnecessary to enumerate all the different Acts of Parliament—though each served the purpose of irritating the general temper—by which "regulation" gradually encroached on rights that nature, time, and charters had all united in making sacred. It is sufficient to say, that the spirit of trade, presuming on its manifest supremacy, which, so far at least as Massachusetts is concerned, had received legislative acknowledgment in the adoption of the Navigation Act, fully carried out the law of its being, and that, invariably proceeding from much to more, it made one trespass the pretext for another, until restriction became onerous, compensation was fast diminishing, and exaction began to wear a threatening look. The system of restriction, in fact, had become so searching, so grasping, and so comprehensive, that, had it been rigidly enforced, the colonies could scarcely have traded at all. The Acts of Trade had followed each other thick and fast. Tobacco, rum, sugar, molasses; wool, fish, timber, and iron,—all, in the course of time, became the subject of English aggrandizement at colonial cost, until, according to Mr. Otis, not even a fleece of wool could be conveyed in a canoe across a river or a brook, without the risk of seizure and forfeiture. The statute book bristled with legislation shoring up the Navigation Acts and the Acts of Trade. As the former aimed at the control of commerce on the high seas, so these, their progeny, sought the control of provincial labor and internal trade.[1]

[1] Exporting wool, contrary to the regulations, involved forfeiture of ship, etc., 12 George II., c. 21, s. 11. No wool, or woollen manufacture of the plantations was to be exported, 10 and 11 Wm. III., c. 10, s. 19. Steel furnaces, slitting mills etc. were not to be erected in the plantations, 23 George II., c.

The result of all this was to excite alarm, and, from making the temper of the colonies sensitive to encroachment, to render it irritable. However, as the political rights of the colonies were untouched, dissatisfaction was limited to commercial exaction; though nothing can be plainer than that irritation respecting one thing, was apt, on the slightest provocation, to extend to another. Still, no one had the intention of doing more than, by protesting and by showing a bold front, to maintain chartered rights. It was when the anxiety of the colonies in reference to their commercial future was fully aroused, that there occurred what may well be called the forerunner of the Revolution. From the first it was no more than of the bigness of a man's hand, and it speedily resolved itself into thin air before the chilling blast of Otis' logic. But, nevertheless, it too plainly betrayed the drift of government, and the apprehension it left behind grew into actual alarm when more portentous clouds, one after another, rose above the horizon. It served the unfortunate purpose of raising the appearance of antagonism between the government and colonists, it placed them in the attitude of confronting each other, and set the latter to watching for encroachments, and pondering on the means of opposing them :—yet no such thing as actual conflict was so much as dreamed of by either. This harbinger of strife was the attempt of the government to enforce the Acts of Trade by Writs of Assistance.

In his work, previously alluded to, Ashley had made the following remarks : "The laws now in being for the regulation of the plantation trade, namely the 14th of Charles II., chap. 2, sec. 2, 3, 9, 10 ; 7 and 8 William III., chap. 22, sec. 5, 6 ; 6 George II., chap. 13,[1] are very well calculated, and were they put in execution as they ought to be, would, in a great measure, put an end to the mischiefs here complained of. If the several officers of the customs would see that all entries of sugar, rum, and molasses were made conformable to the directions of those laws ; and let every entry of such goods distinguish expressly, what are of British growth and produce, and what are of foreign growth and produce ; and let the whole cargo of sugar, penneles, rum,

---

29, s. 9. Hats were not to be exported from one colony to another, 5 George II., c. 22 ; nor were hatters to have more than two apprentices, 5 Geo. II., c. 22, s. 7. And furs were to be taken to Great Britain, 8 Geo. I., c. 15, s. 24.

[1] See Appendix F.

spirits, molasses, and syrup, be inserted at large in the manifest and clearance of every ship or vessel, under office seal, or be liable to the same duties or penalties as such goods of foreign growth are liable to, this would very much balk the progress of those who carry on this illicit trade, and be agreeable and advantageous to all fair traders. And all masters and skippers of boats in all the plantations should give some reasonable security, not to take in any such goods of foreign growth from any vessel not duly entered at the custom-house, in order to land the same, or put the same on board any other ship or vessel, without a warrant or sufferance from a proper officer. * * * In fine, I would humbly propose that the duties on foreign sugar and rum imposed by the before-mentioned act of the 6th of King George II. remain as they are, and also the duty on molasses, so far as concerns the importations into the sugar colonies ; but that there be an abatement of the duty on molasses imported into the northern colonies, so far as to give the British planters a reasonable advantage over foreigners, and what may bear some proportion to the charge, risk, and inconvenience of running it in the manner they now do, or after the proposed regulation shall be put in execution. Whether this duty shall be one, two, or three pence, sterling money of Great Britain, per gallon, may be a matter of consideration."

It is easy to see Ashley's idea : The trade with the West Indies, and the great demand from the continental colonies for sugar and the different articles derived from it, or into which it entered, made "the Molasses Acts," as they were called, very important ones. By these Acts it was provided, among other things, that molasses, rum, sugar, etc., brought from foreign colonies into the British American, should pay certain specified duties. The most important of these Acts was one enacted in the time of George II., and which is remarkable from the fact, that it was the only single Act of Trade, prior to the Stamp Act epoch, that contained the terminology of a revenue act. Revenue acts usually began by stating the reasons which called for the existence and the necessity of revenue, and always terminated this statement by saying, that, for remedy whereof, the Commons "have *given and granted*" to his Majesty the respective rates and duties thereinafter expressed. So rigorous was the application of this language, that it became technical, and had all the force technicality could give, and lawyer and statesman alike joined in pronouncing an act containing, in the customary relations, these significant words, a revenue act; while one wanting these words, was as emphatically declared not to be a revenue act. Positive as this rule may be, it may be modified by attendant circumstances; such as the language of the title, which, in revenue acts, always expressed the object to be "an aid to his Majesty," or something to that effect. The other acts specified by Ashley, of Charles II., and William and Mary, also gave duties; but in these neither their titles purported their being grants, nor did the words "give and grant" precede the enacting parts. Of course any interpretation of these as revenue acts, under the accepted rule, was out of the question, and as to the one of George the Second, the government listened with favoring ear to the construction put upon it by the colonies. This was, that, as the title, which was simply "an act for the better securing of the trade of his Majesty's sugar colonies in America," did not contain a single word from which a grant could be implied, but, on the contrary, purported only a commercial regulation; and inasmuch as the act was a kind of compromise, and, being enacted at the express desire of a part of the colonies themselves, might be said to be with their consent, therefore, it was the title that expressed the real meaning of those who called the act into existence, and its language should govern to the exclusion of the words of gift and grant which followed. This view, strained as it was, was promptly acquiesced in by the government, whose policy was to shun colonial politics, which such a thing as revenue plainly smacked of. It was dangerous ground, and they gladly made use of the bridge built for their retreat.

It is plain, that the government, by discarding its acquiescence and taking advantage of the terminology of the act of George II., would have a revenue act at hand, by which it could raise a large sum in the present, and on which it could build a system, which, like the future toward which it looked, would take care of itself. This is precisely the scheme of Ashley, who, at a dash of the pen, lumped the sugar acts, and made them all stand on the Act of George II. He knew that whatever the title of an act which contained words of gift and grant, or what the circumstances that produced it, really and truly it was, what Otis afterward asserted it to be, a revenue act, a taxation law. That it was an unconsti-

tutional law, a law subversive of every end of society and government, and that it was as good as null and void, and no better;
concerning this view of the enactment, he had nothing to say.
It stood ready at hand; its misinterpretation in the interests of
peace and good-will stood in the way, and to Ashley and the
crowd of revenue seekers at his back, it was only a part of the
system they wished to overturn, and no more.

So long as Ashley's aims were confined to Ashley, the colonists
cared little, but the knowledge that he was the latest exponent of
a class who were clamoring for American revenue, and who
might possibly gain the control of Parliament, made the thing
serious. However, the government continued to adhere to the
view it had adopted of the act of George II., until what was feared
by the colonists became reality, and the progeny of the Childs,
the Gees, and the Ashleys pushed its honorable policy from its
moorings. This deplorable event occurred when it was announced that "the Molasses Acts" would thenceforward be
strictly enforced. Great was the apprehension expressed in the
colonies, and great the alarm—"greater," says Judge Minot,[1]
"than the taking of Fort William Henry caused in the year 1757."
New England was thrown into a state of excitement, out of which
arose a case in the Massachusetts courts, in which the constitu-
tionality of this act, and even the Navigation and Trade Acts
themselves, was attacked by James Otis in a manner that will
render him immortal.

The question turned upon *writs of assistance*, which were process, as the lawyers term it, of occasional issue from the Court of
Exchequer in England. These writs imposed upon the customs
officers the odious task of intruding into the private affairs of the
defendants named in them, of entering private buildings and even
dwellings, and, once there, of breaking open chests, trunks, boxes,
or any thing that afforded a concealment for smuggled goods.
For, in an act of 14th Charles II., which had been extended to the
colonies, there was a clause authorizing this very violence, if committed by any one armed with a "writ of assistance under the
seal of his Majesty's Court of Exchequer." These warrants were

---

[1] "History of Massachusetts Bay," 140. "This I fully believe," says John
Adams, quoting the above words, "and certainly know to be true, for I was an
eye and ear witness to both of these alarms." "Life and Works," x, 345. For
Molasses Act, see Appendix E; 6 Geo. II., c. 13.

in the nature of those general warrants, which so shook the kingdom, a short time afterward, and were, of course, highly arbitrary.

It need hardly be said, that nothing could be more offensive to
a people, to whom the infraction of domestic privacy was almost
a thing unknown, than such a measure, and inquiry at once resolved itself into the questions : What are Writs of Assistance?
and Are they of force in Massachusetts?   The government lawyers were ready with such information as they had in answer to
the first question, but their efforts to answer the second affirma-
tively proved ludicrously futile before the overwhelming denial
maintained by Otis, whose argument was as follows :

First, he explained why he appeared in opposition to the crown
so shortly after being the Advocate-General in his Majesty's Court
of Admiralty.   This was, that his cause was in favor of British
liberty, and in opposition to a kind of power, the exercise of
which had already cost one king of England his throne, and
another his head.

He then advanced to a consideration of the natural rights of
man,—those individual rights which are inherent and inalienable,
and of which he proved the right of property to be one.   From
these rights, which belonged to individuals, he passed to those
belonging to society, and which, termed social rights, are likewise
natural and inalienable: for, the surrender of them would be of no
greater validity in point of evidence than are the acts of madmen
or those surprised by fraud, and, being therefore worthless, are of no
avail against the inalienability of these rights ; that, in short, such
rights are as natural and as incapable of divestiture as the others.

Having thus defined those individual and social rights which are
natural and inalienable, he showed how, from time immemorial,
they had been recognized and protected by the British Constitution as fundamental laws ; how, indeed, the Constitution itself
was founded on them, and he called to the proof of his position
the whole range of British legislation and British exploit, from the
old Saxon laws and Magna Charta to the Bill of Rights and the
Revolution of the seventeenth century ; how, as British subjects,
the colonists were as much entitled to all the rights of British
freemen by the law of nature, the Constitution, and the express
guarantees of the colonial charters, as the freemen of England
were ; and how no fiction of law, such as that of "virtual represen-

tation," nor any thing else, was of the least avail against these
rights.

Thus claiming for the colonists, from the outset, the birthrights
of an Englishman, he proceeded to take up, one by one, the Acts
of Trade, and demonstrated, that, if they were to be enforced as
revenue laws, there was an end at once to all security of property,
liberty, and life, to every right of nature, to the English Constitution and to the Charter of the province. He scouted the distinction, then so popular and commonplace, between "external and
internal taxes," and asserted that there was no such distinction in
theory, nor upon any principle but that of "necessity." That
the need of having the commerce of the empire under one direction, was obvious, and that so sensible had the Americans been of
this necessity, that they had actually tolerated the distinction between external and internal taxes, and had submitted to the Acts
of Trade as regulations of commerce ; but never, be it observed,
as taxations or as revenue laws. Nor had the government itself
regarded these enactments as revenue laws, but, on the contrary,
had never so much as attempted to enforce them as such, but had
suffered them to lie dormant in that character for wellnigh a
century. And well it did so ! for the whole power of Great
Britain would be ineffectual to enforce them. Nay, if the king of
England himself, were in person encamped on Boston Common,
at the head of twenty thousand men, with all his navy on our
coast, he would not be able to execute these laws. That it was
true, the Navigation Act was binding upon Massachusetts, but for
the reason only that Massachusetts had adopted it by her own act.
He then commented on this statute, and, while he would not deny
its efficacy as a political policy, nor even controvert the necessity
of it, he expatiated on its narrow, selfish, and exclusive spirit.
He declared, that the act of its adoption and the obedience rendered unto it were a sacrifice to the mother-country on the part of
the colonies, and that it was sufficient to satisfy the cupidity of any
mother, especially one whose children had always been so fondly
disposed to acknowledge the condescending tenderness of that
mother.

Considering the nature of the Navigation Act, he said, that it
was wholly and simply prohibitory. It abounded indeed with
penalties and forfeitures, and with bribes to governors and in-

formers, to custom-house officers, naval officers, and commanders, —but it imposed no taxes. Subsequent acts of trade contained these in abundance, but this act laid none. Nevertheless, this was one of the acts that were to be carried into strict execution by writs of assistance, and houses were to be broken open, and if a piece of Dutch linen could be found, from the cellar to the cockloft, it was to be seized, and become the prey of governors, informers, and majesty.

Then recurring to the Acts of Trade, which were the progeny of the Navigation Act, he pointed out the different features which marked the offspring. These, he contended, did impose taxes; enormous, burdensome, ruinous, intolerable taxes. And here giving a loose reign to his genius, he launched out into bitter invective against the tyranny of taxation without representation. One after another, these acts were taken up, scrutinized, analyzed, criticised, only to be flung to the winds with scorn. The burden of his song was, " writs of assistance." All these rigorous statutes were now to be enforced by the still more rigorous instruments of arbitrary power. What were writs of assistance ? Where were they to be found ? When, where, and by what authority had they been invented, created, established ? No one could answer. Neither the Chief Justice nor his associates had ever seen such a writ, or knew any thing about it. Otis declared boldly, that there was no such a thing known to the law of the land ; and neither bench nor bar ventured to confute him. He went farther, and asserted that there was no color of authority for this writ, except in one statute offered by the crown officers, and that one contained the words, " writ of assistance under the seal of his Majesty's Court of Exchequer." There being such a thing, then, exclaimed Otis, where is your seal of his Majesty's Court of Exchequer !   And what has the Court of Exchequer to do here ?

Since the writ had no such seal, and inasmuch as, even if it had, the jurisdiction of the Court of Exchequer did not extend to the colonies and therefore could give it no force, and, further, as no tribunal or office existed, which, by law or implication, could. be construed as taking the place of such court, and from which such writ could issue, the questions were unanswerable, and no reply was given.

In tossing over the acts from which the crown lawyers pretended to derive the writs of assistance, Otis had much sport. He allowed his humor, wit, and irony free play, when the acts regulating the trade of Bay-making in Colchester, and of Kidderminster stuffs, and prohibiting the importation of bone-lace, cutwork, embroidery, fringe, band-strings, buttons, and needlework, were gravely offered in support of a writ which neither Rastell, Coke, nor Fitzherbert, could show. Upon the principle of construction which would make precedents of these and similar enactments, he argued that the jurisdiction of the Court of King's Bench, and of the Court of Common Pleas might be extended to the colonies ; and all the sanguinary statutes against crimes and misdemeanors, and all the church establishment of archbishops and bishops, deans and chapters, priests and deacons, and all the statutes of uniformity, and all the acts against conventicles.

He admitted, of course, that writs of one kind may be legal ; that is, a special writ, directed to a special officer, and to search certain houses specially set forth in the writ. Such a writ could be granted by the Court of Exchequer in England, upon oath made before the Lord Treasurer by the person who asks it, that he suspects such goods to be concealed in those very places he desires to search. And in this light the writ appears like a warrant from a Justice of the Peace to search for stolen goods. In the old books are precedents of general warrants to search suspected houses, but in the modern books only special warrants are to be found, and it has been adjudged that special warrants only are legal. In the same manner he relied upon it, that the writ prayed for in the petition in question, being general, was illegal. In the first place, then, the writ before them being universal, or general, every one with this writ might be a tyrant. In the next place, it was perpetual. There was no return to be made, and thus the holder of it was accountable to no one, and might reign secure in his petty tyranny. In the third place, a person with this writ might enter all houses, shops, etc., in the daytime, at will, and command all to assist him. Fourthly, by this writ, not only deputies, but even their menial servants could lord it over the people. Now one of the most essential branches of English liberty is the freedom of one's house. A man's house is his castle ; and so long as he is quiet, he is as well guarded as a prince in his castle. This writ, if declared legal, would totally annihilate this right.   Bare suspicion without oath would be sufficient, and that the wanton exercise of this power was not the chimerical suggestion of a heated brain, he gave instances of it which had actually occurred in the neighborhood.

Reason and the Constitution, then, were both against this writ. Only one instance of it could be found in the law-books, and that was in the zenith of arbitrary power, during the reign of Charles II., when star-chamber powers were pushed to extremity by some ignorant clerk of the exchequer.   But, had this writ been in any book whatever, it would have been illegal.   All precedents are under the control of the principles of law, and no Act of Parliament can establish such a writ, for an act against the Constitution is void.   The act of William III., therefore, is confined to the sense of special writs : that an officer should show probable ground ; should take his oath of it ; should do this before a magistrate ; and that such magistrate, if he think proper, should issue a special warrant to a constable to search the place.   Any thing and every thing in the nature of a general warrant was void and of no effect.

He did not, however, stop here, but turning to the literature illustrative of the spirit which animated the Acts of Trade, and would enforce their execution as revenue laws, he paid his compliments, in no measured terms, to the galaxy in which shone a Child, a Gee, and an Ashley. " I cannot pretend," says John Adams, from whom we have the only report of this argument worthy of the name,—" I cannot pretend to remember these observations verbatim and with precision. I can only say that they struck me very forcibly : Tacitus himself could not express more in fewer words." Otis had no thanks for the knight for his compliments to New England at the expense of Virginia, and he stigmatized, as it deserved, the inference, that colonies were to be sacrificed for being industrious and frugal, wise and virtuous, while others were to be encouraged and fostered for laziness, vice, and profligacy.   But when he came to the part William had acted in this business, the scorn of the orator burst forth : A Stadtholder adopting the system of St. John and Downing, of Child and Charles the Second ; a system having for its result the destruction of his native country, to which he owed not only his existence, but all his power and importance besides ! Proh Pudor !

The very effigies of the Stuarts that beamed from the walls of the council chamber must have wreathed their smiles in disdain of the Dutch apostate.

Turning to the laws relating to the internal policy of the colonies and their domestic manufactures, Otis alternately laughed at and raged against them all. One member of Parliament, he said, had declared that even a hob-nail should not be manufactured in America ; another had moved that the Americans should be compelled by act of Parliament to send their horses to England to be shod—but this last was a man of sense, and meant by this admirable irony to cast ridicule on the whole selfish, partial, arbitrary and contracted system of Parliamentary regulation in America. Every one of these regulations of internal policy he pronounced null and void by the law of nature, by the English Constitution, and by the American charters, because America was not represented in Parliament.

This led him to remark upon the charters, whose history he glanced at, and from which he drew the conclusion, that, as neither James I. nor Charles I. could have wished the Parliaments they hated to share with them the government of the colonies and the enjoyment of royal prerogatives ; and as neither Pym, Hampden, Sir Harry Vane, nor Cromwell could surely have desired the subjection of a country they had once regarded as an asylum, to the arbitrary jurisdiction of the one they had wished to fly from, it must have been to Charles II. and his yearning for a personal government that we owed the royal assent to the Navigation Act in which King and Parliament were associated together. That association, he maintained, was forced on a monarch who had learned from doleful experience that Parliaments were not to despised, but who, though compelled to a union he abhorred, accepted it with the purpose of making his coadjutor his instrument in the accomplishment of his designs. Charles II., he said, courted Parliament as a mistress ; his successors embraced her as a wife, at least for the purpose of enslaving America. From that unhappy union had flowed all the ill which a Parliamentary government, not their own, could inflict. In short, the attempt now being made was simply one of arbitrary power against the natural self-government of the people.   Suffer it to be done, and colonial liberty was at an end.[1]

Such is the imperfect sketch of an argument which placed its maker, at one bound, at the head of colonial advocates, elevated him to a place in the highest rank of patriots, and enrolled him among the Americans whose fame is deathless.   This is all that is left to us of what produced a most powerful effect upon those who heard it, and of what unquestionably changed the destiny of this country.   We cannot possibly now reproduce this speech from what we have of it.   It was not committed to writing, nor was it reported.   All we have are the notes jotted down at the time by a young man, who, swayed by the overpowering eloquence of the orator, was unable to keep up with his work; the partial reproduction of the speech by the same youth in after life,[2] and his recollections, given when an octogenarian and fifty-seven years after its delivery.   Yet even then, though in the meantime he had himself become one of his country's greatest orators, and was one to whom the eloquence of the greatest and best of the civilized world had become familiar, even then the breast of the old man was instinct with the memories of that day, and the aged heart of John Adams was fired anew at the recollection of James Otis' denunciation of the writs of assistance. After that lapse of time, the wonder is, not that we have an imperfect sketch, but that we have any, and were it not for the remarkable intellect of him who sought to transmit it, we should have none.

Whether the colonists, whose prejudices were naturally in favor of the orator, exaggerated the excellence of his speech, or, whether, astonished and delighted at such unaccustomed elo-

---

[1] In giving this sketch of Otis' speech, I have adopted as nearly as possible the notes and accounts of John Adams, even in language.   Adams made minutes of the speech during its delivery, though, as he says in his autobiography, " I was much more attentive to the information and the eloquence of the speaker than to my minutes, and too much alarmed at the prospect that was opened before me to care much about writing a report of the controversy."   " Diary, Life and Works," ii, 124, n.   Then comes the speech as given in Minot's " History," which may be found, expurgated from interpolations, in the same work, Appendix A, 523.   This is also attributed to Mr. Adams.   And lastly, his sketch of it given in his letters to Judge Tudor, fifty-seven years after its delivery, which are to be found in the same work, x, pp. 314, *et seq.*

[2] *Id.* ii, Appendix A, 523.

quence, they magnified its worth, we have now no means of judging. There is, however, no mistaking its effect. The judge appointed for the purpose of sanctioning the writ was dumb before the orator, the bar hung upon every word, the audience was still to catch every breath, and his very opponent, once his master in the law, could not conceal his delight in meeting a foeman so worthy of his steel, nor restrain his generous exultation at the glory and triumph of his pupil.

But it was upon the people throughout the colonies that this speech wrought its greatest effect ; an effect which deepened its channel as it made its way. The patience which had taken apart, analyzed and compared the different statutes, and then had gathered them together into one system, had not been wasted. The clearness with which the facts were stated and the inferences drawn, had not been in vain. The passionate appeal to justice fell not to the ground, nor did the scorn which lashed the evil-wishers of his country lie dead in the ears of its friends. Although the question was one which arose in Massachusetts only, its importance was felt to the uttermost bounds of the colonies. Attention was at once turned upon the subject of colonial relations with the mother-country ; a subject which nearly all had slept upon, until Otis broke this dangerous slumber, and bade them awake. Then all awoke : those who were not of the mercantile interest as well as those who were ; and these relations, what they were, what their nature, were they proper, and, if not, what the remedies readiest for their restoration, but, if they were, what the defences best for their protection,—these, and a hundred questions more, became the subjects of universal comment and reflection. Henceforth it will be seen not only that the colonists acted as those who had studied their ground, but that the indifference or ignorance of the old world concerning their attainments, or even their existence, gave way to admiration for the extent of their researches and the depth of their learning. This result, especially in the northern colonies, where the illustration stood ready for the argument, was due to the eloquence and logic of James Otis. When he sat down the American Revolution had been inaugurated. Doubtless neither he, his hearers, the people, nor the government, suspected such a thing : but we now know it to be the fact. The war which, in securing our independence, gained the name of Revolution, was but the last expression of that mighty change of which Otis' was the first. That terminated what this began,[1] but this was what foretold the coming storm, and the last words of the orator had hardly died away, before the real American Revolution had set in.[2]

---

[1] Les révolutions que conforme la liberté ne sont qu' une confirmation de la liberté." " Esprit des Lois," liv. xix, chap. xxvii.

[2] "I shall only say, and I do say in the most solemn manner, that Mr. Otis' oration against the Writs of Assistance breathed into this nation the breath of life." "Life and Works of John Adams," x, 276.

CHAPTER X.

The Conflict with Absolutism.

AT the next term the court decided, that, inasmuch as it appeared that such writs issued from the Exchequer when applied for, the like practice in the province was warranted[1]; yet the government found no advantage in a decision robbed beforehand of its effect. It, accordingly, desisted from this attempt, and, while there may have been applications, no such writ ever issued.

The government held the position, but could make no use of it further than as a ground on which to parade the rights adjudicated in their favor by judges, whom the irritated people regarded as commissioned for the purpose of deciding as they did. This half-way course of action was the most ill-judged one that could be adopted. One only of two things should have been done : either to enforce the writ now that the court had decided they were in the right, or openly to abandon a policy which had been proved to be odious. If the former had been adopted, the colonists would have at once been driven to submission or resistance. Resistance was out of the question, for the cause of Massachusetts not being a common one, except in sentiment not yet fully formed, she would have had to stand alone, and, incapable of resisting singly, submission would have been her fate, and the power of the government would have been established. If the latter course had been pursued, Massachusetts would have had nothing to oppose, but on the contrary there would have been every consideration of gratitude to bind her with hooks of steel to a parent who, with the right to pursue her course solemnly adjudicated, had

---

[1] Hutchinson's "Hist. of Mass.," iii, 94.

generously renounced a policy distasteful to her offspring. But, the truth is, that the government did not fully appreciate the importance of the occasion and the need of discretion. Three thousand miles of ocean and the lapse of a month's duration so deadened the waves of colonial excitement, that, when they fell upon the ear in Whitehall, they hardly created a sensation. The government was continually seeking increase of revenue in one quarter or another, and disappointment was a common affair. This Boston matter was one of a dozen such cases, and no more. " The people do not like this way of raising revenue, though the courts say we are right! Well, we are constantly humoring others, and we suppose we must humor these. Do not act on this decision of the court, then, but hold it in reserve, and, in the meantime, let us try something else." Such was, in effect, the way the matter was regarded and acted upon, and, like all half-measures, this indefinite way of settling a question produced bitter fruit. To the Bostonians, this pigeon-holing what to them was of the greatest interest and of the highest importance, was either incomprehensible or offensive. Was the government irresolute ? was it indifferent? Was it letting I would, wait upon I dare not ? Had it abandoned the offensive policy? or was it holding it like a sword over their heads in case future exactions brought no favorable answers ?

During this state of uncertainty a general sense of uneasiness spread over the colonies. For the first time something had really come between the mother and her children, and distrust had taken root. The attempt to enforce the Sugar Acts as revenue laws could not be forgotten in a day ; indeed, there was nothing to hinder its repetition, and it was but too apparent, that, instead of being one and the same with that of England, the spirit of the colonies was now something different. Dissension had entered the camp, and, though there was no conflict, there were, without contradiction, two parties whose leaders, while on their faces friends, mistrusted each other in their hearts, and sulked in their tents. Confidence was gone. What will the government do next? was the apprehensive whisper throughout America. What next step toward revenue from the colonies shall we take ? was the question asked at Westminster.

George Grenville, at that time the leader of the ministry, was

the man who answered these questions. He was intelligent, educated, well-meaning, honest, and of official experience, but he was
narrow. He was ambitious, but lacking in judgment, and was
more disposed to found the acts of his administration on legislation,
than on the qualities of human nature. Indeed, his great fault
seems to have been his over-weening faith in legislation being the
do-all of government; for he was of those, says Burke, who are apt
to believe regulation to be commerce, and taxes to be revenue,[1]
and, he might have added, who believe legislation to be government. Among regulations, none stood so high in Grenville's
estimation as the Navigation Act, and, confounding causes with
effects, like many of his countrymen, he considered those elements
of prosperity which gave efficacy to the Navigation Act, the legitimate results of the Act itself.

Mr. Grenville's idea seems to have been, that the late war between England and France had been undertaken as much for the
benefit of the colonies as for that of Great Britain, and that it was
nothing more than just, that they who shared the benefits should
also bear a part of the burdens it had brought. No position
could be more substantial than this, and, had he confined himself
to it, no fault could have been found ; for their sense of oneness
with Great Britain, as we can see for ourselves, did impress them
with the belief, that what was done for the mother-country was
done, too, for them, and that, consequently, the burden must be
shared as well as the benefit. But when he took the ground, that
the colonies had not done their share, but were reaping the benefit without dividing the burden, he went further than the facts
warranted his going, and his position became untenable. For, in
the prosecution of that war, as well as others, the Americans had
not only suffered great losses of men and property, but they had
incurred debts, the greater part of which fell on the northern
colonies, who had promptly met them, and who, even at that time,
were steadily paying them off. This very colony of Massachusetts, for instance, at the time of the Port Duty act, was annually
raising what, for the time and place, was the large sum of £37,500
sterling for sinking her debt, and this she expected and intended
to do for four years longer, or until it was entirely cleared off.

Thus Mr. Grenville acted on premises that were radically

---

[1] Speech "On American Taxation."

wrong. He beheld what did not exist, and saw not what did. What alone was perfectly clear to him, was his inability to meet the annual demands of the public debt, and the scene presented to his eyes embraced an enlarged military and naval establishment on a new footing, an enormous increase of Great Britain's indebtedness, and an insufficient revenue.[1] Beyond this valley of Desolation, however, stretched the pleasant land of Beulah, where the colonists, untaxed for revenue, were rapidly rolling up wealth. To a man whose notions of prosperity were limited to the effects of a Navigation Act, the sight was tantalizing, and the thought naturally recurred, Why should these people go scot free, while we are still bearing the burdens imposed by their defence?

Now, as we have seen, they were not going scot free; for these people were at that time bearing their share of the burden by paying debts, to sink which they were annually taxing themselves; were paying vast profits to England on their trade, which, without her, they would not have had to pay; and were subject to enormous indirect taxation besides.[2] Nor was that war nor any other, fought for the defence of the colonies, but solely for the purposes of the home government; purposes with which the colonists had no more to do than the people of the United States to-day have to do with those of Downing Street, but which they were compelled to further, unless they would have their commerce endangered, their frontiers ablaze, and their homes at the mercy of the savage. In America, the armies of England were not defensive but invading armies, and, for the purpose of defence, the colonist had to rely upon himself alone. But it is none the less a fact, that, at that time, the burden of the colonists was really lighter than the burden of those who had caused its imposition; for, with their debts reduced by actual payment, and with the future certain to supply what was needed for their extinction, they had nothing but a short probation of indebtedness to undergo, and nothing more to fear than creditors whose only ill-nature might arise from the impending termination of loans they could not expect to renew. This happy result had been attained by their having promptly

---

[1] The English debt was doubled by the expenses of the war, and amounted to £140,000,000.—Parl. Hist.: "Mag. of Am. Hist.," 341. Burke's "Speech on American Taxation."

[2] The colonies annually consumed British produce and manufactures to the value of £3,000,000.—"Am. Reg.," part 1, 1764.

faced and ascertained their liabilities, by their careful collection of taxes, by their economy, by the assistance brought by immigration, and by the absence of internal distraction which the confidence, everywhere reposed in charters guarding them in their rights and exempting them from imperial taxation, secured. Thus it will be seen, that the colonists, whose generous conduct during the war found its acknowledgment in the reimbursements to them by Great Britain of advances made by them,[1] were now bearing the part of their burden which remained, and that, though the mother-country might not be, they were entitled to the full enjoyment of their share of the benefits accrued, less their share of the common burden still remaining. It was the sight of this enjoyment, almost at its full, and the contrast it presented to her

---

[1] "26 April, 1759. The King sent a message to the House of Commons requesting them to enable him to compensate the North American colonies for 'the expenses incurred by the respective Provinces, in the Levying, Clothing, and Pay of the troops raised by the same.' The motive assigned was 'the zeal and vigor with which his faithful subjects in North America have exerted themselves in defence of His Majesty's just rights and Possessions.' Upon which, April 30, the House resolved an appropriation of £200,000. This message and resolution was repeated yearly thereafter, and though this compensation did not exceed one-fourth of their expenditure, they were satisfied with 'these most honorable of all testimonies.' "—"A True State of the Proceedings," etc., 1774.

As early as the beginning of the century, concerning New England's action respecting the Canada expeditions, Dummer says : " It has been acknowledged to me by English gentlemen who were then on the spot and well experienced in these things, that such a fleet and army wanting the necessaries they did, could not have been dispatched on so short warning from any port in England."— "Defence of the N. E. Charters," 40 ; and see Otis' "Vindication," etc., 9.

" Massachusetts raised 500 men for the Cuba [Jamaica, 1703] expedition, of whom not 50 returned."—" Observations relating to the Present Circumstances of Mass. Bay," 4. " The most expensive expedition was that to Cape Breton, in which Massachusetts expended almost 2,000,000, old tenor, a sum vastly exceeding its ability, and which nothing but the last extremity could excuse : an extremity not only affecting Massachusetts, but the whole continent besides, and in which *the trade of the English nation, both with regard to the cod fishery, and also its Navigation to the Northern Colonies, was deeply interested.* In this Expedition we almost made ourselves Bankrupts, not only with respect to money, but also with regard to Labour, the worst bankruptcy that a community can suffer ; for we expended thousands of lives, which were lost on the surrender of Louisburg, who were some of the Flower of the People.

"Another expedition in which we were at great expense was that designed for Canada, and recommended from the Crown, and although the scheme was not executed, yet Bounty money and billeting 2,000 men could be very ill spared by a people already drained of men and money."—*Id.*, 4, 5.

The colonists rallied to the support of Pitt with enthusiasm. They vied in voting men and money. Dr. Franklin says that the number of Americans or Provincials employed in the war was greater than that of the regulars, and elsewhere, that " the Colonies had raised, paid, and clothed near 25,000 men, a number equal to those sent from Great Britain, and far beyond their proportion."—" Mag. of Am. Hist.," i, 338, 339.

own condition, that had much to do with stimulating England to take from America what the latter had earned and was fairly entitled to.

It has always been a marvel, and one, too, that will never be explained, how the eyes of the minister could have been blind to the fact, which stared him in the face on each recurring budget, that the Americans had really borne more than their share of the war, and that Great Britain was so sensible of this, as actually to reimburse them for their over-payments. But so it was, and possessed with the conviction, that, on the score of the war, it was America that was in debt to England and not England to America, he set to work to devise means of drawing revenue from the colonies.

It will be observed, that, heretofore, the administration had limited its experiments to what already existed, and, seeking to enforce those acts of revenue only which were then upon the statute book, had directed its procedure against a single colony. The boundaries of its operations were thus defined beforehand, and, notwithstanding the lack of absolute certainty, this self-imposed restraint lent some assurance to the future. The cabinet, however, was not permitted to long retain the passive attitude it had assumed after its failure. The need of revenue daily became more pressing, until at last something had to be done and a decisive step be taken : a bill was accordingly introduced and passed "granting duties in the colonies and plantations of America." This occurred in 1764, and the act imposed other port duties than those already laid. Strange to say, the enactment of this bill, known as the *Port Duty Act* provoked little censure in America, although, in addition to its ominous title, it declared, "that it was just and necessary that a *revenue* should be raised there," and contained the positive words of donation, namely, "giving and granting"; and this, too, notwithstanding the wording of the preamble, that the Commons were "desirous to make *some* provision in the *present* session of Parliament *towards* raising the said *revenue*," should have warned the colonists that Parliament, which thus asserted its supremacy, was already committing their fortunes to the uncertain fluctuations of future need. Such, however, was the fact, and expressions soon to be recurred to in wrath and passion fell almost unnoticed.

This marvel may be accounted for by reason of the attack not being a direct one, by the principle not being objectionable, by the process being one to which the colonists were more or less accustomed, and by the distinction between external and internal taxes operating in its favor. Thus, though disguised by a new title and differing in features from its predecessors, the measure met with customary recognition.[1] The most probable reason, however, is, that it was lost to view or confounded with what appeared simultaneously with it, and which, applying to all the colonies alike, raised such a gust of passionate protestation, that every thing that concerned the subject was borne before the blast in one commingled cloud. A great storm was now impending.

This commotion was excited by the passage of a *Resolution* which set forth, that, in the colonies, "it may be proper to charge certain stamp duties as are now paid in England," and which contained a notice that a bill to that effect would be introduced during the ensuing year.

Mr. Grenville cannot certainly be charged with making haste to do evil. His march was as deliberate as was his determination to cast off the old policy and to adopt the new. Under the guise of giving the colonies ample notice to adapt their affairs to the new order of things, he reserved to himself all the time he desired to observe the effect of his shot. It must not be supposed, however, that he was wedded to Stamp duties to the exclusion of any other means of raising revenue. These were adopted only because they appeared at the time to be the best of all the means

---

[1] Burke, "Speech on Am. Taxation." In Massachusetts, however, where Otis had enlightened the people, the protest was emphatic enough, as the following resolution of its Assembly shows:—"That the sole right of giving and granting the Money of the people of that province was vested in them as their legal representatives ; and that the imposition of Duties and Taxes, by the Parliament of Great Britain, upon a people who are not represented in the House of Commons, is absolutely irreconcilable with their rights. That no man can justly take the property of another without his consent, upon which original principle the right of representation in the same body which exercises the power of making laws for levying taxes, one of the main Pillars of the British constitution, is evidently founded : That the extension of the Powers of the Court of Admiralty within this Province is a most violent infraction of the trial by Jury,—a right which this house, upon the principles of their British Ancestors, hold most dear and sacred, it being the only security of the lives, liberties, and property of his Majesty's subjects : That this House owe the strictest allegiance to his most sacred Majesty, King George III.—and that they have the greatest veneration for the Parliament." "A true State of the Proceedings in the Parliament, and in the Mass.-Bay," 5, 6.

proposed. He was perfectly willing to substitute another which would produce the same results, and he even assured a member of Parliament, as well as the agents of the colonies, whom he brought together for the purpose, that, if they would name any other duty equally productive, but more to their taste, he would readily comply with their wishes. One thing, though, was to be well understood, that this was only a choice of taxes, and must not become a question of principle, for on that point his mind was made up, and if the Americans objected to being taxed by Parliament, they might save themselves the trouble of discussing what he had already determined upon.[1]

After this curt announcement that the ancient system, which regarded the colonies as tributary to England only in respect of commerce, was at an end, and that the government had already substituted another under which they were to be viewed likewise as sources of revenue, there was nothing left for the colonists to do but to look out for themselves. The feeling which was aroused by the news burst forth at once from every part of the land. Unlike the case of the Writs of Assistance, this was a measure which concerned all the colonies alike.[2] The colonists everywhere took but one ground—that their territory was a part of the British Empire; that they themselves were British subjects; that Britons could not be taxed without representation; that they were not represented; and that, consequently, this Act, in taxing them without their consent, was illegal and tyrannical.[3] Should the secretary of state request aid, as heretofore, in the king's name, their legislatures would grant it; but that must be their own act, and not another's. The tribal love of self-government had never before spoken out more distinctly or more positively. Massachusetts and New York sent remonstrances—they were laid on the table; Connecticut, Rhode Island, Virginia, South Carolina, and

[1] "In regard to the fifteenth resolution relating to the Stamp duty, it will certainly pass next session unless the Americans offer a more certain duty. Had not William Allen Esq., been here indefatigable in opposing it, and happily made acquaintances with the first personages in the Kingdom and the greater part of the House of Commons, it would certainly have passed this session." "Lett. fr. London," *N. Y. Mercury*, June 4. 1764. And see Ld. Mahon's "Hist. Engd.," chap. xliii, and Burke's "Speech on Am. Taxation."

[2] See Otis' "Rights of the British Colonies Asserted and Proved"; though he admits the right to tax.

[3] See the "Virginia Resolves," passed the following spring.

Jamaica presented petitions—they were rejected in scorn without a reading, they were not so much as received, and, on the 22d of March, 1765, by a Parliament which had been deaf to Barré, and whose average attendance was not increased by the consciousness of any measure of especial importance being before it, the *Stamp Act* was passed,[1] and the members went tranquilly home. The ministry was delighted, and the king gave a joyful assent.

It was not until October, that England heard of the reception the Act was meeting in America ; and what she heard was simply amazing : Parliamentary absolutism had met a rebuff at the very outset. Had a volcano suddenly upheaved the quiet fields of Warwickshire, the spectacle could not be more bewildering to English minds than what the drowsy communities of merchants and planters across the Atlantic then presented. Commotion reigned from one end of the country to the other. Deep, intense feeling prevaded all ranks, and for a time, it appears, profound silence had brooded over the land. Then, as with a rush of mighty waters, the whole mass was in motion. Tolling bells called the people together, who, in injured tones, broke away from the calm expostulation of decorous petition, and spoke, in indignant accents, the broken utterances of outraged feelings. Sons of Liberty harangued clubs of patriots. Flags were at half-mast. Bands paraded the streets playing dirges. Death's heads grinned from the newspapers, above whose heavy black lines stretched a serpent in pieces, with the motto, "Join or Die !" Ships were stopped in the lower bays until search proved them harmless. The effigies of tax-collectors hung from trees ; those of a hated ministry went up in showers of sparks and cinders from pyres around which the rabble jeered and hooted. Mobs roared in the streets, and honored officials, whose only crime lay in the fact, that, if this obnoxious law were carried out, they were the ones to execute it, were cut by their neighbors, insulted by the populace, and at last forced to precipitate flight. Governors, the representatives of Majesty itself, leaped from the rear of buildings whose fronts were already smashed in, and whose contents, five minutes after, were piled in the mud in indistinguishable heaps ; and custom-house officers, trembling at the sight of the halter, which dangled from the tree before the door, called God to wit-

[1] See Appendix G.

ness that they had already sent in their resignations. The whole land was seething and boiling over. This species of violence, however, was merely sporadic in a country which had no violent classes, save in the seaports, and it was soon over. It quieted down beneath the firm and determined pressure of law and order, and gave way to conduct much more significant. Solemn meetings were held, where the painful silence was broken by the tremulous tones of those who rose to lay before their neighbors their rights as subjects, and to insist upon the necessity of maintaining them. The coolest and best were there, and all of these were there; the professional men and merchants in the North, the planters in the South. The legislatures resolved, remonstrated, and appointed committees to correspond with each other. Some strange things appeared: the word "American" began to be used for "colonist," and in the Virginia House of Burgesses there was a flash of lightning so vivid that dazed and startled members actually cried out, Treason!— and were told to make the most of it. But, whether the assembly was parliamentary or whether it was merely popular, it was all one. The government party gave way before the rush. People and legislators[1] had but one notion of the Stamp Act, and came to but one resolution respecting it: that the thing was accursed, and that they would have none of it. Whereupon, when Parliament met, this was the state of things the colonies presented—no man dared to take it upon himself to distribute the stamps; the offices and some of the courts were closed, and no public business could be transacted; private business was wellnigh suspended, and all America was as one man against the government.

But the people by no means confined themselves to an attitude of passive resistance. A very positive and significant fact appeared. Nine of the colonies were actually sitting together in congress in New York: the four remaining being in full sympathy with them, and absent only through the successful intrigue of the ministry party. This congress, a stormy one, united in an address to the King and a petition to the House of Commons, both of which were rejected, and a hearing refused, on the ground that they emanated from a body unknown to the Constitution; a good

---

[1] As an evidence of the rapid progress of public opinion, the resolutions of the Massachusetts House were adopted unanimously; though Hutchinson says that three fourths of those who voted them had, only a session before, voted an address distinctly recognizing the right of Parliament to tax the colonies.

reason for a doubtful act. This congress, and the word "American," were the most ominous things of all the apparitions which walked the earth the dark night of the Stamp Act.

No wonder England stood aghast. She had, however, two things in her favor: time for the sober second thought, and a change in the ministry already accomplished. Parliament would not sit for business until the 14th of the following January, and Grenville had gone out and Rockingham was in. This change in the administration could not but be acceptable to the Americans, and common-sense would have a chance to declare itself during the time that remained of the recess. Both conjectures proved true. The friends of the colonies worked hard to arouse public opinion, and the first efforts were soon seen in the respectful hearing given to English merchants, who were received with attention at the door where seven great colonies had been turned away. The session of 1766 is memorable for the debates on the Stamp Act. Pitt urged repeal, immediate repeal, and Rockingham, Dowdeswell, and Conway seconded him with all their might; even Charles Townshend voted for it. The House was in earnest, and promptly consigned the subject to a committee, who, for six weeks, industriously collected evidence and thoroughly considered the matter. Then, upon their report, the old British self-control and common-sense asserted itself. By a majority, said Burke, that will redeem all the acts ever done by majorities in Parliament, it repealed the Act, and the ancient colonial system was reinstated. By this time all England was aroused, and the crowd which filled the lobbies in breathless expectation, burst into cheers when the result was announced.

The news was sent off to the colonies. There went with it, it is true, a *Declaratory Act* which asserted the right to tax; but in the joy of the moment this was regarded merely as a bridge prudently built for a flying enemy, and, pushed out of sight, was as speedily out of mind. Every ear heard but the cheers in the lobbies, and every tongue rung but one word "repeal." The Americans were again free Britons, and in the common gladness, bonfires blazed in their streets, and the peals from the steeples of Christ Church and the Old South answered the merry-go-round of Bow Bells. At once the agitation ceased. People and Legislature outvied each other in assurances of reverence for the Parliament that had saved their liberties from itself, and in protestations of loyalty to the best of kings, who could hardly control himself sufficiently to sign the "fatal compliance." God had interposed in their behalf ; the Prince of Peace himself had walked the waters, and, at his word, the winds went down and the waves were still.

Four new facts, which were powerfully to affect the destinies of America, constituted the outcome of the Stamp Act matter. The first was the awakening of the colonies to the existence of absolutism which had for its object the curtailment of their rights. The second was a sense of capacity to take care of themselves in the senate as effectually as they had already demonstrated their ability to defend themselves in the field. The third was the universal acceptation of what until then had been doubted and opposed, that, in the union of the colonies was strength. The fourth was, that two great parties sprung into existence in America. To these may be added, not as a positive force, but as an accretion which had its favorable influences, the greater appreciation in England of American character, and a more lively sense of kinship with Americans. The colonists then became recognized, by the Whigs, at least, as something more than mere extremities of the body of which England was the head, as something more than mere feeders to the general system, and as having brains and character of their own. Between them and the Whigs there sprung up a strong feeling of alliance, and the time was not far distant when statesmen like Chatham and Burke shocked insular prejudice by mentioning their senates and those of Athens and Rome in the same breath.

But, alas for the Declaratory Act ! It was the wicked fairy that set at naught all the precious gifts the good fairies had given the little princess. When they had departed, she remained, and when the joy over what had been lost and was found again had died away, this it was that then began to make mischief. In looking back upon the story of those days, the conviction cannot be avoided, that had it not been for the Declaratory Act, the independence of the colonies had never occurred. There would have been no necessity, no provocation for such a step. Without that Act the triumph over absolutism would have been decisive. The struggle would have been brief and even less eventful than the Revolution of 1688 ; yet the result would have been as effectual. But, as it was, when the smoke of the bonfires had drifted away and men could see clearly, it was evident, that, though the measure had been defeated, the hostile principle remained. Indeed, it was too plain, that, in the Declaratory Act, absolutism had made another positive assertion of its determina-" tion to rule ; that in fact, it had taken a long step forward. 'This was a great gain, when it is considered, that, for the first time since the days of the Tudors, absolutism was favorably recognized by the people of England themselves, and that their determination to enforce it had been actually enrolled in their archives. Heretofore, it had been but a disputed question ; now, it became a living force and a rule of action for British power. There it stood, pro-, claimed to the world, and no one could go behind it or around it. Absolutism had the oyster and liberty held the shell.

Nevertheless the people both in America and England thought that they had settled things on the old foundation. They were not permitted to hug their delusion long. In a short time Pitt entered the Lords, and Townshend led the Commons.

Charles Townshend was a man whose versatility of genius was only equalled by his versatility in trimming. He was not fickle ; on the contrary, he was steady in his contempt of principle and in his resolution to do the best for himself with whatever happened to be at hand. There was no such thing in the man's whole character as one fixed and stable political principle, unless it were that all profit, and all glory, should enure to the benefit of England, cost what it might to the rest of the British possessions ; that all power should centre in the throne ; and that all distinction should rest upon himself. His contemporaries styled him "the Weathercock." and it is doubtless to his vacillating disposition which, in making him "every thing by turns and nothing long," prevented the identity of his name with any one great principle, that is owing the fact of his posthumous fame being wholly incommensurate with that which he enjoyed in his lifetime. For, the man who carried the House with him whenever he opened his lips, and whose memory compelled the panegyric of Burke, did enjoy a great, a very great reputation. The very audacity with which Townshend flung his glove into the lists challenged the admiration of the spectators. His methods were violent. He was a bundle of contrarities ; on the one hand he courted opposition, and on the other he clung to the majority. He took delight in coolly shocking received notions of political conduct, and found exquisite pleasure in the commotion his effrontery excited. Arrogant, imperious, with him defiance was the sport of the hour. If there was one impulse in this political ruffler more powerful than selfishness, it was his devotion to absolutism. This was the sole mistress to whom he was constant.

Such was the leader of the House of Commons at a time when, above all others, it was necessary that the true relations between the mother-country and the colonies should be steadily kept in view, when the temper of Britons at home and abroad should be thoroughly understood, when, if any new maxim of administration were to be adopted, it should be that of Bear and Forbear, and when the art of healing was more loudly demanded than that of estranging. No sooner did this mischief-maker become the master spirit of the cabinet than he showed his hand ; and thus he did it :

"It has long been my opinion," said he when addressing the House a few months after the repeal, "that America should be regulated and deprived of its militating and contradictory charters, and its royal governors, judges, and attorneys be rendered independent of the people. I, therefore, expect that the present administration will, in the recess of Parliament, take all necessary previous steps for compassing so desirable an event. * * * If I should differ in judgment from the present administration on this point, I now declare that I must withdraw. * * * I hope and expect otherwise, trusting that I shall be an instrument among them of preparing a new system."[1] He declared himself ready, if called upon, to use the army in collecting the revenue, and, that there should be no misconstruction put upon his vote for repeal, he averred that he voted for it, not because the Stamp Act was not a good measure, but because repeal was expedient. Repeating this assertion for the benefit of the galleries, he added : "After that, I do not expect to have any statue erected in America."

Accordingly, in May, 1767, there were introduced into Parlia-

---

[1] From manuscript report in "Bancroft," vi, 10, quoted in "Frothingham," 203.

ment what are now known as the *Townshend Acts.* They were passed and received the royal assent, though, as had been the case with the Stamp Act, they were not to go into force until the November following their passage. These acts imposed duties on glass, paper, painters' colors, and tea; they established a Board of Customs at Boston for the collection of revenue throughout America, and they legalized the Writs of Assistance. It will be seen that Townshend did not deal in half-way measures; he went back to the beginning, and he went, too, further forward than any one had ventured to suggest. Not only was revenue directed to be collected, but the machinery for collecting it went out in the same vessel that carried the authority; and, that nothing be left upon which to found a protest or an evasion, the odious Writs of Assistance were brought to life again and legalized. But the Act which imposed duties did not stop at mere revenue: it went further. At one stroke it centralized all power in the imperial government and boldly established English supremacy. This was done at a stroke by stating in the preamble, that the ensuing duties were laid for the purpose of providing a fund wherewith to maintain the colonial governments and the colonial defence; the inference to be drawn being, that the act would enure to the benefit of the colonies, inasmuch as it was intended to expend there the moneys so raised, in paying the expenses of the governments and of the courts, and in maintaining the common defence.

Thus a people who needed no defence, and who jealously held sacred the right of maintaining their own courts and governments, were to be bribed into acquiescence to despotism by the promise of getting back the money unlawfully wrung from them. No more artful trick whereby to rob free people of their liberty, and no more unworthy one ever disgraced a minister or legislature. The scheme was simply this—to establish a despotism by an appeal to the avarice of those despoiled. To uphold such a project, it was fitting that recourse should be had to the bad and ignoble qualities of human nature rather than to the good and noble. Heretofore, the internal governments of the colonies had been their own. They themselves paid their governors, their legislatures, their judges, and it was they who provided for their own defence; they were, as we have seen, self-governed. Now, on the contrary, it appeared that the right of self-defence was to be taken away, that their courts were to be constituted of those who had deprived them of this right, and that their governments were to be made independent of them and placed absolutely in the hands of their rulers ; and for all this they were to pay with their own substance. There was no pretence of commercial regulation ; that idea was scouted. The Townshend Acts were political ; there was no mincing of words about it, and the avowed object was the centralization of power into the hands of Parliament. Absolutism had thrown down the gauntlet : it would now attack by storm what it had previously been content to gain by sap.[1]

Before the acts went into effect Charles Townshend died, and the administration staggered on, deprived of the guidance of Lord Chatham, who, for more than two years, was held in the strictest seclusion by reason of ill-health : a great calamity for England, for now, more than at any time since the days of the Stuarts, she was to need coolness of judgment, tact, prudence, and firmness in action, self-control, and the exercise of that rarest of arts in governing, the art of waiting in calm and serene patience. But, as the event proved, she was as ill provided in moral qualifications for the task she had set herself to perform as the colonists afterward were in physical means for the struggle which closed the conflict. The battle was, after all, not to the strong in arms but to the strong in spirit.

At once the war between parliamentary absolutism and local self-government broke out with a stubbornness which lasted until one side had, by the accomplishment of its political independence, acquired the victory over the other. Virginia and Massachusetts came to the front. Agreements not to import the products of Great Britain were eagerly signed in the colonies, and were lived up to with a consistency and spirit which is wonderful when it is considered how irksome and galling this deprivation of home comforts and personal necessities must have been. From Pennsylvania "The Farmer's Letters" of John Dickinson circulated throughout the whole country with a rapidity which showed how all-engrossing was the subject then uppermost in the public mind, and met with a welcome whose warmth displayed the enthusiasm of the people, and their determination to maintain their rights.

---

[1] Knox's " Extra-official Papers," ii, 26.

The Legislature of Massachusetts sent a Circular Letter to the Assemblies of the other colonies, in which was set forth the necessity of all acting together harmoniously, and of freely communicating the mind of each to the others. The course Massachusetts had pursued was described, with the contents of the petition and letters which had been written, and with the hope expressed that she would have their cordial co-operation in resistance to the ministerial measures. The notion that political independence was aimed at was strenuously denied, and the trust was uttered that what had been done would meet the approval of their "common head and father," and that the liberties of the colonies would be confirmed. This Letter elicited response from some, others returned none officially, but all who answered replied favorably. It gave, however, the greatest offence to the ministry, and particularly to Lord Hillsborough, the Secretary of State for the Colonies. It seems that he read it entirely by the light which a letter from Governor Bernard to Lord Barrington had shed upon it. This epistle declared the real motive of the colonies to be a determination to be independent. Hillsborough, filled with this idea, communicated it to the other members of the cabinet, and thus the Circular Letter was laid prejudged before them. It was determined that it merited notice, but that the only notice to be given it should be one of censure, and, on the spur of the moment, they resolved upon two things : to require the Massachusetts Assembly to rescind the Letter, and to require the other legislatures before whom it had been laid to reject it. This was done, and the consequences were, that the General Court, or Legislature, of Massachusetts voted, by ninety-two to seventeen, that they would do nothing of the kind, and that the other legislatures gave the outcast a hearty welcome. As for the people, they showed their approval of their representatives by toasting, from one end of the country to the other, " The unrescinding Ninety-two," with whom was coupled the number Forty-five, or that of the famous " North Briton"; while the Bostonians added fuel to the flame by a riot on the score of the sloop *Liberty*, in which they attacked the houses of the Commissioners of the Customs, and made a bonfire of the Collector's boat. Shortly afterward, (but not by reason of the riot), four ships of war anchored in Boston harbor, and two regiments of soldiers were quartered on the town.

The Circular Letter, the action of the legislatures, and the general contumacy of the people, attracted the attention of all western Europe, and when Parliament met in 1769, its agitation at once showed its deep feeling of resentment against the colonies, and particularly against Massachusetts and the city of Boston. The absence of Lord Chatham at this juncture cannot be too deeply deplored. None but he was capable of awing the resentful into prudence. The king called attention in his speech to what had been done in Boston as subversive of the Constitution, and indicative of a tendency to independence of Great Britain. Sixty papers bearing upon colonial affairs, and all condemnatory of the late doings, were laid before Parliament, which, in both Houses, expressed its opinion, that the action of Massachusetts was derogatory of the dignity and rights of the Crown and Parliament. Lord Mansfield gave it as his opinion, that the members of the General Court had been guilty of contumacy in refusing to rescind the Circular Letter, in sitting in a self-called convention, and in various other ways, and that they should be summoned to England to account for their conduct. Whereupon, Lord Hillsborough moved, that censure be passed on that body, and also upon the Boston town-meeting, which was done ; and the Duke of Bedford, smarting under the action of the Grand Jury, which had separated without bringing in true bills against the rioters, pushed through a joint Address to the King, begging His Majesty to obtain the fullest information, so that, in case of sufficient grounds, the statute of 35 Henry VIII. might be enforced, and the offenders brought to trial in England, before a special commission. To point the moral, the king knighted Bernard.

This revival of the law of Henry VIII., which had become obsolete, from the very fact that it was a part of that despotism, which for generations had not dared to show its head in England, was neither politic nor justifiable. It is due to a portion of the English press to say, that this step of Bedford excited alarm, and that it met with vigorous protestations, in which it was averred, that the bloody axe of Henry VIII. had been scoured up and whetted for the necks of poor Americans. One might suppose that the sight of this engine of despotism so quickly dragged out of its hiding-place, would have inspired salutary reflection. Free people have no use for such things, and the question might naturally arise,

What is the meaning of this, and here among a free people? That such thoughts did intrude themselves, there is no doubt; but there are none so blind to despotism as those who desire it and those who enforce it. King, Parliament, and people, all were seeking to make their power felt by their dependencies; so far forth they wished a despotism, and, having one, were bent upon imposing it on those whom they deemed powerless to help themselves. England's head was turned by the glories of the late war, and the magnitude of her armament. Her pride no longer lay in dispensing the bounty and extending the protection of a mother, but in making her children feel the weight of her power. It is a sad state of affairs, when a parent had rather that her child be bound to her by fear than by affection; yet, such was now the spirit that pervaded the mother-country.

The colonies might well have been appalled. With an armed force quartered on their soil, with the people of England united in indignation against them, with the King never mentioning them except in terms of bitterness, with the Commons' table loaded with bills aimed at their liberties, and with even the names of their leaders bandied about the floor as the names of men for whom the gallows was waiting, it was now their turn to stand aghast. But they did nothing of the kind. Massachusetts turned her head in mute appeal. It was not in vain: Virginia stepped promptly forward, and opposed her breast to the blast.

For many years Virginia had been without a governor. It was deemed a happy stroke of policy at this time, to send her one whose amiable disposition would give assurance of the kindness still felt for the colonies in the royal closet from which he was dispatched. There can be no question of Lord Botetourt's appointment being a conciliatory act; nor of its being, as far as it went, a politic act. Though he lacked force, his gentleness, amiability, and dignity made up the deficiency, and, altogether, he was one who would have been in every way suited to a people who delighted in the courtesy of *l' ancien régime*, had the times been such as to give to manners the precedence of principles. That the appointment was a pleasing one, is shown by the fact, that though Botetourt came in a whirlwind and departed in one, the Virginians gave him what Charles Townshend declared he did not expect for himself, a statue. But, welcome as the new governor might be, the gale held on its course.   The planters heard with polite deference the whisper that his Excellency would be gratified if they kept silent on political questions, and answered it by the Resolves of May 16, 1769, which were received with one acclaim throughout the colonies.

They resolved : that the sole right of imposing taxes upon them lay in themselves ; that it was their undoubted privilege to petition their sovereign for redress of grievances, and to procure the concurrence of His Majesty's other colonies, in dutiful addresses, praying the royal interposition in favor of the violated rights of America ; that all trials for any crime whatsoever done in the colonies ought of right to be had before the colonial courts, according to the fixed and known course of proceeding, and that seizing any persons suspected and sending them beyond the sea to be tried, was highly derogatory of the rights of British subjects, as thereby the inestimable privilege of being tried by a jury from the vicinage, as well as the liberty of summoning and producing witnesses, would be taken away from the party accused ; that an address be prepared assuring His Majesty of their inviolable attachment to him and his government, and to beseech his royal interposition, as the father of all his people, to quiet the minds of his loyal subjects of that colony, and to avert from them those dangers and miseries which would ensue from the seizing and carrying beyond sea any person residing in America, suspected of any crime whatsoever, to be tried in any other manner than by the ancient and long-established course of proceeding.   And they ordered their Speaker to transmit, without delay, to the Speakers of the other legislatures, a copy of the resolutions, and a request for their concurrence.   Whereupon, the amazed Botetourt could only gasp out his abhorrence of the whole proceeding, and tell the planters to go home.

The Virginians being in no mood for returning home in such a fashion, held a meeting in "the Apollo," and united into an association to carry out the non-importation agreement ; an example speedily followed by all the other colonies, but one.   As for the legislatures appealed to, they concurred heartily.

Although both sides were now confronting each other as antagonists, actual hostility was something which came much later. The policy of Great Britain was indeed inimical to the liberty and

peace of America, but this enmity was not yet shown by her deeds,
—though these were unquestionably becoming threatening. On
the contrary, it accorded with this policy to assume and maintain
as long as possible a conciliatory aspect: it was the colonies who
were to wear the appearance of being in the wrong, not England.
Nothing was easier to effect than this, inasmuch as, so long as the
Declaratory Act stood on the statute book, measures might be
changed at will. The appointment of Lord Botetourt, as has been
seen, was one of those conciliatory acts which left the principle as
unfettered and vigorous as ever; the recall of Bernard was an·
other, and we have now to notice still another of the series, which
continued until they and the odious principle they masked were
at last contemptuously flung to the ground together.

In the spring of 1770, Lord North took advantage of a petition
from the London merchants to modify his policy by moving a
partial repeal of the act imposing revenue. This motion was not
made until after full deliberation and a consultation which revealed a great division of opinion in the cabinet. The question
before the ministers was, Shall or shall not the imposition of the
new import duties laid upon America be persevered in? Lord
Chatham was still absent, but the Duke of Grafton was for repeal
and total repeal. Lord North, too, was for repeal, but for repeal
of such a sort as would not reflect in the slightest degree on the
principle involved. This, he thought, could be effected by the
retention of the duty on tea, which was not a British product, and
which would preserve the principle of the right to tax while the
measure would be shorn of its obnoxious features. The king
thought so too; "there must always be one tax," said he, "to
keep up the right." On the question being put to vote it was
determined, by a majority of one only, that the policy should
be persevered in, but that the measure should be modified.
The king and his advisers took great credit to themselves for
this concession and for the self-control and magnanimity it involved.

Accordingly the Act was thus partially repealed, though the
whole Opposition, except Grenville, who, by not voting, displayed
irresolution, were for absolute repeal. The right was but a
shadow, they said, the profit but a peppercorn: and well might
they say so, for, during the past financial year, the duty on tea

from all America had produced less than three hundred pounds sterling.[1]

But that the right was a shadow only, was by no means so considered by the absolutists, who proceeded to prove, in the most positive way absolutism has ever been able to adopt, how substantial it was. Henceforth the government of the colonies was, as far as it could be effected, a government of ukase, of imperial rescript, or, as then termed, of Royal Order. From this time there issued directly to the governors *Royal Instructions*, under the king's signature, and with the privy seal annexed. The position was taken, that though the king, like his subjects, was under the law in England, he was above it in the colonies. Lord Granville said to Franklin, that the king's instructions, when received by the governors, were laws of the land, "for the King is the legislator of the colonies"[2]; an expression to be considered as conflicting with the doctrine of parliamentary supremacy, were it not that such supremacy really meant absolutism which acted through Parliament, but which had its true source in the throne. It was not the first time the throne had made the imperial legislature its instrument, but it was the first time it had succeeded in using the people of England themselves. That such was the case is disclosed by the language of the people everywhere no less than by the action of their representatives in Parliament. Monopoly, as has been seen, upon a former time, moved from the corporations and nobles to the commonalty, and now absolutism had stepped from the throne to the streets. Every Englishman demanded that the Americans look upon him as one of their sovereigns. "Every man in England," said Franklin, "* * * seems to jostle himself into the throne with the King, and talks of

---

[1] Ald. Beckford's statement, "Cav. Deb.," i, 400. During this year, 1770, George Grenville died. He was not a great man, but he was earnest, and, at heart, disposed to do good : but he did not know how to effect his ends, and he was continually under the delusion that government lay solely in Acts of Parliament and Orders in Council. He was a functionary, not a statesman. One cannot read his last recorded expression on American taxation without feeling that he was conscious of the great mistake he had made. "Nothing," said he, "could induce me to tax America again, but the united consent of King, Lords, and Commons, supported by the united voice of the people of England. * * * I will never lend my hands toward forging chains for America, lest in so doing I should forge them for myself."—"Cav. Deb.," i, 496. Were the conditions omitted from this acknowledgment, the Americans would regard his atonement as complete.

[2] Sparks' "Works of Franklin," vii, 550.

our subjects in America."[1] With the moral support of Lords and Commons thus offered it, the King found no opposition at home thrown in the way of his Royal Instructions.

These instructions followed each other thick and fast, and were as various as the circumstances which demanded them. No two were alike for two places, for diversity was sought as a feature favorable to the prevention of a general issue by the colonists. They ignored colonial laws, required the dissolution of the legislatures, removed them from their accustomed places, negatived their choice of speakers, directed the governors to withhold their assent from tax bills, and seemed to be formed on the assumption that all power was to emanate from the royal closet, that a personal government was the one ordained of God for the colonies, and that constitutional liberty did not exist for those who dwelt beyond the boundaries of the British Isles. The bureaucracy meddled with every thing; even in support of the slave trade, which called forth the indignant protests of Virginia and Massachusetts against that inhuman traffic. Whenever absolutism once feels the ground growing firm beneath its feet, it takes upon itself the shape of a personal government, with all those features, so odious to the Saxon mind, of direct action, absence of parliamentary deliberation, secrecy, and closet administration. Nothing discloses the subordinate and instrumental part played by Parliament so well as these Royal Instructions. As soon as the crown felt itself strong enough, it ignored the notion of a parliamentary government as much as the Americans did, and had not the English people been blinded by their arrogance, they would have seen how purely artificial the term parliamentary absolutism is. Reflection should have taught them from their own history, that there is really but one continuing absolutism, the one which appears on the throne the moment the iron is magnetized enough to draw the particles; that the absolutism of a people is not a persistent active force, but a temporary disorder which in time corrects itself, and that the only part they or the Parliament which represents them can play, is that of being the tool of him who holds the actual power. However, though free themselves, the English were now enjoying the intoxication of playing despot to others, and there was no hand to stay them; for, from Grenville's last

---

[1] *Id.*, vii, 468.

words in Parliament, there seems to have been but one man of all those who wrought the mischief sober enough to suspect, that, in forging chains for others, he might be forging them for himself.

For awhile the ukase administration seemed to be acceptable even to the victims.   Under the intolerable pressure of personal deprivation, the non-importation agreement was broken, and the colonists fell to quarrelling among themselves and calling each other hard names.   The Boston massacre, which had created intense excitement in both countries, appears to have served the purpose in America of relieving the public mind of the hatred then poured out on England and every thing English.   But the troops had been withdrawn, and a disposition to let things alone, bad as they were, began to make itself felt.   Repeal, such as it was, was having its effect, and the ministry party in the colonies began to flatter themselves, that "the reaction," that dream of Bourbonism, which always takes hope when revolution stops to take breath, had surely set in.

One great effect of the Stamp Act had been to call into existence two parties in America, which, like those of England, were called Whig and Tory.   So distinct, however, were the provinces, and so sluggish the disposition to unite, that, in the Whig or patriot party, there was little concert of action.   There could not be ; for what existed of that party in each colony was bounded by the limits of that colony, and, in fact, there may be said to have been as many such parties as there were provinces.   Apathy had fallen upon the land, but the apathetic pauses of revolution are invariably brooding, and this was one of them.   The American leaders were none the less conscious that something had to be done to deliver the people from the body of that death, notwithstanding that the people were muttering for a little more slumber, a little more folding of the hands to rest.   For the moment it seemed as if there was nothing which was available to break the dangerous lethargy.   The pertinacity of the cabinet, however, soon came to their relief.   Though the duties on glass, paper, and paint, had been repealed, the preamble of the Act imposing them had not been, and the purpose to make the colonial governments and courts English instead of American still stood out boldly from the statute book.   That purpose was now to be enforced through an order of Hillsborough, that the judges and their subordinates should be paid from the imperial treasury. This was followed by a declaration of Lord Dartmouth, that the King had the right to make such provision. "The blind may see, the callous must feel, the spirited will act," cried Josiah Quincy; and Samuel Adams, seeing that the hour had struck, now bent himself to the task of organizing one party throughout America. At a town-meeting, called to consider this salary question, Adams moved that a committee of correspondence be appointed. The motion was carried. This example was everywhere followed throughout New England, and eventually in the other provinces, and henceforward the "committees of correspondence" figure on every page of the revolution. This movement, even when still confined to New England, was formidable, and the astute and far-reaching Hutchinson, delaying not for instructions from London, boldly threw himself in its path and denounced the committees of correspondence as hostile to the Constitution. The encounter which ensued was eagerly observed from both sides of the Atlantic. To the annoyance of the cabinet, it brought out that dread of absolutism, a discussion of first principles, before which the unsupported Hutchinson at last had to retire, covered with the ridicule of enemies and the reproaches of friends.

Still the remaining colonies did not evince a disposition to throw off their indifference, and the Bostonians were yielding to disappointment, when a Royal Instruction arrived creating a Commission to inquire into the circumstances which resulted in the burning of His Majesty's schooner *Gaspee* in the Rhode Island waters, to order the arrest of the parties charged, together with the witnesses, and to call for assistance, if any were needed, upon the commander of the army in America, who was instructed to supply it. When the arrests were made, the parties arrested were to be sent to England for trial.

This actual violation of the right to trial by jury, with the spectacle of the British army in readiness to strike the right down should it attempt to assert itself, aroused every instinct of the freeman. Nevertheless, the tameness of overawed Rhode Island was such as to provoke a taunt from Greene, the future antagonist of Cornwallis in the Carolinas. Virginia, however, took up the matter at once, and, through her young progressives, sounded the alarm to all the colonies in a set of resolutions, which, for the first time, referred to the action of all the British colonies in America, without limitation.   These resolutions, which were unanimously adopted, provided for a standing committee "to keep up and maintain a correspondence and communication with her sister colonies," and was the first effective legislative action of the kind. "Full scope," wrote Richard Henry Lee, "is given to a large and thorough union of the colonies, though our language is so contrived as to prevent the enemies of America from hurrying this transaction into the vortex of treason."   Five colonies at once responded with resolutions to coöperate.   The silence of irresolution hung over the remaining seven.   Another aggression was needed to stir timidity into boldness.   It soon came, and the prolonged quiet was abruptly broken by an affair which riveted attention upon the colonies, and did much to hasten their revolt.

CHAPTER XI.

The Conflict with Absolutism—Continued.

THE affairs of the East India Company had fallen into bad shape. Child's panegyric had been written in vain. Their embarrassments were attributed to bad management and to the refusal of one of their best markets, the American, to take their teas on any terms so long as they were burthened with duties. The colonists drank tea none the less, it is true, but they smuggled it from the rivals of the East India Company, the Dutch ; a fact which only served to aggravate the evil. Two things occurred, in consequence, to embarrass the company : an enormous glut which crammed the warehouses, and an empty money-chest. In its distress the company appealed to the government, who undertook to relieve it by a loan of £1,500,000 sterling. In order to reim·bursement, however, it was necessary to take another step, namely, to effect the sale of the teas. In 1772, on a renewal of the Tea Act, an act granting a drawback of three fifths of the English duties of customs on all teas sent to the colonies was passed. Still the Americans would not take the teas. In order to over-come this perversity, Lord North now, April 27, 1773, proposed a drawback on teas going to America of the whole duty payable in England, and that the company should be at liberty to export its teas directly to the colonies, which, under the Navigation Acts, as we have seen, could not then be done. In this case, the teas, when landed on American wharves, would be subject only to the duty of three pence imposed by the Act of 1767. As this would en-able the Americans to get their teas cheaper than from the Dutch, no doubt was entertained of the colonial market opening itself to the company, which, in turn, would be relieved of its surplus, and reimbursement would be assured, while the three pence, which would not be felt in the paying, would be enough to keep the flag of principle flying, and satisfy the royal mind respecting the one tax necessary to maintain the right.

It will be observed, that in this, as in every measure brought to bear upon them, the Americans were to admit the right of Great Britain to tax them without representation, as a first step, and, as a second, they were to pay in cash for making the admission. So long as the colonies were maintained by England for commercial reasons, it was natural and proper that her legislation should bear the ear-marks of trade. But when, in addition to commercial regulation, she adopted a policy purely political, it is but reasonable to expect that her action in that respect should be free from even the suspicion of thrift. This, it seems, was to expect too much. " They have no idea," wrote Franklin, " that any people can act from any other principle than that of interest," and, accordingly, all of England's dealings with her colonies are marred by those offensive peculiarities which smack of the shop. This was galling in the extreme to a people who, outside of their few seaports, had no trading classes, and it served to aggravate the irritation every measure of this commercial power excited.[1]

---

[1] During the year 1773 there occurred two expressions of feeling which displayed the sense of injury felt by one side, and the contempt entertained by the other. The first was the publication of two satires by Dr. Franklin, then residing in England as a colonial agent, entitled respectively, " Edict of the King of Prussia," in which Prussia exacts revenue from the people of England on the ground of their Teutonic origin, and " Rules for reducing a Great Empire to a Small One," the tenor of which may be judged from the following paragraph : "In the first place, gentlemen, you are to consider that a great empire, like a great cake, is most easily diminished at the edges. Turn your attention, therefore, first to your remotest provinces, that, as you get rid of them, the rest may follow in order."—" Works," iv, 387.

The second was one in which the same person figured, but in a different capacity from that of author. A Mr. Thomas Whately, formerly private secretary of Mr. Grenville, and later Under Secretary of State, died, leaving among his effects a package of personal correspondence with Gov. Hutchinson and Lt. Gov. Oliver, of Massachusetts. These letters, in some mysterious way, came into the hands of Dr. Franklin, under an injunction of secrecy and a pledge that he would never reveal the name of him who disclosed them. This pledge Dr Franklin kept, but he forwarded the letters, or a copy of them, to the Speaker of the Massachusetts House of Assembly, still under the imposition of secrecy. Another copy, however, coming under no condition of secrecy, as it was alleged, was published. The effect was, to cause such indignation that a petition was ordered by the Assembly to be transmitted to Dr. Franklin for presentation to the king, asking the removal of Hutchinson and Oliver. The matter was referred to the Council, before whom the petitioners appeared by their counsel, Lee and Dunning, and Hutchinson and Oliver by their counsel,

. Had the Boston Caucus and the young progressives of "the Raleigh" deliberated a lifetime, they could not have gained their object so speedily and effectually as the sight of a ship loaded with East India tea did for them. What legislative resolutions, circular letters, and all the devices of politicians had failed to do, this visible, sensible, palpable fact effected in the twinkling of an eye. The old Stamp-Act feeling burst forth stronger than ever. At Boston, the people pitched the tea overboard; a deed which was greeted throughout the colonies by the ringing of bells, and the stoppage of the tea ships before they touched the wharves. The committees of correspondence sat from day to day, "like a little senate," as Hutchinson said. The popular party everywhere acquired great strength, and when the legislatures next came together, six more colonies were in solemn though active coöperation with Virginia. The colonies were practically united, and men again began talking of a congress.

The news of the reception the tea had met with in America had a natural but none the less unhappy effect on the government and the people of England. Heretofore, they reasoned, those contumacious people have confined their opposition to paper demonstrations—for the Boston massacre was in the nature of a riot rather than a rebellion—demonstrations, which, though aggravating, have nevertheless not been hostile, and their resistance has been of that

Wedderburne. The affair caused great talk in London, and the room was crowded with the leaders of the Whigs and Tories. From the very beginning it was apparent that the Council regarded the doubtful mode by which the letters were obtained as something of much greater importance than the question at issue, viz.: whether or no the misrepresentations and animosity revealed in the correspondence justified the retention of the accused in positions requiring so much judgment and impartiality as those they then filled. Wedderburne, sustained by the unconcealed sympathy of the Council, was in his element. He scowled and roared. He did not stop with making fun of the doctor and joking about philosophers acting as go-betweens. He pilloried him for the contempt of the world as one who in ancient Rome would be called the man of three letters, and he held the Yankees up to the ridicule of judges who received his buffoonery with roars of laughter, and who answered his malignity with sarcastic witticisms. Finally the scene was brought to a close, and a decision was entered in favor of Hutchinson and Oliver, with the extra judicial opinion appended, that the petition was based on "false and enormous allegations, and was groundless, vexatious, and scandalous." Two days afterward, Franklin, who was likewise a postmaster-general in the colonies, was informed that the king had no further need of his services. For once the philosophical character of this remarkable man did not attain to perfect self-control; from that day he was the bitter, unrelenting enemy of king and Tory.

passive sort which all people are at liberty to make use of by way of disapproval. Now, however, resistance is become active. Property has been destroyed, and those who destroy property are on the high road to the destruction of life. Active resistance smacks of rebellion. The thing is becoming ominously grave, especially when it is considered, that it is the most portentous of a series of acts, all of which have steadily gone from bad to worse. On the assembling of Parliament for business in 1774, the king laid before it the information he had received, and urged that the most serious consideration be given it. That England was stung to the quick, was shown in the vehemence with which her wrath broke forth on the floor of Parliament. Blind with that wrath, she committed the mistake she had made before of directing it entirely against the city of Boston, and of ignoring the fact that the opposition to parliamentary rule was general throughout America. Venn shrieked, *Delenda est Carthago!* and, before the hurricane which bent its force on Massachusetts, the Whigs were silent, or opened their lips only to timorously mutter that the Americans had "gone too far" and done "too much."

On the 14th March, Lord North brought in the *Boston Port Bill*, which within a fortnight was passed with very little debate, and received the king's signature March 31, 1774. After setting forth that the condition of the town of Boston was such that the commerce of his Majesty's subjects could not be safely carried on, or the customs be duly collected, it provided, that, from the first of June following, it should not be lawful for any person to lade or unlade, to ship or unship any goods from any quay or wharf within that harbor, and constituted Marblehead a port of entry, and Salem the seat of government : but a power was reserved to the king in Council, after compensation had been made to the East India Company, and peace and order had been established, to restore the town its trade. It was further announced, that the fleet and army would be employed to enforce the act : "Whatever may be the consequences," said the Prime Minister, "we must do something ; if we do not, all is over."[1]

Dowdeswell, Burke, and Fox offered resistance to the bill on the ground that Boston was not bound to render compensation for the property destroyed, and that the display of force preceded

[1] "Parl. Hist.," xvii, 1164, 1479.

instead of following the demand for compensation. Chatham did not speak, and the bill passed whereby sentence of death was passed upon the city. Before its passage, however, another bill, styled the *Massachusetts Government Bill or Regulating Act*, was introduced, whereby the charter of that province was to be altered by making the Council appointive instead of elective, and by ren.' dering the magistracy wholly dependent on the governor, who in certain cases could remove incumbents without the assent of the Council. Thus, at a time of intense excitement, when the irritated colonists were protesting violently against the right of strangers to their soil exercising the power of taxing them, the government impetuously undertook to deprive them of even the appearance of self-government. This might be gratifying to passion, but it was certainly very impolitic. Still another bill enacted, that for the next three years the governor might, in his discretion, send any persons accused of complicity in the late disturbances to any other colony for trial, or even to England ; and still another was passed, giving all lands not embraced in any other charter to the Province of Quebec ; a measure which excited the angry zeal of every Protestant in Protestant New England.

During this legislation the news came that the Bostonians had emptied another cargo into the harbor. Evidently these people had doomed themselves to destruction. Their case was hopeless, and there was now nothing to do but to let the wrath of a justly exasperated parent take its course.

Throughout the course of this arbitrary policy, it never seems to have entered the English mind that this sad state of affairs was due solely to the existence of the *paternal* government they had set up for the colonies in defiance of their own rejection of it in 1688. If a paternal government was hateful and altogether abominable to Britons in England, why should it not be to Britons in America ? That the tribe in America was doing in 1774 only what the tribe in England had done in 1688, seems never to have crossed their minds, and they blindly rushed on in the path which had led the Stuarts to the fate presented them by the fathers of these very Englishmen.

It is evident, that when the mass of the English people could be got not only to look with indifference upon the imposition of

arbitrary power upon Britons, but even to support and encourage
it, with no compensation for the danger of the experiment except
the gratification of a sense of power, it is evident that public sentiment in England was on a lower level than it had been in 1688,
that it had declined, and that to regain the point whence it had
descended would be for Great Britain a positive advance from her
present position. On the other hand it is equally as plain, that the
Americans, in combating absolutism and seeking to establish their
liberties on the basis of 1688, were the ones who were really advancing. But what especially denotes the inoculation of absolutism is, that what is now so clear, was at that time totally ob-
scured to the English eye, and that Great Britain was deeming
her honor to lie more in a display of force than in the maintenance
of those humane principles which, until then, she had upheld so
bravely. Had the English people been true to their own history
and made the cause of the Americans their own ; had they met
absolutism with the assertion that constitutional liberty was not
for a day nor for a locality, but for all time and for wherever an
Englishman could set his foot on British soil, the two peoples
would have met at one point, they would have acted together, and
the cause of constitutional liberty would have expanded with a
growing empire, which there would have been every reason to
keep bound together, and no excuse for disrupting. The Quebec
act, by giving the Canadians what they wanted, bound Canada to
England by a tie yet unbroken. Had the English people done
as much for their free kindred as they did for the conquered
French, and recognized in them the same inheritance of liberty
they themselves enjoyed—which was all that was asked,—what
resulted in Canada would have unquestionably resulted in the
rest of the British possessions, in spite of that bursting sense of
maturity which cannot be omitted as one of the incentives of
American independence. The recognition of the Roman Catholic
religion, a religion to which England was bitterly hostile, could
not have been an agreeable task to English representatives, yet we
see them of their own accord hastening to do what was almost as
needless as it was painful, rather than to do what was just. There
can be no more convincing evidence that, at this last great crisis
of Anglican liberty, England had fallen behind her principles,
and that absolutism had poisoned her blood.

But it must be plainly spoken ; throughout this dreary conflict Americans had no help from the English masses, nor even their sympathy.   The lesson of the Revolution of 1688 seems to have been absolutely forgotten by the descendants of those who accomplished it, and resting content with the posession of liberty in themselves, they wasted not a thought on that of their dependencies, but either stood by with folded arms, or afforded substantial aid to absolutism by lending it the assistance of Parliament.   It was enough for them to know that it was not their ox that was being gored.   When the conflict actually broke out between local self-government and absolutism, the English people were on the side of absolutism, and "the violent measures were fairly adopted by a majority of individuals of all ranks, professions, or occupations in this country" of England.[1]   Thus the Revolution of 1688 had no effect in arousing the sympathy of the people of England for those engaged in a struggle with arbitrary power like that which they had themselves brought to so glorious a conclusion. What effect it had, even when exerted by such men as Chatham and Burke, was powerless to arouse a nation of traders to any view of the situation which was broader than the pages of their ledgers ; and, in this respect, as far as any benefit to the colonies is concerned, the Revolution of 1688 might as well have never occurred.   In fact, the Revolution of 1776 would have taken place had that of 1688 never figured in the British annals ; it was the fight of Americans with absolutism abetted by the English people, and was won by the Americans in spite of the English.   When prudence was a virtue, a charge to this effect was stricken from the rough draft of the Declaration of Independence.   If, however, the truth is ever to be uttered, it may now be told.

The Boston Port Bill was received in America with honors not accorded even to the Stamp Act.   It was cried through the streets as "A barbarous, cruel, bloody, and inhuman murder," and was burnt by the common hangman on a scaffold forty-five feet high.   The people of Boston gathered together in town-meeting at Faneuil Hall, and expresses were sent off with an appeal to all Americans throughout America.   The responses from the neighborhood came like snow-flakes.   Marblehead offered the use

---

[1] Rockingham to Burke, " Burke's Corresp.," ii, 68.

of its wharves to the Boston merchants ; Salem averred that it would be lost to all feelings of humanity were it to raise its fortunes on the ruins of its neighbor. Newburyport voted to break off trade with Great Britain, and to lay up its ships. Connecticut, as her wont is, when moved to any vital occurrence, betook herself to prayer and humiliation, first, however, ordering an inventory to be taken of her cannon and military stores. Virginia, likewise. resolved to invoke the divine interposition, but, before another resolution which called for a Congress could be introduced, her House was precipitately dissolved ; whereupon the resolution was brought up and passed at a meeting called in "the Apollo," where it was further declared that an attack on one colony was an attack upon all. Two days later the Massachusetts letter itself was received, upon which the Virginians called a convention. From all parts contributions in money poured into Boston, and resolutions were everywhere passed, declaring that no obedience was due the late acts of Parliament ; that the right of imperial taxation did not exist ; that those who had accepted office under pay of the king had violated their public duty ; that the Quebec act establishing Roman Catholicism in Canada was hostile to the Protestant religion, and that the inhabitants of the colonies should use their utmost diligence to acquaint themselves with the art of war, and for that purpose should turn out under arms at least once a week. In the fulness of time, a cordon of ships was drawn around the town, and six regiments and a train of artillery were encamped on Boston Common—the only spot in the thirteen colonies where the government could enforce an order.

The conflict between constitutional liberty and absolutism had now reached that dangerous point where physical force became one of its elements. The colonists had used force in the destruction of property, and the mother-country had retaliated by a display, in their very midst, of force which threatened the destruction of life. Absolutism was quick with the last argument of kings. The situation was at once recognized throughout the colonies, and the knowledge that in union there is strength, manifested itself in one general impulse toward a Colonial Congress. Committees of Correspondence were organized in every county, and throngs attended the public meetings. "One great, wise, and noble spirit ; one masterly soul animating one vigorous body," was the way John Adams described this impulse. The Canadas alone remained inanimate. Having obtained what they wanted, there was no reason for their moving in the matter, and belonging for the most part to a race of absolutists, it is not to be wondered at, that they withheld sympathy from those who were combating what was natural to them, and that they flatly refused to budge.

But not so those to whom constitutional liberty was as the breath of life. On the 17th of June (1774) the Massachusetts Assembly, which had been removed by a royal order to Salem, answered Virginia by resolving on a call for a Continental Congress at Philadelphia. The governor, hearing of what was going on, sent the secretary of the colony to dissolve the Assembly, but, finding the doors shut upon him, he had to content himself with reading the message to the crowd outside. The House went on with its work, while, at the same time, a great meeting, with John Adams in the chair, was being held at Boston in Faneuil Hall. Twelve colonies agreed to send delegates to a Continental Congress to be held at Philadelphia in September. In this movement the action of Virginia had great weight ; not that it was more conspicuous than the rest, nor for those tame sentiments which Mr. Jefferson afterward said he believed were wisely preferred, but for the deep, underlying tone of resistance heard on every hand, and which made itself felt to the farthest bounds of the land. The instructions which had been prepared, but which prudence suppressed, were eagerly taken home to the bosoms of men, and were reproduced in England under a title conferred upon them by Edmund Burke. This "Summary View of the Rights of British America" spoke the heartfelt sentiments of the Virginians, and ran like wildfire through the colonies. Their influence was all the more felt for not being official.

The Tea Act, the Boston Port Bill, and the Massachussetts Government or Regulating Act had accomplished an end not dreamed of by their creators. They erased from the colonial mind the last vestige of the right of the British Parliament to tax America, and they called into being a creature hitherto unknown, a Parliament of the colonies themselves. This stranger to the structure of British polity was, from the circumstances which gave it life, antagonistic to the Parliament of Great Britain. It had been created to protect American society from the attacks of absolutism ; its further object was to foster America and every thing American, and to neutralize and resist all encroachments upon the welfare of its own creators. In this work its first attitude was necessarily that of antagonism to a Parliament bent on asserting its power to rule the colonies. Thus they were by nature and circumstance antagonistic to each other, and, for the moment, hostile. The two could not occupy the same place at the same time ; one or the other had to give way. They represented their peoples, and in representing them, represented, too, the conflict which was known of all men.

The tribe was divided : there were now two Parliaments, one in England and the other in America. In the autumn of 1774 the Americans bent their steps toward Philadelphia, and, amid breathless expectation, on the 5th of September, fifty-five representatives sat down in Carpenters' Hall. Virginia, in the person of Peyton Randolph, was in the chair. It need hardly be said, that the Congress was composed almost to a man of members of the Whig party, within whose limits, however, two divisions at once manifested their presence, the Moderates and the Extremists. The former, who had John Dickinson of Pennsylvania for their leader, though exacting in the redress of grievances, were not yet for severing the connection with Great Britain. The latter, who were led by a majority of the Virginians and all the Massachusetts men, looked the event of separation in the face, and were prepared to meet it ; though, aware that public sentiment had not yet caught up with them, they made no motion toward that end. The Moderates, consequently, controlled the action of this First Congress, and all being restricted to the common ground of redress of grievances, every thing was conducted with the appearance of harmony and unanimity.

On the 17th of September the County of Suffolk, in Massachusetts, resolved, that the people owed an indispensable duty to God and their country to preserve those liberties for which their fathers fought and bled, expressed the determination of the inhabitants to oppose the acts altering their charter, and promised cheerful submission to whatever the Continental Congress should recommend. To this Congress replied, unanimously expressing feeling for the sufferings of their countrymen in Massachusetts, approved the course which had been taken to oppose the measures of the ministry, and recommended perseverance in the same firm and temperate conduct. These resolutions, together with those of Suffolk County, were ordered to be printed.

In the meantime, General Gage, who was in command of the troops in Boston, began to fortify his position, a procedure which gave great offence to the people : whereupon Congress resolved, " That this Congress approve of the opposition made by the inhabitants of Massachusetts Bay to the execution of the late acts of Parliament ; and if the same shall be attempted to be carried into execution by force, in such case all America ought to support them in their opposition." Slight though it was in comparison with what was afterward displayed, this was the most conspicuous indication of a rebellious spirit that appears on the record, and, after a quiet session of less than two months, on the 26th of October, Congress adjourned to meet on the 10th of May following. It gave to the world, however, a Bill of Rights ; entered into a non-importation, non-consumption, and non-exportation association ; issued an address to the people of Great Britain and a memorial to the people of British America ; sent a letter to the people of Quebec and the rest of Canada ; prepared a loyal petition to the king and gratefully thanked the noble advocates of civil and religious liberty in and out of Parliament.

The Whigs were enthusiastic in their praise of what the Congress had done : their adversaries, the Tories, were bitter in their condemnation. As the former greatly outnumbered the latter, and were increasing as these decreased, the measures of Congress were warmly welcomed by the people. Certainly, an atmosphere of dignity, of purity, of self-control, and of mutual concession rested over the session, and invested every thing they did with a gravity no American has yet been irreverent enough to make light of. " When your lordships," said Chatham, " look at the papers, when you consider their decency, firmness, and wisdom, you cannot but respect their cause and wish to make it your own. For myself, I must declare and avow, that, in all my reading and observation—and it has been my favorite study : I have read Thucydides, and have studied and admired the master states of the world,—that, for solidity of reasoning, force of sagacity, and wisdom of conclusion, under such a complication of circumstances, no nation or body of men can stand in preference to the general Congress at Philadelphia." This judgment has been confirmed by the settled opinion of another century and of a wider world. That faith in this Congress, as well as admiration for it, was not wanting to the Americans at that time, is shown by the eagerness with which its recommendations were everywhere acted upon, and by the universal testimony that it had uttered the sincere convictions which now reigned in every heart.

In accordance with these recommendations, Massachusetts resolved to stand solely on the defensive. For the purposes of self-protection, she and other colonies reorganized their obsolete militia ; and the minute-men are now first heard of. The Massachusetts legislature, in further provision for the future, now that the government of the crown was daily becoming further and further removed from the people, appointed a Committee of Safety : a body which speedily found counterparts in the other colonies, and which afterward became the model for the famous *Comités du Salut Public* of France. To set at naught this rude organization for defence, Great Britain prohibited the export of arms and munitions of war to the colonies.

While affairs were thus going from bad to worse in America, England had the further excitement of a bitterly contested election. The ministry were everywhere successful. Burke had been returned from Bristol only after a sharp contest, and after having been previously rejected in Westminster. In the city of London, where public opinion was strongly on the side of the colonies, four members hostile to Lord North were returned, and, as a still further expression of opposition to the ministry, Wilkes was elected Lord Mayor. But the result was altogether in favor of the Administration, and the king saw with intense satisfaction an increased ministerial majority. When, then, Parliament met in November, there were only eighty-six votes in both Houses which could be rallied in opposition to the Administration on colonial measures : thirteen in the Lords, and seventy-three in the Commons. If Parliament really represented the English people, the Americans could look to them for few friends. But Parliament at that time did not represent the people. It represented few constituencies other than certain families. Nevertheless, it cannot be denied, that, at the very time when it was hostile to popular rights at home and was striving to prevent the liberty of the press, to suppress free speech, and even to take from the people the right of saying who their representatives should be, those same people were sustaining it in its attacks on the liberties of kindred but distant freemen.

There was one man, however, who, whatever his personal imperiousness and his exaggerated notions of imperial power over the dependencies might be, saw clearly that this was a conflict between constitutional liberty and absolutism, and ranged himself with unfaltering fidelity on the side of freedom. This man was Lord Chatham, who again on the floor of the House of Lords, resolved on instant action. Accordingly, on the 20th January, 1775, he moved an address to the king, praying that, in order to open a way to the restoration of peace and quiet in America, and to soften animosity, his Majesty should order the troops to remove as soon as possible from the town of Boston. In this motion he was supported by the Lords Rockingham, Cambden, and Shelburne. But the ministry retorted, that, instead of withdrawing the troops that were there, they should rather send more, and, on a division, only eighteen peers could be found to support the motion, among whom were the Duke of Cumberland and Lord Grosvenor. Sixty-eight lords voted against the motion.

But this resolute man was not to be rebuffed when he had once taken a stand for constitutional liberty. He betook himself forthwith to the preparation of "A provisional Bill for settling the Troubles in America," and that he might not err from ignorance of the real feelings of the Americans toward England, he personally sought the counsel of Dr. Franklin: "I am come," said he, "to set my judgment by yours as men set their watches by a regulator." Having carefully considered its provisions, he laid the bill on the table of the House of Lords. It declared in plain terms the dependence of the colonies on the crown, and their subordination to the British Parliament in all matters touching the general weal of the empire, and above all in the regulation of trade. But it proposed, no less explicitly, that no tax nor talliage, or other charge for the revenue, should be levied from any body of British freemen in America without the consent of its own representative assembly. It further declared, that delegates from the several colonies, lately assembled at Philadelphia, should, as they desired, meet at the same town and hold another Congress on the 9th of May ensuing : then to consider, first, the making due recognition of the supreme legislative authority of Parliament, and, next, of making, over and above the usual charges for the support of civil government in the respective colonies, a free grant to the king of a certain perpetual revenue toward the alleviation of the national debt.   But it was also provided, that the relinquishment of the right of taxation to the provincial assemblies should not take effect unless Congress first unqualifiedly recognized the legislative authority of Parliament as supreme.   The bill further provided, that the Admiralty courts in America should be restrained to their ancient limits ; that it should not in future be lawful to send persons indicted to another colony or to Great Britain for trial ; that the acts of Parliament relating to America since 1764 were to be wholly repealed ; that the colonial judges were to hold their places during good behavior and not during the pleasure of the crown, and that the charters and constitutions of the several provinces were not again to be invaded, unless on some legal ground of forfeiture.   " So," ran the concluding words of the bill, "so shall true reconcilement avert impending calamities."

Lord Mahon thinks,[1] that had this bill become a law, the Americans would have accepted it cheerfully, and it would have been effectual. " The sword was then slumbering in the scabbard." But, was it now possible for the colonists to accept these provisions cheerfully, and for the bill to be effectual ?   It is true it guaranteed, as far as it was worth, the independence of the judges, and the restriction of the Admiralty courts to ancient limits, and it reinstated matters where they stood in 1764.   But, would not the Americans, after going so far in their opposition to parliamentary rule, have asked themselves, What is the guaranty of an Act of Parliament worth, if the charters, long since become a part of the British Constitution itself, cannot protect themselves ? The Parliament which violated the charters can repeal this guaranty and violate them again ; this is but placing the sheep in the care of the wolves.   Again : it is true that this bill recognized the Congress, but in the same breath it required the colonies in Con-

---

[1] " Hist.," cap. li.

gress assembled to concede the very point at issue, the right of the British Parliament to rule them. This, of course, was utterly out of the question. Moreover, in so doing, the colonists were not only to concede this supremacy in the home Parliament, but to concede to the General Colonial Parliament the right to express that concession. This, in the absence of any special delegation of power to Congress by the individual colonies, would not have been permitted. It was simply asking all to concede what each had already refused to yield, or, worse still, it was empowering the creature to grant what the creators had hitherto denied. The Colonial Congress was the creature of certain local self-governments, created to effect certain objects which each had in common with the rest, and which objects were specified in the credentials of its representatives. It was not intended to meddle with those subjects that properly belonged to individual legislation. Yet this bill, in recognizing the Congress, ignored its authors, and thus conferred on the creature powers the creators had not endued it with. It is hardly possible that, at that stage of parliamentary conflict, the colonists were prepared to accept two parliamentary rulers when they were rejecting one, but rather, that, in spite of the great name which vouched for its honesty, the bill would have been tainted with the suspicion of an alliance between the two Parliaments. It must be borne in mind, that legislation and ruling are two different things, and that the opposition of the Americans was to Parliament as a ruler and not as a legislator. When its legislation took on itself the character of imperial decrees, then it was that opposition to Parliament broke forth. They would have opposed their own Congress in the same way the moment it usurped functions that had not been granted it. In this bill parliamentary supremacy remained untouched, and so long as that was the case, the Americans would not have been content.

However, after a debate characterized by great excitement, the English settled the question for themselves by defeating the bill, though the minority rose to nearly double its former number. This measure had one good effect: it set men to devising schemes of conciliation. Lord North tried his hand at it. His scheme was this: that the colonial assemblies should look after the common defence of the colonies, and each provide for the civil government of its own province, and, so long as the king and Parliament approved of such action, so long Parliament should forbear to lay any tax or duty within such province. This met with great opposition. The extremists, so blinded with rancor that they could not recognize an old friend in a new guise, opposed it as being a concession, while the Whigs of course refused to have any thing to do with so well-known an enemy.

But a greater than North tried what he could do. Edmund Burke introduced resolutions having for their distinct object conciliation with America. He, too, failed; but the effort which gave the world his immortal speech will never be deemed by posterity to have been entirely vain.

All attempts toward conciliation having failed, the tide rolled on. In retaliation for the non-importation and non-exportation agreements, Parliament closed the New England ports to trade, and the naval forces on that coast were increased by two thousand, and the land forces by more than four thousand men.

In conformity with their plan for self-protection, the Massachusetts men had gathered together some military stores at a place called Concord. Gage now determined to destroy these stores, and it must be admitted that every motive of military prudence justified him in doing so. But the times had now become such that the slightest act of military caution was the signal for putting the torch to the magazine. No sooner was it known that troops were to leave Boston for Concord, than expresses rode forth by night, and when the day dawned the yeomanry of the neighborhood were getting under arms on their village greens. At sunrise on the morning of the nineteenth of April (1775), the detachment, which had moved out under cover of the darkness, in order the better to effect its object by surprise, reached Lexington, a small village eleven miles from Boston, on the road to Concord, from which place it was distant six miles. There a squad of countrymen was already gathering. A collision ensued; the troops fired and several men fell dead, while others were stretched on the ground sorely wounded. The resistance, however, was not great enough to stay the progress of the troops, who continued their march to Concord. Here they destroyed the stores, and, after another encounter with the farmers, set out on their return to Boston. But the alarm throughout the country side having become general, they found the road obstructed by parties of minute-men, who, wrought to frenzy by the slaughter of their kindred and neighbors in the morning, had hurried across the fields from every direction, each man bent on avenging his relative or friend by a shot at the red-coats. The column was galled from the stone fences on its flanks by an incessant fire, which could not be returned with effect. The loss became steady, yet, as their numbers diminished, the English did not dare to halt and defend themselves, much less attack. Time was fast becoming every thing ; the command was losing discipline, it began to huddle together, and it pressed confusedly forward, its assailants gaining in numbers and boldness as they neared Lexington. It was now evident, that, without relief, the column must either cut its way through a fast-thickening enemy, or die on the green it had strewn with bodies in the morning. The retreat was rapidly degenerating into a rout that augured ill for a single man of them ever regaining Boston, when the head of the column joyfully rushed into the protecting ranks of a hollow square, which, under Lord Percy, had been prudently drawn up to receive them. Here they threw themselves on the ground, "their tongues hanging out of their mouths like those of dogs after a chase," said an eye-witness.[1] But little time could be afforded for rest, and the sore-beset and weary column again took up its march. Discipline and Percy's reinforcements, however, told in its favor. It pushed its way through the irritated swarms, who taunted them with the changed fortunes of the day, and who kept calling out to Percy : "Chevy Chase! Chevy Chase!" and toward sunset it reached Boston, pursued up to the very fortifications by the countrymen, now frantic that "these murderers," as they called them, should escape. Nearly three hundred of the English were dead or wounded, since, by way of bravado, their band at daybreak had played "Yankee Doodle" on the road to Lexington.

The affair of Lexington and Concord acted upon the sensitive people like a shock of electricity. The intense emotion that possessed North and South alike revealed a sense of kinship the colonists had never before entertained, and, as this burst forth, the sense of kinship with Great Britain sank suddenly down into

[1] Stedman's " Hist. Am. War," i, 118.

dead ashes. The New England militia flocked together from all quarters, and Boston speedily found itself beleaguered by its own countrymen ; nearly twenty thousand occupied the heights overlooking the town. With an imprudence,[1] which Congress, who stood solely on the defensive, would have liked to reprove, Ticonderoga and Crown Point were surprised and taken, May 14th, the same day the Second Congress met at the State House in Philadelphia, when twelve colonies sat down together. A few days later, Massachusetts took the chair in the person of John Hancock. The proposal of Lord North was rejected in a report which assigned the following reasons for its rejection : that it was a high breach of the privilege of determining the purposes for which moneys should be granted ; that it was unreasonable, inasmuch as it compelled the colonies to purchase the favor of Parliament without knowing the price ; that it insidiously sought to divide the colonies and set them against each other ; that it was offered in the presence of fleets and armies, which at that moment were being reinforced ; that it was unnecessary, unsatisfactory, and unjust, and a violation of their natural plan of government, and that it was deceptive, inasmuch as, under a question which appeared to be one merely of laying taxes, there was really hidden the claim of a right to alter charters and to rule absolutely. In conclusion, the report expressed the conviction, that the Americans had only themselves to rely upon to defeat the ministry and render their liberties secure.

Though blood had been shed—and more still was shed on the 17th of June, at Bunker Hill,—it will be observed, that there was no expression indicative of a desire, much less a determination, to be politically independent. On the contrary, the Conservatives, led by Dickinson, still held the floor, and while measures were taken for defence, Congress still clung to the hope of securing their rights as members of the British Empire. It was with this hope, yet possessing strength but daily weakening, that they resolved on another petition to the king. The anxious hopes of the whole country once more fixed themselves on this often tried but never successful expedient, and acrimony and revolution paused to observe its effect. In this petition, which was drawn

---

[1] The event justified the affair. But, as an act of active hostility, the Congress, for some time, was much embarrassed by it.

by Mr. Dickinson, the most affectionate terms were employed respecting the king. It declared that the colonists entertained too tender a regard for the kingdom from which they derived their origin ever to seek such a reconciliation as would be inconsistent with her dignity or her welfare, and it simply besought his Majesty that he would be pleased to designate some mode by which a happy reconciliation could be effected. After all the delegates had signed it, it was entrusted to Richard Penn, one of the proprietaries and a loyalist, to bear to the throne, when the responsibility would be upon the king. Penn departed on his healing mission, and Congress adjourned to the fifth of September.

During its session, however, Congress, stimulated by the action of Bunker Hill, which had occurred in the meanwhile, had prepared for the worst. It organized a common force, for the purposes of defence only, under the name of the Continental Army. Of this army it made George Washington, a representative of the land-holding interest in the South, commander-in-chief. It then adopted certain measures designed to help the colonies and to hamper any course adverse to the general welfare : such as the prohibition of supplies to the British fishing fleet, and to colonies not acting with them, and, of course, to the military and naval forces then in possession of Boston and the adjacent waters. It forbade the negotiation of bills of exchange drawn by British officers. It declared that no obedience was due to any act of Parliament altering or repealing the charter of Massachusetts, and it recommended to the people of that colony to exercise for themselves the powers of government until their charter was restored to them. In order to further the common ends, notes on the joint credit of the colonies were authorized to be issued, and from that time the country made use of Continental money.

Congress reassembled on the 5th of September, but so few members were present that it adjourned to the 13th, when, for the first time, Georgia having arrived, the Thirteen Colonies came together and proceeded to business. In the meantime, all hearts had followed Penn, who bore what Franklin, who had now come home, pithily styled " the *last* petition." They were doomed to disappointment. It was received with a silence which was broken only by the announcement that his Majesty would decline answering it, and, as if to forestall any effect it might produce in favor of the petitioners, the very day it was presented to the minister, the Proclamation for suppressing rebellion and sedition issued to the heralds. These, a few days afterward, proclaimed in due form at Westminster, Temple Bar, the Royal Exchange, and other accustomed places, that, whereas many subjects in divers parts of the colonies of North America, forgetting their allegiance, and after obstructing the lawful commerce of loyal subjects, had proceeded to open and avowed rebellion, and that this rebellion had been promoted by the counsels of divers wicked and desperate persons within the realm of England, now it was commanded all civil and military officers, and all loyal subjects, to use their utmost endeavors to suppress this rebellion, and to give full information of all persons corresponding with the persons in arms in North America, in order to bring them to condign punishment.

The news of the rejection of the petition, and that they had been actually proclaimed rebels, reached the colonies accompanied with the further information, that ten thousand mercenaries were also to be used against them. As indication of a vigorous policy, Lord George Germain was made head of the American department, in place of Dartmouth, and Gage, who had been slow to wrath, was recalled, and the Howes placed in command of the forces. These signs were ominous, but the most hopeless feature of all was the unanimity of the English people against America. It is true, that the Proclamation had been hissed on the steps of the Exchange, and that Wilkes would not permit the mace to be borne during the ceremony, but loyal addresses to the king poured in from all classes, the ministry party in Parliament was compact and overwhelmingly great, the Opposition was small and feeble, and Lord Rockingham was perfectly warranted in writing to Edmund Burke, that "the violent measures toward America are fairly adopted and countenanced by a majority of individuals of all ranks, professions, or occupations in this country." [1]

The king's speech came later and left no room for either doubt or hope. It inveighed against the "desperate conspiracy" and "general revolt," and announced a large increase of the land and naval forces in America. But one man among the ministers seems to have appreciated the danger and to have been governed

---

[1] Burke's ' Corresp.," ii, 68.

by discretion—Grafton resigned, and, in resigning, told the king, that, deluded themselves, his ministers were deluding him.

The Opposition tried to bring up the petition Penn had brought over, as ground for conciliation, and, in both Houses, started debate on the employment of mercenaries. They were over-whelmingly defeated, and Parliament proceeded to secure the colonies by a persistent course of legislation, which made Burke say, a year or two afterward : " It affords no matter for very pleas-ing reflection to observe, that our subjects diminish as our laws increase."[1]

While Parliament was thus attempting to legislate peace into the colonies, and absolute rule into itself, Congress was acting its part. Proclaimed as rebels, repelled from the throne, and with the door of Parliament to be opened to them only in the case of abject submission, the condition of the colonies was des-perate indeed. But, left to themselves, they acted for themselves. From one position they rapidly advanced to another, their deter-mination to remain free grew more and more fixed, and it was in answer to popular sentiment that Congress advised resistance at Charleston, created a naval code, organized a committee of cor-respondence with foreign powers, and recommended several colo-nies to set up governments for themselves. Men now talked openly of independence.

Still the varying fortunes of war—for such it now was—had the effect to keep alive the necessity, if not the desire, of leaving open a way to reconciliation. The Assembly of Pennsylvania, through the inspiration of Mr. Dickinson, gave expression to this pru-dence, by instructing its delegates to "dissent from and utterly reject any propositions, should such be made, that may cause or lead to a separation from our mother-country, or a change of the form of this government." New Jersey, Maryland, Delaware, and New York expressed their opinion in nearly the same terms, and thus the Middle Colonies, arrayed in mass on the side of conserva-tism, maintained, or endeavored to maintain, an equipoise between the extremes.

But there happened at this time, that is, in January, 1776, an event which, perhaps, had more to do with bringing about the im-mediate result of independence than any thing else, and that was

---

[1] " Lett. to Sheriffs of Bristol," 1777.

the publication of Tom Paine's "Common Sense." Paine himself was but a new-comer, without means, without an established character or name, and his book is deficient in scope and logic, and marred, moreover, by coarseness. And yet the effect of the work is beyond dispute. It did more to accomplish the immediate fact of independence than all the grave deliberations and eloquent outpourings of a senate, at whose door its author was hardly worthy to stand. No one now reads "Common Sense," except from curiosity or historical inquiry : but, the production of the moment, it was just what the moment demanded, and its welcome was enthusiastic. It was published in Philadelphia, where conservatism had its stronghold, and it was thus at once brought face to face with the garrison. Much of its effect must be attributed to its being published anonymously. That effect was great, and in the temper the colonists then were, the printing-press was kept day and night throwing off copies. The work may be briefly described as a plea for independence and a continental government. So far, opinion had gone no further than to a mere confederation, but Paine took a bold stand for an actual, positive central government. In their eagerness to discuss the advantages or disadvantages of such a government, men did not notice that they had tacitly conceded independence, and when they awoke to that fact, they were already too familiar with the thought ever to relinquish it. In this way the notion of independence became fixed in the public mind, and the effect "Common Sense" wrought, was simply to provoke the action of forces which, hesitating until then, were now ready and eager to act.

Dickinson, with the conservatives at his back, resisted the pressure for independence with a force to which the purity of his own character and that of his following lent great weight. But in revolutionary times nothing can stay those advances which are compelled by the exigencies of the moment. The very men who hesitate the most are forced by the present necessity to do things which the next instant become precedents against them, and, thus, in spite of themselves, they are hurried along to the point they are striving to avoid. Hence, the daily necessity of defence, by compelling these conservatives to acts of sovereignty which they would have eschewed, compelled them, too, to that final assertion of sovereignty, a declaration of independence. During the winter, Congress, in self-defence, had to order the disarming of the Tories, the equipment of privateers, the opening of the ports to all nations, and had to deal directly with foreign powers. All these things, and many more, embraced the exercise of sovereignty, and, as each occurred, it straightway became a precedent which promptly arrayed itself on the side of independence. "There is a rapid increase," wrote Franklin, in April, "of the formerly small party who were for an independent government."

This progress of public sentiment is clearly illustrated by the Resolution of the 15th of May. Congress had heretofore been very chary in advising individual colonies to exercise any thing like sovereign powers, but in this Resolution it was recommended to *all* the colonies, wherever it should be considered necessary, to form such governments as might conduce to their happiness in particular, and that of America in general. This was, in effect, telling the colonies that they were sovereigns, that they were to look to no one but themselves for political organization, and that they should set up for themselves. Practically, it was an intimation to each colony to declare itself independent.

This resolution was strenuously resisted by the Conservatives, whose vehemence was augmented by the fact, that the preamble declared it irreconcilable with conscience to take oaths to support the crown. As far as solidity of argument is concerned, and familiarity with the principles of government, the Moderates, in this instance at least, certainly outshone their opponents. But the time for conservatism had gone by, and henceforward the Progressives had the upper hand in the votes, if not in the arguments. The tide of revolution was now in full sweep.

In order to have the sustaining force of public opinion in the course thus foreshadowed, and which none were so blind but that they could see, the members of Congress began asking the Assemblies which had elected them what their opinion respecting independence was, and what the best course for Congress to pursue ; and some of them, to make sure of the desired answer, themselves wrote energetic letters to influence the minds of those who were to instruct them. North Carolina was the first to answer, and replies from three others were in by the middle of May. They were for independence. The rest did not answer before

,the Progressives determined to force matters, and on the 7th of June (1776), Richard Henry Lee, in behalf of the Virginia delegates, submitted resolutions concerning independence, confederation, and foreign alliances. Prefacing his motion with a speech, he offered the following :

" That these Colonies are, and of right ought to be, free and independent States ; that they are absolved from all allegiance to the British Crown ; and that all political connection between them and the State of Great Britain is, and ought to be, totally dissolved.

" That it is expedient forthwith to take the most effectual measures for forming foreign alliances.

" That a plan of confederation be prepared and transmitted to the respective Colonies for their consideration and approbation."

It will be noticed, that, in spite of " Common Sense," the local self-governments went no further than mere confederation. John Adams seconded the motion, and its consideration was postponed until the following morning, when the members were ordered to attend punctually.

The next morning these resolutions were referred to the Committee of the Whole, and were debated with closed doors, as was the custom, until seven in the evening, when an adjournment was had until Monday. On Monday the debate again continued until evening, when it being thought best to await the fast-maturing minds of a few colonies, it was resolved to postpone the resolution agreed upon until the 1st of July, and in the meanwhile, that no time be lost, a committee be appointed to prepare a declaration in conformity to it. On the next day a committee was chosen to perform this duty.

Of this great and anxious debate we have not a single word by direct report. We have nothing but the entries in the journal, eked out by the recollections of some of the surviving actors years afterward. We know the substance of what was said by some, and a few expressions, as used by such or such a man, are to be found here and there in the writings of these men, but given entirely from memory. But, from the lips of those who hung upon each other's words from Saturday morning until Monday night, and who wrought such mighty deeds in Israel, there has not come down to us one single sentence.

On the 12th of June a committee of one from each colony was chosen to report the form of a confederation, and a committee of five to prepare treaties with foreign powers.

By the last week in June the question of independence or no independence, was virtually settled in the affirmative in every colony, except New York. The time, foreseen at the adjournment of the subject to a future day, had now arrived, and, accordingly, the draft of a Declaration of Independence, of which Thomas Jefferson was the author, was reported on the 28th of June, and was laid on the table. On the first of July, Congress voted "to resolve itself into a committee of the whole to take into consideration 'the resolution respecting independency,' and to refer 'the draft of the declaration' to this committee." On the importunity of fresh delegates from New Jersey, the subject was discussed anew, John Adams speaking in favor of separation. John Dickinson replied to him with consummate ability and force, and based his argument on the inexpediency of independence at that time. Adams rejoined, and was followed by others for and against the measure. The New York members were, in view of their instructions, excused from voting, but the resolution was agreed to on a division, though the final question was postponed until the following day, the 2d, when twelve colonies (New York, as has been seen, not voting) resolved "that these United Colonies are and of right ought to be free and independent States ; that they are absolved from all allegiance to the British crown, and that all political connection between them and the State of Great Britain is and ought to be totally dissolved."

From that time forth the word "colonies" gave place to the word "States" in America.

The draft of the Declaration of Independence was immediately taken up and considered, and on the evening of the fourth of July, the committee rose, and Harrison reported the Declaration as having been agreed upon. It was then unanimously adopted : Great Britain was divested of her sovereignty, the people of the different States, each one for itself, assumed it, and the Revolution was accomplished in every thing save the proof of physical ability to maintain its results against the world.

During the weary years that followed, the conflict of constitutional liberty with absolutism was transferred from the closet and the senate to the field, where the fate of British absolutism was finally sealed by defeat.   Local self-government won the day.

Free inquiry had done its work in America.   It had passed from the religious subjects of our Puritan age to the secular ones of the Age of State Development, and, in doing so, had brought about the same revolution in politics here as it had done in England : that is to say, it had created and brought to a similar conclusion a warfare between prerogative and popular freedom in this country as it had once done in Great Britain.   There it terminated in the Revolution of 1688, which established definitely the limitations of the prerogative, or that element of sovereignty, which, outside of popular self-government, had ever displayed its hostility to free institutions by claiming to be above and independent of them, and free from any accountability whatever.   From the Revolution of 1688, the government of England became, in truth, for the first time, a constitutional government.   With that achievement the forces of free inquiry in English politics altered their course ; they abandoned their warlike attitude and rested content in securing and preserving what they had acquired. Henceforth, the growth of their possessions was due, not to the arts of war, but to the arts of peace.   But, in America, the attempts of arbitrary power to enlarge itself at the expense of local self-government, though interrupted, were persistent.   Absolutism looked on this country as a field in which to regain the footing it had lost on the soil of England.   It did not act blindly, but chose its instruments with a cunning which would have been successful but for the obstinacy of personal liberty.   It worked on the colonies through Parliament and commerce ; this secured America to Great Britain by the bonds of interest, that by those of political dependence.

The colonists left England with a conviction of the omnipotence of Parliament.   The struggles of generations had at last ended in the establishment of a free legislature, and the emigrants went forth with the notion, that, now that this had been accomplished, nothing more remained to be done ; the security of liberty was rendered certain, and the highest good of free government was attained.   Nothing was so great in their eyes as the

Parliament of England, and the notion, that what made Parliament so great to Britons made also the Parliament of a petty colony just as great to its handful of people, had yet to be wrung from hard destiny and the slow-evolving years. The crown saw its opportunity, and it was quick to foster the sentiment that the Parliament of England was naturally the Parliament of all the British possessions. That principle once expanded into a principle of statecraft, absolutism would have had nothing further to do than to rule America by act of Parliament.

The extent to which this notion reached is astonishing, and it only goes to show how dangerous to liberty are its own friends; for here we behold a free Parliament, the last great triumph of self-government, itself used against freedom. Had this widespread idea been acted upon in the days of the Writs of Assistance, we now see clearly that absolutism would have got such a foothold in our country as it never, in human probability, would have lost, and America might to-day have been the seat of that personal rule in government which the Revolution of 1688 had effectually destroyed in the British Isles: for, with this notion of the supremacy of Britain's Parliament, there went, as part of it, the further notion, that it was to apply a different set of principles to the government of the colonies from what it did to the government of England. But the bold tongue of James Otis sounded the inquiry which forever rejected the doctrine of parliamentary supremacy in the provinces, which placed that supremacy in the provincial Parliaments, and, in so doing, secured the provincial liberties. Otis himself, great as he was and conscious of the magnitude of his work, still, as other agents of liberty have been, hardly knew what he did. He died in the belief that the Parliament of England was something greater than the Parliament of Massachusetts: but when, in his all-compelling argument, he showed forth the Writs as the instruments of an absolutism which was using Parliament for its own ends, and when he traced those encroachments of prerogative back to Charles II., and declared that that monarch had courted Parliament as a mistress, he exposed the whole plan, and he dragged it forth into the pure air only that it should crumble into dust. Free inquiry at once roused itself to action. What was this Parliament, and what had it to do with the colonies? were the questions heard on every side. What was this prerogative, and what had sucn a questionable shape to do in America.? Though, in spite of reason, the vague and groping notion that the Parliament of England must be something greater than the Parliament of Virginia or the Parliament of Massachusetts stuck tenaciously, it finally gave way, and parliamentary freedom at last established itself on American soil as a purely local self-government. Instead of existing for one people only and in one locality, this freedom was to exist for all who spoke the English tongue wherever it had an abiding place, and who could show they were fit to have it by asserting its existence among them. Instead of dwelling only in Westminster Hall, it was to find a habitation in thirteen different commonwealths at once, and the rule was laid down, that no autonomy based on the Teutonic principle of local self-government should so much as be considered free, until the absolute freedom of its own Parliament, a freedom restricted by race, tribal and physical limitations only, was guaranteed it in advance, and maintained inviolate from the beginning.

Free inquiry gave England a constitution, and it did the same for America. Applied to government it had for its results the limitation of the prerogative, the annihilation of arbitrary power, and the expansion of the liberty of the individual : pushed to the last extremity, it turned not upon its tracks, but hewed its way by boldly vesting the sovereignty itself in the citizen. The conflict by which these results were simultaneously attained continued until its climax was reached in the American Revolution, whereby the supremacy of local self-government was assured, and constitutional government, on the basis of individual liberty, was firmly established. Thus the Revolution of 1776 gave to America what the Revolution of 1688 gave to England, constitutional, local self-government.

In looking back to the period when the English people, still under the influence of the Reformation, took upon themselves a new character, and felt the impulse which directed them across the Atlantic to found new States in the Western Hemisphere, it is well to inquire what has been the Motive of their Development ? The answer from first to last, from the convocation of Pym's Parliament and before, to the achievement of American Independence, is the Assertion of Individuality. First, that assertion in matters of conscience ; lastly, that assertion in matters of government.

When the English tribe started on its career through these generations, it was submissive to credulity in religion and submissive to unaccountable power in the state. Its social form was a political tyranny, erected upon religious credulity. When it emerged from the conflicts of these ages, its whole character was changed. In England, in the place of intolerance, conscience is free, and the church instead of using the civil power to enforce its decrees, is but a mere appendage of a government which, in turn, uses it for its own purposes : while in the place of unaccountable power, there stands a parliamentary or representative government, with prerogative shorn of its terrors. There, the social form has become one in which the Freedom of the Citizen is founded upon Freedom of Conscience. In America we behold a like spectacle. Here, too, intolerance has given way to a freedom of conscience which will not even listen to a union of Church and State, or any thing in the nature of any connection whatever. In the eye of government there is no Church but churches, which, under the law, are simply corporate aggregations of individuals, and which are entitled only to the protection accorded to all corporations alike. In the place of unaccountable power we behold a purely representative government, and here, too, the social form is one where the Freedom of the Citizen is built upon Freedom of Conscience. The tables are completely turned.

In observing the successive stages of this mighty change, we see that the Spirit of Liberty which moved Individuality to action, first acted toward the establishment of a Constitutional Government in England ; that, the work having been accomplished there, she next betook herself westward to the silent culture of States from colonies ; and, lastly, that when the time of their maturity had come, she fiercely drew the sword, and, asserting their existence, took a step still further, and boldly transferred the sovereignty from the throne to the people.

In all this course, we behold the expansion of individual rights at the cost of unaccountable power, whether that power be in Church or State. It is the history, for the time being, of the career of the Spirit of Liberty as it existed in the English tribe. First of her works came Freedom of Conscience ; next came the culture of Tribal Institutions in a desert where there was nothing to hinder their growth ; and, last of all, came Popular Sovereignty founded upon Freedom of Conscience, and sustained by institutions as old and as free as the tribe itself. This trilogy of Eras covers the most glorious period of the English race known to history.

APPENDIX.

303

APPENDIX A.

THE BOARD OF LORDS OF TRADE AND PLANTATIONS.

The general supervision and management of the British plantations in America and elsewhere was entrusted by King Charles II., by royal commission, dated 1 Dec., 1660, to a standing council, who were instructed to correspond with the several governors, etc., and in general to dispose of all matters relating to the good government and improvement of the colonies. Subsequent commissions were from time to time issued to various individuals, substantially of the same tenor, constituting them a Council of Foreign Plantations for the time being. On the 21st December, 1674, the king revoked the commission for the existing council, and directed their books and papers to be delivered to the clerk of the Privy Council. By order in council, 12 March, 1765, King Charles II. referred whatever matters had been under the cognizance of the late Council of Trade and Foreign Plantations to a committee of the Privy Council, * * * and directed them to meet once a week, and report their proceedings to the king in council. During the reign of James II. the affairs of the plantations continued to be managed by a similar committee of the Privy Council. * * * Upon the accession of King William III., in February, 1689, a committee of the Privy Council continued to manage the affairs of the plantations, until their growing importance suggested the necessity of a separate and distinct department of government for their direction.

The year 1696 is the era of the permanent organization of what is familiarly known to our historians as the "Board of Trade." On the 15th May in that year King William III., by royal commission, constituted and appointed the great officers of state, for the time being, and certain other persons, "Commissioners during the royal pleasure, for promoting the trade of the kingdom, and for inspecting and improving the plantations in America and elsewhere." This board was empowered and required to examine into the general condition of the trade of England and of foreign parts, and to make representations to the king thereupon ; to take into their custody all letters and papers belonging to the Plantation Office ; to inquire into the condition of the plantations ; to examine into the instructions of the governors, etc., and report their conduct to the king ; to present the names of proper persons for governors and secretaries, etc., in the colonies, to the king in council ; to examine into and consider the

acts passed in the colonies ; to hear complaints, and make representations thereupon, etc.; and with power to send for persons and papers. The Board of
Trade and Plantations, as thus organized, was continued through the successive
reigns by royal commissions, until its final dissolution by Act of Parliament, in
July, 1782.—Brodhead's " Report to the Governor of the State of New York,"
1845, 1 ; "Docs. relating to the Colonial Hist. of N. Y., Genl. Introd," pp.
xxviii, *et seq. ;* see also *Id.,* vol. iii, Introd., xv.

It was only in matters of great secrecy and concern that the Provincial Governors were required to correspond directly with the Secretaries of State.—*Id.,*
i, xxix.

On the suppression of the Board in 1782, the business was transferred to the
Secretaries of State.

APPENDIX B.

EXTRACTS RELATING TO FREEDOM OF CONSCIENCE, FROM "THE
GREAT LAW, OR, THE BODY OF LAWS OF THE PROVINCE OF
PENNSYLVANIA AND TERRITORIES THEREUNTO BELONGING,
PASSED AT AN ASSEMBLY AT CHESTER, ALIAS UPLANDS, THE
7TH DAY OF THE 10TH MONTH, DECEMBER, 1682."

" Whereas the glory of Almighty God, and the good of mankind, is the
reason and end of government, and therefore government, in itself, is a venerable ordinance of God ; and forasmuch as it is principally desired and intended
by the proprietary and governor, and the freemen of the province of Pennsylvania and territories thereunto belonging, to make and establish such laws as
shall best preserve true Christian and civil liberty, in opposition to all unchris-
tian, licentious, and unjust practices, whereby God may have his due, Cæsar his
due, and the people their due, from tyranny and oppression of the one side, and
insolency and licentiousness of the other, so that the best and firmest foundation may be laid for the present and future happiness of both the governor and
people of this province and territories aforesaid, and their posterity. Be it
therefore enacted, by William Penn, proprietary and governor, by and with the
advice and consent of the deputies of the freemen of this province, and counties
aforesaid, in assembly met, and by the authority of the same, that these following chapters and paragraphs shall be the laws of Pennsylvania and the territories thereof.

1. "Almighty God being only Lord of conscience, father of lights and
spirits, and the author as well as object of all divine knowledge, faith, and worship, who only can enlighten the mind, and persuade and convince the understanding of people, in due reverence to his sovereignty over the souls of mankind:
It is enacted by the authority aforesaid, that no person now or at any time hereafter living in this province, who shall confess and acknowledge one Almighty
God to be the creator, upholder, and ruler of the world, and that professeth

nim or herself obliged in conscience to live peaceably and justly under the civil government, shall in anywise be molested or prejudiced for his or her conscientious persuasion or practice, nor shall he or she at any time be compelled to frequent or maintain any religious worship, place, or ministry whatever, contrary to his or her mind, but shall freely and fully enjoy his or her Christian liberty in that respect, without any interruption or reflection ; and if any person shall abuse or deride any other for his or her different persuasion and practice in matter of religion, such shall be looked upon as a disturber of the peace, and be punished accordingly. * * *

2. "And be it further enacted, by the authority aforesaid, that all officers and persons commissionated and employed in the service of the government of this province, and all members and deputies elected to serve in assembly thereof, and all that have right to elect such deputies, shall be such as profess and declare they believe in Jesus Christ to be the son of God, and Saviour of the world, and that are not convicted of ill-fame, or unsober and dishonest conversation, and that are of one and twenty years of age at least." * * *

APPENDIX C.

INTOLERANCE OF AMERICAN PURITANISM.

" Most of the early Reformers were intolerant. Most bitter was the persecution, in the Low Countries, of the Arminians by the Calvinists, who had very recently been delivered from persecution themselves. * * *

" The celebrated ' Pilgrim Fathers,' who fled from the tyranny of Laud and his abettors, to America, and are described as having ' sought only freedom to *worship God*,' had no notion of allowing the same freedom to others, but enacted and enforced the most severe penalties against all who differed from them, and compelled the ever-venerated Roger Williams, the great champion of toleration, to fly from them to Rhode Island, where he founded a colony on his own truly Christian system. One of the principal founders of the New England colony [Sir Richard Saltonstall], remonstrated with these persecutors, saying (in a letter given in a late number of the *Edinburgh Review* [Oct., 1855, p. 564, and in Hildreth's " Hist. U. S." i, 382, 383,]) : ' Reverend and dear sirs, whom I unfeignedly love and respect, it doth not a little grieve my spirit to hear what sad things are reported daily of your tyranny and persecution in New England, as that you fine, whip, and imprison men for their consciences. First, you compel such to come into your assemblies as you know will not join you in your worship ; and when they show their dislike thereof, or witness against it, then you stir up your magistrates to punish them, for such, as you conceive, their public affronts. Truly, friends, this your practice of compelling any, in matters of worship, to that whereof they are not fully persuaded, is to make them sin ; for so the Apostle (Romans, xiv, 23), tells us ; and many are made hypocrites thereby, conforming in their outward acts for fear of pun-

ishment. We pray for you, and wish you prosperity every way; hoping the
Lord would have given you so much light and love there, that you might
have been eyes to God's people here, and not to practise those courses in the
wilderness which you went so far to prevent.' They [Wilson and Cotton], replied: 'Better be hypocrites than profane persons. Hypocrites give God part
of his due—the outward man; but the profane person giveth God neither outward nor inward man. You know not if you think we came into this wilderness to practise those courses which we fled from in England. We believe
there is a vast difference between men's inventions and God's inventions; we
fled from men's inventions, to which we else should have been compelled; we
compel none to men's inventions.'

"About the same time Williams sent a warm remonstrance to his old friend
and governor, Endicott, against these violent proceedings. The Massachusetts
theocracy could not complain that none showed them their error; they did not
persevere in the system of persecution without having its wrongfulness pointed
out.

"'Had Bunyan,' said the Reviewer, 'opened his conventicle in Boston, he
would have been banished, if not whipped; had Lord Baltimore appeared
there, he would have been liable to perpetual imprisonment. If Penn had
escaped with either of his ears, the more pertinacious Fox would, doubtless,
have ended by mounting the gallows, with Marmaduke Stephenson or William
Leddra. Yet the authors of these extremities would have had no admissible pretext. They were not instigated by the dread of similar persecution, or by the
impulse to retaliate. There was no hierarchy to invite them to the plains of
Armageddon; there was no Agag to hew in pieces, or kings and nobles to bind
with links of iron. They persecuted spontaneously, deliberately, and securely.
Or rather, it might be said, they were cruel under difficulties. They trod the
grapes of their wine press in a city of refuge, and converted their Zoar into a
house of Egyptian bondage; and, in this respect, we conceive they are without a parallel in history.'"—Bacon's "Essays," Annotations by Archbishop
Whately to Essay V, "Of Adversity."

"Your New England ministers, so-called, seem to have much zeal for religion,
but have a peculiar talent in the application and practice; and by looking no
farther than their own narrow limits, do not consider the universality of God's
love to the creation, and how pleasing it is in his sight that we carry a moral
and civil respect and love to our fellow-creatures, as brethren by creation and
the workmanship of his hands, all of a piece as to our naturals."—Extract from
letter of Isaac Norris, A.D., 1700.—"Penn. Corresp., Memoirs of Hist. Soc.
of Penna.," ix, 23.

What must have been the psychological condition of a people whose most
precious specimen of literature at that time, 1647,—one of the few specimens
extant,—breathed the spirit emanating from the following quotations from
Nathaniel Ward's "Simple Cobbler of Agawam"? It was a great book in its
day—it ran through four editions in the first year,—and unquestionably reflects
truly the moral and mental condition of those to whom it was addressed, and

who took it to their bosoms. Cotton, with all his learning and good antecedents, was bad enough, but, of all the bigots who left their mark on the unformed character of the youthful colony, none surpassed Ward in intolerance. Yet this man had had every thing to make him good; all, in fact, that ability, learning, travel, good society, and the companionship of such men as Lord Bacon, Usher, and David Paraeus could do. They were all in vain. The more light thrown on his mind, the more it contracted. He may have done some good by helping the simple laws of the colony on their feet, despotic and cruel though they were, but that was all, and, after remaining in this country twelve years, the bigot returned to England. Here are a few specimens extracted from Tyler's "History of American Literature," i, pp. 230, *et seq.*, the italics being my own. It may be said of him, what he said of the Devil, "Sathan is now in his passions * * * he loves to fish in roiled waters."

"We have been reputed a colluvies of wild opinionists swarmed into a remote wilderness, to find elbow-room for our fanatic doctrines and practices. I trust our diligence past, and constant sedulity against such persons and courses will plead better things for us. I dare take upon me to be the herald of New England so far as to proclaim to the world, in the name of our colony, that *all Familists, Antinomians, Anabaptists, and other enthusiasts, shall have free liberty—to keep away from us ; and such as will come—to be gone as fast as they can, the sooner the better.*" Toleration, he tells us, is "profaneness," laying "religious foundations on the ruin of true religion ; which strictly binds every conscience to contend earnestly for the truth, to preserve unity of spirit, faith, and ordinances, to be all like-minded, of one accord : *every man to take his brother unto his Christian care * * * and, by no means to permit heresies or erroneous opinions. * * ** My heart hath naturally detested four things : the standing of the Apocrypha in the Bible, *foreigners dwelling in my country to crowd our native subjects into the corners of the earth,* alchemized coins, *toleration of divers religions or of one religion in segregant shapes. * * * Polypiety is the greatest impiety in the world. * * ** To authorize an untruth by a toleration of state, is to build a sconce against the walls of heaven, to batter God out of his chair. * * * He that is willing to tolerate any religion or discrepant way of religion, besides his own, unless it be in matters merely indifferent, either doubts of his own, or is not sincere in it. He that is willing to tolerate any unsound opinion, that his own may also be tolerated, though never so sound, will for a need hang God's Bible at the Devil's girdle. * * * It is said that men ought to have liberty of their conscience, and that it is persecution to debar them of it. * * * Let all the wits under the heavens lay their heads together and find an assertion worse than this (one excepted,) [and] I will petition to be chosen the universal idiot of the world. * * * Since I knew what to fear, my timorous heart hath dreaded three things : a blazing star appearing in the air ; a state-comet, I mean a favorite, rising in a kingdom ; *a new opinion spreading in religion. * * ** If the whole conclave of hell can so compromise exadverse and diametrical contradictions as to compolitize such a multimonstrous maufrey of heteroclites and quicquidlibets quietly, I trust I may say with all humble reverence, they can do more than the senate of heaven."

Here is the soul of Torquemada and the buffoonery of Tetzel. Mr. Tyler, however, cites a redeeming passage, which in justice to Ward should be given, though he significantly points out how annihilating it is to Ward's own doctrine against toleration : "Ye will find it a far easier field to wage war against all the armies that ever were or will be on earth, and all the angels of heaven, than to take up arms against any truth of God."

With the annihilation of his book by the only good thing in it, let us leave him ; not, however, without giving the full title of the greatest literary effort of its day in Massachusetts : "The Simple Cobbler of Agawam in America : willing to help 'mend his native country, lamentably tattered both in the upper-leather and sole, with all the honest stitches he can take ; and as willing never to be paid for his work by old English wonted pay. It is his trade to patch all the year long gratis. Therefore I pray gentlemen keep your purses. By Theodore de la Guard. 'In rebus arduis ac tenui spe, fortissima quaeque consilia tutissima sunt,'—Cic. In English :

> When boots and shoes are torn up to the lefts,
> Cobblers must thrust their awls up to the hefts;
> This is no time to fear Apelles' gramm :
> Ne sutor quidem ultra crepidam.'

London. Printed by J. D. and R. I. for Stephen Bowtell, at the sign of the Bible, in Pope's Head Alley, 1647." For sentiments similar to those of Ward, see the elder Winthrop, Cotton, Dudley, and Norton.

APPENDIX D.

EXTRACTS FROM A REPORT OF THE LORDS COMMISSIONERS OF TRADE AND PLANTATIONS, TO THE HOUSE OF COMMONS. DATED YE 27TH OF MARCH, 1701.

We have on many occasions represented to his majesty, as we did likewise in our report to the late House of Commons, the state of such plantations in America as are under the government of proprietors and charters, and how inconsistent such governments are with the trade and welfare of this kingdom.

That these Colonies in general have noways answered the chief design for which such large tracts of land and privileges and immunities were granted by the crown.

That they have not conformed themselves to the several acts of Parliament for regulating trade and navigation, to which they ought to pay the same obedience and submit to the same restrictions as the other plantations, which are subject to his majesty's immediate governments ; though, on the contrary, in most of those proprietary and charter governments, the Governors have not applied themselves to his majesty for his approbation, nor have taken the oaths required by the Acts of Trade, both which qualifications are made necessary by the late act for preventing frauds and regulating abuses in the plantation trade.

That they have assumed to themselves a power to make laws contrary and repugnant to the laws of England, and directly prejudicial to our trade, some of them having refused to send hither such laws as they have there enacted, or have sent them very imperfectly.

That divers of them having denied appeals to his majesty in council, by which not only the inhabitants of those Colonies, but others, his majesty's subjects, are deprived of that benefit enjoyed in the plantations, under his majesty's immediate government, and the parties aggrieved without remedy from the illegal proceedings of their courts.

That these Colonies continue to be the refuge and retreat of pirates and illegal traders, and the receptacle of goods imported thither from foreign parts, contrary to the law, no return of which commodities, those [*obliterated*] all of which is much encouraged by their not admitting of appeals as aforesaid.

That by raising and lowering their coin from time to time, to their particular advantage, and the prejudice of other Colonies, by exempting their inhabitants from duties and customs to which other Colonies are subject, and by harboring of servants and fugitives, these governments tend greatly to the undermining the trade of the other plantations, and entice and draw away the people thereof, which diminution of hands in Colonies more beneficial to the Crown, and do very much [*obliterated*]. Independent Colonies do turn the course of trade to [*obliterated*] propagating woollens and other manufactures proper to England, and not of applying their thoughts and endeavors to such as are fit to be encouraged in those parts, according to the true design and intention of those settlements.

That these governments do not put themselves in a state of defence against an enemy, nor do they sufficiently provide themselves with arms and ammunition, many of them not having a regular militia, being no otherwise at present but in a state of anarchy and confusion. To cure these and other great mischiefs in these Colonies, and to introduce such administration of government and fit regulations of trade as may make them duly subservient and useful to England, we have humbly offered our opinion that the charters of several proprietors and other instituting them to a right of government, should be resumed to the crown, and these Colonies put into the same state of dependency as those of his majesty's other plantations, without further prejudice to every man's particular property and freehold, which we conceive cannot otherwise be well effected than by the legislative power of this kingdom.—"Memoirs of Hist. Soc. of Pa.," vol. ix. Appendix, pp. 379, 380.

In this connection, it may be well to read the passages bearing on this subject in the "Diary" of Evelyn, who was one of the original members of what was known as the Board of Trade and Plantations. From these it will appear that alarm and mistrust respecting New England were constant :

" —but what we most insisted on was to know the condition of New England, which appearing to be very independent as to their regard to Old England or his Majesty, rich and strong as they now were, there were greate debates in what style to write to them, for the condition of that colony was such that they were able to contest with all other Plantations about them, and there was feare of their breaking from all dependance on this nation * * * some of our Council were for sending them a menacing letter, which those who better understood the peevish and touchy humor of that Colonie, were utterly against."—Evelyn's "Diary," May 26, 1671.　First meeting of the Commissioners of Trade and Plantations.

"I went to Council, where was produc'd a most exact and ample information of the state of Jamaica, and of the best expedients as to New England, * * * since we understood they were a people almost upon the very brink of renouncing any dependance on the Crowne."—*Id.*, June 6, 1671.

" —the Council concluded that in the first place a letter of amnestie should be dispatch'd."—*Id.*, June 21, 1671.

" "A full appearance at the Council.　The matter in debate was whether we should send a Deputy to New England, requiring them of the Massachusets to restore such to their limits and respective possessions as had petition'd the Council ; this to be the open Commission only, but in truth with seacret instructions to informe the Council of the condition of those Colonies, and whether they were of such power as to be able to resist his Majesty and declare for themselves as independent of the Crowne, which we were told, and of which of late years made them refractorie.　Coll. Middleton being call'd in, assur'd us they might be curb'd by a few of his Majesty's first rate fregates, to spoil their trade with the islands ; but tho' my Lo. President [the Earl of Sandwich,] was not satisfied, the rest were, and we did resolve to advise his Majesty to send Commissioners with a formal Commission for adjusting boundaries, etc., with some other instructions."—*Id.*, August 3, 1671.

" We also deliberated on some fit person to go as Commissioner to inspect their actions in New England, and from time to time report how that people stood affected."—*Id.*, Feb. 12, 1672.

" Now our Council of Plantations met at Lord Shaftesbury's (Chancellor of the Exchequer) to reade and reforme the Draught of our new Patent, joyning the Council of Trade to our political capacities."—*Id.*, Sept. 1, 1672.

In 1701 this same board declared, that, " the independency the colonies thirst after, is notorious."

In 1703, Quarry wrote : "Commonwealth notions improve daily, and, if it be not checked in time, the rights and privileges of English subjects will be thought too narrow."

In 1705, the following occurs :—"The colonists will, in process of time, cast off their allegiance to England and set up a government of their own," * * * and that "their increasing numbers and wealth, joined to their great distance from Britain, would give them an opportunity, in the course of some years, to throw off their dependence on the nation, and declare themselves a free state, if not curbed in time, by being made entirely subject to the crown.—Some great men professed their belief of the feasibleness of it, and the probability of its some time or other actually coming to pass."—"Defence of the New England Charters," Jeremiah Dummer, 32, 33.

"We have caught them at last," said Choiseul, Bancroft's "Hist. U. S.," chap. xx, and Lord Mansfield declared, that, "ever since the Peace of Paris, he always thought the northern Colonies were meditating a state of independency on Great Britain."—*Id., id.*

But, though such expressions were used here and abroad, and such desires undoubtedly did exist in the breasts of individuals, nothing like a wish for political independence was at all general among the people, and I have no doubt that John Adams expressed the feeling exactly in the following words :— "There is great ambiguity in the expression, 'there existed in the Colonies a desire of independence.' It is true there always existed in the Colonies a desire of *independence of Parliament* in the articles of internal taxation and internal policy, and a very general, if not a universal opinion, that they were constitutionally entitled to it, and as general a determination, if possible, to maintain and defend it. But there never existed a desire of *independence of the crown*, or of general regulations of commerce for the equal and impartial benefit of all parts of the empire. It is true, there might be times and circumstances in which an individual or a few individuals, might entertain and express a wish that America was independent in all respects, but these were '*rari nantes in gurgite vasto.*' For example, in one thousand seven hundred and fifty-six, seven, and eight, the conduct of the British generals Shirley, Braddock, Loudon, Webb, and Abercrombie was so absurd, disastrous, and destructive, that a very general opinion prevailed that the war was conducted by a mixture of ignorance, treachery, and cowardice ; and some persons wished we had nothing to do with Great Britain forever. Of this number I distinctly remember I was myself one, fully believing that we were able to defend ourselves against the French and Indians, without any assistance or embarrassment from Great Britain. * * * *That there existed a general desire of independence of the crown in any part of America before the Revolution, is as far from the truth as the zenith is from the nadir.* That the encroaching disposition of Great Britian would one day attempt to enslave them by an unlimited submission to Parliament and rule them with a rod of iron, was early foreseen by many wise men in all the States ; that this attempt would produce resistance on the part of America, and an awful struggle, was also foreseen, but dreaded and deprecated as the greatest calamity that could befall them. For my own part, there was not a moment during the Revolution, when I would not have given every thing I ever possessed for a restoration to the state of things before the contest began, provided we could have had any efficient security for its continuance."—Letter to George Alexander Otis, "Life and Works of John Adams," x, 394, 395 ; dated 9 February, 1821. And see letter from same to William Tudor, *Id.*, x, 373, in which is also quoted [pp. 372, 373] the following paragraph from a letter to *Dennys de Berdt*, authorized by the committee composed of J. Otis, Sam. Adams, Col. Otis, Maj. Hawley, and Samuel Dexter :—

"When we mention the rights of the subjects in America, and the interest we have in the British constitution, in common with all other British subjects, we cannot justly be suspected of the most distant thought of an independency on Great Britain. Some, we know, have imagined this of the colonists ; and others, perhaps, may have industriously propagated it, to raise groundless and unreasonable jealousies of them ; but it is so far from the truth, that we apprehend the colonies would refuse it, if offered to them, and would even deem it the greatest misfortune to be obliged to accept it. They are far from being insensible of their happiness in being connected with the mother country, and of the mutual benefits derived from it to both."

After the temper of the colonies had been ruffled by the Stamp Act, there are to be found expressions, such as this extract from *The American Whig*, A. D., 1769 (New York), contains, though they were, as John Adams says, confined to individual and not general opinion.

" This country will shortly become a great and flourishing empire, independent of Great Britain ; enjoying its civil and religious liberty, uncontaminated and deserted of all control from bishops, the curse of curses, and from the subjection of all earthly kings. The corner-stones of this great structure are already laid, the materials are preparing, and before six years roll about, the great, the noble, the stupendous fabric will be executed."

APPENDIX E.

THE THREE ACTS.

THE ACT OF NAVIGATION.

STAT. 12 CAR. II., C. 18.—A.D. 1660.

" An act for the encouraging and increasing of shipping and navigation.

" For the increase of shipping and encouragement of the navigation of this nation, wherein, under the good Providence and protection of God, the wealth, safety, and strength of this kingdom is so much concerned, be it enacted, that from and after the first day of December, 1660, and from thence forward, no goods or commodities, whatsoever, shall be imported into, or exported out of, any lands, islands, plantations, or territories, to his Majesty belonging, or in his possession, or which may hereafter belong unto or be in the possession of his Majesty, his heirs and successors in Asia, Africa, or America, in any other ship or ships, vessel or vessels, whatsoever, but in such ships or vessels, as do truly and without fraud, belong only to the people of England and Ireland, dominion of Wales, or town of Berwick-upon-Tweed, or are of the build of, and belonging to, any of the said lands, islands, plantations, or territories, as the proprietors and right owners thereof, and whereof the master, and three fourths of the mariners, at least, are English ; under the penalty of the forfeiture and loss of all the goods and commodities which shall be imported into, or exported out of any of the aforesaid places, in any other ship or vessel, as also of the ship or vessel, with all its guns, furniture, tackle, ammunition, and apparel ; one third part thereof to his Majesty, his heirs and successors ; one third part to the governor of such land, plantation, island, or territory, where such default shall be committed, in case the said ship or goods be there seized : or, otherwise, that third part also to his Majesty, his heirs, and successors ; and the other third part to him or them who shall seize, inform, or sue, for the same in any court of record, by bill, information, plaint, or other action, wherein no essoin, protection, or wager of law shall be allowed. And all admirals, and other commanders at sea, of any of the ships of war, or other ships, having commission from his Majesty, or from his heirs or successors, are hereby authorized and strictly required to seize and bring in as prize all such ships or vessels as shall have offended contrary hereunto, and deliver them to the Courts of Admiralty, there to be proceeded against ; and in case of condemnation, one moiety of such forfeitures shall be to the use of such admirals, or commanders, and their companies, to be divided and proportioned among them, according to the rules and orders of the sea, in case of ships taken prize ; and the other moiety to the use of his majesty, his heirs and successors."

Section second enacts, that all governors shall take a solemn oath to do their utmost, that every clause shall be punctually obeyed.

Section third. And it is further enacted by the Authority aforesaid that no goods or commodities whatsoever of the growth, production, or manufacture of Africa, Asia, or America, or any part thereof, or which are described or laid down in the usual maps or cards of those places, be imported into England, Ireland, or Wales, islands of Guernsey or Jersey, or town of Berwick-upon-Tweed, in any other ship or ship's vessel or vessels whatsoever, but in such as do truly and without fraud belong only to the people of England or Ireland, dominion of Wales, or town of Berwick-upon-Tweed, or of the lands, islands, plantations, or territories in Asia, Africa, or America, to his Majesty belonging, as the proprietors and right owners thereof, and whereof the master and three fourths at least of the mariners are English under penalty, etc.

Section fourth. And it is further enacted by the Authority aforesaid that no goods or commodities that are of foreign growth, production, or manufacture, and which are to be brought into England, Ireland, Wales, the islands of Guernsey and Jersey, or town of Berwick-upon-Tweed, in English-built shipping or other shipping belonging to some of the aforesaid places and navigated by English mariners, as aforesaid, shall be shipped or brought from any other place or places, country or countries, but only from those of their said growth, production, or manufacture, or from those ports where the said goods and commodities can only, or are, or usually have been first shipped for transportation and from none other places or countries, under the penalty of the forfeiture of all such of the aforesaid goods as shall be imported from any other place or country contrary to the true intent and meaning thereof, as also of the ship in which they were imported, etc.

Section eighteenth. And it is further enacted by the Authority aforesaid that from and after the first day of April, which shall be in the year of our Lord 1661, no sugars, tobacco, cotton, wool, indigoes, ginger, fustick, or other dyeing wood of the growth, production, or manufacture of an English plantation in America, Asia, or Africa, shall be shipped, carried, conveyed, or transported from any of the said English plantations to any land, island, territory, dominion, port, or place whatsoever other than to such English plantations as do belong to his Majesty, his heirs and successors, or to the kingdom of England or Ireland or principality of Wales, or town of Berwick-upon-Tweed, there to be laid on shore under the penalty of the forfeiture of the said goods or the full value thereof, as also of the ship, with all her guns, etc.

Section nineteenth. And be it further enacted by the authority aforesaid, that for every ship or vessel which, from and after the 25th day of December, 1660, shall set sail out of or from England, Ireland, Wales, or town of Berwick-upon-Tweed for any English plantations in America, Asia, or Africa, sufficient bond shall be given, with one surety, to the chief officer of the custom-house of such port or place from whence the said ship shall set sail, to the value of one thousand pounds, if the ship be of less burthen than one hundred tons, and of the sum of two thousand pounds if the ship shall be of greater burthen. That in case the said ship or vessel shall load any of the said commodities at any of the said English plantations, that the same commodities shall be by the said ship brought to some port of England, Ireland, Wales, or to the port or town of Berwick-upon-Tweed, and shall there unload and put on shore the same, the danger of the seas only excepted. And for all ships coming from any other port or place to any of the aforesaid plantations who by this act are permitted to trade there, that the governor of such English plantation shall, before the said ship or vessel be permitted to load on board any of the said commodities, take bond in manner and to the value aforesaid for each respective ship or vessel that such ship or vessel shall carry all the aforesaid goods that shall be laden on board in the said ship to some other of his Majesty's English plantations, or to England, Ireland, Wales, or town of Berwick-upon-Tweed. And that every ship or vessel that shall load or take on board any of the aforesaid goods, until such bond given to the said governor, or certificate produced from the officers of any custom-house of England, Ireland, Wales, or of the town of Berwick, that such bond have been there duly given, shall be forfeited, with all her guns, etc. * * * And the said governors and every of them shall twice in every year, return true copies of all such bonds by him so taken to the chief officers of the customs in London.

Rot. Parl., 12 *C.* II., *p.* 2, *nu.* 6.   5 *Statutes of the Realm*, 246.

STATUTE 15, CAR. II., C. 7—A.D. 1663.

" An act for the encouragement of trade."

Section fifth. " And in regard his Majesty's plantations beyond the seas are inhabited and peopled by his subjects of this his kingdom of England, for the maintaining a greater correspondence and kindness between them, and keeping them in a firmer dependence upon it, and rendering them yet more beneficial and advantageous unto it, in the further employment and increase of English shipping and seamen, vent of English woolen and other manufactures and commodities, rendering the navigation to and from the same more cheap and safe, and making this kingdom a staple, not only of the commodities of those plantations, but also of the commodities of other countries and places, for the supplying of them ; and it being the usage of other nations to keep their plantations' trades to themselves.".

Section sixth. " Be it enacted, etc., that no commodity of the growth, production, or manufacture of Europe, shall be imported into any land, island, plantation, colony, territory, or place, to his Majesty belonging, or which shall hereafter belong unto or be in possession of his Majesty, his heirs and successors, in Asia, Africa, or America (Tangiers only excepted), but which shall be *bona fide*, and without fraud, laden and shipped in England, Wales, or the town of Berwick-upon-Tweed, and in English-built shipping, and which were *bona fide* bought before the 1st of October, 1662, and had such certificate thereof as is directed in one act, passed the last session of the present Parliament, entitled, '*An act for preventing frauds and regulating abuses in his Majesty's customs*'; and whereof the master and three fourths of the mariners, at least, are English, and which shall be carried directly thence to the said lands, islands, plantations, colonies, territories, or places, and from no other place or places whatsoever ; any law, statute, or usage to the contrary notwithstanding ; under the penalty of the loss of all such commodities of the growth, production, or manufacture of Europe, as shall be imported into any of them, from any other place whatsoever, by land or water ; and if by water, of the ship or vessel, also, in which they were imported, with all her guns, tackle, furniture, ammunition, and apparel ; one third part to his Majesty, his heirs and successors ; one third part to the governor of such land, island, plantation, colony, territory, or place into which such goods were imported, if the said ship, vessel, or goods, be there seized, or informed against and sued for ; or, otherwise, that third part, also, to his Majesty, his heirs and successors ; and the other third part to him or them who shall seize, inform, or sue for the same in any of his Majesty's courts in such of the said lands, islands, colonies, plantations, territories, or places where the offence was committed, or in any court of record in England, by bill, information, plaint, or other action, wherein no essoin, protection, or wager of law shall be allowed."

The other sections prescribe the oaths and penalties.

STAT. 25 CAR. II., C. 7.—A.D. 1672.

" An Act for the encouragement of the Greenland and Eastlard Trades, and for the better securing of the Plantation Trade."

The first four sections relate solely to the fisheries—to train oil, blubber, whale-fins, and the like.

Section fifth. And whereas, by one Act passed in this present Parliament, in the twelfth year of your Majesty's reign, entitled, An Act for Encouragement of Shipping and Navigation, and by several other laws passed since that time, it is permitted to ship, carry, convey, and transport sugar, tobacco, cotton, wool, indigo, ginger, fustick, and all other dyeing wood, or the growth, production, and manufacture of your Majesty's plantations in America, Asia, or Africa from the places of their growth, production, and manufacture, to any other of your

Majesty's plantations in those parts (Tangiers only excepted), and that without paying of customs for the same, either at the loading or unloading of the said commodities, by means whereof the trade and navigation in those commodities from one plantation to another is greatly increased, and the inhabitants of diverse of those colonies, not contenting themselves with being supplied with those commodities for their own use, free from all customs (while the subjects of this your kingdom of England have paid great customs and impositions for what of them have been sent here), but contrary to the express letter of the aforesaid laws have brought into diverse parts of Europe great quantities thereof, and also daily vend great quantities thereof to the shipping of other nations, who bring them into diverse parts of Europe, to the great hurt and diminution of your Majesty's customs and of the trade and navigation of this your kingdom: For the prevention thereof we your Majesty's Commons, in Parliament assembled, do pray that it may be enacted, and be it enacted by the King's most excellent Majesty, by and with the advice and consent of the Lords Spiritual and Temporal and Commons in this present Parliament assembled, and by authority of the same, that from and after the first day of September, 1673, if any ship or vessel which by law may trade in any of your Majesty's plantations shall come to any of them to ship and take on board any of the aforesaid commodities, and that bond shall not be first given with one sufficient surety to bring the same to England or Wales, or the town of Berwick-upon-Tweed, and to no other place, and there to unload and put the same on shore (the danger of the sea only excepted), that there shall be answered and paid to your Majesty, your heirs and successors, for so much of the said commodities as shall be loaded and put on board such ship or vessel, these following rates and duties, that is to say, etc.

Section sixth. Duty to be levied by Commissioners of the Customs in England.

Section seventh. If party have not ready money, Commissioners may take a proportion of the commodities.

Sections eighth and ninth. Relate to Eastland trade.

Rot. Parl. 25 *Car.* II., *nu.* 7   5 *Statutes of the Realm*, 793.

APPENDIX F.

STAT. 13 AND 14 CAR. II., CH. IITH.

"An Act to prevent frauds, and regulating abuses in his Majesty's customs."

Section fifth. "And be it further enacted by the authority aforesaid, that in case, after the clearing of any ship or vessel, by the person or persons which are or shall be appointed by his Majesty for managing the customs, or any their deputies, and discharging the watchmen and tidesmen from attendance thereupon, there shall be found on board such ship or vessel, any goods, wares, or merchandises, which have been concealed from the knowledge of the said person or persons, which are or shall be so appointed to manage the customs, and for which the custom, subsidy, and other duties upon the importation thereof have not been paid ; then the master, purser, or other person taking charge of said ship or vessel, shall forfeit the sum of one hundred pounds ; and it shall be lawful to or for any person or persons authorized by *writ of assistance under the seal of his Majesty's court of exchequer*, to take a constable, headborough, or other public officer, inhabiting near unto the place, and in the daytime to enter and go into any house, shop, cellar, warehouse, or room, or other place ; and in case of resistance, to break open doors, chests, trunks, and other packages, there to seize, and from thence to bring any kind of goods or merchandise whatsoever, prohibited and uncustomed, and to put and secure the same in his Majesty's storehouse in the port next to the place where such seizures shall be made."

"Here," says John Adams, "is all the color for writs of assistance, which the officers of the crown, aided by the researches of their learned counsel, Mr. Gridley, could produce."   " Life and Works," x, 323.

In the attempt to support the petition to the colonial court for writs of assistance, the crown officers presented, among others, acts, whose contents were, on examination, discovered to be as incongruous as their titles ; a few of which are here given :—" An act for regulating the trade of Bay-making in the Dutch Bay-hall in Colchester."   " An act for the regulating the making of Kidderminster stuffs."   " An act for granting to his Majesty an imposition upon all wines and vinegar," etc.   " An act for granting to his Majesty an imposition upon all tobacco and sugar imported," and finally, " An act for prohibiting the importation of foreign bone-lace, cutwork, embroidery, fringe, band-strings, buttons, and needlework."   In times when titles were given to acts of Parliament to conceal, not reveal the contents, it certainly behoved a faithful attorney for the crown to be blind to the ridiculousness of what really were, no doubt, useful subjects, and offer all he could, be it ridiculous or not.   But, when, as it turned out, these acts, at least for the most part, did not extend to America, were not made for the colonies there, and had no more application to Massachusetts than to Soudan, these offers and persistence of the crown become in the highest degree reprehensible.

STAT. 7 AND 8, W. III., C. 22.

"An Act for preventing frauds, and regulating abuses in the plantation trade."

": Whereas, notwithstanding divers acts made for the encouragement of the navigation of this kingdom, and for the better securing and regulating the plantation trade, more especially one act of Parliament made in the 12th year of the reign of the late King Charles II., instituted an act for the increasing of shipping and navigation ; another act, made in the 15th year of the reign of his said late Majesty, instituted an act for the encouragement of trade ; another act made in the 22d and 23d years of his said late Majesty's reign, instituted an act to prevent the planting of tobacco in England, and for regulation of the plantation trade ; another act, made in the 25th year of the reign of his said late Majesty, instituted an act for the encouragement of the Greenland and East-land fisheries, and for the better securing the plantation trade, great abuses are daily committed to the prejudice of the English navigation and the loss of a great part of the plantation trade to this kingdom by the artifice and cunning of ill-disposed persons, for remedy whereof for the future," etc. * * *

Section sixth. "And for the more effectual preventing of frauds and regulating abuses in the plantation trade in America, be it further enacted by the authority aforesaid, that all ships coming into, or going out of any of the said plantations, and lading or unlading any goods or commodities, whether the same be his Majesty's ships of war or merchant ships, and the masters and commanders thereof, and their ladings, shall be subject and liable to the same rules, visita-tions, searches, penalties, and forfeitures, as to the entering, landing, and dis-charging their respective ships and ladings, as ships and their ladings, and the commanders and masters of ships, are subject and liable unto in this kingdom, by virtue of an act of Parliament made in the fourteenth year of the reign of King Charles II., instituted an act for preventing frauds and regulating abuses in his Majesty's customs. And that the officers for collecting and managing his Majesty's revenue, and inspecting the plantation trade, and in any of the said plantations, shall have the same powers and authorities for visiting and searching of ships, and taking their entries, and for seizing and securing, or bringing on shore any of the goods prohibited to be imported or exported into or out of any the said plantations, or for which any duties are payable, or ought to have been paid, by any of the before mentioned acts, as are provided for the officers of the customs in England by the said last mentioned act, made in the fourteenth year of the reign of King Charles II.; and also to enter houses or warehouses, to search for and seize any such goods ; and that all the wharfingers and owners of keys and wharves, or any lightermen, bargemen, watermen, porters, or other persons assisting in the conveyance, concealment, or rescue of any of the said goods, or in the hindering or resistance of any of the said officers in the performance of their duty, and the boats, barges, lighters, or other vessels employed in the conveyance of such goods, shall be subject to the like pains and penalties, as are provided by the same act made in the fourteenth year of the reign of King Charles II., in relation to prohibited or unaccustomed goods in this kingdom ; and that *the like assistance* shall be given to the said officers in the execution of their office, as by the said last mentioned act is pro-vided for the officers in England ; and, also, that the said officers shall be sub-ject to the same penalties and forfeitures, for any corruptions, frauds, couni-vances, or concealments, in violation of any the before mentioned laws, as any officers of the customs in England are liable to, by virtue of the last mentioned act ; and, also, that in case any officer or officers in the plantations shall be seized or molested for anything done in the execution of their office, the said officer shall and may plead the general issue, and shall give this or other cus-tom-acts in evidence, and the judge to allow thereof, have and enjoy the like privileges and advantages as are allowed by law to the officers of his Majesty's customs in England."

STAT. 6, GEOR. II., CHAP. 13.

"An act for the better securing and encouraging the trade of his Majesty's sugar colonies in America.

Section first. "Whereas, the welfare and prosperity of your Majesty's sugar colonies in America are of the greatest consequence and importance to the trade, navigation, and strength of this kingdom ; and whereas, the planters of the said sugar colonies have of late years fallen under such great discouragements, that they are unable to improve or carry on the sugar trade upon an equal footing with the foreign sugar colonies, without some advantage and relief be given to them from Great Britain ; for remedy whereof, and for the good and welfare of your Majesty's subjects, we, your Majesty's most dutiful and loyal subjects, the commons of Great Britain, assembled in Parliament, have given and granted unto your Majesty the several and respective rates and duties hereinafter mentioned, and in such manner and form as is hereinafter expressed ; and do most humbly beseech your Majesty that it may be enacted, and be it enacted by the king's most excellent Majesty, by and with the consent of the lords, spiritual and temporal, and commons, in the present Parliament assembled, and by the authority of the same, that from and after the twenty-fifth day of December, one thousand seven hundred and thirty-three, there shall be raised, levied, collected and paid unto, and for the use of his Majesty, his heirs and successors, upon all rum or spirits of the produce or manufacture of any of the colonies or plantations in America, not in the possession or under the dominion of his Majesty, his heirs and successors, which at any time or times, within or during the continuance of this act, shall be imported or brought into any of the colonies or plantations in America, which now are, or hereafter may be, in the possession or under the dominion of his Majesty, his heirs or successors, the sum of ninepence, money of Great Britain, to be paid according to the proportion and value of five shillings and sixpence the ounce in silver, for every gallon thereof, and after that rate for any greater or lesser quantity ; and upon all molasses or syrups of such foreign produce or manufacture, as aforesaid, which shall be imported or brought into any of the said colonies of or belonging to his Majesty, the sum of sixpence of like money for every gallon thereof, and after that rate for any greater or lesser quantity ; and upon all sugars and paneles of such foreign growth, produce, or manufacture, as aforesaid, which shall be imported into any of the said colonies or plantations of, or belonging to his majesty, a duty after the rate of five shillings of like money for every hundred weight avoirdupois of the said sugar and paneles, and after that rate for a greater or lesser quantity."

Section second. Enacts simply that all duties imposed by the first section shall be paid down by the importer before landing.

Section third. "And be it further enacted, that in case any of the said commodities shall be landed, or put on shore in any of his Majesty's said colonies or plantations in America, out of any ship or vessel before due entry be made thereof, at the port or place where the same shall be imported, and before the duties by this act charged or chargeable thereupon shall be duly paid, or without a war-

rant for the landing and delivering the same, first signed by the collector or impost officer, or other proper officer or officers of the custom or excise, belonging
to such port or place respectively, all such goods as shall be so landed or put on
shore, or the value of the same shall be forfeited ; and all and every such goods
as shall be so landed or put on shore, contrary to the true intent and meaning
of this act, shall, and may be seized by the governor or commander-in-chief, for
the time being, of the colonies or plantations where the same shall be so landed
or put on shore, or any person or persons by them authorized in that behalf, or
by warrant of any justice of the peace or other magistrate (which warrant such
justice or magistrate is hereby empowered and required to give upon request),
or by any custom-house officer, impost, or excise officer, or any person or persons him or them accompanying, aiding, and assisting ; and all and every such
offence and forfeiture, shall, and may be prosecuted for and recovered in any
court of admiralty in his majesty's colonies or plantations in America (which
court of admiralty is hereby authorized, empowered, and required to proceed to
hear, and finally determine the same), or in any court of record in the said colonies or plantations where such offence is committed, at the election of the in-
former or prosecutor, according to the course and method used and practised
there in prosecution for offences against penal laws relating to customs or excise ; and such penalties and forfeitures so recovered there shall be divided as
follows," etc., etc.

The remaining sections have reference only to the penalties, *onus probandi*,
and charge of prosecution.

APPENDIX G.

PREAMBLE TO THE STAMP ACT.

'An Act for granting and applying certain Stamp Duties, and other Duties,
in the British Colonies and Plantations in America, toward further defraying
the Expenses of defending, protecting, and securing the same ; and for amend-
ing such Parts of the several Acts of Parliament relating to the Trade and
Revenues of the said Colonies and Plantations, as direct the Manner of determining and recovering the penalties and forfeitures therein mentioned."

[The great length of the act, which covers thirty-nine pages of large 12mo,
precludes the possibility of its repetition here.]

INDEX.

Abercrombie's campaign, 52 n. . 311
Absolutism, of the Restoration, feeble, 8 ; Anglican, overthrow of, 7, 300; conflict with, 247, *et seq.*; conflict with, transferred from the closet to the field, 297, 298; acting through Parliament, . 299, 300
Acrelius, Israel . . 161 n.
Act of 35 Henry VIII. . . 264
Act of Navigation, 142, Appendix E, 312, 313, 314 ; 186 *et seq.*; effect of, on commerce, 189 ; origin of, 190, 191 ; effect of, on colonies, 191, 192 ; upon Protestantism, 192, 193 ; upon monopoly, 193 ; John Adams' view of, 195 n.; reënacted, 191, 196 ; changed relations of colonies to England, 214, 216, 222 ; corner-stone of colonial policy, 221 ; interpretation of, by government, 239; reënacted by Massachusetts, 239 ; prohibitory in nature, 239, 240. See tit. " Restrictive system"; "Child"; " Gee"; "Ashley"; "Otis."
Acts of Trade, multiplication of, under William III., 15 ; colonial indebtedness when attributed to, 141, 142 ; design of, 186, 187 ; legislation of, The Three Acts,195 *et seq.*, 312, 313, 314, 315, 316 ; treatises upon, 205 *et seq.*; motive of 221 ; interpretation of, by government, 237, 239 ; comments of Otis upon, 240, 242, 243. See appendices E and F, and tit. " Restrictive system " ; "Ashley "; "Otis." . . . . .

Acts for revenue. See tit. " Revenue."
Adams, Abigail, letters of . 180 n.
Adams, John, notion of Revolution, 24 n.; on governors' commissions, 39 n.; impression of Pennsylvania Dutch, 163 n.; his Five advantages of New England, 164 *et seq.*; his encounter with Pemberton, 166 n., 189 n., 190 n.; his views of Acts of Navigation and Trade in relation to Am. Revolution, 195 n.; on commercial literature, 219 n.; on grants in charters, 220 n.; reports Otis' argument, 244 ; his opinion of it, 245 n.; speaks in favor of independence, 297 ; true description of colonial desire for independence 311
Adams, Samuel, moves Committee of Correspondence . 271
Allen, William, opposes Grenville's policy . . . 254 n.
America, Discovery of, effects of, upon commerce . . . 187
American colonists, character of 21, 22, 23
American Whig,The, prediction of 312
Annapolis, life at . . 139, 140
Anne, Queen, policy of, favorable to colonies, 16 ; purity of language previous to reign of, 130 ; foreign travel in South increased during reign of . . 130, 131
Ashley, John, his book, 219; advocates colonies as sources of revenue, disdains the charters, 219 ; on the regulation of colonial trade, the Molasses Act 234, 235

Assets, land as 183
Baltimore, Lord, see tit. "Calvert, George."
Barbadoes, The, Child's description of settlers in . . . 208
Barclay, Robert, notion of the Scriptures . . . 64 n.
Barré, Colonel 255
Berkeley, Sir William, convenes the legislature of Virginia . 42
Bernard, Governor, his letter to Lord Barrington, 263 ; knighted 264
Bill or Declaration of Rights, 12 ; colonial liberty destitute of, 14 ; passed by First Congress . 283
Black, William, his Journal, 158 *et seq.*
Blackstone, Sir William, on common law in colonies . 40 n.
Board of Lords of Trade and Plantations, established by Chas. II., revived by William III., 15 ; Appendix B ; Evelyn, member of, 309, 310 ; extracts from report of, 308, Appendix D ; ultimate object of 15, 16, 221
Boston, see tit. " Massachusetts," " Stamp Act," " Port Bill," " Regulating Act," etc.
Boston Port Bill, 276 ; how received in America . . . 279
Botetourt, Lord, character of, appointed governor of Virginia, 265 ; dissolves House of Burgesses, 266 ; his appointment a conciliatory act, 265, 267 ; the Virginians erect a statue to him 265
Braddock's defeat . 52 n., 311
Bristol, sympathy of, with colonies, 18 ; controls, with London, colonial trade, 57 ; Burke elected member from . . . 284
Brownists, The, denied right of state to impose religion, 60 ; called Separatists, 61, 90 ; did not disapprove of expulsion of Roger Williams, 61 ; settled at Plymouth, Mass., 61, 84 ; the Pilgrims were, 84, 90 ; asserted autonomy in Mayflower compact, 86 ; their autonomy a theocratic oligarchy, 86, 87 ; motive of their emigration . 92
Bunker Hill, fight of . . . 290
Burke, Edmund, his six sources of freedom in the colonies, 29 *et seq.*; on material progress of colonies, 203 n.; on colonial

imports, 211 n.; on Port Duty Act, 253 n.; resists Boston Port Bill, 276 ; summary view of rights of America, 281 ; elected from Bristol, 284 ; introduces resolutions for conciliation . 288
Burnaby, his opinion of Rhode Island government, 45 n.; on the political and commercial character of the Virginians, 134 n.; on the Pennsylvanians 163 n.
Calvert, George, origin and character of, 118, 119 ; becomes a Romanist and turns his attention to America, 118, 119, 121 ; founds Maryland, procures a charter with remarkable grants, 121, 122 ; his relations to freedom of conscience, death . 123
Cambden, Lord, supports Chatham 285
Canada, French occupation of, 49, 50, 51, 52 ; effect of destruction of French power in, 185, 186, the Quebec Act, 277, 278, 280
Carolinas, North and South, Proprietary, afterward Royal Governments, 36, 45 ; self-government in, vanity of Locke's constitution 45
Caucus, The . . . 176 n.
Charles I., 6, 8 ; attempts monopoly of tobacco, 47, 48 ; Virginia acquires representative government under . . 48
Charles II., assents to the Habeas Corpus Act, 12 ; reenactment of Navigation Act under, 191, 196 ; unmasked by Otis 243, 299
Charters, The, Dr. Robertson's remark concerning, commented upon, 37, 38 ; construed as compacts, 38, 220, and n.; favorable to liberty, 38, 39 ; of Virginia, 41 ; of Maryland, 43, 121, 122 ; of Massachusetts, 43, 44 ; of Connecticut, 44 ; of Rhode Island, 44, 69 ; difference between, 121 ; grants and exemptions in . 210 n , 220 n
Chatham, Lord, on colonial trade, 213 n.; on Stamp Act, 217 n.; on Restriction, 221 ; on Declaratory Act, 227 ; enthusiastic support of, by colo-

nists, 251 n. ; urges repeal of Stamp Act, 257 ; enters House of Lords, 259 ; deplorable absence of, 262, 264 ; opinion of the First Congress, 283, 284 ; bill for settlement of troubles, takes counsel of Franklin . 285

Chesapeake Bay, effect of, upon Virginia and Maryland 125 *et seq.*

Chester, The Great Law of, 76 *et seq.*; Appendix B.

Child, Sir Josiah, 206 ; his treatise, 207 *et seq.* ; his postulates, 210, 211 ; analysis of his argument, 212 ; his disregard of the charters, 211, 213 ; unfriendly to the colonies, 213, 214 ; is knighted, 215 ; merit and mischief of his book, 215 ; Otis' comments upon . . . 242

Choiseul, his significant exclamation 310

Church of England, establishment of, not burdensome to the colonies, 14 ; mild intolerance of 62

Church of Rome, Anglican and Puritan horror of, 89, 90 ; disabilities of Roman Catholics in England, 119, 120, and n.

Cigars, late introduction of 132 n.

Circular Letter, The . . 263

Coke, Sir Edward, assists Roger Williams, 107 ; his decision against monopoly . . 198 n.

Colleges, colonial . . 171, 172

Colonies (and Colonists), The English, in America, motive of, 5 ; results of expansive movement following the Reformation, 5 ; effects of the Revolution of 1688 upon, 13 ; in what Rev. of 1688 did not affect them, 13 ; how they early acquired liberties, 13, 14 ; liberty of, destitute of constitutional guaranties, 14 ; the Habeas Corpus Act did not extend to them, 14 ; two conditions in, favorable to liberty, 14 ; how the Rev. of 1688 injured them, 15 ; American liberty favored by French occupation, not favored by William III., Board of Lords of Trade and Plantations established for, 15 ; prosperity of, under Queen Anne, 16 ; absolutism under George III., begins with assault upon, 16, 17 ; absolutism aided by disdain of provincials, 17, 18 ; popular sentiment in England adverse to, 18 ; negative character of history of, previous to Am. Revolution, 20 *et seq.* ; why they took up arms, 21 ; their happy lot, 21, 204, 205 ; unsuspected advantages possessed by, 22 ; familiarity with science of government, 23 ; English nature of, 24 ; successive eras of their development, 25 ; Roman, 31, 32 ; Grecian, 33, 34 ; three kinds of American, 35, 36 ; institutional nature of, 48, 49, 50 ; French, 33, 49, 50, 51, 52 ; self-government in, 43, 44, 54, 55, 56, 58, 217 n. ; absence of centralization, political or social, in Southern, 133 ; feeders to British trade and manufacture, 195, 199, 216, *et seq.* ; as sources of revenue, 216 ; not attached to any realm, 217 ; their support of English foreign policy, their money accounts with England, 249, 250, 251, and n., 252 ; remonstrate against being made sources of revenue, 254, 255 ; their reception of Stamp Act, 255, 256 ; convene a Congress, 256 ; their reception of Boston Port Bill, 279 ; the Thirteen first assemble in the Second Congress, 291 ; "colonies" give place to "States" . . 297

Commercial relations, colonial . 29

Commissions of governors, custom lent the force of charters to . . . . 39 and n.

Committee of safety, 284 ; of confederation, of treaties . 297

Committees of correspondence, 256, 271

Common law, The, brought with the colonists, 40, 42 ; Mansfield concerning . . 40 n.

"Common Sense," Paine's work, its effect 294

Commonwealth and Churches, another name for Church and State 111

Compacts, the charters construed as, 38, 220 n. ; the Mayflower C., 84 *et seq.*

Concord, Affair of, 288, 289; effect of . . 289, 290

Congress, nine colonies meet in New York, 256; general impulse toward, 275, 280; the First, 281; Chatham's opinion of the First, 283, 284; the Second 291

Connecticut, a charter government, 36; democratic, 44; remonstrates against Port Duty Act 254

Conscience, see tit. "Freedom of C."

Conservatives or ..oderates, The 282

Conway, for repeal of Stamp Act 257

Cotton, John, titles of some of his books, 104 n.; on Williams' expulsion 110

Cromwell, Oliver, character of his dictatorship, 8; condition in which his death left the Revolution, 8; confirms Baltimore's patent 68

Crown Point, Surprise of . . 290

Dartmouth, Lord, significant declaration of, 271; displaced . 292

Davenant, Charles . . . 206

Debating society, an institution, 104; effect of . . . 105

Declaratory act, 257, 258, 259; Chatham's opinion of . . 227 n.

Delaware, a proprietary government, 36; self-government in, 43; qualified toleration under Swedish occupation of . 67 and n.

Descent, one of Burke's six sources, etc., 29; considered, 30; race purity . . 164, 165

De Tocqueville, on the township . . . . 175 n.

Development, Historical plan or law of, the standard of, 95; how the true condition of a people is to be ascertained, 96; homogeneity of the law of, 96, 97; slow action of, 97; illustrated from English history, 97, 98; d. of New England character . 99

Dialects, effect of negro and Indian, upon the English language 130

Dickinson, John, his "Farmer's Letters," 262; leader of the Moderates, 282; draws petition to the king, 290; instructions to Pennsylvania delegates, 293; resists the Progressives . 294

Discussion, theological, in New England, 100, 101, 102, 103, 104, 105; political, in the South 132

Disdain of provincials, a support to absolutism, 17; an incentive to colonial independence . 56, 57

Disputation among American Puritans, 100; its uses, 102, 103, 104; it becomes secular, 104, 105, 114; see tit. "Debating Society."

Dissent, nature of, 60 *et. seq.*; in Virginia at time of Revolution . . . . 145 n.

Distinctness of colonial autonomy . . . . 36 *et seq.*

Distribution, of land and water, see tit. "Chesapeake Bay," "Virginia," "Maryland"; of population, 126, 127; causes of d. of population, 128; isolation in the South, and effects, 128, 129, 130, 131, 133; concentration in New England, *id.*, 168, 169; of land in estates, 181; of intestates' estates, 182; land as assets . 183

Divisions of society, not obstructive, in America . . . 14

Domestic life in South . 134 *et seq.*

Dowdeswell, urges repeal of Stamp Act, 257; resists passage of Boston Port Bill . 276

Dummer, Jeremiah, on the grants in charters, 220 n. . . 221 n.

Dutch, The, maritime supremacy of, 187, 188; decline of . 189, 192

Dutch, Pennsylvania . 147, 163 n.

Edonton, population of . . 128 n.

Edwards, Jonathan, 104; his citations from Shepard . . 104 n.

Elections, in the South . . 133

Eliot, John, acquires the Indian tongues . . . . 88, --6

Ellenborough, Lord, on the common law in colonies . . 40 n.

Emigration, the great Anglican, 5; homogeneity of, 24; from Ireland begins . . . 121 n.

English officers, conduct of, toward colonial troops . 153, 185 n.

English people, The, their sense of superiority to colonists, 17; abetted absolutism, 265, 277, 278, 279; when not represented by Parliament . . . 284

Eras, of English history from beginning of Reformation, 5, 6,

7 ; the destructive, 6 *et seq. ;* the constructive, 8 ; of effort, 12 ; of colonial development, 25 ; their motives and characteristics, 25, 26 ; the expansive force of colonial, 25 ; how this force acted, 25, 26 ; the trilogy of, necessary to comprehension of American Revolution, 26 ; review of . 300, 301

Established Church (Establishment), see tit. "Church of England."

Evelyn, John, member of Board of Lords of Trade and Plantations, quotations from . 309, 310

Extremists or Progressives, The . 282

Family, The, unit of Southern society 134

Farmer's letters, The, . . 262

Fisheries, The, Coke on monopoly of, 198 n ; Child upon, 210 ; right of, granted in charter 210 n.

Forms of, colonial governments, one of Burke's six sources, 29 ; consideration of . 31 *et seq.*

Fortescue, Sir Maurice, letter to Chesterfield . . . 120 n.

Fox, Charles James, resists passage of Boston Port Bill . . 276

Fox, George, founds Society of Friends, 63 ; his denial of authority in matters of conscience, 64 ; answered by Roger Williams 66

Franchises, growth of, 38, 39 ; forfeiture of Virginia's, 41 ; profuse dispensation of, 54 ; granted in charters . . 210 n.

Franklin, Benjamin, Hume's opinion of, 157 ; his printing press, 160 ; statement concerning colonial aid to England, 251 n.; his observation on public feeling in England, 268, 274 ; political publications of, 274 n.; before the Council, 274 n.; discharged from office, 275 n.; consulted by Chatham . . 285

Free Inquiry, its advance during the Protectorate, 7 ; review of its work, 298 *et seq.*; see tit. "Freedom of Conscience."

Free trade 206

Freedom of Conscience, first establishment of, in England, 7 ; first appearance there, 97 ; of what era the mastering spirit, .

25 ; includes free action of the mind, 25 ; the prominent feature of religion in the North, 59 ; American colonies apparently unfavorable to, 59, 60, 62 ; short duration of unfavorable conditions, 60, 62 ; dissent heretical, 60 ; subordination of the State to the Church, 60, 61 ; rule for ascertaining presence of toleration or of intolerance, 62, 111 ; Maryland and Pennsylvania notable exceptions to prevailing intolerance, 62 ; greatest, in Rhode Island, 69 ; condition of, when Quakers settled Pennsylvania, 66, 67, 68, 69 ; arrival of Quakers turns the tide in favor of, 60, 62, 68, 69 ; declaration of, in West Jersey, 70 ; assertion of, in Pennsylvania, 72, 75 ; Quakerism necessarily favorable to, 72, 73 ; restriction upon, in Pennsylvania, 76, 77, 78 ; passiveness of Quakerism aided, 81 ; settlement of Massachusetts stimulated by intolerance, 83, 84, 87 ; hostility of Puritanism in America to, 92 *et seq., sparsim ;* course and historical development of, in England, 97, 98 ; not thoroughly understood by those first maintaining it, 98 ; slow to become a social force, 98 ; rapid development of, after the Reformation, 98 ; not yet a principle of action at period of Anglican migration, 98 ; becomes such during English civil war, 98 ; notion of, before and after advent of Roger Williams, 106 ; Massachusetts Puritans distrusted principle of, 108 ; this principle involved in trial of Roger Williams, 110, 111 ; this trial discloses existence and condition of, in Massachusetts, 110 ; is the starting-point of, as a social force, 111 ; soul-liberty, 112 ; divorce of Church and State, 112, 113 ; theological dispute gives way to secular debate, 114 ; the Ship of State, 115 n.; causes of, North and South, 123 ; review of its work in America. . . 300 301

French in America, The, a men-
ace, 16 ; their colonies, 49 ;
non-institutional character of,
49, 50, 51, 52 ; effect of destruction of French power in
America   .   .   185, 186
Friends, Society of, see tit.
"Quakerism."
Frontier, The, 147 *et seq.;* the
frontiersman, 148, 149, 150 ;
life of, favorable to personal
freedom and local self-govern-
ment   .   .   .   152, 153
Gage, General, fortifies, 283 ; is
recalled   292
Galloway, Joseph, on mutual independence of colonies   .   36 n.
Gaspee, The affair of   .   . 271
Gee, Joshua, 215 ; his treatise,
215, 216 ; the first writer to advocate making the colonies
sources of revenue, 216 ; his
scheme approved, and work re-
published   218
George II., prudent course respecting the colonies, Adams'
commendation of   .   226 n.
George III., methods of absolutism under, 16 *et seq.*; insists
upon revenues from colonies   . 267
Georgia, a royal government, 36;
scanty colonial life, 45 ; takes
its place in Second Congress   . 291
Germain, Lord George   .   . 292
Governments, Colonial, Forms of
the ; see tit. "Forms of Colonial Governments."
Governors, Commissions of, a
substitute for charters   . 39 and n.
Grafton, Duke of, for repeal of
Revenue Acts   .   .   . 267
Granville, Lord, on Royal Instructions   268
Greece, its colonies   .   33, 34
Greene, Nathaniel, taunt of   . 271
Grenville, George, how he lost
America, 227 ; character of,
249, 268 n.; his notion of colonial obligation, 249 ; wherein
erroneous, 250, 251 ; determines
upon making the colonies
sources of revenue, 253, 254 ;
irresolution of, 267 ; last speech
and death of   .   .   268 n.
Habeas Corpus Act, passed un-
der Charles II., 12 ; of no force
in the colonies, 14 ; refused to
America by William III.   .   . 15

Harrison, reports that a Declaration of Independence has been
agreed upon   .   .   . 297
Harvard University, library of,
88 ; character of   .   . 171
Henry, Patrick, startles the
House of Burgesses   .   . 256
Hicks, Elias, notion of the Scriptures, 64 n.; seeks to restore
Quakerism   65
Hillsborough, Lord, Secretary of
State for the colonies, offended
by the Circular Letter, 263 ;
issues order for payment of
colonial judges from imperial
treasury   271
Hooke, William, apostrophe to
Old England   .   .   82 n.
House of Stuart, colonization
chiefly effected under, 53 ; services of, to freedom of conscience, 63 ; the Quakers' re-
gard for   80
Howes, The, in command of the
American forces   .   . 292
Hume, David   .   .   . 157
Hutchinson, Thomas, on domin-
ion, 35 n.; on effect of governors' commissions, 39 n.; on
force of Acts of Parliament in
America, 202 n.; opinion of, respecting Committee of Correspondence, 271 ; intercepted
letters of, brings Franklin before the Council   .   . 274
Independence, movements toward, 293, 294, 295 ; resolutions
and debate concerning, 296 ;
new discussion of, question of,
settled, 297 ; Declaration of   . 297
Independents; see tit. "Brownists."
Individuality in Southern character, 133 ; moved to act as a
social force   3
Institutions, definition of, 48, 49 ;
institutional nature of English
colonies, 48 ; a tribal characteristic, 49 ; non-institutional nature of French colonies, 49,
50, 51, 52 ; natural development of English, 49 *et seq.*;
antiquity of American, 52, 53 ;
have their root in local self-
government, 54 ; and in love of
the soil, 55 ; appear simultaneously with the settlers, 56 ; of
New England, 164, 166 ; development of tribal   .   . 25, 301

Intolerance ; see tit. "Freedom of Conscience."

Ireland, Emigration from, began 121 n.

Jamaica remonstrates against Port Duty Act 255

Jefferson, Thomas, on intolerance in Virginia, 67 n., 146 ; his reason for absence of boroughs in Virginia, 127 n.; on parishes, House of Delegates, 132 n.; opinion of Virginia resolution for a Congress . . . 281

Judges, The, not independent of the crown, 14 ; became so, 205 ; independence of, threatened, 245 ; payment out of imperial treasury ordered . . . 271

Juries of the vicinage . . 205

Keith, Sir William, proposes to derive revenue from the colonies, Walpole's reply . . 227

Laissez-faire policy, The, 31, 56 ; the best policy . 225, 226, 227

Land as assets 183

Language, Purity of, in the South 129, 130, 131

Learning in New England 88, 100, 101, 102, 103

Lee, Richard Henry, seeks the union of the colonies, 272 ; submits resolutions respecting independence . . . 296

Lexington, Affair of, 288, 289; effect of . . . 289, 290

Library, City, of Philadelphia 157 et seq.

Libraries, in New England, beginnings of 88

Local self-government, 48 et seq. ; a race-craving, 57, 58, 204, 205. See tit. "Love of the Soil," "Institutions," "Frontier," etc.

Locke's constitution, vanity of . 45

Logan, James, his love of books, 156 ; the Loganian collection 157 and n.

London, sympathized with the colonies, 18 ; controlled, with Bristol, colonial trade . . 57

Mahon, Lord, on provincialism of English gentry of 18th century, 144 ; on convict transportation to colonies, 224 n.; opinion of Chatham's Bill . . . 286

Manners in the Southern Provinces, one of Burke's six

sources, 124 ; consideration of . . . 124 et seq.

Mansfield, Lord, on the common law in the colonies, 40 n. ; his opinion concerning contumacy of Massachusetts Legislature, 264 ; concerning intention of colonies to be independent . 310

Manufacturing system, The . 206

Marblehead, offers the Bostonians the use of its wharves . 280

Maryland, see tit. "Freedom of Conscience"; a Proprietary Government, 36 ; charter of self-government, 43, 121, 122 ; the first to guarantee religious liberty, 60, 121, 122 ; orderly settlement of, 78, 79 ; Puritans in, 68 ; faith in, 117 et seq. ; Calvert, founder of, 118; topography of . . . 125 et seq.

Massachusetts, see tit. "Puritanism," "Freedom of Conscience," etc. ; a Charter Government, 36 ; self-government in, 44 ; intolerance in, 59, 83, 84, 87, 92 et seq. sparsim, 108, 110, 111 ; oligarchy in, 86, 87, 108 ; education in, 100, 101, 167, 163 ; pays her advancements to England, and her indebtedness, 249 ; protests against Port Duty Act, 253 n. ; her Circular Letter, 263, 264; Government Bill or Regulating Act, 277 ; Legislature removed to Salem . 281

Mather, Cotton, his literary fecundity . . . . 104 n.

Mauduit, Israel, on grants in charters . . 38 n., 220 n.

Mayflower Compact, The, 84 ; Mr. Justice Story's opinion of, commented upon, 85; analyzed and discussed . 85, 86, 87

Mennonites, The, settled Germantown 161

Mental action, of a people, law of its advance and retrogression 12, 13

Mercantile system, The . 206

Migration, The Anglican, 5 ; the Brownist, Independent, or Pilgrim, 84 ; the Puritan, 83, 87 et seq.

Moderates or Conservatives, The, led by Dickinson, 282 ; course of 293

Molasses or Sugar Acts, The, 234, 235, 236 ; interpretation of, by

government, 235 ; really revenue acts, 236 ; enforcement of. 237
Monopoly, when popularized, 7 ;
of tobacco, 46, 47, 48 ; effect
of Navigation Act upon, 193 ;
of fisheries, 198 n. ; nature of
English, 193, 194 ; under Acts
of Navigation and Trade . 222
Montcalm, Marquis de, could not
save French power in America,
50 ; this power fell with him . 51
Montesquieu, his notion of the
colonies . . . 195 n.
Movement, The Great, or Revolution, 5 *et seq. ;* nomenclature
of, 8 ; different phases of, 9 *et
seq. ;* critical deductions from,
12, 13 ; its effect upon American character, 13 ; the means
it employed . . . 10, 11
Mun, Thomas . . . 206
Murray, Lindley . . . 161
Navigation Act, see tit. " Act of
Navigation."
Newcastle, Duke of . . . 18
New England, 13 ; self-government in, 43 ; see diff. tit. of
N. E. Colonies, " Puritanism,"
" Freedom of Conscience " ; rationalism in, 82 *et seq. ;* her
five advantages, 164 *et seq. ;*
Child's description of people
of, products same as those of
England, 210 ; competitor with
England, 210, 211 ; her charters,
210 n.; increase of trade of . 211
New Hampshire, a Royal Government, 36 ; self-government
in, 44 ; churchly, not Puritan . 44
New Jersey, Proprietary, afterward a Royal Government, 36 ;
self-government in, 43 ; West
Jersey, democracy, popular government, freedom of conscience,
Quakerism in, . . 69, 70, 72
New York, a Royal Government,
self-government in, 36, 45 ; intolerance in, 67 ; remonstrates
against Port Duty Act, 254 ;
nine colonies convene at city
of, 256 ; excused from voting
on question of independence . 297
Non - importation, associations,
262 ; broken, 270 ; renewed,
273 ; Congress enters into . 283
Norfolk, Population of . 128 n.
North, Lord, for partial repeal
of revenue acts, 267 ; effects

drawbacks on teas, 273 ; endeavors to conciliate . . 287
Old Colony, Plymouth settlement called 88
Oliver, Lt.-Governor, letters intercepted 274
Otis, James, his interpretation of
English writings respecting the
colonies, 208 ; his argument
against Writs of Assistance,
237–244 ; speech minuted by
Adams, 244 and n. ; effect of
argument upon the colonists,
245 ; a forerunner of revolution, 245, 246 ; John Adams'
opinion of the argument, 246
n. ; overthrew doctrine of parliamentary supremacy . . 299
Paine, Thomas, his work " Common Sense " 294
Parishes, in the South . 132 n.
Parliament, how far authority of,
extended to colonies, 217 n. ;
when it did not represent the
people, 284; notion of supremacy of, 298, 299 ; the instrument
of absolutism, 299; freedom of . 300
Pemberton, Israel, his encounter
with John Adams on the subject of toleration . . 166 n.
Penn, William, see tit. " Quakerism," " Pennsylvania," " Freedom of Conscience."
Penn, Richard, bears petition to
the king 291
Pennsylvania, settlement of, a
direct result of moral agitation
in Europe, 13 ; a Proprietary
Government, 36 ; self-government in, 43, 160 ; foundation
of, 73 ; origin of name, 73 n. ;
charter of, tenure of land of,
73, 74 ; freedom of conscience
permitted but not asserted by
charter, 74 ; prudence in settlement of, 75, 78, 79 ; freedom of conscience asserted by
legislation, 75, 76 ; restricted
immediately by the people, 76;
the Great Law of Chester, 76,
77, 78 ; humane motive in settlement of, 78 n. ; popular
government in, origin of, 81 ;
University of, 157 ; agriculture, commerce, 159, 160 ; education in, 161 ; mixed population of, 161, 162 ; spirit of
liberty in 163

Percy, Lord, commands retreat
from Lexington . . . 289
Petty, Sir William . . . 206
Philadelphia, progressive party
in, 154, 155; character of,
155; trade, elegance, learning,
156; 157; libraries, learned
societies, 157, 160; social life
of, 158, 159; Congress meets
in 282
Philadelphia City Library . 157 *et seq.*
Piedmont of Virginia, The, how
and when settled, 144, 145;
conflict with Church and State,
145, 146; dissent in, 145 n.;
more democratic than lowlands
146, 147
Pitt, William, see tit. " Lord
Chatham " . . . .
Planter, The Southern, his life,
habits, character, 130 *et seq.*;
his land speculations, 135, 136;
field sports of, 136, 137; his
respect for woman, 137, 138;
hospitality, social life of, 138,
139; his refinement, 139; his
winter visit to the capital, 139,
140; his home, patriarchial
life, 140, 141; his commerce
with England, 141, 142; the
squirearchy, English and American . . . 142, 143, 144
Plymouth or Pilgrim settlement,
The, 43; the Old Colony, 88;
a Brownist settlement, 84, 88 n., 90
Political Economists, Early English 206
Policy of Great Britain toward
the colonies, 31, 56, 225, 226,
227; change in . 16, 227, 228
Port Duty Act 252
Praemunire, Writ of, 119; for
what it issued, 119, 120; pains
of 120
Presbyterianism (Presbyterians),
organizes into a party, 89; sympathy between, and Puritans . 90
Privy Council 15
Proclamation of Rebellion . 292
Progressives or Extremists, The,
282; course of . 295, 296
Protective System, The . 206
Puritanism (Puritans), what it
was, and what it did for England, 9 *et seq.*; defence of political P., 10, 11; early P. not
dissent, 60; in America, expelled Roger Williams, 61; P.

in Maryland, 68; American P.
the same as English, 83; settlement in Massachusetts, 83, 84,
87; P. emigrants socially of a
higher class than the Pilgrims,
87, 88; learning of N. Eng.
P., 88; early English P. merely
reform, 8, 89, 91, 107; sympathy between P. and Presbyterians, 90; not when Brownists
left England, 90; horror of
Rome and of Brownists, 90, 91;
first reform, afterward dissent,
91; the second N. E. emigration absolutely Puritan, 91;
colonization of N. E. due to P.,
91, 92; real P. emigration when,
92; P. emigration impelled by
no lofty or humane motives, 92,
93; monarchical and conformist, 93; their notion of freedom
imperfect and of slow growth,
93, 94; unsocial disposition of,
94, 95; early history in America
uneventful, 99; its theological strife, 100; great learning,
but no literary class among,
100, 101; character of its literature, 102; rage for disputation among, 102, 103; the purposes subserved by this disputation, 103, 104; theological
subjects give way to secular,
105; view of Roger Williams'
case from P. standpoint, 108,
109; intolerance of P. oligarchy.
111; and see Appendix C.
Quakerism, an example of conscience and State instead of
Church and State, 63; its advent in America propitious to
freedom of conscience, 63, 68;
mystical nature of, 64, 65, 66;
the Inner Light, and denial of
dogmatic authority, 64; pre-
supposes freedom of conscience,
64, 72; its passiveness, 64;
failure of, in practical life, 65;
seeks the Middle Colonies, 66;
reasons for this step, 66, 67;
distressed condition of toleration when Quakerism appeared,
68; it turned the day in favor
of freedom of conscience, 69;
the Quakers settle WEST JER-
SEY, 69; their assertion of power in the people, 69, 70; their
assertion of absolute freedom of

conscience, 70 ; popular form of their government, 70, 71 ; their political constitution criticised, 71, 72 ; their commonwealth a pure democracy, 71, 72; the Quakers settle PENNSYLVANIA, 72 ; Pennsylvania a result of West Jersey, 72 ; historical importance of Quakerism in Pennsylvania, 72; finds a necessary expression in freedom of conscience, 72, 73 ; fidelity of, to this principle, 72, 73 ; Penn's charter, 73, 74 ; it does not assure freedom of conscience in terms, 74 ; that assurance given in the laws, 75, 76 ; the broad principle of the founder not maintained in the legislation of the people, 76, 77, 78 ; the Great Law of Chester, 76, 77, 78 ; order a characteristic of, 79, 80 ; friendly to the House of Stuart, 80 ; passiveness of, a constitutional force, 80, 81 ; how it aided freedom of conscience, 81 ; America indebted to Q., 81; mentioned by Child 209

Quebec Act, The . 277, 278, 280

Randolph, Peyton, chairman of First Congress . . . 282

Regulating Act or, Massachusetts Government Bill . . . 277

Regulation ; see tit. " Restrictive System."

Religion in the Northern Provinces, one of Burke's six sources, 29 ; consideration of . . . . . 59 *et seq.*

Remoteness of Situation, one of Burke's six sources, 30 ; a cause of the *Laissez-faire* policy, 31 ; contributes to self-government, 56 ; compensation for restriction not a result of . . 204

Representation, early in Virginia, 41, 47, 48 ; generally acquired soon, 43, 44, 45, 46 ; granted in Maryland Charter, 122 ; in Pennsylvania, 43, 160; colonial, in British Parliament impracticable, 204 ; for, in the several colonies, see . . . 43–45

Resolve of 15th May, 1776 . 295

Resolves of Suffolk County . 282

Resolves, The Virginia . . 266

Restrictive System, The, see tit.

"Act of Navigation," "Acts of Trade," " Trade," " Child," " Gee," " Ashley," etc. ; increase of English trade under, 192 n.; what the system was, 198, 199 ; pecuniary compensation for, 199 *et seq. ;* political compensation for, 203 *et seq. ;* literature of, 205 *et seq.;* changed colonial relations to England, 214, 216 ; consideration of, 221 *et seq. ;* imposed new character upon colonies, 222 ; controlling principle of, 222; not censurable by colonists, 223 ; defects of, 224 ; enlargement of, 233 ; extremes of, . . 233 n., 234 n.

Revolution, The Great, see tit "Movement, The Great, or R."

Revolution of 1688, what it was, and what it did for England, 8 11, 12, 298 ; its effects upon America indirect, 13 ; did not give America constitutional government, 13, 14 ; how it injured colonial liberty . . . 14, 15

Revolution of 1776, arbitrary taxation the immediate cause of, 19 ; at first an attempt to redress grievances only, 19 ; a manifestation of same force which produced R. of 1688, 19; necessary sequence to R. of 1688 ; resulted in transferring sovereignty from throne to people, 19 ; moral effect of upon other peoples, 20 ; character of actors and of the cause, 20, 21, 22, 23 ; beginning of, 246 ; termination of, 23 ; qualities in which it was rich, 24 ; Trilogy of Eras preceding, 25 ; knowledge of, necessary to comprehend, 26 ; gave America constitutional government . 300

Revolutions, Character of, 23 ; when they terminate . . 23

Rhode Island, a Charter Government, 36 ; self-government in, 44, 45 ; freedom of conscience in, 59 ; rationalism of, 63; Quakerism debated in, 66 ; remonstrates against Port Duty Act, 254 ; overawed . . . 271

Richard II., Navigation Act of . 186

Robertson, Dr., his surprise concerning the charters, commented upon . . . 37 *et seq.*

Rockingham, Lord, administration of, 257; supports Chatham, 285 ; his description of public feeling. . . 279, 292

Roman Catholics, burdened condition of, in England, 119, 120 n.; seek Maryland . 117, 118

Rome, its colonies . 31 *et seq.*

Royal Instructions 268, 269, 270

Salem, generous conduct of, toward Boston, 280 ; legislature removed to 281

Saltonstall, Sir Richard, remonstrance against intolerance, . . . 305, Appendix C.

Sandys, Sir Edwin. protects Virginian tobacco . . . 46

Schools ; see tit. ' Massachusetts," " Pennsylvania," " Virginia," etc.

Shelburne, Lord, supports Chatham 285

Shepard, Thomas . . 104 n.

Smith, Adam, his notion of the colonies . . . 195 n.

Soul-liberty (Roger Williams'), ... 112, 113

South Carolina remonstrates against Port Duty Act . . 254

Sovereignty transferred from throne to people . . 19, 301

Spain, her colonial policy, spirit of 17

St. John, Henry, Act of Navigation attributed to . . . . . . 190, and also n., 191, 196

Stamp Act, Appendix G ; passed, 255 ; reception of, in America, 255 ; repealed, 257 ; effects of, 258, 270 ; Chatham upon, 217 ; preamble of . 320, Appendix G.

Story, Mr. Justice, his view of Mayflower Compact controverted . . . . 85 *et seq.*

Suffolk, County of, Resolutions of 282

Sugar Acts, The, see tit. " Molasses Acts."

Taxation, unlawful, immediate cause of colonial revolt, 19 ; colonies exempt from imperial, ... 45, 46

Tea Act, see tit. " Townshend Acts"; retention of duty on tea, 267 ; concedes drawback to Americans, 273 ; in aid of East India Company, 273 ; reception of ships in America . . 275

Ticonderoga, Fort, surprise of . 290

Toleration, see tit. " Freedom of Conscience." . . . .

Topography of Maryland and Virginia . . . 125 *et seq.*

Townshend, Charles, votes for repeal of Stamp Act, 257 ; character of, 259, 260 ; policy of, 260 ; death of 262

Townshend Acts, 260, 261; effect of 261

Township, The, 164, 174 *et seq.* ; the unit of Northern society, 174; an autonomy, 174; source of political vitality, 174, 175 ; representative and executive forces, 175, 176 ; favorable to development of high forms of citizenship, 177 ; division and concentration of power, 177 ; a local self-government, 177, 178 ; develops practical art of governing, 178, 179,180; attachment of citizen to, 179 ; reality of, 180 ; favorable to fierceness of freedom . 180, 181

Trade, see tit. "Acts of Trade"; increase of English, 192 n.; legislation concerning, 195, etc. ; treatises concerning, 205 *et seq.* ; increase of N. England . . 211

Union, general movement toward, 275, 280, 281 ; the Thirteen Colonies unite in Second Congress 291

United States, The, results of the Great Movement . . 5, 6

Universities and Colleges 171, 172

Venn, his *delenda est Carthago !* . 276

Virginia, a Royal Government, 36 ; forfeiture of her franchises, 41 ; conservative and aristocratic, 42 ; resists revenue system, 46 ; early representation in, 41, 47, 48 ; intolerance in, 67 and n. ; topography of, 125 *et seq.;* Burnaby's character of the Virginians, 134 n. ; education in, 168, 169 ; Child's character of, 208 ; remonstrates against being made a source of revenue, 254, 256; the Resolves, 266 ; creates a committee of correspondence . . . 272

Walpole, Sir Robert, corruption under, 16 ; prepares the way for absolutism of George III., 16, 18 ; his *laissez-faire* policy in respect to the colonies, his answer to Keith . . . 227

Ward, Nathaniel, intolerance of, quotations from his "Simple Cobbler of Agawam," Appendix C.

Washington, George, is made commander-in-chief . . 291

Wilkes, John, elected Lord Mayor, 284; refuses the mace at proclamation of rebellion ; 292

William The Third, no friend to American colonies, 15; character of colonial administration under, 15; Otis' denunciation of 242

Williams, Roger, see tit. "Freedom of Conscience," "Brownists," "Puritans," etc.; disputes Quakerism, replies to George Fox, 66; appears in Boston, 106; his life-work, the first to make freedom of conscience a constitutional principle, the First of the Americans, 106; origin of, 107; change of religious views, character of, at time of arrival in America, 107; expulsion from Massachusetts, 108; facts of the case, justification of expulsion from Puritan standpoint, 108, 109; the party that really deserves censure, 110; significance of the trial, it discloses

the existence of toleration, 110; toleration and intolerance involved in the trial, 111; starting-point of freedom of conscience as a social force, 111; soul-liberty, 112; divorce of Church and State, 112, 113; trial causes theological debate to give way to secular, 114; the Ship of State, 115 n.; the friend of the Indians, 115, 116; character of, effect of his teachings, 116, 117; remonstrates with Endicott 306

Williamsburg, Population of, 128 n.; life at . . . 139, 140

Winslow, Edward, opinion of Roger Williams . . . 107

Winthrop, John, conformist and monarchist, 93; the Winthrop immigration . . 88, 92

Woman, condition of, in the South . . . 137, 138

Writs of Assistance, Otis' Argument concerning, 237 et seq.; the Court sustains, 247; argument upon, overthrew doctrine of parliamentary supremacy . 299

Yale College, Library of, 88; character of 171

www.ingramcontent.com/pod-product-compliance
Lightning Source LLC
Chambersburg PA
CBHW021113270326
41929CB00009B/853